Healing Our Planet Healing Our Selves

The Power of Change Within to Change the World

edited by
DAWSON CHURCH & GERALYN GENDREAU

www.HealingC

Elite Books
Author's Publishing Cooperative
Fulton, CA 95439
www.EliteBooks.biz

Library of Congress Cataloging-in-Publication Data

Healing our planet, healing our selves: the power of change within to change the world / edited by Dawson Church & Geralyn Gendreau.

p. cm.

Includes bibliographical references.

ISBN 0-9720028-4-7

1. Health. 2. World health. 3. Humanity. I. Church, Dawson, 1956- II. Gendreau, Geralyn.

RA776.H4325 2005

362.1--dc22

2004026324

Cover and Interior Design by Dawson Church
Typeset in Mona Lisa and Book Antiqua by Nan Sea Love
Cover Design by Vicki Valentine
Printed in USA
First Edition

10 9 8 7 6 5 4 3 2 1

Contents

Dedication

This book is dedicated to the many people who
in their smallest of daily thoughts and actions
with no thought of reward or acknowledgment
join the unseen multitude who strive
consciously, deliberately,
with the conviction of ultimate success
for the highest good of all.

Acknowledgments

Thanks to the many people who helped midwife this book. Thanks first to the many co-authors, who gave generously in order to contribute their voices to this vital global dialog. It has been a magnificent experience to immerse ourselves in this stream of fresh new ideas that hold out such hope for our collective future.

Many thanks to Neale Donald Walsch. After we interviewed him in his home, he e-mailed many of his best-selling author friends, and requested that they contribute to this book. His generosity saved us many days of research, and hours of supplication!

Thanks too to the people who supported us emotionally, financially and spiritually during the sometimes-trying twelve months that it took to bring the project to fruition. Thanks especially to Gordon Feller, who organized the Gregory Bateson Centennial Conference at the University of California at Berkeley, who put us in contact with many of the conference presenters, and is the most remarkable teacher (by example) of positive revisioning. Thanks to the sales staff at Midpoint Trade, who have enthusiastically encouraged us in producing this series of anthologies. Thanks also to Norman Shealy, Ann and Bob Nunley, Bob Matusiak, and the inspired staff of Holos University. The work of Holos is destined to bring significant positive changes in the spiritual and emotional growth of our profession.

Thanks to Carol Gendron for her love and support, to Greg Gendron for his patience, to Mary, Jeremy, Molly, and Robin, to Stuart Sovatsky for his heart of gold and discerning mind, to Hari and Maximillian Meyers for advice and perspective. Thanks to Michael Heumann, Rob Calef, Lion Goodman, Rocky Kemp, Gita Orchier, Debra Guisti, William Joyus Lippincott, Homi Shivaie, and Chuck Henderson. Thanks also to Blake More, for constant inspiration, and to Anthony Wright for deep counsel and harp music.

—Dawson Church and Geralyn Gendreau

Part One

The Guiding Light of Spirit

Barbara Marx Hubbard: Bringing God Home

The universe works in spirals. One such spiral is the story of evolution. It begins in the void, the mind of God, and the field of all possibilities. The first turn on the spiral is the Big Bang, the formation of the universe. The second turn on the spiral is the formation of matter, and then Earth. The third turn is the formation of life. The fourth turn is the formation of animal life. The fifth turn is the formation of human life.

The sixth major turn on the spiral is, I believe, the formation of a universal human life. The planetary crisis we find ourselves in today is, in fact, the transition from one stage of human evolution to the next.

We are currently near the end of a forty-thousand-year period of individuation and separation from nature. In the myth of the Garden of Eden, the "fall from grace" can be understood as the separation of humans from nature, and the origin of self-consciousness. "Leaving the garden" is a metaphor for separation from the state of being embedded in spirit, the unconscious children of God. For the last forty thousand years, our human journey has been toward the development of civilization. Today, with the advent of science and technology, we have gained the powers that we used to attribute to our gods.

The year 1945 was a significant marker. When the U.S. dropped the atomic bomb on Japan, it signified the handwriting on the wall. It was a signal to all of humanity that if we continue in the illusion of separation from nature, from each other, and from the deeper patterns of creation, we are capable of destroying our planetary life-support systems, and

Barbara Marx Hubbard has been a pioneer in positive options for the future of humanity for forty years. A public speaker, author, and social innovator, she is president and executive director of the Foundation for Conscious Evolution. She has been instrumental in the founding of many future-oriented organizations, including the World Future Society, New Dimensions Radio, Global Family, The Foundation for the Future, and the Association for Global New Thought. Among her books are *Emergence* (Hampton Roads, 2001), and *Conscious Evolution* (New World Library, 1998). For more information visit her website at www.barbaramarxhubbard.com.

killing the human species altogether. Discovering that we had these powers in 1945 marked another turn on the spiral.

Each decade of planetary evolution during this sixth turn of the spiral has produced noteworthy events that have transformed our world. In the 1950s, it was the discovery of DNA, the development of television, of computers, and of contraceptives. The 1960s brought the Apollo program, making us a universal species, at least physically. That decade also witnessed the beginning of the human potential movement, as well as the rapid awakening of the women of our species, plus an urgent new awareness of the fragility of our planetary environment.

A spiral has both an inner ring and an outer ring. The outer ring is planetary evolution. The inner ring is personal evolution. Starting around the year 2000, the acceleration of social and planetary change increased. We entered what Ervin Laszlo calls a "macro shift," in which the whole civilization is under stress. The process of individual self-evolution began accelerating rapidly. But individual psycho-spiritual evolution is proceeding much faster than social evolution. Despite our personal growth, as a society we're not yet transforming the educational system, the political system, or the economic system. While creative solutions to social problems can be found everywhere, they are not yet connected. There are many innovations here and there, but they haven't added up to systemic change. This is producing an entire civilization and environment tilted out of balance. The disequilibrium is accelerating. It shows up in the eruption of violence between groups and cultures, environmental upheavals, and in the form of economic and political inequity.

-§-
Today, with the advent of science and technology, we have gained the powers that we used to attribute to our gods.
-§-

As individuals, we have varying degrees of awareness of this acceleration. To some, it takes the form of confusion, desperation, frustration, or alienation. But for many others, it has taken the form of an awakening of spirit within. From this perspective it feels like humans are bringing the gods home. We are awakening to a profound desire to participate in the process of creation, to restore the Earth, to heal the terrible inequities we see, to free people to be themselves, and to explore the universe. The inner ring on the evolutionary spiral contains all the individual stories that are part of the planetary story.

Many of us hear an inner voice giving us guidance from our higher self. We may call that presence by many different names—the voice of the Higher Self, the inner guide, the Christ. If we give that inner voice our full attention, if we recognize it as our deep Self, then a momentous evolutionary change occurs. Gradually we find that we are no longer a local personality seeing the divine. Rather we become an incarnation of the divine, educating the local personality. I call this "the shift from ego to essence."

Between the inner ring of self-evolution, and the outer ring of social evolution, there is a third ring that I think of as *vocational evolution.* Each of us has, within us, a genius code, just like we have a genetic code. The genius code is the blueprint for your unique creativity. As the situation on Earth becomes increasingly interactive, as we increasingly experience our interconnectivity in the form of pain and danger—as well as potential—inner vocational stirrings are waking up. This doesn't mean that people are feeling called to be yet another ordinary "doctor, lawyer, or Indian chief."

-§-

Despite our personal growth, as a society we're not yet transforming the educational system, the political system, or the economic system.

-§-

These new vocations are often hybrids. They are *callings* rather than jobs and professions. They fill us with desire to give our best within the social whole. Our vocations are so unique to each person that they can rarely be identified by a neat occupational label. Just as many of the new functions that people do today—biotechnician, telecommunication specialist, nanotechnologist, environmentalist, futurist, medical ethicist, desktop publisher—didn't exist in the 1950s, the job descriptions that reflect our emerging evolutionary vocations or callings are yet to be defined.

For me, finding my vocation began in 1966, when I started to catch the implications of this evolutionary potential. At the time, I had a very conventional social role. I was a wife, and the mother of five children. Yet in the midst of this settled reality I began to wake up to the magnitude of my vocation, which is to be a communicator of evolutionary potential. The way I heard the call was in these words: "Barbara, go tell the story of the birth of a Universal Humanity."

Vocation is a projection of the most authentic self. And that projection takes the form of projects. Our projects are projections of self. As the self evolves, and becomes more and more "we-sponsible," it incarnates its own identity in outer expression, rather than projecting its sense of divine identity onto some outside person. We bring God home.

The creator within us wants to create a better world. Our projects can become the creator within expressing its unique creativity in relationship to self and social evolution. When we say, "Yes!" to our life's purpose and our calling, it actualizes potential in our environment to create our authentic vocation. Your growth depends on incarnating that greater Self, and then expressing that greater Self in the evolution and healing of our world. Those of us who are awakening find ourselves powerfully called into creative action.

When you say, "Yes!" to your inner calling, it's like falling in love. You fall in love with your intrinsic potential. Then you join your genius with that of others, in order to co-create. You develop a new form of love, one I call supra-sexual co-creation. The purpose of this new kind of love is not to reproduce the species; it's to evolve the Self and express that Self in the form of outer work. As we have fewer children and live longer lives, the drive to self-purpose is harnessed to express creative love. In the old language, you're "one with the will of God." In the new language, you're "expressing the deeper pattern of creation in a personalized form."

As I've put more and more attention on that deep self, I've shifted my identity to that self. It now resides in the center of my being. If my local personalities have anxieties or get into distress, they turn to the essential self for healing. And that's the start of healing the world around you. If you can't identify with your own essence, you can't heal your local self, or the larger world. The blueprints for healing—for both the world and your local selves—are coded inside that greater essence. They are Evolutionary Codes. Jesus said, "If I be lifted up, all will be lifted up unto me." The "I" that's doing the lifting is that internal essence.

-§-

We are no longer a local personality seeing the divine. Rather we become an incarnation of the divine, educating the local personality.

-§-

When you learn to shift your identity to the essential self, the wisdom for healing your local self is present. When you place your attention within the essential self, you feel warm, you feel whole, and you feel at peace. You feel loved and loving. You feel all the qualities of being that you might desperately seek outside yourself as a local self trapped in the illusion of separateness.

The embodiment of personal selfhood, and collective social transformation, is leading us to a quantum shift that has only been envisioned by the mystics and seers of humanity. They have revealed to us such images as "the new heavens and the new Earth," Paradise, or the New Jerusalem. As we combine an evolved consciousness—what we might call a Christ Consciousness or God Consciousness—with the new technologies—nanotech, biotech, quantum computing, genetic medicine, space colonization and others—the end result is a species so powerful that our entire physical world—including our bodies—can be transformed.

Right now we're in a global crisis, an emergency filled with terrible and dangerous symptoms: violence, environmental destruction, proliferation of weapons of mass destruction, dire poverty and the suffering of billions. It can either be an apocalyptic crisis of destruction; or it can become a crisis of birth—a beginning rather than an end. If we can get through the planetary crisis quickly enough so that we don't destroy our own life-support system, or blow ourselves up, then we can see immense possibilities for a positive future. If we combine our higher consciousness with our new and evolutionary capacities, both social and technological, we can jump to the next stage of human evolution. We can become what I think of as a Universal Humanity—a new civilization co-created by Universal Humans, humans connected through the heart to the whole of life, humans awakening from within to the impulse of self and social evolution, bringing the gods home as our own developmental potential to evolve.

The transition to the future human is full of emergencies. We could destroy our own life-support system within the lifetime of living generations. In the same time frame, we see emergent potentials—innovations and creative solutions—everywhere, in every field and function. The emerging innovations are quantum capacities—like tapping into zero point energy, radical life extension, and the enhancement of intelligence—that bypass the entire old system. But we can't jump to the quantum capacities without facing the emergencies and the emergence. You can't send a newborn to university. The baby has to breathe first.

We need to develop a whole system approach to the whole system crisis. We need to apply the best that we know about social networking, design science, non-linear and synergistic processes, collective envisioning, intention, mass resonance events, the maturation of the mass media to communicate our growth potential, and much more. All of this is in the works. In the same twenty to thirty years in which we could destroy ourselves, we could experience a shift of consciousness and connectivity to the positive, which would send us in the direction of a future that matches the aspirations of the human spirit.

-§-

Vocation is a projection of the most authentic self.

-§-

Most of the problems we are facing on Earth are the critical hygienic conditions of a planetary species undergoing the crisis of our birth to the next stage of evolution. Solving our immediate problems is vital, but is not our end goal, any more than the goal of the newborn baby is to breathe, nurse, and eliminate. Certainly, unless the baby learns to breathe, nurse, and eliminate, it will die, just as if we don't handle our emergencies, we won't make it either. But handling our emergencies is simply a natural stage in our learning curve toward becoming a universal humanity applying our spiritual, social, scientific, and technological capacities harmoniously.

The growth path once we leave the emergency room requires a new step in personal evolution. As an individual human being creates a deeper self-identity, and incarnates that fully, that person's outer projects reflect the shift. Carl Jung calls this "the continuing incarnation of the Self." The evolutionary process we are going through is the securing of that divine identity internally. We heal the local self, which then becomes transparent to the impulse of the essential self that is guided by the deeper processes of creation. The beauty of operating from within is that you're already rewarded, you're already at peace, and you're already fulfilled! You are Self-rewarded. Your external projects simply reveal the expression of your deeper Self.

Before I realized this, no matter how hard I worked as a good egoic personality, following the commands of my essential self, but separated from it, I was always late, I was always behind, I was always incomplete. So I tried harder to follow the higher guidance—the ego is insatiable. Yet it cannot succeed when in a state of separation from the source of its being. I felt I was failing to transform anything. The ego is never fulfilled, even if you achieve great things. The next day, it requires a new goal. Successful people often feel this pressure even more acutely than unsuccessful ones!

I had to stop my efforts, and allow my attention to be in accord with my guidance. I keep a journal, and write in it frequently. Whenever I'd feel this guidance, I'd put double brackets around the words I was writing. When I looked back at those journals—all 152 volumes of them—I realized that what was common to all the highlighted passages was a feeling tone of peace, wholeness, oneness, joy, and wisdom. I started to put my attention each day on the *feeling* of receiving guidance, not on the specific guidance itself.

-§-

When you learn to shift your identity to the essential self, the wisdom for healing your local self is present.

-§-

You have a highly sophisticated biofeedback mechanism in your own body. When you reside in this essential self, the whole biochemistry of your body changes. Endorphins flow. You are at peace, as the design of your deeper life purpose starts to unfold in social action. You perform actions with what Joseph Chilton Pearce calls "unconflicted behavior," as the life purpose of your essential self begins to flow. Within that essential self are evolutionary codes, dormant potentials that are actualized naturally as you express the creativity of the essential self. When you join in co-creation with other people who are also tapping into the inner self, you experience a feeling of joy and ease and rightness as those shared codes unfold gracefully and effortlessly. You get over your own self-consciousness; you get past the boundaries of your egoic self, exhausted by its efforts to act separate from the greater flow. As the ego comes to rest in the vibrational field of the higher self, it loses its illusion of separation, which is the source of most human problems anyway. Depression and physical illness can be interpreted as signals that we're not accessing the deep codes of our creative selves. Cancer can be interpreted as the body's effort to grow, but without a plan. Misfortune can be a way of nudging you into paying attention.

My experience is that we are giving birth to a universal human within ourselves. This universal human has a conception, at the time of our first unitive experiences. It has a gestation period. You know it's happening when you suddenly get turned on, and you can't live your old life anymore. You can't go back to your old ideas, your old teachers, your old books. Then the universal human has a birth period, when the ego realizes it can't tolerate being separate from source anymore. The ego makes a fateful choice to invite the essential self, the guide, the inner voice to come in the whole way and to take dominion within the household of selves.

Sometimes I forget all this and go at life the old way, and it's hopeless; it's simply impossible. I remind myself not to do anything when I feel reactive and separated from my own essential self. When the local self resonates with our own essence, this essence penetrates body and mind utterly.

This gestation has happened on a collective scale through the great religions. While their founders brought forth their higher selves, their followers could not. They became mired in dogmatic separation. For this reason, the organized religions cannot lead us across the great divide to the next stage of evolution. Only individuals can do that, through inner evolution. When this inner incarnation occurs, social action emerges spontaneously, naturally and creatively. The universe finds ways to support the fulfillment of these individual actions, because they fit the emerging new pattern.

-§-

The transition to the future human is full of emergencies.

-§-

On the spiral, more and more human beings are becoming unwilling to operate as separated egos seeking the divine. We're unwilling because it does not work, it is painful, and it causes dis-ease, depression, and alienation. It's not that we become idealistic; it's simply that the old way does not work for us. Around the year 2000, more and more people became unwilling to operate as separated egos seeking the divine. The deepest wellspring of evolution is pushing us in this direction.

There's organic cohesion between the individual social actions performed in this way. Rather than being isolated endeavors, they possess an organic unity. Nature has been forming whole systems for billions of years, and is pressing through us to form a whole system out of us, instead of contending parts. So when we identify with the inner self and reside in there, and let the biochemical shift occur that makes this our natural state, then our outer expression begins to conform to that organic pattern.

How can you do this each day? The first priority is to pay attention to those flashes of knowing. Focus on that experience. Let that Self into your heart and solar plexus, until you begin to feel peace and joy, oneness and wholeness, throughout your body.

Once that happens, your local self begins to resonate with the vibration of your higher self. That higher self is potently attractive; for the local self it's like spending time with a master, a guru, a great teacher. This isn't you temporarily taking on the personality of a master, whose presence helps you reorganize your energy into a more elevated constellation. This teacher's message is a perfect fit, entirely customized for you. It is You!

It's uniquely you as an expression of universal creativity. It's the creator within as you. When the local self resonates with that, you experience the bliss of union. The longer your personality stays in the "rose chamber of union"; the longer you let your local self be "off duty," not getting anything done; not rushing about, the more it falls in love with the essential self. That's the first level of resonance.

The second level of resonance occurs after you stabilize the experience of the local self being one with the essential self. It occurs where two or more such beings are gathered, resonating with each other in a co-creative pattern. This is the next stage of sexuality; Nature's purpose, as you shift from procreation to co-creation, is to get you to join your genius with another. The union is explosive; it gives rise to the next level of potential in both partners, the level of divine work. Work has a whole different flavor when you do it as part of the unfolding implicate order of nature.

In this young stage, your best course is to draw people into small groups where you all can stabilize in the experience. Jesus told us not to go forth alone, but to go in twos. I believe that he said this because it takes two or more gathered in the name of the Self to "hold the morphic field" and to express the reality of the universal process of creation that resides at the heart of each person. If you harmonize with your essential self, then go out into the world ready for action alone, you face a dissonance so great that unless you are an accomplished master of the very highest order, like Gandhi or Nelson Mandela or Mother Teresa, you quickly lose your resonance amid the dissonance of the world.

-§-

Depression and physical illness can be interpreted as signals that we're not accessing the deep codes of our creative selves.

-§-

We need an image of ourselves at the next stage of evolution that is attractive enough to move us toward it. One of my life's purposes is to articulate a vision of our future collective possibility that is so compelling that it irresistibly calls to us to throw off the shackles of our old consciousness, and be attracted toward it.

As we synergize and connect the elements that are creative and positive in every field, a vision of the new world takes shape. It's one in which individual genius is unlocked, and we become self-evolving, self-governing, self-authorizing, and infinitely creative. In this new world, the Universal Human might have continuity of consciousness through many physical bodies. The resurrected body of Jesus might be a prototype, a model, for everyone else. Our bodies might become so sensitive to thought that we can materialize and dematerialize at will.

I believe that we can completely restore our planetary environment. I believe that we will develop renewable and eventually zero point energy systems, which will liberate us from an economic model based on scarcity. I believe that we will develop the skills required to heal virtually every disease. I believe that we will learn to live and work in space, becoming an Earth-space species. I believe that we will voyage beyond our own solar system, eventually becoming a true universal species. I believe that we will find we are not alone in the universe. I think we'll find that, in a literal sense, "mother" Earth is giving birth to a universal species. That birth process is the next turn in the spiral, beyond the transition that we are in now, and toward a universal species. The following huge step will be to discover that we are not alone, as we contact other universal species.

-§-

The first higher life form we meet has to be ourselves.

-§-

Yet the first higher life form we meet has to be ourselves. The first encounter has to be with our own kind, the Universal Human. When we finally see that image of ourselves, not displaced into a vision of life after death, or a vision of the risen Christ, but a vision of the risen humanity, then we will be ready for the next steps in our maturation.

Neale Donald Walsch: Tomorrow's God in Action

In the last couple of years, a wave of shock and horror has gone through the hearts and minds of people all over the globe as they have witnessed innocent people being beheaded by extremists in the Middle East. We are compelled to ask, "What could cause human beings to do such a thing?"

We asked ourselves similar questions after the cataclysmic events of September 11, 2001. What state of mind could produce an action like flying a planeload of civilians into a building? On television, we saw crowds of people in the Middle East cheering and dancing in the streets in response. Our culture realized that the hijacking wasn't just the action of nineteen men. We sat in stunned silence as we realized that not only could this event occur, but that thousands of people could agree with it. A whole swath of humanity has collectively created a state of being that allows them to embrace mass murder with joy and celebration.

These events have prompted philosophers and spiritual leaders to ask us all, "What role, if any, do you think that you or your society have played in the creation of this extraordinary event?" Astute people began to see that personal responsibility isn't just a concept without functional reality; there's a direct connection between the mental and spiritual health of the planet and the individual health of the people on it.

We are in a time of introspection, in which individuals have begun to see the connection between planetary health and vibrance, and the health of the human species; the views of individuals, assembled into a

Neale Donald Walsch is the author of fifteen books, and founder of the nonprofit Conversations With God Foundation. In 1992, after four failed marriages, poor health, spotty relationships with his children, and losing his job, he fired off an angry letter to God—and to his surprise, received an answer filled with profound truths. Those answers have touched the lives of millions of people through his books, most recently *When Everything Changes, Change Everything* (Hampton Roads, 2009). He recently created Humanity's Team, a worldwide grassroots movement to catalyze the emergence of a new form of spirituality on Earth. Full information is found at www.HumanitysTeam.com.

consciousness held by a large number of people, becomes our collectively created experience. Right now, you could walk down the street in many cities and not find a single person who understands that it is the most sacred beliefs of individuals in the world that create our collective behavior. The beliefs that humanity currently holds about itself are simply no longer viable and no longer serve us.

Where do we start? There are five fallacies about God, and five fallacies about life, that create dysfunction, violence, conflict, and a state of continuing turmoil on this planet. The five fallacies about God are:

1. Humans believe that God needs something.
2. Humans believe that God can fail to get what He needs.
3. Humans believe that God has separated them from Him because they have not given Him what He needs.
4. Humans believe that God still needs what He needs so badly that God now requires them, from their separated position, to give it to Him.
5. Humans believe that God will destroy them if they do not meet His requirements.

It's important to draw the connection between cause and effect, to show how a belief in *this* creates an outcome called *that.* The first fallacy, that God needs something, is a self-destructive belief. As soon as we construct a God who needs something in particular in order to be happy, in the absence of which He will be unhappy and send down His wrath, we set up a damaging idea of deity itself. The consequence of this belief is that it gives us human beings the moral authority to act in similar ways toward each other—and consider it normal.

-§-
There's a direct connection between the mental and spiritual health of the planet and the individual health of the people on it.
-§-

We then construct our social conventions, our legal systems, our political realities, our economic models—in fact the whole fabric of human interactions—based on the moral authority we gather from a God who behaves in this way. We allow ourselves to say, for instance, that, "If you don't fulfill my needs in this relationship I will also punish and condemn you. It may even be perfectly okay to kill you, because sacred scripture authorizes me to do so." Virtually every scripture—the Koran, the Bible, the Bhagavad Gita, and the Book of Mormon—talks about a God who not only becomes angry and kills people, but instructs all other humans to kill them as well. So just that one single idea, that God needs something to be happy, sends people running to the hills, trying to figure out, "What is it that God needs?"

Eight different people will provide eight different answers to that question. Who has it right? Once we've chosen one, we hope that we made the correct choice. Then, most dangerously, we turn around and call the other seven wrong, and decide what their punishment should be for being wrong. We look to the same misunderstandings and the same fallacious beliefs to determine that punishment as we did to discover our original idea of God. We pile fallacy upon fallacy, error upon error, mistake upon mistake. We look to the same God we misunderstood in the first place to help us understand the answer to the question, "What shall we do with those who don't understand you?" Those outcomes can range anywhere from a simple admonition to something far more drastic, like crucifixion.

Every human construction, our entire global system, is based on fallacious fundamental beliefs that have no basis in ultimate reality. The five fallacies about life are:

1. Human beings are separate from each other.
2. There is not enough of what human beings need to be happy.
3. To get the stuff of which there is not enough, human beings must compete with each other.
4. Some human beings are better than other human beings.
5. It is appropriate for human beings to resolve severe differences created by all the other fallacies by killing each other.

These flawed perceptions began when we were in very primitive stages of development as a species. During the earliest days of humanity's evolution, the world outside of us was largely outside of our understanding and comprehension. We simply saw what we saw. We did not know why things happened the way they did.

-§-
The beliefs that humanity|currently holds about itself are simply no longer viable and no longer serve us.
-§-

In those very early days we knew that there was something out there. What it was, we did not know. And with the first lightning bolt that struck, with the first peal of thunder, we were clear that it was more powerful than us. When we saw a volcano erupt, when we saw a shooting star, we said, "That's a lot bigger than me. I can't make something like that happen. What did make it happen?" Quite naturally, early humans came to the assumption that there was something in the universe larger than themselves. From there it was a very short leap to asking, "How can I please that force, so the rain will come and I can grow my crops? How can I control these effects I see in my exterior world? There must be some way."

What you think becomes your reality. That's true whether it's practiced in the year 2005, 21 B.C. or 2 million years ago. In this day and age, when the thinkers are of relatively high consciousness, this can be a plus, but the process can be a minus if the people doing the thinking are just barely evolved enough to grapple with these ideas. So if our ancestors, when they saw fire in the sky, did a little dance, and the fire stopped, from that day on they connected their dance with the fire stopping.

I once gave a lecture at the Church of Today in Michigan. This church was in an old building with a tin roof, and it started to rain. Even with amplification, the congregation couldn't hear me. I watched all 1,400 faces look up at the roof when the rain began. It was 11 o'clock in the morning of an all-day retreat, and I realized I'd lost my audience.

I said—as loudly as I could—into my microphone, "The rain is really hard to hear over, isn't it?" Nods said, "Yes." It was coming down in sheets. I jokingly said, "Not to worry, I'll make it stop." At that moment it stopped. The whole audience was awed. After that they hung on every word I said.

-§-

We're going to create a new God, tomorrow's God, right here on earth during the course of the next twenty-five years. We're going to create a less dysfunctional one.

-§-

That's how shamanism got started. No one back then had the consciousness to know any better, not even the shaman. He also thought, "This how it happens." He was so convinced that his dance was making it rain, that the next five times he danced, four out of those five times the rain began. Your thought creates your reality. The thought became the reality which became the thought which became the reality. That's how the cycle began. There was so much faith put in the healer, the medicine man, that he became effective by virtue of that first accident and the shared belief that arose from it. Eventually these attempts to control our exterior environment became mythologies, and the mythologies turned into religions. People believed that It, whatever It was, needed something in order to feel better. Since we humans needed things in order to be happy, we thought God must be the same way. We created God in the image and likeness of man.

We create God. And we're going to create a new God, tomorrow's God, right here on earth during the course of the next twenty-five years. We're going to create a less dysfunctional one. In my book *The New Revelations,* I invite you to take the Five Steps to Peace. In taking these steps, you:

1. Acknowledge that some of your old beliefs about God and about Life are no longer working.
2. Acknowledge that there is something you do not understand about God and about Life, the understanding of which will change everything.
3. Are willing for a new understanding of God and Life to now be brought forth, an understanding that could produce a new way of life on the earth.

4. Are courageous enough to explore and examine this new understanding, and, if it aligns with your inner truth and knowing, to enlarge your belief system to include it.
5. Live your life as a demonstration of your highest and grandest beliefs, rather than as a denial of them.

What religion needs now is what Sir John Templeton calls "Humility Theology." He defines this as "a theology that is willing to admit it does not have all the answers and is willing to live within the question." Our idea that we have all the answers—about God, about life, and about each other—is killing us. Yet fallibility is the one thing religious leaders can't admit to. The first of the Five Steps to Peace that I identify in my work is, "Some of our old beliefs aren't working." The second is, "We choose to acknowledge there is something we don't understand about God and about life, the understanding of which could change everything." Can you imagine the pope saying that? In the same spirit that Martin Luther asked his congregation to tack The Ninety-Five Theses on church doors all over Europe in 1517, I invite you to copy the Five Steps to Peace out of this book, and tack them to the church doors.

-§-
Our idea that we have all the answers—about God, about life, and about each other—is killing us.
-§-

Most of humanity is sleepwalking. People can be aroused out of that sleep. The process happens largely through the entertainment industry: books, songs, television, and motion pictures are key means by which people are participating in the great awakening. And that process is exponential. It's not a 1, 2, 3, 4 progression. It's a 2, 4, 8, 16, 32 progression as people influence each other.

The Conversations With God books have sold upwards of seven million copies in thirty-four languages. Those seven million people are talking to seven million more. So suddenly you're looking at fourteen, then twenty-eight million people who are impacted by these messages. That's not a small number of people. When you multiply that by the number of message centers, the Deepak Chopras, the Marianne Williamsons, you're suddenly talking 100 or 150 million people. Pretty soon, we're approaching critical mass and all the dominos begin to fall.

Jean Houston uses the phrase, "jump time." At jump time, humanity does not evolve in a slow, upward climb. It hits critical mass and then does a very rapid jump. As our consciousness changes, our institutions change. At jump time, we create a whole new cosmology that results in the construction of new collective realities around politics, economics, education, government. The way we live our lives, collectively, shifts and changes during jump time. It happens relatively quickly. Over a period of a decade or two we see enormous changes, and by the end of a quarter century—just twenty-five years—virtually everything is different.

The last great, true jump was the Renaissance. In a period of just twenty-five to thirty years, everything was different. Society's attitudes toward sexuality, our beliefs about God, science and society, everything changed, just like that. Many sociologists now agree that we are very close to the next jump time. Cosmologists refer to it as an evolutionary leap; religionists call it a quickening of the spirit; I call it the Great Awakening.

-§-

At jump time, we create a whole new cosmology that results in the construction of new collective realities around politics, economics, education, government.

-§-

How can you play a part in this? You do it by taking personal responsibility for making the people whose lives you touch aware that it is time to wake up. You choose to participate in the Great Awakening as an awakener. You embrace the personal intention of waking up as many people as you can. I've made that the intention of my life and I suspect that I've touched some seven million people in that process. It doesn't matter if you just touch a dozen, because your reach extends far beyond what you might imagine. I make this point more directly and more specifically in each of my books. In the most recent one, *Tomorrow's God,* I say it right in the Introduction:

"This book has come to tell you that you can change the course of humanity.

"You.

"Not only the people who run governments or own corporations or lead movements or write books or are influential for some other reason. Not only those people.

"You.

"You can change the course of human history.

"This is not an exaggeration. Please believe me. This in not an exaggeration.

"This book calls you to that singular undertaking. It invites you now to internalize the wisdom of both ancient and contemporary masters found here; not merely to hear it again, but now to *receive* it, to *take it in,* to absorb it at the deepest level of your being, until it becomes the essence of who you are at the cellular level.

"Life will be inviting you over the years immediately ahead to act and respond from this level of Deep Knowing. What you place there now in terms of the things you profoundly believe, and how far you spread the messages found here through the living of your life in a new way, will make all the difference *in* the world *to* the world.

"Yet do not feel that you have to do all this by yourself. Perhaps the most uplifting and exciting part of the message that is brought to us in this book is that now, none of us have to 'go it alone.' We have teammates, and we can join them and call them to us, to rally around humanity's greatest cause: changing ourselves and changing our world."

I'm not the only one who is issuing calls like this. Happily, these calls are being issued from pulpits and from lecterns. Spiritual writers and spiritual messengers all over the world are echoing them. Even some politicians are beginning to say these words. We are beginning to create true mass movement. The idea that each of us is collectively responsible is gaining traction.

-§-
If we trace a behavior back to the belief that sponsored it, and correct our belief, we have a chance to correct the behavior.
-§-

But these efforts cannot be undertaken simply at the level of behavior. If a leader suggests we need to change at the level of behavior, it is like putting a Band-Aid on an open wound. What people who are currently entrenched in the system need to understand is that the solution is not found at the level of *behavior*. The solution is found at the level of *belief*. Every behavior springs from—and is given birth by—a belief. If we trace a behavior back to the belief that sponsored it, and correct our belief, we have a chance to correct the behavior.

Try this simple exercise. Write a list of the last five disasters in your life. As candidly as you can, on the left side of a piece of paper, list the last five bad decisions you made, poor choices, walls you've walked into, major problems you've had.

Now draw a line down the middle. On the other side of the page, write down what you believed that caused you to do that. What belief was behind that choice or decision?

Now cross out the left hand side of the page. It is irrelevant. It's the right hand side of your page that not only sponsored these, but lesser behaviors; perhaps they didn't create catastrophes but they are not doing you any good. Go down that hall of mirrors to discover what belief sponsored this particular disaster, which belief sponsored that one. When we do this in workshops anywhere in the world, participants get huge "A-ha's" when they see the connections.

I've set up a global educational undertaking called Humanity's Team. The stated mission of Humanity's Team (www.HumanitysTeam.com) is simply to free humanity from the oppression of its beliefs—about God, about life, and about each other—in order to create a different world and facilitate the Great Awakening. We've created New Spirituality study groups, and New Spirituality emotional support groups. Our first and primary program is education. The vision of Humanity's Team is to create workshops, seminars, and educational opportunities based on the New Spirituality. Jimmy Breslin, the *New York Times* columnist, wrote, "The civil are not organized, and the organized are not civil." Humanity's Team organizes the civil around principles upon which the largest number of people can honestly agree.

I have a one-word definition for wellness: Peace. The degree to which you exhibit and experience peace—which is another word for love—is the essence of personal wellness. The same definition can be applied to planetary wellness. The degree to which the planet experiences being at peace is the degree to which it's well. The degree to which it lacks peace is the degree to which it lacks wellness. The world's environmental health, its economic health, its political health, its sociological health, and its spiritual health, are all a cumulative reflection of our collectively created reality. Wellness equals peace on the planetary as well as on the individual level.

-§-

The degree to which the planet experiences being at peace is the degree to which it's well.

-§-

The place where individual health meets planetary health is the level of our individual beliefs, as well as the collective beliefs embraced by humanity. If we as nationalities, as religious groups, as political parties, have the courage to examine the most sacred of our beliefs, we will discover the source of our behavior. Considering the possibility that there may be another way to hold reality is the key to the golden door of peace on this planet.

Saniel Bonder: Healing the Roots of Fundamentalism

Religious believers who take every word of their scriptures as literal, absolute truths are often called "fundamentalists." They see a black and white world. They state convictions such as: "If you don't follow these scriptural precepts absolutely, you are sinning against the one true God."

"Either you are one of the chosen or you are among the heathen."

And, usually: "If you are not saved, you will go to hell."

No matter how much his doctrines and prejudices flout common sense, current science, and the parameters of reason and civility, the fundamentalist believes he alone is right and all who disagree are wrong—and damned. The syndrome appears in all religions: my maternal grandfather was an Orthodox Jewish fundamentalist.

Those with less rigid beliefs suffer questions that don't trouble these literalists. Secretly, though, in our psychic backwaters, we hide similar rigidity and cling fiercely to irrational prejudices. If we look closely, we may find that these "fundamental" assumptions govern our lives. Just because they're not written down in a holy book doesn't prevent us from imposing primitive belief systems on reality as if our survival depended on their being absolutely true.

What if this generic fundamentalism is universal to humanity, and threatening or even lethal to life on Earth?

Saniel Bonder has helped hundreds achieve embodied spiritual enlightenment—and then discover how to live an awakened life together on Earth. A neo-shaman and tantric, he is author of *Great Relief* (New Leaf Distributing Company, 2004), *Healing the Spirit/Matter Split*, and *The Tantra of Trust*, and founder of the Awakening Mutuality work (www.wakingdown.org, 888.741.5000). He's also a devoted husband to his beloved, Linda Groves; an avid golfer and flute player; a grateful Gold Ambassador in John Easterling's Amazon Herb Company; and a proud activist with Dr. Helen Caldicott's Nuclear Policy Research Institute. For more information see www.sanielbonder.net or call 1.888.657.7020.

Chapter Three

A Shocking Crime

One weekday morning in late 2003, "James" lured a teenage girl standing at a suburban bus stop into his pickup, offering her a ride. Zonked on drugs, he molested her while driving. A chase ensued, and James was eventually arrested. Suddenly, this man with no criminal record was headed to prison.

When we heard the news, my wife Linda and I were stunned. We'd known James as a reliable, honest tradesman, a good person. In fact, he'd begun to apologize immediately upon being apprehended. But his crime was the kind that turns up the volume on everyone's fears: not only fears about random violence, but also the fear that anyone could crack and do something horrible, even you or me.

Linda and I knew James did not have a foundation of inner work to stand on. With his outer life in wreckage, we feared for his sanity – even his survival.

Fundamentalism in Our Souls

Stories of crack-ups like this scream out of the news almost daily. We can see these acts as eruptions of fundamentalist chaos in the psyche, whether or not the perpetrator is a "religious fanatic." James wasn't.

What more can that perspective reveal?

My reflections here come mainly from in-the-trenches transformational work with individuals and groups over a dozen years. I've been sobered by pervasive fundamentalism in others – and in myself.

When we dive deeply into the roots of our fundamentalism, our feeling-insight can become like a red-hot ball of psychic iron burning down to basic foundations of the soul. Wherever our character is built on fundamentalist fear and absolutism, that red-hot ball can blaze through flooring and drop into a deeper basement.

-§-

No matter how much his doctrines and prejudices flout common sense, current science, and the parameters of reason and civility, the fundamentalist believes he alone is right.

-§-

Along this fiery, startling course, we discover sub-basements beneath the personality. Those underground rooms each give structural integrity to the total house of who we are. But they're not the foundation of our character or its ills. We need to keep burning through false foundations until we hit bottom and stand on solid, conscious ground.

An Astonishing Transformation

James's crime rocked everyone close to him to the core. It dealt a fatal blow to his business. And what of the young girl whose life he had shattered? As a husband, a father, and a now-disgraced businessman, James suffered suicidal depression for months after his crime.

However, before I first visited him in jail later, his wife said that he was having an "awakening." Sure enough, sitting in his orange jail jumpsuit, James looked as if several layers of dead skin had been scraped off his face. Even in those horrific circumstances, he was going through a resurrection.

When he told me why his crime occurred, and what had happened since, his transformation began to make sense.

The First Basement: Broken Zones and Broken Souls

When James got stoned and did that terrible thing, where did reliable, sensible James go?

"Saniel—I'm broken!" Years ago a woman dear to me shouted those words from a foot in front of my face. Her anguished cry opened a gateway through which I tumbled and have not stopped falling.

With colleagues, I have been charting the terrain of human brokenness ever since. We try to work from an embodied spiritual perspective that encounters and holds our psychic madness without violent recoil or subtle judgment.

What do I mean by "broken"? Our psyches, even our souls, suffer discontinuities in life. The central feeling-sense of "I" or "me" crucial to managing daily life is compromised in almost every human being.

Even balanced, healthy egos also have psychic "broken zones," places or times of severe disconnection from that generally sunny, positive "I."

Others have survived with no such functional, balanced, central self. I call them "broken souls."

-§-

We need to keep burning through false foundations until we hit bottom and stand on solid, conscious ground.

-§-

In workshops, I suggest that healthy egos have typically suffered ordinary setbacks and less-than-horrific abuse. From childhood they've more or less continually come forward into life. Yes, they have their crises and issues. Healthy egos also have broken zones: distressed identity fragments cut off from their central, characteristic self and, for survival's sake, surrounded by defenses. But their functional ego has grown stronger.

Broken souls are different. To illustrate, I pick up a big object and say to workshop participants, "The ego of the broken soul is like a little plant, just germinating or still fragile. It's standing there, small, delicate, bright green, when"—I drop the heavy object—"*BAM!* Someone or something slams it back deep underground. And that often happens again and again."

Many broken souls have experienced massive doses of such violence. If not physical or sexual, it's almost always emotional and verbal.

Strong egos can also become broken souls at any time, in reaction to shattering experiences. Holocaust survivors are one example.

Even so, many broken souls galvanize amazing energy to survive and flourish. Some people who look to be most "together," the most creative, effective, and attractive among us, are secretly broken souls.

This includes many of our leaders, secular and spiritual. When a leader requires others to hold him as flawless, or simply unaccountable, his flock becomes self-toxifying. The ideal of a leader's untouchable superiority betrays brokenness in all willing participants. Such societies become like extended dysfunctional families. Their "children" shoulder unbearable pressures of both their own shadowy brokenness and that of their "parents." These collectives often embody the worst attributes of what we fear as cults. However, many of them flourish not only in marginal spiritual or political communes, but also in corporate high-rises, respectable churches and synagogues, and halls of government—all over the planet.

-§-

Healthy egos also have broken zones: distressed identity fragments cut off from their central, characteristic self and, for survival's sake, surrounded by defenses.

-§-

Every Broken Zone Has Its Own Fundamentalist Mind

Where we are broken, we are drowning and gasping for breath, or exploding with volcanic intensity. We are so dissociated from actual events around and within us that we can't recognize them. The world, to our brokenness, is black or white; good or evil; sacred or sinful. There is no middle ground. At the core are primal emotional reactivity and a pitched battle to survive against odds.

Every broken zone has its own fundamentalist mind. Every broken zone is a rigid fanatic. Every broken zone fiercely projects a fantasy of absolute, simplistic ideals upon whatever relative, complex reality it encounters. Broken zones cannot meet the multi-faceted, *present* mystery and paradoxes of the self, the other, or the world. If it feels seriously threatened, every broken zone may be tempted to do almost anything to stay alive.

It's a huge battle. No wonder our broken parts have to work so hard just to survive. Yet they are the very parts that made survival possible, long before a central self could integrate our traumas. They don't need to be transcended (read: exterminated). They need to be heard, welcomed into the whole self, honored, and *integrated.* That is what relieves them of their sociopathic fierceness.

The more one meets broken identity fragments in others and oneself, the more the whole world of human psyches looks like a collection of walking Picassos. *Guernicas,* actually: bombed-out war zones, devastated by our brokenness and its inherent fundamentalism.

However, we can't fully account for our fundamentalist madness with histories of our traumas. James's earlier life doesn't explain how he became a suicidal and eventually violent broken soul. *He had never suffered any proportional, causative trauma.* So we may need to let that molten ball of deeply felt insight burn down further, below brokenness.

An Atrocious Way to Die While Alive

During our first visit in jail, James said that since high school, he knew he would someday kill himself. Marrying, having children, creating a successful company, enjoying his sporting life, none of that changed this core conviction. He was living on borrowed time.

He also felt squeezed into a box. Going through the motions of family and business life, he was missing in action. Before his crime, James was running on fumes. No one knew he was strung out on drugs. His suicidal impulse was driving him to the edge. That fateful day, over he went.

In a bizarre way, James did die: in one atrocious act, he destroyed the outer shell of his life forever.

-§-

When a leader requires others to hold him as flawless, or simply unaccountable, his flock becomes self-toxifying.

-§-

Yet now he was undergoing a rebirth.

Meditating, keeping a journal, he lived a day at a time. He was remorseful about his crime and felt he deserved to pay his dues. But facing a long prison term – maybe life – he was, for the first time, experiencing meaning and feeling from the heart. He honored others' beliefs in God, but as for himself, he tapped his chest: "I have to find out who I am first." There in a county jail, James was consciously birthing his soul into his body.

The Second Basement: The Spirit/Matter Split

Perhaps James's brokenness expresses an underlying human fracture, "the Spirit/Matter split." Simply put, in this split we regard Spirit as good and matter (unworthy of a capital "M") as bad; Spirit as divine, flesh as weak and sinful; the limitless as positive and all limitations, even the Earth and our personal, concrete desires and reactions, as negative, dangerous to our souls, even evil.

James was not struggling with such beliefs – but this split underlies belief and disbelief. It is a pre-conceptual, fearful, sometimes physically violent revulsion to all that is material, limited, and mortal. I put it this way in my book, *Healing the Spirit/Matter Split:*

> Since ancient times, both the enlightenment traditions of the East and the religious traditions of the West have sprung from, and perpetuated, a chasm at the very core of human life and awareness. That rift is so foundational to postmodern people that even our secular sciences and our ways of sensing and knowing the world are suffused by it.... I call that chasm "the Spirit/Matter split." (p. x)

The Spirit/Matter split is like a primary fault line in our being. Branching up from it are secondary faults of our broken zones and the underground caverns of broken souls. The Spirit/Matter split begins at the place in Being where transcendental and cosmic reality gives rise to individual soul-nature and personhood. It is more basic to us than our broken zones and personal fundamentalisms.

-§-
The whole world of human psyches looks like a collection of walking Picassos. Guernicas, actually: bombed-out war zones.
-§-

If we are deeply materialistic, we doubt Spirit, God, Consciousness. If we're ambivalent, we may *believe* in spiritual or religious conceptions, but we can't *embody* them. And if we're deeply spiritual or religious, we often can't hold dense matter to be as Godly and real as radiant Light. We fear it and regard material life as tempting, sinful, dangerous.

Bizarrely, our greatest geniuses and heroes, including enlightened spiritual leaders and "non-dualist" teachers, are often severely split. An overwhelming majority of our social, political, and ecological catastrophes can be traced to the Spirit/Matter split in individuals and in societies.

Hypermasculine Dissociation Equals Original Sin?

The feminine impulse in our natures seeks to merge, feel, receive, and surrender; the masculine, to differentiate, analyze, penetrate, and control.

Another phrase I use for the Spirit/Matter split is "hypermasculine dissociation." Early humanity did not suffer this split—but it wasn't enjoying what we today would romantically envisage as "enlightened harmony before the fall." We might call that early condition "hyperfeminine," an unconscious, murky latency of spirit in "Mater," Earthly matter. We participated in both physical and psychic realms, but without masculine individuation or self-conscious intelligence.

Anthropologists agree that five to ten thousand years ago humanity dramatically evolved. All around the Earth, human beings differentiated their consciousness from Earthen and tribal realms in which it had been embedded for untold millennia.

But the wrenching evolutionary force of that passage took humanity beyond *masculine differentiation* into *hypermasculine dissociation.* In the classic East this detaching impulse became a violent will to separate spirit from the physical and psychic world, seeking "liberation from the wheel of birth and death." Later, in the classic West, this same hypermasculine dissociation became an equally violent mental will to stand free of and understand the world, thus to control, manipulate, and subdue it.

-§-

An overwhelming majority of our social, political, and ecological catastrophes can be traced to the Spirit/Matter split in individuals and in societies.

-§-

Thus, the onset of the hypermasculine epoch may have first triggered in human consciousness a sense that there's something fundamentally *wrong* with us. Hyperfeminine humanity, merged in terrestrial Mater (Mother Earth) without self-consciousness, suffered no such primal self-division and distress. The Spirit/Matter split or hypermasculine dissociation, in other words, may be the source of "original sin" as a feeling-assumption about ourselves, deeper than thought and perception. Our religious and spiritual traditions have then interpreted that assumption for millennia as actual sin, active "missing of the mark" of our right relationship with God, Reality, ultimate Being. In postmodern humans, this has become rampant alienation even from our own bodies and souls.

James's crime was a violent outburst of unbridled hypermasculine estrangement.

Since then he has been uniting Matter and Spirit in his life with humility and strength.

What resource is he drawing on?

Or, what is underneath the Spirit/Matter split?

Time to let that red-hot iron ball of feeling-insight smoke and burn yet deeper.

Reality Sets In Even More

As the months wore on, James's prospects did not look good. The District Attorney's office would not plea bargain.

Even so, other prisoners and the guards noticed James' uncommon disposition. Fellow prisoners sought him out for advice and solace. Without fanfare, James was becoming a guide and teacher.

His mother and sister stood by him, but things became difficult with his wife.

In the face of the District Attorney's refusal to negotiate, James and his lawyer decided to risk a trial: James pleaded not guilty by virtue of temporary insanity.

The Foundation Level: The Core Wound

While entering his plea, James was becoming saner than ever.

I was then publishing a book, *Great Relief: Nine Sacred Secrets Your Body Wants You to Know About Freedom, Love, and Trust.* It's a primer on the "Core Wound" of our lives.

The "Core Wound" is not a psychological issue or birth trauma, but the fundamental mystery of our existence. It is our subjective registration of always being material and spiritual, finite and non-finite. We are at once limitless—at least, we yearn and strive for limitlessness—and limited.

After visiting with James, I decided to devote much of the book's final chapter to his story. In disgrace and confinement, untutored, he was spontaneously adapting to the simultaneous anxiety and ecstasy of his most fundamental condition, the Core Wound. From *Great Relief:*

> This contradiction between the obvious limits we confront at all times and the impulse to know or get or be something limitless, or far less limited, triggers a perpetual conflict at the core of our lives.
>
> In most cases we don't personally experience it as a conflict or dilemma that we can think about and name as such. Rather, we feel it more like a wound, an inexplicable, almost unnameable pain. We endure it as something like a gash in the most intimate, private, core tissue of our being.
>
> Our limits are all associated with having or being a finite body. (Mind and emotions are as anchored to the body as leaves to a tree.) But if we were content, truly OK with these limits, then we would be at peace or at home in life as it already is. Our impulse toward the limitless continually translates as the feeling, "This is not enough." The helpless, perpetual mix of obvious limits and the impulse toward limitlessness makes for living as this core wound.
>
> *The core wound is the engine of human evolution.* It appears to me that, uniquely among living creatures, human beings suffer this wound, conflict, or contradiction. As a species, it makes it impossible for us to stay still. And it makes it extremely difficult for us to ever know who we really are.
>
> I suggest that everything every human being has ever done has been a reaction to that wound itself.

> Everybody suffers it. Every *body*. And every body is suffering *as* this existential wound. It is not happening *to* us. It *is* not something we are *experiencing*. It is what we are *being*. (pp. 99-101)

Fundamentalism and the Core Wound

Fundamentalism festers like lethal bacteria in the stagnant waters of our broken zones. Those waters originally stream from a more primal dissociation, the Spirit/Matter split. Originating deep within, this split is a violent fault fracturing reactively out of the molten reality of the Core Wound. That Wound is like white-hot magma under the crust, at our hearts. It's the fire of the Sun in the center of Earthen being—an utter mystery.

Hyperfeminine, prehistoric humanity had its own primitive fundamentalisms. But as the Spirit/Matter split became dominant, it spawned many peripheral fractures in our psyches. The current pandemic of fundamentalist brokenness is like a hypermasculine autoimmune disorder of the soul. It allows many opportunistic psychic dis-eases to flourish.

The governing force of this split has steadily magnified over generations. We've added to it immense reactions of interior isolation and fragmentation; massive, toxic judgments of self, other, and world; whole societal and cultural machines built on hidden fear and bewilderment. Underneath, that primitive sense of fundamentally missing the mark, of estrangement, and alienation, has intensified—original sin or karma.

But even that primordial sense of wrongness is unnecessary pain we add to the inevitable pain of the Core Wound:

> The core wound is not evidence of a degraded human estate. On the contrary, I hold it to be an evolutionary hallmark of our humanness. The more sensitive you become to and *as* this core wound, the more you advance in human evolution.
>
> Thus, the root of our suffering, this core wound, is not evil, and it's not sin. It constitutes the marrow of our true dignity as human beings—even when we appear to have no dignity at all. (p. 2)

A Compassionate Choice With Hard Consequences

James found jury selection unnerving. The courtroom was wall-to-wall people, many openly hostile to him. Once the jury was in place, the trial began that same day.

James went into shock. He couldn't breathe, couldn't show his face, and couldn't even cry. To him, the District Attorney's opening statement was like a bomb exploding in the courtroom.

Back in his cell afterward, stunned, James could not stop feeling badly for his victim. She would have to take the stand and testify. The thought of putting her through that, and of how she must be dreading it, was more devastating to him than his own prospects.

James took charge. He told his attorney to change his plea to guilty and accepted a deal that would give him a minimum of 15 years to life.

As I write, he awaits final sentencing.

Healing Ourselves Before Healing Humanity

Though seared again by internal flames, as he had been that fateful morning in his pickup, this time James took a stand. He stepped beyond his shock and brokenness. Accepting grave consequences, he made one magnificent pass with the suture of self-responsibility. He continued to knit his own Spirit/Matter split into a single fabric of being the best person he could be. In his heart he heard a great secret to freedom, love, trust, and truly great relief—not from the Core Wound, but in it.

If James can do that, in *his* circumstances, who of us can't, in ours?

We may assume we've already dealt with realities of fundamentalism, broken zones and broken souls, and the Spirit/Matter split. We may think we are beyond the Core Wound of Being.

Or, if not us, then surely this saint, that enlightened master, this psychological or philosophical giant—surely they are beyond this diagnosis.

I don't think so.

If there were ever a case of "Physician, heal thyself," dear friends, I think we're looking in a huge mirror here. *All* of us. No exceptions.

This doesn't mean we should stop our wise, heroic efforts toward urgent healings for our planet and ourselves. Not at all!

But "heal" means "to make whole." If we won't look to see how fragmented and twisted we are, authentic realization of the Core Wound and the paradoxical wholeness it grants will forever elude us.

If we are leading-edge healers of humanity, then our fellow humans will be deprived of a healing we presumed we had no need for and therefore never experienced.

If our species thus continues in ignorance and grave interior shattering and mistrust, then all life on Earth will go on paying for our incapacity to really know ourselves and to evolve into *trust:* trust of self, trust of others, trust of Being.

Innate to us, the Core Wound cannot be healed. It can be accepted, realized, embodied, celebrated, *lived.* That process heals the Spirit/Matter split and weaves our brokenness into integrated selfhood. From straitjacketed fundamentalism, it liberates us into wisdom and compassion.

In this light, prideful denial of our hidden fundamentalism, brokenness, and deep splits is as violent a bane upon Earth as nuclear fallout and genocide. That denial is an ongoing root cause of such visible horrors. And that denial guarantees more of the same—for our planet and for our selves.

-§-
It takes already-realized consciousness to really heal our bodies and souls.
-§-

Healing the Earth of pandemic human fundamentalism takes place from two grounds up.

The first is the living Earth itself—*Herself*—the Material Ground on Whom we physically stand.

The second is Spiritual Consciousness, often symbolized by "Father Sun" and regarded as a primordial male principle. It—symbolically, *He*—is the invisible, Nonmaterial Ground in Whom we spiritually stand.

We once evolved into a Spirit/Matter split that divided the singularity of unconscious being. Now we are reuniting these two grounds of being and consciously evolving:

> [F]inite Matter is every bit as real, divine, and important as Infinite Spirit. This discovery is not abstract.... In fact, ending the ancient "holy war" against earthly life has a paradoxical effect for many. It does not weaken or sabotage but rather empowers our human capacity to commune with and realize infinite Spirit. In that passage we not only feel the presence of Spirit. We become that great Oneness of Spirit and Matter, unshakably. (pp. ix-x)

The process of human transformation is not just evolutionary—*it is itself evolving.*

Today we are uncovering the pernicious presence of fundamentalism, brokenness, and the Spirit/Matter split in our philosophies, psychologies, practices and disciplines, even our venerable spiritual traditions, and nearly all of our cultural and social customs.

Paradoxically, healing these ills may first require basic *embodied* and *enlightened* wholeness. Achieving that disproves long-standing views of human psycho-spiritual development, which propose enlightenment can come only *after* psycho-emotional transformation. We can learn how to simultaneously *be* both the personal, material ground, with all our flaws and limitations, and the impersonal, spiritual ground, with all its sublimity and grace.

Outgrowing these syndromes requires embodied enlightenment as a foundation, not a result. It takes already-realized consciousness to really heal our bodies and souls. Disproving long-standing dogmas, people are evolving on this integrative basis today. When we are being both the material Ground, with our personal flaws, and the spiritual Ground, with its impersonal sublimity, our basic awakeness catalyzes evolutionary healing.

We will question many cherished beliefs and principles. The conscious marriage of spirit and matter forces us to reconsider every value that even subtly favors either principle. What if every reference to a God apart from us, every casting of the eyes upward when thinking or speaking of Spirit, reinforces a primordial crack in our feeling of Being? And compounds our sinful ("mark-missing") violence upon both our bodies and the Earth?

This evolutionary shift drives an unrelenting redesign of our entire lives and all consciousness and culture. It forces a both cellular and transcendent reconsideration of primitive assumptions that "something is wrong here." Instead we come to this realization:

There is no problem in Being. To be human is to endure, at once ecstatic and devastated, always gloriously whole and strangely, gloriously broken. All that frightful madness about being fundamentally wrong, sinful, karmic, and limited, upon which we've built entire religions and societies, is itself what's wrong—along with hypermasculine cartoon-dreams of an absolutely blissful salvation, liberation, and harmony, here or elsewhere. We are OK. Life and death are OK. And we can learn, together, how to abide in natural agony/ecstasy. We can stop adding unnecessary pain to inevitable pain.

Even as we heal beautifully, scars and tremors of our brokenness remain. We accept simultaneous brokenness and wholeness in the Core Wound as the yin and yang of real life. The wound becomes a gorgeous, living paradox. Cycling like seeds and then flowers in the sunshine of inherent wellness, we fall and rot,-rise and bloom again and again, into ever-fuller divine humanity. Our presence, to one another and to all life, becomes a benediction.

Our planet may require nothing less.

So may our selves.

What Can We Do Next?

While draining away a lot of bathwater, we also take forward great "baby" virtues and benefits from the hypermasculine epoch of human culture, including innumerable advances that civilization as we know it has made possible.

In addition to developing new material, psychological, and spiritual technologies to meet our immense evolutionary tasks, we humans need to grow into a global sobriety: If we don't address these underlying, species-wide ills, anything else we do to heal our planet may be superficial

—jeopardized or even doomed by what we have not confronted and healed in ourselves, heart by heart. Yet it is entirely possible for us to curb the plague of human fundamentalism and its deeper ills within decades—and to eradicate it within the twenty-first century. We not only can do this: we *must.* Only thus can we guarantee humanity and life on Earth a viable future in the twenty-second century and beyond.

Two generations ago Nobel laureate William Faulkner declared, "Humanity will prevail."

No, it won't.

Humanity will simply evolve.

May we accept the dignity and peace that naturally anoint our hearts when we become thus true to our planet—and to our selves. That's what my friend and teacher James is doing behind bars. If he can do it there—where can't we?

Huston Smith: The News of Eternity

I taught for a time at Syracuse University. One semester, I invited the author Saul Bellow to appear for three weeks as a guest lecturer. He was a big fish for that area, so the Syracuse press corps mounted a press conference to interview him. When the journalists had assembled, the leader of the press corps asked, "Mr. Bellow, we are all writers here, and you are a writer. What's the difference between us?"

Without batting an eyelid, Bellow replied, "Reporters are interested in the news of the day. Novelists, if they're worthy of their salt, are interested in news of eternity."

We live in a world in flames. There is no issue that calls for more serious thinking than the difference between the news of the day and the news of eternity. When we look at Islam today, the news of the day is dismal, all the way through. But what do the religions have to say about eternity? Here they are in full agreement. The message in Christianity is one of peace, with Jesus as the Prince of Peace. The core of the Koran is similar. It is an absolutely solid message of peace.

What about the jihad that fundamentalist Islamists believe they are waging against the West? The word jihad is usually translated as holy war. But the literal meaning of the word is effort. What's wrong with effort? When people are at war, then effort is directed at furthering their aims in the conflict.

Christianity, too, has a doctrine of a holy war, a righteous war. It's spelled out in the Catholic doctrine of the Just War. What the Catholic

Huston Smith, Ph.D., is a retired professor of philosophy and religion whose teaching appointments include MIT and the University of California at Berkeley. His twelve books include *The World's Religions* (HarperSanFrancisco, 1991), *The Way Things Are* (University of California Press, 2003), and *Why Religion Matters* (HarperSanFrancisco, 2001). In 1996 Bill Moyers featured his life and career in a PBS series, *The Wisdom of Faith.* His documentary films on Hinduism, Buddhism and Islam all won international awards, and *The Journal of Ethnomusicology* cited his discovery of Tibetan multiphonic chanting as an important landmark. More at www.hustonsmith.net.

church teaches about a holy war, and what Islam teaches about a jihad, bear a great deal of resemblance to each other. Yet religion can be hijacked by politics, and used to stir up conflict and violence. In a time of war, each side needs power. The greatest power is to be sanctioned by God. Each side wants to set up a pipeline from God, the greatest power, down to their political maneuvers. This results in both sides claiming to be on God's side.

It's interesting to go back in history and discover the origin of this word jihad in relation to war. It stems from a time when Mohammed and his followers were returning from fighting a war. For ten years, the Meccans were trying to wipe Mohammed and his followers in the city of Medina off the map, because they had stood up for justice. After ten years of battle raging back and forth between Medina and Mecca, Mohammed was victorious. When he got home, Mohammed declared, "We have returned from the lesser jihad to the greater jihad." By the greater jihad, he meant the evil that dwells in the heart of every one of us. He saw the inner struggle, the inner effort, as an infinitely greater battle than the outer one—a historical reality that is missed by all the current press reporting on jihad.

-§-
Institutions and nations are always selfish and self-interested, and...usually coerce individuals to behave in immoral ways.
-§-

Reinhold Niebuhr, a theologian powerfully affected by World War I, wrote a remarkable book called *Moral Man and Immoral Society.* Hearsay has it that Fidel Castro, John F. Kennedy, and Che Guevara were all reading it at the same time. Niebuhr's thesis is that individuals are moral in and of themselves, and often make selfless choices. But larger groupings like institutions and nations are always selfish and self-interested, and—because they have both power and social momentum on their side—usually coerce individuals to behave in immoral ways.

The faith traditions help us with these behaviors, because they inspire us to do better. They lay down guidelines for societal actions. These traditions are the practices that can transform this selfish behavior, affecting the whole landscape of problems we face.

Rev. William Sloane Coffin, who served as Chaplain of Yale University during the Vietnam War and later founded one of the largest peace organizations in the U.S., was asked what Christianity has to say about war and peace, he quoted the biblical prophet Amos: "Let justice run down like water, and righteousness like a mighty stream."

But when pressed for specifics, he said that Christianity gives us the mighty stream, but it doesn't give us a whole irrigation system; that we have to build for ourselves. The wisdom traditions give us inspiration and comfort, but we have to apply them to our daily lives. Every morning, wherever I am, I read two or three pages from one of the great wisdom traditions. That's my irrigation system. In Robert Frost's phrase, "Everyone must work the ounces of his own strength on the world in his own way." You have to begin with what you have.

A critical turning point for me came in the spring of my junior year in college. It was a day that changed my life forever.

There were only six hundred students in this little college. My major was Activities; I wanted to be a Big Man On Campus, and to do that I thought I needed to be visible, and join as many societies as possible.

The professor who taught philosophy selected the students who showed a genuine interest in philosophy, and set up a monthly class in his home. Each meeting, one of us composed and read a short paper, three to five pages in length, on some philosophical topic. The whole group would then discuss the idea of the day over cherry pie a la mode, made by the professor's wife.

-§-
I felt as though I were in a tunnel, traveling rapidly through the universe of ideas, with ideas streaking toward me like points of light.
-§-

This particular night, my interest in the topic kept mounting, even after we left the professor's house. On the way back to the dormitory we continued the discussion. A little knot of three or four of us talked till midnight, then went to bed.

I turned off the light but I could not sleep. My head would not stop churning. The whole night, I felt as though I were in a tunnel, traveling rapidly through the universe of ideas, with ideas streaking toward me like points of light, some large, some small, then receding into the distance.

When I got up the next morning I was a changed student. I spent the next year-and-a-half getting myself out of all the organizations, so that I could throw myself into the world of ideas. I've been immersed in them ever since.

The list of problems our world faces is endless, from global warming to pollution to economic inequality to hunger to war. One of my books is entitled *Why Religion Matters.* After September 11, my eyes fell on that title, and I reflected that the ideas in the religious traditions surely matter a great deal, because they have endless resources for helping us with our individual spiritual growth, and providing a guideline for society as it confronts its challenges.

One of these challenges is keeping the enormous powers of destruction that technology has given us under our control, and utilizing them for human well-being. Scientist James Lovelock, developer of the Gaia theory, gave our planet only a fifty percent chance of making it through this century. Our consciousness has not caught up with our technology.

Modern society aims for knowledge through science. Science is empirical, meaning that it studies what our sense receptors pick up. The whole panoply of science is an extrapolation from things that our eyes can see. But our sense receptors are not our only receptors. Nobody has ever seen a thought. Nobody has ever seen a feeling, yet that's what our existential lives are awash with. Because modernity makes science the big picture, consciousness—which cannot be seen—has received short shrift. Science believes that matter is the most fundamental stuff of the universe. That's dead wrong.

All the great religions and wisdom traditions turn that belief exactly on its head. They tell us that what's fundamental is consciousness. In the beginning, God. God is consciousness. The heavens and earth—and all the material things that science knows how to deal with—came later. So the truth of the matter is that consciousness is not only all there is, but consciousness is primary, while matter obtrudes into this vast sea of consciousness. This mundane world is just a shadow, like the shadows on the cave walls in Plato's oft-quoted allegory. That's the basic story line of religion, developed in a thousand ways.

I've been involved with science for a long time. I taught at the Massachusetts Institute of Technology for sixteen years. All of my students were scientists. A large number of my colleagues were world class scientists. Science is good.

-§-

The religious traditions surely matter, because they have endless resources for... providing a guideline for society as it confronts its challenges.

-§-

Scientism, though, is bad. What's the difference? Science is the positive finding, through controlled experiment, of truths about the physical universe—and that's good. Scientism, by way of contrast, says two things. The first is that science is the best if not only probe of truth. The second fallacy of scientism is that it holds that the most fundamental substance in the universe is what scientists deal with, namely matter. There is no scientific basis for those two corollaries. They're a philosophical assumption and a matter of opinion. But this distinction has not been made. I don't want to paint scientists as white-jacketed bad guys. This isn't something that scientists have done to us; we've done it to ourselves. We've wanted all the benefits of science; rapid reproduction of goods, the reduction of drudgery, increases in life expectancy, and so on. But we've wanted these good things about science so much that we've forgotten that these practices deal only with the material aspects of life. We've sold ourselves a bill of goods, and it's pulled our culture askew. It has spawned the most secular culture history has ever witnessed.

I did my doctoral work at the University of Chicago. At that time, academics believed that science had the ability to explain everything. My teachers had persuaded me that science is the big picture; my world view was the scientific world view.

Then, one evening, four months before I was due to complete my dissertation and get my degree, I came upon a book by a mystic. Mysticism is everywhere now, but it wasn't so back then. I started reading. By page two, I realized that this material had nothing to do with my dissertation. I kept on reading that book, and my scientific world view collapsed like a house of cards. I realized that I was a mystic, and that mystics had a depth and accuracy that I'd never heard before.

I've never looked back. I quit philosophy, which has sold out to the scientists and lost touch with the big picture. I went to China and India and Nepal, and found profound ideals there. If you try and understand these great truths on your own, without the guidance of these great traditions, there's no hope. You just wander around and get no place.

At the start of my journey, I apprenticed myself to the most profound thinkers in each of the eight great wisdom traditions. I read their books and contemplated their practices. For instance, while studying Hinduism, I read the Upanishads and studied the Bhagavad Gita. Having done my homework, then I went to study with the teachers of these traditions in person. I focused myself for between two years (the shortest) and fifteen years (the longest) and the wisdom afforded to me through these minds became my guide. At the top of each tradition are the mystics. Whatever the religion, they all speak the same language, with only small differences between them. In this way, I found myself standing at the convergence of the wisdom of all the great traditions.

-§-

Because modernity makes science the big picture, consciousness—which cannot be seen—has received short shrift.

-§-

Truth holds together. You can't fill in all the interstices with just one religion. I haven't found anything in the other religions that are incompatible with my own Christianity. What I learned from Taoism, for instance, is not at all in conflict with the teachings of Jesus. It augments my Christianity by fleshing out different crevices of my experience that I didn't hear Christianity speaking to with the same precision. An example is the Four Yogas of Hinduism. The four ways to God in this tradition are through knowledge (jnana yoga), though love (bhakti yoga), through service (karma yoga), and through meditation (raja yoga).

The same idea appears in the twelfth chapter of Mark's Gospel: "Thou shalt love the lord thy God with all thy heart [bhakti yoga], with all thy soul [raja yoga], with all thy mind, [jnana yoga] and with all thy strength [karma yoga]. Those four ideas are present in both religions. In the Bible, they're dealt with in one verse, whereas in Hinduism, they're explicated in many books of scripture. So the guideline I've discovered is that truth holds together.

There's a fundamental divide in religious people between the mystics, and those that are not of that bent. The minds of mystics work differently. Mystics are comfortable with abstractions. Religious people who are not mystics don't work with abstractions. C. S. Lewis, a great Christian thinker and writer in the mid 1900s, put it very vividly. He said, "When I was a boy, my parents drilled into me, 'Don't attribute a form to God, because God is infinite, beyond all boundaries of form.' I tried and tried to think of a formless God. But the closest I could come was an infinite sea of gray tapioca." A concrete mind needs something concrete to latch onto. And that's the basic difference between the mystics and orthodox practitioners. The mystics have all the orthodox knowledge too, but they also have the experience of intuitive insight into truths that cannot even be put into words, because words are forms and forms have their boundaries. All the core truths of the wisdom traditions are united in the experience of the mystics.

-§-

At the top of each tradition are the mystics. Whatever the religion, they all speak the same language.

-§-

The big question is this: What is the nature of ultimate reality? How can we best comport our lives in keeping with it? These are the great issues with which the traditional religions and philosophies have never lost touch. Man does not live by bread alone. An upward tilt toward the better is built into us humans. It's a part of our nature. So spirit, and the lord of the spirit will be here no matter what happens. Spirit and its cultivation is the most important pursuit we could possibly undertake. Our work is to tend that life-giving lamp.

Part Two

Catalyzing Social and Political Transformation

Mary Catherine Bateson: Cybernetics and Trust Between Nations

My father Gregory Bateson referred to cybernetics as "the biggest bite out of the fruit of the Tree of Knowledge that mankind has taken in the last 2,000 years." (Bateson 1966 in Bateson 1972: 484) He had grown up with the Biblical story of the Fall and knew that such bites are often ambiguous, carrying both risk and promise. Writing in 1966, he paired the development of cybernetics with the Treaty of Versailles as the two most significant events of the twentieth century, but he pointed to the Treaty of Versailles as disastrously reducing the possibility of trust and was hopeful about the possibilities of cybernetics. By cybernetics, he did not refer narrowly to computers, but to the once-integrated field that studied communication and control in organisms and social organizations as well as in machines, now sometimes called systems theory.

The treaties that followed the First World War, especially the draconian peace imposed on Germany in the Treaty of Versailles, set the stage for many of the conflicts that have occurred since, including World War II. The conflicts in the Balkans have been déjà vu all over again. But Gregory's argument was more subtle: the Treaty of Versailles, cruel and punitive as it was, was especially destructive because it was imposed in the context created by American President Woodrow Wilson's Fourteen Points, which had proposed a non-punitive peace settlement. The demoralization of Germany that led to the rise of Nazism was triggered by a sense of betrayal, not by hardship.

Gregory seems to have incorporated the communications aspect of cybernetics in his thinking earlier and more deeply than the systems

Mary Catherine Bateson is a writer and cultural anthropologist. She has written and co-authored many books and articles, lectures across the U.S. and internationally, and is president of the Institute for Intercultural Studies in New York City. Until recently she was the Clarence J. Robinson Professor in Anthropology and English at George Mason University; she recently completed three years as a Visiting Professor at the Harvard Graduate School of Education. This chapter is based on a talk she gave at Foundation2020, Brioni Islands, Croatia, in May 2004. She can be found on the web at www.marycatherinebateson.com. Photo courtesy of George Mason University.

aspects. The Theory of Logical Types developed by Whitehead and Russell (1910–13) was an early influence on the Macy Conferences (von Foerster, editor, 1950–56) and the basic element in Gregory's theoretical thinking right through the 'sixties, underpinning his theories about learning and about schizophrenia.

Cybernetics has had a variety of influences on foreign policy, especially through games theory and economics, as well as analyses of the effects of positive and negative feedback on such symmetrical processes as arms races, another subject of early interest to Gregory. At the Foundation2020 conference in 2003, for instance, I drew on Gregory's work in arguing that the effort to make Croatia "competitive" framed Croatia's relations with other nations symmetrically, and that for stability such symmetrical relations should be balanced by complementary relations expressed in terms of "distinctiveness" and the possibility of playing a unique or indispensable role. Interestingly, Gregory argued at different stages in his career that both symmetry and complementarity are potentially subject to regenerative feedback and potentially lead to runaway change.

-§-
The demoralization of Germany that led to the rise of Nazism was triggered by a sense of betrayal, not by hardship.
-§-

But the Logical Types have been less central in thinking about international relations and need to be looked at today as we face the problem of creating trust between nations, especially those with a long history of mutual conflict or of betrayal. The end of the Cold War and the creation of the European Union have led to novel—almost startling—levels of cooperation in Europe, but the fear of terrorism and the American preference for going it alone have undermined transatlantic trust. Can a nation-state be said to trust (or distrust) another? What can weave the fabric of future cooperation in the Balkans? In the spring of 2004, in the Brioni Islands of Croatia, Foundation2020 decided to celebrate the Bateson centennial by applying Bateson's thinking to the nations of former Yugoslavia as they move toward European integration. Four presidents and three foreign ministers were present for portions of the discussions focused on the question: "How can we trust each other?"

There is a story that keeps coming into my mind as I try to think about the issue of trust, a story told by Sister Souljah, an African American woman, in her memoir (1994: 8). She had had a relatively secure early childhood, but when her father became ill and unemployed the family moved into a housing project and her parents divorced. One day her father took her to a playground, encouraged her to climb up on the slide, and held out his arms, promising to catch her. She was four years old. When she zoomed down the slide he stepped back and let her fall on her head. After he had comforted her in her tears he said, "I told you not to trust anybody."

It seems to me that, as we go back and forth between talking about trust and how trust or distrust might be learned, some story like that, painful as it is, should be in the back of our minds. It is, of course, a classic double bind, because the injunction to distrust is framed by the parental premise demanding trust: "Whatever I do to you, or for you, is for your own good." The father is betraying her "for her own good"—so that she will learn that, as a black child growing up in white America, she should not trust. Yet she is required to trust him in spite of what looks like clearly abusive treatment. Do we learn trust? Or do we start from innate trust and learn distrust? How does this aspect of learning shape all other kinds of learning?

The Brioni sessions included a video presentation. On the left side of the screen were images, many of them historical. On the right side of the screen, the word "trust" appeared, then, occasionally, "change." Trust. Trust. Change. As we think about the state of the world in this time of very rapid and unpredictable change, we need to investigate the relationships among trust and change, betrayal and learning, and the relationship of all these to our capacity for adaptation.

-§-
The end of the Cold War and the creation of the European Union have led to novel—almost startling—levels of cooperation in Europe.
-§-

In the second half of the twentieth century, cybernetics offered a new way of looking at adaptation, in terms of constancies maintained by homeostasis, in systems in which some variable is kept steady by constant small corrections, and unwanted change is prevented by corrective feedback. But cybernetics has also provided tools for thinking about runaway change, change accelerated by regenerative feedback, as in epidemics and population explosions.

A participant asserted during the conference sessions that an infant is born with the capacity to trust. I'm not sure that's strictly true, because infants don't have an alternative, so there is no selective pressure for the initial presence of trust. Unlike the young of many other species, the human infant doesn't have to recognize the mother immediately. Unlike newly hatched chicks, a human baby can't walk away and get lost; it's the mother who can walk away and has to learn to connect with the infant. But certainly, normal human infants are born with the capacity to *learn* to trust. It is critical for human infants to have the repeated—many, many times repeated—experience of feeling discomfort or need that is then met. Having that need met, whoever does it, is critical. It seems probable that that experience of dependable, reliable, many-times-repeated care really is the basis for the capacity to trust.

Trust is learned and relearned over time, moderated and contextualized. If you watch infants, they go through periods of being very anxious when exposed to anyone new or strange. Continuity is the basis for trust: that which you can depend upon, that which is predictable. There is an important tension here, because the need for continuity co-exists with another characteristic we share with other primates, which is curiosity and the enjoyment of stimulation. One would want to specify that discontinuity and unfamiliarity are enjoyable only as long as the infant's experience of continuity supports a sense of basic trust. Within limits, even painful experiences do not subvert the capacity for trust or extinguish curiosity. Change, experienced as difference or unfamiliarity, is both threatening and stimulating.When I am speaking about how people adapt to change, there will almost always in an American audience be someone who puts up a hand and says, "But aren't there some things that don't change?" I know from experience that this is intended as a theological question, for one of the things that monotheists have traditionally said about God is that God is entirely trustworthy and unchanging, the Rock that is not moved.

-§-
In the last couple of centuries we have begun to think of change as a good thing....That is a fairly new idea for human beings to have.
-§-

For most people, most of the time, change is bad news. If you think about the way we value gold because it is incorruptible, the way we value the hardness of diamonds as well as their light, you get a sense of the anxiety that has attached to the experience of change. I'm speaking of history, however, not as if we were taking a poll of the population today. In the last couple of centuries we have begun to think of change as a good thing (and to call it "progress"), and indeed to think of accelerating change as an even better thing, while stability has come to be viewed as stagnation. That is a fairly new idea for human beings to have. In Arabic, a single root is the basis for words for both "change" and "heresy." That which is given and known is what is true. That which is new is necessarily a deviation. And change is scary. Change is rot and corruption, illness and death.

Today we romanticize change. When people use the much-quoted saying of my mother's, Margaret Mead, "Never doubt that a small group of thoughtful committed citizens can change the world; in fact, it's the only thing that ever has," are they saying what a bad thing that is? No. Implied in the very saying is the notion that we might want to change the world, and that change will be for the better. Poor old world.

Furthermore, we tend to believe that change for the better will come about through the increase and diffusion of knowledge. We imagine improving our society by improving our educational systems, and people who go into education see themselves as world changers, as people who will help children to think in new ways. This is another fairly new and rare human idea. What most human beings have wanted to do with their children in ages past is to bring them up to look at the world the way they do, not differently; to do what their elders tell them to do. Our drive to encourage our children to think, the positive fruit we hope to pluck from scientific research, and the sense that, the further education spreads around the globe, the better our chance of building a better world, are fairly new ideas. Even though most of the time I buy into the belief that knowledge will solve our problems and make us free, I think it's important to remember the centuries when people felt differently. Accepting new ways of thinking is a form of change and depends on a willingness to *be* changed in partly unpredictable ways. We need to remember that our enthusiasm for change is a rather odd idea that needs examining, and that new knowledge, including cybernetics, can be dangerous.

One of the earliest stages of Gregory's work was an analysis of the logical levels of learning. Most of what is learned in schools is what he called Learning I. He also spoke about something he called Learning II or Deutero-Learning, which is often translated or explained as meaning "learning to learn," and then translated in schools of education into such goals as the acquisition of study skills. That was not what he had in mind. What he had in mind was the acquisition of basic premises, basic ways of experiencing contexts that then became contexts for learning. When a child has learned to trust the reliable care of a parent, this is Learning II and that learning becomes basic to the child's character. The child has also learned to trust the things that the parent says as reliable, and to trust and accept things that are learned from parental substitutes, surrogates of various sorts. The thing that is so horrifying about that little story of the playground is that the father is acting as a parent in taking the child to the park. He's claiming that not only is he babysitting the little girl, he's teaching her a valuable life lesson. He is claiming their interaction as a context where trust is appropriate and in which she should learn, and then he is violating that trust. He apparently believes he is imparting useful information about the oppressive and dangerous world in which she must live, but in fact he may be changing her basic premises about life and learning. The premises implied by methods of education and the classroom context are often taken in at a far deeper level than simply absorbing what the teacher *says.*

-§-

In Arabic, a single root is the basis for words for both "change" and "heresy."

-§-

The playground story is apparently isomorphic with the paradox of Epimenides the Cretan, who said, "All Cretans are liars." But for that four-year-old child, this is not simply a matter of intellectual interest in the logical structure of paradox. This child may be protected from later disappointments by a habit of distrust, but along with her capacity to trust, her capacity to learn is also likely to be damaged, because learning from others depends upon a degree of trust.

In the peace settlement at the end of World War I, the warring powers, which were perfectly capable of deception and knew better than to trust each other within the context of warfare, accepted a series of statements (Wilson's Fourteen Points), not as part of that context, but as outside of it and defining it. The European allies then treated the Fourteen Points as a tactic of warfare, but in doing so they violated a trust that transcended warfare and subverted the possibility of trust for many years to come. Traditionally, "a message *about* war [was] not part *of* the war." (Bateson 1974: 483). Although Gregory did not connect this episode directly with his work on schizophrenia, he did describe it as creating a kind of insanity.

When people ask, "Aren't there some things that don't change?" I think they are raising a very fundamental problem about the nature of human learning and the human capacity to change. They are saying, I believe, "We can take the risk of embracing change because we believe we are in the care of an unchanging God." Yet it is also the case that around the world people are rejecting change of any kind, including exposure to new ideas, as a way of protecting basic religious convictions and ethnic loyalties.

-§-

The premises implied by methods of education and the classroom context are often taken in at a far deeper level than simply absorbing what the teacher says.

-§-

Gregory used to play with the French maxim, *plus ça change, plus c'est la méme chose,* "the more it changes, the more it's the same." And he would ask, of any given change: What is the continuity that is being maintained by that change? That's how a thermostat works. It is self-correcting system that keeps the temperature steady (nearly unchanging) by switching the heat on and off in a particular pattern of change called oscillation. Change is the way that self-correcting systems approximate constancy. If I get cold and put my jacket on, I may look very different superficially, but I'm doing it to maintain a more fundamental constancy of body temperature and comfort. So every time people make a change, it's reasonable to ask what they are trying to maintain or continue by making that change.

Gregory also used to cite the reverse of that maxim: *plus c'est la méme chose, plus ca change,* "the more it's the same, the more it changes." (Bateson 1974: 447) The example I use for that is the way, for instance, the special garments that used to be worn by Catholic nuns were held constant and unchanging for centuries. Because the context was changing, however, and everyone else's clothing was changing, a kind of garment that once represented a standardized modest version of an ordinary woman's clothing became exotic and frightening and created distance rather than trust. In that example, holding a superficial characteristic constant actually produces profound change at a different logical level. The changed relationship between the nuns and the children they look after is more fundamental than the way a garment is cut and sewn. The effect of freezing the garment was to interfere with relationships and create distance and distrust, which probably affected other aspects of life as well.

A related aspect of fundamentalism is that it asserts the present truth of statements that were originally made in the context of earlier ideas about the nature of truth. The Creationists have absorbed the new ideas about scientific truth and are inappropriately applying them to old ideas about creation that were originally believed in a rather different sense.

The other example that Gregory used in talking about this, which applies both to individual adaptations and to evolutionary patterns, is that of a tightrope walker in the circus, who commonly carries a long, thin bamboo rod. He corrects his balance with tiny movements of the rod. The truth that is kept constant is that he is able to walk and not fall. It is his position on the wire that is constant. The movements of the rod, the tiny adaptations, are changes that maintain the more fundamental truth of his position on that wire. If you were to freeze the position of the rod, he would fall. The steering on a bicycle is similar.

The tightrope walker who is successfully staying on the high wire is an example of *plus ça change:* the more it changes, the more it stays the same. But if you freeze the part of the system that might allow for adaptation—if you freeze the bamboo, or you freeze the handlebars, or you freeze the conventional clothing worn by the nuns—then what changes, changes at a more profound level.

Thus, in the human pattern of building a basic sense of trust on sameness and continuity, we have a recurrent point of vulnerability leading to dangerous conflicts. Almost everywhere in the world where there have been extreme outbreaks of ethnocentrism and genocidal attacks on other groups, the context has been one of anxiety about change. At base, ethnocentrism is an affirmation—an embrace—of something as familiar as possible. If we are hoping to create a world of peaceful co-existence in spite of high diversity and rapid change, it becomes really important to look at the human capacity for relearning the contexts that classify experience, like the context of reliable care in infancy. We need to affirm deep continuities in human relations in spite of frightening superficial change or difference. In the Balkans, the loss of the context created by the Yugoslav state created huge anxiety about ethnic and religious differences and the other changes on the horizon, anxiety often expressed as rage. Under present circumstances, the potential stabilizing context of the European Union may make the divisions in the Balkans tolerable.

Let me go back to the answer that I give when somebody asks, "Aren't there some things that don't change?" I look for the circumstances in which human beings, whatever their technological level, in fact do steadily accept change. The most important one is with a child. The nature of caring for a child is caring for someone who is changing from day to day—changes of the type we call development or learning or growth. Instead of making a commitment to someone unchanging, you are committed to someone who is unfolding in only partly predictable ways. This to me is a parable of what we have learned to do in celebrating the unfolding possibilities in a constantly changing society. We have learned to celebrate change rather than constancy, and this is a higher level of abstraction than adapting to any particular change. It's not a trivial problem. And of course we need to reinforce curiosity, which gives a positive value to change and difference.

-§-

The potential stabilizing context of the European Union may make the divisions in the Balkans tolerable.

-§-

You can call the Deutero-Learned character trait of welcoming change optimism or flexibility, and you can see it expressed in boosterism. It is surely part of what has made it possible to bring together European nations that were enemies in the last century and to overcome various kinds of bigotry and distrust. Yet there are also grave dangers inherent in this celebration of change and even of accelerating change. Especially in relation to technology, we do not approach the new with sufficient caution.

Nevertheless, we have built into our culture a willingness to learn that combines trust and curiosity, which I believe is the best basis for hope that we will be able to make the changes and adaptations that will sustain us, not on a high wire in the circus but in the natural environment in which our species lives. The biosphere is the larger context of which we must become increasingly aware. Because as Gregory pointed out, the unit of survival is not the organism; it's not you or me, my friends. It's not the species, *it's the species in its environment.* It's that relationship that can be modified in many ways but that must supply the underlying constancy that keeps us on that high wire and that sustains us in the larger system of which we are a part.

Nan Sea Love 200

The Dalai Lama: Compassion in Action

Q: I can understand how my own mind and actions can affect my own causes and conditions. Can they also affect world conditions like hunger, poverty, and other great sufferings of beings everywhere? How?

A: Initiative must come from individuals. Unless each individual develops a sense of responsibility, the whole community cannot move. So therefore, it is very essential that we should not feel that individual effort is meaningless. The movement of the society, community or group of people means joining individuals. Society means a collection of individuals.

Q: If you returned to an independent Tibet, would it be difficult to reconcile the Buddhist principles of compassion with the reality of governing a state with a large Chinese non-Buddhist population?

A: I have already noticed during the last few decades so much degeneration in Tibetan culture and the Tibetan way of life. Besides our Chinese brothers and sisters, even among Tibetans it seems there is some danger. Take, for example, some young Tibetans who have escaped from Tibet in the last few years—although their sense of being a Tibetan is strong and very good, certain aspects of their behavior make me grow more anxious. They immediately fight or use force. Every other aspect of their motivation is excellent, but there is so much degeneration in their humbleness or honesty and compassionate attitude. But then that's reality, so we have to face it. Still, I believe that when we have freedom—freedom of speech, freedom of thought, freedom of movement—we can minimize these

Tenzin Gyatso, the Fourteenth Dalai Lama and revered leader of Buddhism worldwide, is one of the greatest champions of humankind's precious right to live one's life according to one's own values and customs. Former head of the Tibetan state, he sought accommodation with the Chinese government when it invaded Tibet in 1950. He fled Tibet in 1959 for exile in Dharamsala, India. For his nonviolent resistance to the Chinese occupation, which has killed some one million Tibetans, he was awarded the Nobel Peace Prize in 1989. Text used with permission of China Now magazine, (www.chinanowmag.com); portrait by Nan Sea Love (www.nansealove.com).

things. Although in the future, when we have freedom, I will no longer be the head of the Tibetan government. That is my final decision.

Q: Your Holiness, you said that the changing attitudes of some of your Tibetans makes you anxious. So I wondered why you have decided to give up your historic authority in Tibet when it would seem that young people need spiritual rather than political guidance.

A: The fact that I will no longer be the head of the Tibetan government does not mean that I will give up my moral responsibility or commitment. Of course, being a Tibetan, particularly since I am so trusted, it is my obligation to serve, to help humanity in general, and particularly those people who very much trust me, till my last breath.

Also, if I continue to carry the responsibility, although I think many Tibetans might appreciate this, indirectly it would become an obstacle for the healthy development of democracy. Therefore, I decided I must be out. There is another advantage: if I remain as the head of the government and a problem develops between the Tibetan central government and local people or an administration, then my presence could lead to further complications. If I remain as a third person, then I can work to solve such serious matters.

Q: Your Holiness, wouldn't sacrificing your beliefs in using violence to free Tibet be a worthwhile action, as this would result in the alleviation of suffering of the Tibetan people?

-§-
China and Tibet have to live side by side, whether we like it or not.
-§-

A: No, I don't think so. In that situation, more violence would happen. That may lead to more publicity and that may help. But after all, the most important thing is that China and Tibet have to live side by side, whether we like it or not. Therefore, in order to live harmoniously, in a friendly way, and peacefully in the future, the national struggle through nonviolence is very essential.

Another important matter is that the ultimate agreement or solution must be found by the Chinese and Tibetans themselves. For that we need support from the Chinese side, I mean from the Chinese people's side; that is very essential. In the past, our stand was the genuine nonviolent method; this already creates more Chinese support, not only from the outside but inside China also. There are more supporters amongst the Chinese for our cause. As time goes on, more and more Chinese are expressing their deep appreciation and their sympathy. Sometimes they still find it difficult to support the independence of Tibet, but they appreciate our way of struggle. I consider this to be very precious. If Tibetans take up arms, then I think we will immediately lose this kind of support.

We should also remember that once we cultivate a compassionate attitude, nonviolence comes automatically. Nonviolence is not a diplomatic word, it is compassion in action. If you have hatred in your heart, then very often your actions will be violent, whereas if you have compassion in your heart, your actions will be nonviolent. As I said earlier, as long as human beings remain on this Earth there will always be disagreements and conflicting views. We can take that as given. If we use violence in order to reduce disagreements and conflict, then we must expect violence every day and I think the result of this is terrible. Furthermore, it is actually impossible to eliminate disagreements through violence. Violence only brings even more resentment and dissatisfaction. Nonviolence, on the other hand, means dialogue, it means using language to communicate. And dialogue means compromise: listening to others' views, and respecting others' rights, in a spirit of reconciliation. Nobody will be a 100% winner, and nobody will be a 100% loser. That is the practical way. In fact, that is the only way.

Today, as the world becomes smaller and smaller, the concept of "us" and "them" is almost outdated. If our interests existed independently of those of others, then it would be possible to have a complete winner and a complete loser, but since in reality we all depend on one another, our interests and those of others are very interconnected. Without this approach, reconciliation is impossible. The reality of the world today means that we need to learn to think in this way. This is the basis of my own approach—the "middle way" approach.

-§-
Nonviolence is not a diplomatic word, it is compassion in action.
-§-

I consider human rights violations and similar sorts of problems also as symptoms. For instance, if there is some swelling or pimple on the surface of the skin, it is because something is wrong in the body. It is not sufficient to just treat the symptoms—you must look deeper and try to find the main cause. You should try to change the fundamental causes, so that the symptoms automatically disappear. Similarly, I think that there is something wrong with our basic structure, especially in the field of international relations. I often tell my friends in the United States and here: "You cherish democracy and freedom very much. Yet when you deal with foreign countries, nobody follows the principle of democracy, but rather you look to economic power or military force. Very often in international relations, people are more concerned with force or strength than with democratic principles."

We must do something about these beautiful but awful weapons. Arms and the military establishment are intended to kill. I think that mentally there's something wrong with the concept of war and the military establishment. One way or another, we must make every attempt to reduce the military forces.

Q: What would your Holiness like readers do to help the Tibetan cause?

A: Although I am very, very encouraged to receive great support from many different places like the United States and Britain, we still need more active support. You see, the Tibetan issue is not only a human rights issue, it also involves environmental problems and the issue of decolonization. Whatever way you can show support, we appreciate it very much.

Q: How can meditation help bring about contentment?

A: Generally speaking, when we use the term "meditation" it is quite important to bear in mind that it has many different connotations. For example, meditations can be single-pointed, contemplative, absorptive, analytic, and so forth. Especially in the context of the practice of cultivating contentment, the type of meditation that should be applied or engaged in is more analytical. You reflect upon the destructive consequences of a lack of contentment and the positive benefits of contentment and so forth. By reflecting upon these pros and cons, you can enhance your capacity for contentment. One of the basic Buddhist approaches in meditation is to engage in a form of practice during the meditative session so that it can have a direct impact on one's post-meditative period. For example, on our behavior, our interaction with others, and so on.

-§-

As the world becomes smaller and smaller, the concept of "us" and "them" is almost outdated.

-§-

Q: Karma is the law of cause and effect of our activity. What about the cause and effect of inactivity?

A: Generally speaking, when one talks about the doctrine of karma, especially in relation to negative and positive karma, it is definitely linked with a form of action. But that does not mean that there are neutral actions or neutral karma, which can be seen as a karma of inactivity. For instance, if we are confronted with a situation in which someone is in need of help, suffering, or in a desperate situation, and the circumstances are such that, by being actively engaged or involved in the situation, you can help or relieve the suffering, then if you remain inactive that can have karmic consequences. But a great deal depends upon one's attitude and motivation.

Q: What is the best way to gain confidence in our Buddha Nature?

A: Based on the concept of Emptiness, meaning the objective Clear Light, and also the concept of the subjective Clear Light, we try to develop a deeper understanding of Buddha Nature. It's not easy, but through investigation, I think both intellectually and through making connection with our daily feeling, there is a way to develop some kind of deeper experience or feeling of Buddha Nature.

Q: Your Holiness, why is Buddhism described as a spiritual path when everything revolves around the mind?

A: Yes, it is true that some people describe Buddhism as a science of the mind rather than a religion. In the writings of one of the greatest Buddhist masters, Nagarjuna, it is mentioned that the approach of the Buddhist spiritual path requires the coordinated application of the faculty of faith and intelligence. Although I don't exactly know all the subtle connotations of the English term "religion," I would personally think that Buddhism can be defined as a sort of combination of spiritual path and philosophical system. However, in Buddhism, greater emphasis is given to reason and intelligence than faith. Yet we do see roles for faith. The testimony of Buddha is not taken simply on blind faith just because he is the Buddha, but rather because Buddha's word has been proven reliable in the context of phenomena and topics that are amenable to logical reason and understanding. By inferring that Buddha has been proven reliable in these matters, one can then conclude that Buddha's word can also be taken as valid on issues or topics that are not so immediately obvious to us. Ultimately understanding and investigation are the judge. Buddha gave us liberty to carry out further investigation of his own words. It seems that among humanity, one group of people describe themselves as radical materialists and another group base themselves solely on faith, without much investigation. Here are two worlds or two camps. Buddhism belongs to neither one.

-§-
We must make every attempt to reduce the military forces.
-§-

Q: What do you feel about blind faith in order to reach Enlightenment?

A: I think you should keep in mind compassion with wisdom. It is very important to utilize one's faculty of intelligence to judge the long-term and short-term consequences of one's actions.

Q: What of the case of someone who has no religious faith?

A: Whether we follow a religion or not is a matter of individual right. It is possible to manage without religion, and in some cases it may make life simpler. But when you no longer have any interest in religion, you should not neglect the value of good human qualities. As long as we are human beings, and members of human society, we need human compassion. Without that, you cannot be happy. Since we all want to be happy, and to have a happy family and friends, we have to develop compassion and affection. It is important to recognize that there are two levels of spirituality, one with religious faith, and one without. With the latter, we simply try to be a warm-hearted person.

Helen Caldicott: The Nation that Saved the World?

After the Berlin Wall came down in November 1989, America and Russia began to make peaceful overtures toward one another. People all over the world breathed a huge sigh of relief. No longer did we have two superpowers poised and ready to bomb the whole world into oblivion. The imminent threat of nuclear war that had held all of humanity hostage for decades was over.

Or so we thought.

People believe that the danger has gone away now that the Cold War is over. They think that former U.S. President Clinton's disarmament efforts got rid of the bomb.

They did not. And because the Americans didn't get rid of the bomb, the Russians didn't either. The Cold War ended, but the cold warriors continue. The situation is not unlike a woman who had breast cancer ten years ago. She completed all her treatments, and has been cancer-free since. When I tell her that she has a metastasis and her cancer has now come back, everything in her psyche screams, "No! It can't be true."

Unfortunately, in the case of the nuclear threat, it is true. In fact, the threat is now worse than ever. The situation in Russia is extremely serious. A former colonel in Russia calls me on a regular basis. Each time we speak, he begs me to hold a conference between the powers that be—in Russia and America—to talk about the urgent need to get the warheads off their missiles so they won't go off by accident, or by some terrorist taking over

Helen Caldicott, M.D., is a humanist, physician, and a Nobel Peace Prize nominee. She is recognized worldwide as an impassioned advocate of nuclear disarmament, and has been honored with dozens of awards, including the Gandhi Peace Prize and the SANE Peace Award. She founded and headed Physicians For Social Responsibility and Women's Action For Nuclear Disarmament (WAND). She is the author of several books, as well as developing dozens of documentaries. She has spoken at many universities, and her articles have appeared in virtually every major newspaper and magazine worldwide. You can find her on the web at www.helencaldicott.com.

the missile silos. But I haven't got the funding to host such a conference. Nor have I been able to get the attention of the American media. There is a tremendous resistance to looking at the facts because people simply don't want to experience the fear of eminent nuclear holocaust again. So the media actively denies the existence of a threat. But we are in terrible trouble. Thousands of nuclear weapons remain on hair-trigger alert. Any number of scenarios could trigger their launch and cast us all into the pall of conflagration and nuclear winter.

As citizens of the world and custodians of life on earth, we need to face the truth about the continued threat of nuclear war. There is only one reason to develop our spirituality, and that is to save life on this planet. The purpose of spirituality is not to indulge in hedonism. The purpose of spirituality is to help us get properly grounded so that we can do the necessary work that fulfills our highest destiny—the work of saving the world.

-§-
If you walk into a square anywhere in Europe, you will see a man on a horse—a man who was responsible for killing thousands.
-§-

Albert Einstein said, "You cannot simultaneously prevent and prepare for war. The very prevention of war requires more faith, courage and resolution than are needed to prepare for war."

War is clearly obsolete, and yet men love to kill. In Western society, we have elevated the killers and placed them high on a pedestal. If you walk into a square anywhere in Europe, you will see a man on a horse—a man who was responsible for killing thousands. If you walk around Washington, you will see that almost every single fountain and statue is dedicated to the killers. There is an extraordinary adulation of killers, and this contributes to why men kill. And, as has always been the case, the men who kill claim that God is on their side. But God is on both sides. Some of the greatest music, literature, and art have been written in the name of killing and war, or, in the name of God. The two have become practically interchangeable. We find both superpowers and terrorist extremists claiming to kill under God's commandment and authority.

But why do men kill? My theory looks at this question in terms of sociobiology.

When we were troglodytes, it was appropriate for men to kill marauding tribes and saber tooth tigers to save their babies. But for three million years that killer instinct has not evolved or changed. We are a deeply flawed species if we look at this instinct in light of where we are now. Our brains have not evolved much in this area. The cerebral cortex has developed quite rapidly—so much so, that we use it to justify what our midbrain tells us to do. This is what creates the insanity of ongoing war. If we look at Homo sapiens in light of evolution, we see a very young species. Einstein said it best, "The splitting of the atom changed everything save man's mode of thinking, and thus we drift towards unparalleled catastrophe."

Of course, not all men love to kill. I think of the men of our species in terms of a bell-shaped curve. On the one end of the curve, we find a small minority of men who are very sensitive and who would never hurt a fly. In the middle we find the majority: these men love to watch football, play combat video games, and drive a car up from zero to 100 mph in a matter of seconds. The testosterone factor is what makes these activities pleasurable for the majority of men. These are the men who would go to war and kill, but they come back terribly damaged. At the other end of the bell curve we find another a small minority of men whose reptilian midbrain has a toxic reaction to testosterone. When they are the men inhabiting the Pentagon and the White House, we are in big trouble.

-§-
America is currently designing, developing, testing, and building 500 new hydrogen bombs a year.
-§-

This small minority of men are the ones who put the brain's neocortex to the task of designing weapons that can blow up the planet. And they are still working on it! America is currently designing, developing, testing, and building 500 new hydrogen bombs a year. For these men, the project is great fun. But often, the men who work on the bombs have serious problems. Some have Asberger's Syndrome, or they are autistic. They are brilliant, but they have great difficulty when it comes to forming relationships. William J. Broad has written a book about this called *Star Warriors*. Men like these really need medical attention. They should never be released into labs to do this extraordinary work with no conscience at all.

The people with conscience at the other end of the bell curve are called left-wingers or progressives. They are outside the walls of the Pentagon and the halls of government. Unfortunately, they are not as organized as the right wing. Compared the people who are doing the damage, they are actually very disorganized and somewhat hopeless.

On the other hand, the men who have a toxic reaction to testosterone are very powerful. They will destroy anyone in their path. They get control and will do anything to stay in control. They are the alpha males. It is very deep in us to worship these males because in the past, they were the males who saved us. Watch little girls who have just come into menarche. They get their periods, they start doing their fingernails, and they start scanning for the alpha males to fertilize their eggs. Unfortunately, the men who were once the heroes that could save us are now the ones that could very well destroy us.

These men—a small minority, remember—rise to power and proclaim America the most powerful and the greatest nation on Earth. It is not necessary for America to prove this claim; rather, America needs to demonstrate the qualities of a truly great nation. As Edmond Burke, a member of British Parliament, said two centuries ago, "The only way evil flourishes is for good men to do nothing." It is up to the men and women of the world—Americans, especially—to act.

I speak, therefore, directly to the men and women of America.

You belong to the most powerful nation on Earth, the most powerful nation the world has ever seen. Yours is an immensely wealthy country, a country populated by individuals who want to live with compassion and integrity. You have a great and noble task ahead of you at this moment in history. Each of you can and must be as powerful as the most influential people who have ever lived. If your child and your family were under threat by a lethal disease, you would take every measure within reach to try and save them. This is not merely an analogy; this is precisely the current situation. It is imperative that you now act accordingly in relation to the planetary situation brought about by your country.

-§-
The only way evil flourishes is for good men to do nothing.—Edmond Burke
-§-

What your leaders are doing around the world has created tremendous animosity toward America. I have been to Germany, England, and Holland, and the people in these countries are angry with Americans. Your leaders have brought this down on your heads. You are only 5% of the world's population, a very insignificant percentage, but your country has amassed a huge stockpile of nuclear weapons. That is why you are so powerful.

Together, America and Russia can produce nuclear winter and the end of life on Earth. To look at North Korea or Iraq as a threat to your national security is a diversionary activity, a displacement activity. If you put rats in a cage and threaten them with a lethal situation, they will run away and begin to do something irrelevant to that which threatens them. That is exactly what America is doing at the moment. America has no right to talk about other countries having nuclear weapons. People in glass houses can't throw stones.

In my new book, *The New Nuclear Danger, George Bush's Military Industrial Complex* (The New Press, 2004), I describe in stark detail what will happen if an international incident, or an accident from either human or computer error triggers nuclear war. Material of this nature is hard to hear, but hear we must if we are to understand the peril of our situation and be mobilized to action.

Of the thirty thousand nuclear bombs in the world, America and Russian control 97% of them.

If the proposed START-Three Treaty between Russia and America were to be implemented, it would still allow for 3-5,000 hydrogen bombs to be maintained on alert. The threshold for nuclear winter is 1,000 kiloton bombs blowing up 100 cities—a distinct possibility given current capabilities and targeting plans.

What might be the final outcome to incessant nuclear war planning and the ongoing construction of nuclear weapons? The destruction of the planet could be triggered tonight or tomorrow by human or computer error, or even by a terrorist attack. What would nuclear war be like?

The Reality of Nuclear War

If Russia were to deploy a nuclear weapon, it would explode over an American city—those with population over 100,000 are the most likely targets—approximately thirty minutes after launch. U.S. early warning systems would signal the strategic air command in Colorado of the imminent attack. Officials in Colorado would notify the president of the United States, who, in turn, would have three minutes to make a decision about launching a counterattack. U.S. policy currently embraces a counter force policy in which the President launches U.S. missiles which would pass the Russian missiles mid space during those same thirty minutes. The whole operation, and life as we know it, would be over within one hour.

Nuclear weapons explode over cities with heat equal to that inside the sun. The emergency broadcast system on radio or TV would give the public only minutes to reach the nearest fallout shelter, if such a shelter even exists. Forget about having time to collect the children unless they are already by your side. Most major cities will be hit with more than one explosion. Bombs that land at twenty times the speed of sound if they explode at ground level, gouge out craters 200 feet deep and 1,000 feet in diameter. But most bombs are not programmed to hit the ground; rather, they explode above the ground and produce an airburst. This increases the diameter of destruction but carves out a shallow crater in comparison. All buildings within half a mile of the epicenter will be destroyed. At 1.7 miles out, only reinforced concrete buildings will remain standing. At 2.7 miles out, all single-family residences will have been vaporized, but the bare skeleton of some buildings will still be standing. Fifty percent of the population will be killed in the initial blast. Another forty percent will have sustained severe injuries; most all will suffer severe burns. Bricks, mortar, and building materials become flying artillery traveling at hundreds of miles an hour. Windows will be converted into millions of shards of flying glass by pressures several times that of normal atmospheric pressure. This will cause shocking lacerations and decapitation to the human body. Over pressures will also induce ruptured lungs and eardrums. When a

very small bomb devastated Hiroshima—13 kilotons compared to the current 1,000-kiloton bombs—and a human child actually disappeared. The vaporized child left his shadow behind on the pavement. Dry objects, furniture, clothes and dry wood will spontaneously ignite from the extreme heat. Humans will become walking, flaming torches, or—as took place in Hiroshima in the case of a woman who was running with her baby—charcoal statues. For up to fifty miles from the epicenter, anyone glancing at the flash will be blinded in an instant by retinal burns. Huge firestorms will engulf thousands of square miles. Winds from the explosion exceeding 1,000 miles per hour will fan the firestorms. People in fallout shelters will be asphyxiated as oxygen is sucked out of the shelters by fire.

Fallout

Converted to radioactive dust and shot up in the mushroom cloud, most of the city and its inhabitants will vanish. Depending on prevailing wind and weather conditions, the lethal fallout from this cloud could cover thousands of square miles. People close to the explosion, if any do survive, will suffer acute and encephalopathy syndrome. Doses of 5,000 reds or more (a red is a measure of radiation dose) cause so much damage to the cells of the brain that they begin to swell. But the brain, enclosed as it is in a fixed, bony space, has no room for swelling. As pressure inside the skull rises, symptoms of excitability ensue, then acute nausea, vomiting, diarrhea, severe headache, seizures, coma and death within twenty-four hours. Lower doses of 1,000 reds cause death from gastrointestinal symptoms. Cells in the gut and the stomach lining die. The cells in the bone marrow that build blood, fight infection, and cause blood to clot—all die. Mouth ulcers, loss of appetite, severe abdominal pain, nausea, vomiting, and bloody diarrhea begin within days, leading to death from severe fluid loss, infection, hemorrhage and starvation. At 450 reds, fifty percent of the population exposed to that level of radiation would die. Hair drops out, vomiting and diarrhea occur, as does bleeding under the skin and from the gums. Death occurs from internal hemorrhage and infection.

Severe trauma and injuries exacerbate fallout symptoms, causing patients to die more readily from lower doses of radiation. Infants, children and the elderly are more sensitive to radiation than healthy adults. Virtually no medical care will be available.

Disease

In the aftermath of a nuclear attack, millions of decaying bodies—animal and human alike—will lie and rot. Viruses and bacteria infecting the corpses will mutate in the radioactive environment, becoming even more lethal. Fleas, flies, cockroaches, and lice are naturally resistant to radiation: by the trillions, these insects will transmit disease from the dead to the living. Among the corpses and shattered sewage systems, rodents will multiply by the millions. Disease epidemics now kept in check through immunization and hygiene will reappear: measles, polio, typhoid, cholera, whooping cough, diphtheria, smallpox, plague, tuberculosis, meningitis, malaria and hepatitis. Survivors who make it to a fallout shelters and are not asphyxiated will need to stay there for a minimum of six months while the radiation decays sufficiently for outside survival. Any food that manages to grow will be highly toxic because plants concentrate radioactive elements.

Nuclear Winter

Finally, we must look at the systemic effects of nuclear war. Globally, the effects will be devastating as firestorms consume oil wells, chemical facilities, cities and forests. Our beloved Earth will be covered with a blanket of thick, black, radioactive smoke, reducing sunlight to 17% of normal. A full year will be required for light and temperature to return to normal ranges. But due to depletion of the stratospheric ozone layer resulting in enhanced ultraviolet spectrum, sunlight would return at more than its usual level of intensity. Subfreezing temperatures could very well destroy the entire biological support systems of civilization. Massive starvation, thirst, and hypothermia would result.

In 1985, the White House Office of Science and Technology published a document that stated: "The total loss of human agricultural and societal support systems would result in a loss of almost all humans on earth… equally, amongst combatant and non-combatant countries alike." This aspect of nuclear war is not really understood. Not only are the major combatant countries in danger, the entire human population is vulnerable should superpowers engage the large-scale use of nuclear weapons. We are all, in essence, held hostage by this continuing nuclear madness.

Accidental Nuclear War

On January 25, 1995, a military radar technician in Northern Russia detected a signal from an American missile that had just been launched off the coast of Norway. The Russians had been notified of the launch of a U.S. scientific probe, but the alert had been forgotten, or ignored. Aware that U.S. submarines containing eight deadly hydrogen bombs were just fifteen minutes from Moscow, Russian officials assumed that America had initiated a nuclear attack. For the first time in history, the Russian computer containing top-secret nuclear launch codes was opened. President Boris Yeltsin sat at the computer. Military advisors discussed how to launch a nuclear counterattack. The Russian Chief of Command had all of three minutes to make a decision. At the last moment, the missile veered off course. It became clear that Russia was not under attack.

If Russia had launched its missiles, the U.S. early warning satellites would have detected the launch and notified officials in Colorado. This would have led to President Clinton being notified. He, too, would have had only three minutes to make a decision whether or not to launch a counterattack and allow American missiles to be fired from their silos. We were within minutes of global annihilation that day.

Today, Russia's early warning and nuclear command systems are in a state of deterioration and disrepair. Only one-third of its radars are functional and two of the nine geographical areas covered by its missile warning satellites are not under surveillance for missile detection. The system fails to operate up to seven hours a day. To make matters worse, critical electronic devices and computers sometimes switch to combat mode for no apparent reason. According to the CIA, during the fall of 1996, operations at some Russian nuclear weapons facilities were severely disrupted seven times. Thieves had been attempting to mine copper from critical communications cables. The Russian system is incredibly vulnerable and could easily be stressed by an internal or international political crisis when the danger of accidental or indeed, intentional nuclear war would become very real.

-§-
Russia's early warning and nuclear command systems are in a state of deterioration and disrepair.
-§-

The Unspoken Nuclear War

The United States is currently conducting a nuclear war in Iraq, but most of America is oblivious to the fact. The use of depleted uranium in the bombs being used in Iraq is criminal. A number of soldiers were found to have uranium in their urine, but when I was scheduled to go on national TV to discuss this, the show was cancelled. The American media is actively denying information to the American people who are—by paying their taxes—actually actively causing a huge epidemic of childhood cancer in Basra and Iraq. Over time, the use of depleted uranium will cause epidemics of severe congenital anomalies.

A New Level of Responsibility

Every time I address an audience and speak about these matters, the people immediately understand. American people are tired of being deceived. And while I have some quite influential people around me at the moment, it is not nearly enough. I need access to your media, to your television. I need to be on as frequently as the commentators from right wing think tanks who are feeding the American people lies.

President Eisenhower, in his January 1961 farewell address, warned, "In the councils of government, we must guard against unwarranted influence, whether sought or unsought, by the military industrial complex. The potential for the disastrous rise of misplaced power does exist and will persist. We must never let the weight of this combination endanger our liberties or democratic process."

His prophetic prediction has come to pass.

But the news is not all grim. I am optimistic that we can completely reverse this dreadful situation and all other perils that face us. To do so, however, each of us will need to accept a new level of responsibility and action.

America, as a nation, spends six cents out of every dollar on educating its children, four cents on health care, and fifty cents on the military industrial complex. The $310 billion annual Pentagon budget dwarfs the $44.5 billion the U.S. allocates to the Education Department, and the $20.3 billion that goes to the National Institutes of Health. Annual military expenditures across the globe top $780 billion.

-§-
America, as a nation, spends six cents out of every dollar on educating its children, four cents on health care, and fifty cents on the military industrial complex.
-§-

The total amount required to address mounting global problems—to provide global health care, eliminate starvation and malnutrition, provide clean water and shelter for all, remove land mines, eliminate nuclear weapons, stop deforestation, prevent global warming, ozone depletion and acid rain, retire the paralyzing debt of developing nations, prevent soil erosion, produce safe, clean energies, stop overpopulation and eliminate illiteracy—would be one-third that amount, in the neighborhood of $237.5 billion.

Humanity must put aside the need for superiority over others, and with it, the need to be militarily powerful. We cannot continue to behave as primitive animals killing for pleasure, killing for money, and killing for religious and territorial imperatives. Conflict resolution, peace making and peacekeeping must be our new priorities. Even after the catastrophe at the World Trade Center, it was inappropriate to rush off and kill thousands of innocent people.

America has excellent conflict resolution skills, and these must be deployed. The Pentagon needs to be amalgamated with the United Nations and the military industrial complex ought to be virtually dismantled. U.S. military expertise ought only be used for efficient peace keeping operations sponsored by the U.N. Sixty-eight low intensity wars are currently going on around the world—they demand appropriate attention.

America has the power and resources to reverse global warming, to save the ozone layer, to prevent chemical pollution, stop deforestation, to curb the human overpopulation problem and to prevent the rape of space. Make no mistake—your voice can become loud if you get creative. The money that America invests in killing must now be redirected urgently to the preservation of life. America must rise to its full moral and spiritual height to reach its intended destiny—the nation that saved the world.

Sylvia Haskvitz: Enemy Images

Minneapolis was known as the anti-Semitic capital of the country in the 1950s. As a Jew growing up in a Zionist community, I learned that Arab children are taught to subtract using math problems expressed like this: "If you have five Jews and you kill one, how many do you have left?"

Forty years later, during the time of the Oslo Accords, I was facilitating an Arab-Jewish dialogue group in the San Francisco Bay Area. An Arab man across the room looked at me with an ashen face and said, "I can't believe it! We were taught the same thing about you—that Jews teach their children to subtract by figuring out how many Arabs are left if you start with five and kill one."

This strategy of creating a culture of "us and them" may work to strengthen our communities by making others the "enemy," but is not working if our desire is creating peace. For the past fifteen years, in my work as a facilitator of Compassionate Communication, I have seen that peace between Jews and Arabs emerges naturally when we dismantle our enemy images and learn about the feelings and needs that individuals in both groups share.

In our dialogue group, twenty-five people—both Arabs and Jews—gathered in a different member's home each week. We came together every Sunday to talk and listen and share our stories. For many, just coming to the group brought up a tremendous amount of fear. Might they be endangering themselves or family members back home? After all, the meetings were being held in the home of "the enemy."

Sylvia Haskvitz, M.A., R.D., has been a Certified Trainer with the Center for Nonviolent (Compassionate) Communication since 1989. She is the author of the book, *Eat by Choice, Not by Habit* combining her passions of healthful eating and Compassionate Communication. She co-authored an accompanying *Eat by Choice* guidebook for adults and one to be used with children. She is working with the group Compassionate Communication for the Jewish Soul in supporting people to heal their pasts and access present skills to support continued growth and learning. Check out her websites at ccjewishsoul.com and eatbychoice.net.

As facilitator of the group, I helped establish guidelines to allow people to feel comfortable enough to speak their truth. If a statement could be heard as attacking or blaming, I immediately translated the speaker's message into the universal language of feelings and needs. This process helped bridge the gap between "us and them" by creating what was missing—a human connection.

One participant, Emily, shared how the Israelis had forced her and her family out of their Jerusalem home during the War of Independence in 1948. The distress of that event still weighed on her heavily. She shared the anger and resentment she felt at having seen an Israeli family living in the house her grandfather built, as she described it, "brick by brick." Remembering the trauma of being forced to leave her home at eight years old brought tears to her eyes. Tuning in to sense what she might be experiencing in the moment, I asked, "Emily, thinking back on your childhood experience, are you feeling sad and are you wanting us to be present and hear your story, trusting that you are expressing the truth?"

"Yes, yes," she wailed. "It feels so good to be listened to, to be really heard."

For Emily, it was a new experience to have her story *really heard* by Jews. No one got defensive or negated her experience as she had come to expect. A tremendous space of healing opened for everyone in the room.

-§-
"If you've seen the enemy, you've lost."
—Ram Dass
-§-

For eight hours each Sunday, over a period of one-and-a-half years, this group of twenty-five Arabs and Jews shared their stories, their pain, and their food. As time went by, the group bonded. We cried and laughed together. We got angry and indignant together. We argued over whose culture really did come up with hummus and baba ganoush. And in the end, we realized we were more alike than different.

People's response to a dialogue group is often, "What's the point? How is talking ever going to help?" In the words of Eleanor Roosevelt, "Either we are going to die together, or we are going to learn to live together. And if we are going to live together, we have to talk."

We find peace when we examine our interpretation of other people's motivations and behavior, by understanding their feelings and needs, and by transforming our images of "the enemy" in all its forms. The language of our domination culture has made it easy to embrace enemy images. But a different language can be learned, one that opens a whole new paradigm. By exploring a needs-based language, we discover a place where we are all connected as human beings. By communicating from the heart and listening with empathy, we create the quality of connection for which we all long. In doing so, we help heal the world.

People often ask me, "How do I reach a place of connection with someone whom I believe wronged me?" We can easily turn members of our own family into enemies when we communicate from the paradigm of domination rather than focusing on human needs.

The youngest of three daughters, at age seventeen I was the last of my siblings still living at home. One evening, when my mother and I were cooking dinner, I became bored to tears with the usual conversation. I could not stand all the chitchat about the food we were preparing, and I knew another half hour of standard dinner-table gossip about friends and family members lay ahead. I longed for meaningful connection, but felt I was drowning in meaningless talk. "Can't we talk about anything but food?" I asked, looking for a life-rope to pull me out of my misery.

"What would you like to talk about?" my father barked from the next room in a tone of voice that implied, "I don't want an answer to that question."

Rather than getting into a confrontation, I went to my bedroom to get some peace and quiet. My dad followed. The details of the next half hour are still a little fuzzy. All I remember clearly is that my father and I hit each other. My mother came into the room screaming, "Stop it!" and demanded that my father leave the room.

-§-
"All these religions, all this singing, one song."
—Rumi
-§-

I left my parents' house that night and went to a friend's house for a few days' reprieve. I stopped at the local library and checked out every book on the subject of parent-child relationships that I could get my hands on. I had a strong desire to heal the situation and understand why I felt such pain. I hoped that there were clues in my library treasures.

Upon returning home a few days later, I wrote these words to my father on an index card: "When can we start resolving our differences instead of trying to drown them with time?" (I think I may have been more grown up at seventeen than I am now in my late forties.) I left this card on my dresser. Unbeknownst to me, my boyfriend took it and placed it on the kitchen table. My parents found it before I awoke.

My father responded with a written message that said, "When you apologize, we can talk." I couldn't believe he wanted *me* to apologize. What did I do? Members of my family were not very skilled at taking responsibility for our own part in things. I was livid! That afternoon, I went to the community college where I worked as a lifeguard. When no one was in the pool, I used my time to compile a laundry list of all the injustices I believed my father had carried out against me since I was a small child.

When I returned from work, I asked my dad if he was ready to talk. I still did not apologize. We went into the den and sat down near each other on the couch. I pulled out the piece of butcher-block paper on which I had listed all of my irritations and held it up in front of his face. He was shocked. As we continued to talk, we each found ourselves expressing disbelief. "I can't believe you thought that! This is what I meant…" We spent three hours, back and forth, sharing our different perceptions of shared experiences. In situation after situation, we saw how each of us had perceived what was happening in a very different way than the other. Same event; completely different perspective. What a tremendous relief. The breakdown between us was not a matter of one person being right and the other being wrong; it was about both of us being human in our one-sided perceptions. We cried, we laughed, we hugged. And we each began to see that the world is not so black and white. It was the beginning of a whole new relationship between us.

-§-
We can easily turn members of our own family into enemies when we communicate from the paradigm of domination rather than focusing on human needs.
-§-

I vowed on that day never to avoid a painful conversation with someone I care about again. I had learned the value of communicating to find resolution and connection, rather than avoiding the elephant in the living room. I felt sad when I thought about how much time I had wasted holding onto negative perceptions of my father. So often, when we don't take the time to listen to another—to understand their point of view, to hear their stories—we end up with misunderstanding. On the other hand, when we care enough to listen from our heart, and connect with another in our shared humanness, amazing things happen. That day, thirty years ago, I began to see my father in his humanity and felt the exhilarating joy of honest, compassionate connection.

What Are Enemy Images?

Enemies can be seen in the obvious sense when we are at war as a nation. But we also create enemy images in less obvious ways. We label people mean-spirited, inconsiderate, irresponsible or unhealthy. An enemy image may arise for a person who values the pro-life position when they speak to someone who is pro-choice. Enemy images can arise between two people if their values are on different ends of the political spectrum.

An example of this occurred in my family recently. My partner's sister called me a bitch one afternoon in the intensive care unit at the local hospital. Her mother's life was in jeopardy following heart surgery. I had just reminded her of her mother's request that we do everything possible to keep her alive. My desire was to honor the spoken wish of my partner's mother. Her daughter's desire was to honor and protect her mom, and give her the chance to have a peaceful death. We both had the same need to honor her mother's wishes. But we had different strategies to meet that need. This is often how conflict arises.

I took being called a bitch personally in that moment, and displaced my own pain by labeling her ungrateful, mean-spirited and cruel. This happened in barely an instant inside my mind. I paused to tune in deeper—to what I guessed was the stimulus for her words. I imagined that she was worried that following her mother's wishes would lead to a prolonged death involving breathing tubes and emergency resuscitation. I could see her humanness again and find compassion.

-§-

"When we blame others, we give up the power to change ourselves."
—Marshall Rosenberg, Center for Nonviolent Communication

-§-

All human beings have the same needs. We all share a need for love, attention, appreciation, and acknowledgment. We all desire peace, freedom, and trust. All people need to be heard and valued. And all of us have a need to contribute. When I forget those common needs and judge someone, I fuel the enemy image rather than seeing the real person in front of me.

Enemy images spring out of moralistic thinking that presumes to know the "right" way to behave. When someone behaves in a way we interpret as bad, wrong or inappropriate, we assume we know who that someone is and label them accordingly—inconsiderate, rude, or stupid. Sometimes we go further and avoid the person, or seek out confirmation from others who share our opinion.

Moralistic thinking involves believing we know what's best for others. It can be seen in sentences beginning, "You should..."; "Why do you have to..."; "How come you don't..." and others like them. When someone makes a decision to meet their needs based on strategies we don't agree with or value, we accuse them of being wrong. This keeps separation alive and connection unlikely.

How did we get these enemy images of people? How do we sustain them?

Domination Language and Culture

In *Engaging the Powers: Discernment and Resistance in a World of Domination* (Augsburg Fortress, 1992), Walter Wink writes, "Look at how families are structured here in the United States: the parents claim always to know what's right and set the rules for everybody else's benefit. Look at our schools. Look at our workplaces. Look at our government, our religions. At all levels, you have authorities that impose their will on other people, claiming that it's for everybody's well being. They use punishment and reward as the basic strategy for getting what they want. That's what I mean by domination culture."

The domination culture is reinforced in the very structure of our language. In English, we use the verb "to be" in a manner that makes it easy to objectify others. We summarily blame, shame and criticize. When I say, "You are rude, lame or ridiculous," I fail to see and experience the whole person. A husband says to his wife, "You are selfish. We are strapped for cash and you're splurging on a manicure!" It is difficult to receive a communication like that without taking it personally or feeling the impulse to attack back. Compassionate Communication teaches us to see the vulnerability and pain behind the mask of attack and blame.

Domination culture reinforces and dovetails with the "us and them" paradigm. We believe that in order to live our lives the way we want, we need to have power over others. Getting our needs met is seen as something we must do at the expense of others rather than in cooperation with them. In the short run, dominating someone may get you what you want. In the long run, it rarely does—and we often pay a hidden cost. For example, I once convinced my then-husband to come with me to a workshop he really did not want to attend. I made it easy for him to say yes by agreeing to ride our tandem bike the twenty-five miles to where the workshop would take place. Because he loves cycling, Steve said yes when he really wanted to say no. When the morning arrived, we had a disagreement. We fought the entire ride and arrived at the workshop late. I wished I had gone to the workshop alone. I paid a high price for attempting to get my needs met at his expense.

-§-

When I judge someone, I fuel the enemy image rather than seeing the real person in front of me.

-§-

When we use language that does not take responsibility for our own words or actions, we deny choice. This is another folly of the dominator culture. Making someone else responsible for our behavior—whether it's a boss, a company policy, or orders from "higher up"—we give up our power, living out the language of "he made me do it."

In the workplace, this can lead to even more disconnection and dehumanization. A colleague comes up to me expressing her woes about what the boss has done now. If I respond from the old way of thinking, I might jump right on the boss-bashing bandwagon and announce how much I can relate. Or, I may respond with comments such as, "Cheer up, it's not so bad," or "Maybe you can learn from this experience." But my colleague will usually find it far more helpful if I hear her pain and focus in to sense what she is feeling and needing. Presence in the form of empathy is the real balm that soothes her upset.

How do we transform enemy images, in order to create inner peace, as well as peace on our planet? When we are hurt, we often want people to suffer because we think they caused our pain and deserve to pay for it. Revenge, according to Marshall Rosenberg, Ph.D., the founder of Nonviolent Communication, is a cry for empathy and understanding. But revenge only contributes to a cycle of pain. So how do we interrupt the cycle?

I want to share a story that demonstrates the healing effect of what I call an empathy bath. It is a powerful way to help people relinquish enemy images that are so pervasive in our thinking.

In 1996, I offered a workshop in San Francisco during a Peace Conference that highlighted the Dalai Lama. A number of the participants in my workshop had just come from a session with a famous author. They came in voicing unresolved feelings about what had just happened in the room with this author.

"She was so disrespectful," one of the participants shouted.

"She has a big ego," another person added.

"Were you irritated because you wanted to be treated with respect and to know that your needs were valued?" I asked.

"Yes, and she didn't seem to care what anyone else wanted. She had an agenda that she wanted followed, and that was that," one of them replied.

"So you would have liked more flexibility and a sense of being honored for your unique desires?" I enquired.

After a few interchanges of hearing feelings and needs, we were able to empathize with what may have been going on for this author during the earlier session. We guessed that she might have felt overwhelmed by all the questions being asked, and worried she would not have time to cover her subject adequately. We made a few more guesses about what might be going on in her life to keep her from being as present as workshop participants would have liked.

-§-

Making someone else responsible for our behavior—whether it's a boss, a company policy, or orders from "higher up"—we give up our power.

-§-

Within fifteen minutes, the energy in the room was transformed. The author became human again rather than a beast. Participants felt heard and all was well again with the world.

Ironically, after leaving the conference that day, I was approached by a woman on the street. I tried not to engage with her, imagining that she was homeless and would ask for money. But when I turned to her and looked her in the eyes, she said, "Ma'am, I really like your dress."

The How To of Compassionate Communication

Compassionate Communication is about creating a quality of connection where everyone's needs matter. In addition to the shift in consciousness discussed above, the process has two dynamic parts: speaking from the heart, and listening with empathy.

Speaking From the Heart

To speak authentically about what happened for you in a particular interaction, first direct your attention to what the other person said or did that has your underwear tied in a knot. When you get clear about what action triggered your feelings, then focus on what need of yours was not met by that action. When you tune into that need, a feeling or body sense will likely surface. Express the feeling that is bubbling up inside along with the need that was not met. Then, ask for a connection with the person in the moment. Instead of a future strategy—such as asking the person to promise never to do that again—connect in the moment with a doable request that can be fulfilled in the present. You may ask, "Can you tell me in your own words what you heard me say to see if I was clear?" Or you may say, "Can you tell me how you feel hearing me say that?"

-§-
When we are hurt, we often want people to suffer because we think they caused our pain and deserve to pay for it.
-§-

This is a new strategy. In our culture, we immediately focus on solutions. But this often proves ineffective. When we focus on the end result without willingness to negotiate a win-win, our world becomes one of scarcity. We grapple with power struggles. When we are connected, on the other hand, people want to contribute to each other.

How do you know if you're making a request—or a demand? Here's a test: How willing are you to let go of getting your need met by a specific person? A request conveys that I value both my needs and yours.

My colleagues Ike and Judith Lasater highlight the difference between requests and demands using what Ike calls a duck meter. When Judith asks Ike to take out the garbage, Ike tunes in to his duck meter to assess the situation. A reading of ten on the duck meter is similar to the joy a child feels feeding a hungry duck. A reading of one on the duck meter is equivalent to getting a root canal. Ike chooses to take out the garbage when his meter is running fairly high. If he takes out the garbage when the meter reads a one, it will likely result in him feeling some resentment. His commitment in his marriage is to not exact a cost from his wife by giving when he would rather not. The duck meter helps him do that.

Listening With Empathy

First of all, I encourage you to listen empathetically when you feel an authentic desire to do so. Often, we give to others out of obligation as prescribed by a role—mother, father, counselor, friend—or because we fear hurting their feelings if we say, "No." "Compassion fatigue," or an empathy collision, occurs when we have nothing left to give. Before you can listen empathetically to someone, you may need to fill up your own tank first. Tune into how you feel. If your feeling vocabulary is not as developed as you would like, tune into your body and describe what is happening. Your belly may feel tight or your neck might ache. Or, your body may feel relaxed. All are signs that your needs are either met or unmet. Listen to the signals. Listen for any unexpressed needs to emerge. Developing clarity—and learning to give empathy to *you* first—often brings a sense of relief. More energy returns to the body, and a verbal sigh or softening of the face often occurs.

-§-
Compassion and violence spread at equal speed.
-§-

If and when you have the desire to understand a person who wishes to be heard, offer your presence. Sense what she is experiencing. This empathetic connection is a precious gift. Simply sense what the person feels and needs. Verbalize your guesses about her feelings and needs to assess your understanding and help her get clarity. If you guess inaccurately, she will correct you and give you more information. This type of listening is healing for the speaker as well as the listener by opening the space for the speaker to get to the core of the upset, while allowing the listener to contribute to another's well-being. What comes from the heart enters the heart.

Compassion and violence spread at equal speed. We know where violence leads. And, we have seen the impact of compassion in action. Peace emerges one person at a time. The act of building peace in our selves, in our families, in work groups, neighborhoods, and activist groups, is fundamental to building world peace. The following ten strategies, courtesy of Gary Baran of the Center for Nonviolent Communication, are offered to help us heal our planet and ourselves. They are copyright-free, and you are encouraged to duplicate and use them for the peaceful resolution of conflicts.

Ten Things We Can Do for Peace

1. Spend some time each day quietly reflecting on how you would like to relate to yourself and others.
2. Remember that all human beings have the same needs.
3. Check your intention to see if you are as interested in others getting their needs met as your own.

4. When asking someone to do something, check first to see if you are making a request or a demand.
5. Instead of saying what you *don't* want someone to do, say what you *do* want the person to do.
6. Instead of saying what you want someone to *be,* say what action you'd like the person to take that you hope will help the person be that way.
7. Before agreeing or disagreeing with anyone's opinions, try to tune in to what the person is feeling and needing.
8. Instead of saying No, say what need of yours prevents you from saying Yes.
9. If you are feeling upset, think about what need of yours is not being met, and what you could do to meet it, instead of thinking about what's wrong with others or yourself.
10. Instead of praising someone who did something you like, express your gratitude by telling the person what need of yours that action met.

Debbie Ford: Hate Is Not a Sexy Word

Carl Jung had an expression, "I'd rather be whole than good." These simple words hold a world of meaning, and could open the door to an entirely new world, if we could only drink them in. If we learn to accept the totality of our humanity—both the dark and the light—and take back the parts of ourselves that we project onto other people as hate, we would live in an entirely different world. We'd stop pointing our fingers, we'd stop blaming each other, and we would stop being both the victim and the victimizer. Right now, our world is largely characterized by hate—hate going back and forth between people of different nations, between people of different religions, between people of different ethnicities, but most notably: *between people of different perspectives.*

I was a trial consultant earlier in my life. I got paid to find new perspectives through which to try a case. At a certain point, I had to stop. I simply couldn't do it anymore because I saw that we could manipulate the legal system in unbelievable ways. All a trial consultant has to do is come up with a new perception that people can buy into.

Truth always has a big range. To embrace the full range of the truth is to transform hate. To become whole is to become neutral, to embrace the totality of an issue, not just one piece, one side, or one perspective. Wisdom comes with knowing that our perspective isn't the only true perspective; there are many ways to view any situation. But in a world where the highest value is to be good and not bad, to be right and never wrong, our perceptions quickly shrink and take on unnatural limitations. To be whole is to be both dark and light. If we are accepted for being whole,

Debbie Ford is an internationally recognized expert in the field of personal transformation and human potential. A pioneering force in incorporating the study and integration of the shadow into modern psychological and spiritual practices, Debbie is the founder of the Ford Institute for Integrative Coaching, a personal development organization that provides professional training for individuals who are committed to leading extraordinary lives. A number one *New York Times* best-selling author, Debbie's books and tapes have sold more than one million copies and are used in universities worldwide. For more information visit www.debbieford.com.

rather than for being good—a paradigm that assumes that all of us are both good and bad—it is easy to see and hear what doesn't work. Our perceptions expand to include the whole.

We live in a paradigm that believes that there are good people and bad people. Everyone feels this pressure at some level: not wanting to be found out as one of those bad people. But truth has many sides. Nothing and no-one is all one or the other.

Hate is not a sexy word. People really don't want to hear about it. When speaking to groups of people around the country, I often say, "I want you to get the level where you come face to face with your own hate." Audiences just cringe. They say, "Oh, well, maybe I don't feel that good about myself, but I don't have a problem with hate."

Then I ask, "How many of you embrace your mean self, or your inconsiderate self, or your rude self, or your selfish self? And how many want to get rid of those parts?" People begin to see that they *hate* those parts of themselves. But if you hate anything, you hate everything. We are the world, we're a microcosm of the macrocosm, and hate is a pressing global issue. We have to deal with hate both internally and externally, because not only are we promoting hate unconsciously, but hate is why we don't take care of our families and why our educational system, by and large, is in such a sad state. If we have an internal shift and learn that it's okay to take care of ourselves, then we will start taking better care of our world.

-§-

If we learn to accept the totality of our humanity—and take back the parts of ourselves that we project onto other people as hate, we would live in an entirely different world.

-§-

The process of becoming whole and embracing the totality begins when we stop hating. It is so important that we stop the internal violence that is hate. And the process must begin internally. People hate themselves for not taking care of themselves, for not making their own unique contribution, for not being the greatest expression of who they are. But they don't know what to do with that hate. In most cases, they don't even know that it is hate, so they project it out into the world.

Owning one's projections is crucial for healing. Being able to notice the tendency to transfer parts of oneself onto another requires awareness. And this is a fresh, new awareness; it is not one we have grown into at the level of the collective. But it is coming into our consciousness, and watching the awareness emerge is fascinating. In "Shrek 2," for example, the donkey character says, "Don't you go projecting on me." And even though it slips by 90% of the people watching, that expression would not have been used ten years ago. Nobody would have known what the character was talking about.

Taking responsibility for the projections and being able to withdraw them requires practice. Through practice we mature and gain skill. In the spiritual movement, unfortunately, a lot of people are preaching, "Let's just love one another." But the dark side can't digest that conversation. It is not unlike something Dr. David Simon, Medical Director of the Chopra Center for Wellbeing in Carlsbad, California, pointed out at a recent retreat he and I led together. He said, "People carry around elaborate packages full of all these vitamins and constantly douse themselves with all these expensive nutrients. But the body can't absorb them because it's so toxic." That is what shadow work is about: detoxing the emotional body. Once hate is recognized and seen for what it is, we can begin to digest and eliminate it. Only then can the positive thoughts and affirmations and love really take hold.

-§-

That is what shadow work is about: detoxing the emotional body.

-§-

Detoxing the emotional body is both an intellectual and emotional process. Intellectually, we have to understand the programming called "human" and the whole array that comes with being human. What gets in the way of our healing the most is denial. We all have our foibles and our blind spots. There is only one thing a person can't see—and it's him- or herself. Walk into a room full of a hundred people or a thousand people and there is only one person you can't see and that's you. The external world is a mirror. That is how we see ourselves: by what I love in you, what excites me in you, what I loathe in you, and what disturbs me in you. It is all a reflection of me. Most people aren't willing to go to their co-workers, to their family members, to their children and say, "Do you see something in me that you don't like, or that's disturbing to you?" Wouldn't it be interesting if we asked that question once in a while rather than always attempting to validate our light side?

If we can't see the dark side we cannot harness the power it holds because we displace it with our denial. One client I'm now working with is a woman who hates people who change plans after they are made. She can't see at all the times when she changes a plan. Hate makes it impossible to see where you are that thing you hate, because you've made it wrong. That is what gets in the way of us clearly perceiving: Who Am I? How do I show up for others? What could I alter? What patterns of my own need to be transformed? Instead, most of us are scared of what we might find out.

People attending shadow process workshops often say, "I was thinking about coming for two years, but I was terrified." Basically, they are saying that they're terrified of themselves. And if we're terrified of ourselves, how are we going to interact with the rest of the world?

Denial is rooted in our struggle to be one of the good people. Projection and displacement of our own misbehavior adds to the toxicity of the emotional body. We cannot release what we cannot acknowledge exists. So the first step in emotional detoxing is recognition of the dark. This self-recognition, combined with the larger recognition of the entire range of programming called "human," is a prerequisite to being able to release patterns we have held onto. When we're children, we laugh or cry or scream freely, but as we grow up, we hold our expression in. Then we have to visit the dark side. Detoxing doesn't have to be painful; there are many different ways to do it. But one way or another, we have to do our emotional work.

Projection shows up all the time in politics and international relations. We project our hate onto the terrorists. And they do it back to us; we're the terrible Americans. The projection goes both ways. Human beings have always done this; the players change, but if we look back through history, it is nothing new. The people who support a war make peace activists wrong and the peace activists make the war supporters wrong.

-§-
If we can't see the dark side we cannot harness the power it holds because we displace it with our denial.
-§-

My question is: Is any of that wrong? There have always been wars. There's always been hate and killing. It's just what happens. War and peace—isn't that life? Isn't it part of what happens in the world? Given that this is our collective human experience, how could we evolve, and work out our differences in a more loving way? When we relax out of hating, we can ask the right questions.

This is an internal process. Once we shift internally, we can begin to ask questions that further our social evolution. We can dip into the collective unconscious where all the answers lie. All the answers are within us. Tapping this inner wisdom is vital because we're such an outer-based culture—always looking outside of ourselves for the answers. Deepak Chopra teaches that we must learn self-referral. Without it, we always have outside influences telling us what we should think and how we should feel and what we should do. Learning to go inside to hear the answers, to connect with our wisdom and our own divinity, opens the door to knowledge. Listening inwardly is essential if we are going to shift.

Compassion is the key. Compassion includes tolerance of our humanity, and acceptance of what is inside us—both the dark and the light. Learning to forgive ourselves, to be conscious, aware and gentle with ourselves is vital. If we do that internally we will do it externally as well.

In a Shadow Process workshop I taught a few years ago, a German woman stood out. I asked the critical question: "What is the darkest part of you, the part you're most ashamed of?" She started crying. She shared with the group that her fear was that someone would call her a Nazi, or that she could be viewed as a killer of Jews. Her grandfather had fought in World War II, and she was still carrying the shame and embarrassment of her nation being capable of that kind of hate.

Out of that process, a whole world of new understanding opened up to her. She realized that her entire life up to that point was a reaction to, and a defense against, what she did not want to be. She saw that she had moved to America and decided not to have any German friends. She had cut herself off from her father and didn't have any relationship with her family because she didn't want to be *that.* She had covered all the shame and pain under a blanket of denial. When she forgave herself, and her family for participating in the crimes, it was transformative. She was able to reconnect with her family.

This woman experienced a healing of the heart. We hear a lot of talk about the need to open our hearts, but the truth of the matter is that our hearts are already open. The heart can't close. But we can put walls around it. If we start to melt all those right-wrong interpretations, conclusions, and judgments of what's good and bad, then we can experience the open heart. With an open heart, I can love myself when I'm angry and love myself even when I'm hateful. Hate in itself isn't the problem; it's hating the hate that fuels the fire and causes people to do dreadful things.

-§-
Hate in itself isn't the problem; it's hating the hate that fuels the fire and causes people to do dreadful things.
-§-

Fortunately or unfortunately, pain is a great motivator. More than anything else, pain makes people wake up and open their eyes. When we are comfortable, we don't make changes, look for new answers, or invent new solutions. Pain can also signal the need to embrace a larger perspective: to know that our perceptions aren't the only true perceptions. Imagine if we started teaching children in kindergarten that there is no hard and fast reality. Imagine teaching them the nature of both perception and perspective—how these shape our view of reality. What if, instead of teaching our children to be "right" and "good," we taught them that everybody has a different reality and just because your reality is different from mine doesn't mean that your reality is wrong, it just means that it's different. Teaching just one course—about shifting our perceptions and looking at different perspectives—each school year, would create a whole new human race. It would produce miracles.

In a world without hate upon hate, where people can acknowledge and digest the dark side because they don't have to hide it to prove they are good—mistakes become a catalyst for something great. People who do their emotional work and go through the shadow process—in whatever form—begin living fully. When we start being the best we can be, the world looks like a different place. From this new perspective, we can change the world overnight.

Part Three

Spiritual Activism

Andrew Harvey: Mystical Activism

While in South India making a program for the BBC many years ago, I made the most momentous connection of my whole life. I had the great grace to meet Father Bede Griffith, a man who gave his life to live out the birthing of the new divine humanity. At that time Father Griffith was eighty-five years old, and that birthing was radiating from him in divine beauty, in divine clarity, in divine intensity, and in divine compassion. We spent ten days together talking about his life and the experience of his mystical evolution. Toward the end of those early conversations, he graced me with a terrible and beautiful clue to the time we are living in. Everything I have lived through—and the world has lived through—in the last ten years has proven to me that this conversation came from the heart and mind of God to play a part in the transformation of the world. The time for that transformation is now and there is no time to lose. I wrote the essence of that conversation in my book *A Walk with Four Guides:*

"The whole human race has come to the moment when everything is at stake, when a vast shift of consciousness will have to take place on a massive scale in all societies and religions for the world to survive. Unless human life becomes centered on the awareness of a transcendent reality that embraces all humanity and the whole universe and at the same time always transcends whatever level of consciousness we are in, there is little hope for us."

We are, as a race, going into the eye of an apocalyptic hurricane that will decide the future of the race and the planet. This storm of destruction

Andrew Harvey was born in South India in 1952 and lived there until he was nine years old, a period he credits with shaping his vision of the inner unity of all religions. At the age of twenty-one, at Oxford University, he became the youngest person ever to become a Fellow of All Souls College, England's highest academic honor. He then abandoned academic life to embark on a spiritual search, and was the subject of a 1993 BBC documentary "The Making of a Mystic." His books include *The Direct Path* (Broadway, 2001), and *The Sun at Midnight* (Tarcher, 2002). Find him on the web at www.andrewharvey.net.

will demand everything of all serious seekers who long to see the future transfigured. As the hurricane deepens and darkens, it is critical to know in the deepest part of ourselves that what will look and feel like destruction is actually the necessary stripping away of illusions we do not need anymore, the smashing of fantasies we have outgrown, and the necessary, unavoidable waking up to our true divine power.

The core knowledge and secret that helps us get through this apocalypse and give birth to a new divine humanity is one the great mystical traditions have always known. Enshrined in the depths of all the traditions is the essential secret wisdom that total destruction, absolute stripping, horrible pain, apocalyptic annihilation and death are the birth canal of a wholly new reality. I call it the wisdom of the dark night. It is the wisdom that all the great mystics—like Rumi and Ramakrishna and Teresa of Avila—who have come into the splendor of divine love—have known. Jellaludin Rumi said it this way: "The King never thrashes you without offering you a throne." The secret of the dark night is this: the crucifixion and the resurrection come together.

-§-

Enshrined in the depths of all the traditions is the essential secret wisdom that total destruction, absolute stripping, horrible pain, apocalyptic annihilation and death are the birth canal of a wholly new reality.

-§-

A vast apocalypse is going on. A vast birth is also going on, in and through this apocalypse. Both are manifesting at the same time because both are interdependent. The apocalypse is the birth canal. The sooner we grasp that, the sooner we resonate with all of our being with that, the sooner we can become what we must become—mystical activists and warriors for the new transformation.

The angel of human destiny is standing before every single human being. She is standing uncomfortably close to every being, much closer than the prescribed thirteen inches of personal space. In her hand, she holds a magical mirror, a terrible and beautiful mirror. When she turns the magic mirror to the left, it turns black—revealing a seven-headed snarling beast. This appalling beast of total destruction is menacing all of life on this planet. It is essential that we look into that dark mirror and see each one of these seven heads very, very clearly and stare directly into their eyes.

The first head is a massive, unstoppable explosion of population. By the year 2050, there will be nine billion people on the earth if population continues to expand at the current rate. That is three billion more than the most conservative ecologists believe are supportable. An absolute nightmare which the religions of the world have wholly failed to address, this problem makes nearly all of our agendas pathetic.

The second head is that the environment is already in the midst of Armageddon. It is being massacred. A hundred and twenty species are vanishing into extinction every single day. Nothing real has been done, nothing real has been risked by society, to avert this catastrophe. Every serious person must face this heartbreak.

-§-

The closest most people get to nature is a salad.

-§-

The third head of this seven-headed monster is the growth of fundamentalism. At the very moment at which it is essential that all of the religions of the world pull together, overcome their differences, relinquish their claims of exclusivity, and cry out with one voice to the divine for transformation, all instead have factions that are retreating into a terrifyingly separatist fundamentalism.

The fourth head of this monster makes this separatism even scarier. We are now seeing—on a massive and seemingly unstoppable scale—is the spread of the selling of weapons of mass destruction. There is not necessarily a growth of evil. There is a growth of the absolutely lethal powers that evil now has in its control.

The fifth head is something we are all very well aware of. The technological worldview has created a great cement garden here on the planet. At the very moment when we need to be connected to nature at every level, the closest most people get to nature is a salad. People are perishing from inner meaninglessness and despair at a moment when finding meaning is the source of all hope.

The sixth head of this apocalyptic monster is the media. If the media had any sense of responsibility, any sense of crisis, it would be pouring out the truth about what is happening to the environment, to the poor, and to the defenseless. Instead, media moguls create reality shows. Those voices that are radical, and really empowering—that could teach the mystical truth that could liberate and transform the world—are kept out of mainstream media.

The seventh head keeps people in a state of terrifying anxiety, desperation and fear. In our culture, we have become so hideously busy, so unspeakably hectic, that it is extremely difficult to have any peace of mind, any calm in which to taste the depths of the divine identity which could empower us to transform ourselves and the planet.

This dreadful machine of destruction—an exploding population, combined with an environmental holocaust, the growth of fundamentalism, the proliferation of weapons of mass destruction, technology that alienates on every level, a mass media addicted to triviality, and a human race in a state of perpetual, despairing motion—is a confluence of devastating forces that is supremely intelligent in a black way. This is what the mystics of the Christian tradition call the anti-Christ.

But this is not the only thing that is going on.

For when the angel of human destiny turns the same mirror the other way, it turns into a golden mirror. And in that golden mirror, seven pulsing, interconnected stars appear—the seven stars announcing the birth of divine humanity. This is not something that will happen in ten years, or twenty years. This is happening in me. It is happening in you. It is happening in movements all over the world in astonishing ways.

The first star represents the very extent of the crisis we now face. This crisis is so horrific that it will shake us to our depths and awaken the great slumbering divine secrets that lie at our core. This crisis is a supreme opportunity.

The second star is that the very technology that has created the cement garden is now developing astonishing new advances across the board. It is revolutionizing medicine, shaking loose the potential of quantum physics, and opening up all kinds of new fuel sources. These advances could, if we have the political will, transform everything that we are and do on Earth. One example is the hydrogen economy, which could free us from our dependence on fossil fuel at little cost to the environment—if we have the courage to embrace it.

-§-
This crisis is so horrific that it will shake us to our depths and awaken the great slumbering divine secrets that lie at our core.
-§-

The third star is the media itself. In the last few years the Internet has opened an unprecedented opportunity for the grassroots conveyance of radical information—under the radar of governments and corporations. This opens up the possibility of mobilizing tremendous forces all over the planet.

And the fourth star radiating right at this moment is the great mystical texts of the world's traditions. They have been translated into English and all the other major languages in the last thirty years. Mystical technologies and practices of meditation and inner transformation, kept sacred and secret for very long periods of time, are now open to anyone. This has never happened before. It's no coincidence that right as the apocalypse is shaping, an enormous array of divine power, awareness and knowledge is being given to humanity, to wake us up, to give us courage, to give us joy, and to give us the means to change. This is a huge gift.

The fifth star is one I have devoted my whole waking life to radiating more completely and helping to birth: the return of the divine feminine. For 2,500 years, the bride, the mother aspect of God, has been kept in a dark cellar with her hands and her feet bound. And now, at a time when we need the wisdom of the sacred marriage between heaven and earth, transcendence and immanence, human and divine, body and soul, politics and action, the bride is being brought back in all her wildness and glory, her splendor and fury, and in all her majestic tenderness.

The sixth star in the astounding firmament of birth is the lives of the servants of God's love we witness in action in the world. In the last century we had two World Wars, we had Nagasaki and Hiroshima, we had the horrific exterminations in Nazi Germany, China, Russia and Cambodia. But we were also given in the lives of Gandhi, Martin Luther King, the Dalai Lama, and Nelson Mandela. These lives are examples of how non-violence, when lived with total sincerity and total truth, can transform insuperable difficulties by sheer, holy, God-given power. Gandhi secured the release of India by just standing in place, a semi-naked fakir, radiating the holy knowledge of divine truth and love. Martin Luther King ensured the triumph of a humiliated minority, and ensured the safety of a white population in the middle of a cauldron of hatred on both sides, by preaching and living the truth of Christ. The Dalai Lama, faced with the holocaust of his whole world, has never for one moment lost his unshakeable belief in the transfiguring power of compassion. And in South Africa, we saw a situation that could have degenerated into a total bloodbath transformed by the work of Nelson Mandela and F. W. De Klerk, working together in a spirit of non-violence.

The lives of these people clearly suggest that God is on the side of those who are brave enough to go into the storm with their divine truth and their divine beauty and their divine power radiating from a full heart, mind and body, giving themselves up to be the perfect servants of love that all of us are meant to be.

-§-

For 2,500 years, the bride, the mother aspect of God, has been kept in a dark cellar with her hands and her feet bound.

-§-

The seventh star is one that has blown my mind and my heart and my body and my soul wide open. Rather than a detached spectator watching the play—as the patriarchal traditions tend to think of God—God is also a mother. In the mother aspect, God has an agenda. That agenda is the saving of the human race, the transfiguring of the human race, the co-creation with the human race of a new world. God as mother is protecting us, and pushing us deeper and deeper into divine mischief. Knowing that, we will stop at nothing because we know that the angels and the archangels and the bodhisattvas and all the ascended masters and mistresses are crying out for the transfiguration of the human race and pouring down on the earth blessing and power and protection and knowledge.

Having now seen what is in the black mirror and what is in the golden mirror, we must look at what it takes to align ourselves wholly with those seven stars in the golden mirror. All of these stars are interconnected, part of an enormous mercy being given us. What it takes to galvanize their power and magic is to become a mystical activist.

The future of the planet hinges not on mysticism alone, not on activism alone, but on the inspired marriage of these two potent forces. Mystics, vibrating and bathing the whole cosmos in light, are absolutely adorable. But in a crisis like this, they are so heavenly as to not be of much earthly use. Private pursuit of spiritual experience is absolutely not enough when the world is burning to death. It is absolutely incumbent on every single human being—including the ones who see the light dancing in the trees—to do something real about the real problems in the real world. It is not spiritual to hide from them in a cloud of bliss. The detached, transcendent spiritual ideal which reveals the world as an illusion is not true, because the world is not an illusion. That is bad mysticism. No government and no corporation fears people with Sanskrit names wandering about burning incense, saying, "All is One and we should love everybody."

My first real mystical awakening happened when I was about twenty-one years old. It was winter, and I was a Fellow of All Souls College at Oxford University. I had just been left by someone I was very much in love with and was in a state of extreme suffering and distress. The suffering had gone on for about three weeks of sleeplessness. One particular and devastating night, I woke up after only two hours' sleep, to see the entire world softly coated with fresh snow. Gazing out of the window in the early morning, I experienced the purest and most complete peace and rapture I had ever experienced, far greater than I had imagined possible.

-§-

God is on the side of those who are brave enough to go into the storm with their divine truth and their divine beauty and their divine power radiating from a full heart, mind and body.

-§-

Although I didn't know what was happening at the time, I later realized that at that moment I had touched my own inmost divine being. It was a tremendous experience that opened up all kinds of hungers in me. And it was largely because I had that experience that I found the courage to return to India when I was twenty-five, and start giving up academic life in favor of a larger, mystical life. For once I returned to India, all kinds of mystical experiences started to bombard me and open me. That hour of calm, healed ecstasy gazing at the snow gave me the courage to transform my life later.

To the New Age, and to teachers who purvey the transcendental claptrap that people feed off like heroine addicts to stay in a bliss state while the world burns, I say it is time to realize that there are two initiations on the real path: the initiation into the light which is enormously important and which changes everything, and the initiation into the dark. I am not speaking of something I have not lived. When the dark spears your heart open, the horror and the heartbreak and the pain turns you into a helpless babbler before the awe and majesty and terror of God. Witnessing that real agony of the real world, everything in you cries out to be of use. When those two initiations are combined, a real mystic is born—one whose divine illumination transforms him or her into a fearless love-warrior and love-servant.

Neither can activists change what is happening, for the simple reason that they are fed only by human sources of energy. Their hearts get broken, their wills become exhausted, and their bodies get tired when faced with the prevailing situation on the planet. They give up. Neither mysticism nor activism alone can give us the passion, wisdom, clarity, peace and strength we need. But if we marry a totally lucid, adoring connection with the transcendent in direct relationship with a wild, passionate outraged commitment to correcting the imminent injustice; if we marry the divine energies that are given through a connection to God with a focused plan to unnerve the powerful and the cruel and the destructive on every level—what we will give birth to is a new kind of human being. This birth is what this apocalypse is helping to bring about. The illusions of progress of the activists and the illusions of progress of the mystics must both be shattered. Fusing the two in a massive heartbroken realism can give birth to the power of God in action on Earth.

-§-

We will stop at nothing because we know that the angels and the archangels and the bodhisattvas and all the ascended masters and mistresses are crying out for the transfiguration of the human race.

-§-

This great fusion is the equivalent, in human terms, of the leap from Newton's to Einstein's physics. This fusion asks for nothing less than the abandonment of all the illusions of the past and a seizing of the divine identity at the very core of us. A fusion of that core with a cry for justice for animals and women and gay people and poor people is a revolutionary power that none of the powers of the world can stop. The reign of the dark and of the ignorant, the reign of the demonic, will be over.

Becoming a mystical activist demands blood, sweat, tears, and real hard prayer. It is not a game. It is not something to do after the third vision of the light, it is something to do in total response to a crisis that could destroy everything we hold sacred. Mystical activism is a fusion of the forces of light. It fundamentally threatens all the dark forces that have kept the human race ignorant. In that act of threatening all the dark forces, all the dark forces are aroused against it. That includes all the occult, demonic forces, which means that all of us must get over our naiveté about evil. After the twenty-first century—after Dachau, Hitler, Hiroshima, the desolation of the environment, and all the other atrocities of the last hundred and fifty years—we can no longer paint ourselves into a corner with a koan that says "evil does not exist." Evil is real and terribly powerful in this dimension. It is not so within in the absolute realm, but it is horrifyingly real in its human, its demonic, and its occult forms here and now. At a certain very important stage on the mystical path, we must meet it head on. This is what Rumi did in his dark night, this is what Jesus did in the crucifixion, and this is what is happening on the planet in its dark night. It is very important to become lucid about this and to prepare for this. Otherwise, we will be like lambs going to slaughter.

These are the seven laws of mystical activism:

First, to be mystical activists, we must get real about sacred practice. We don't have a hope in the real world, dealing with real problems, and real people with destructive agendas, unless we are rooted in sacred practice. Develop a profound practice which grounds you and irrigates you with holy intensity every single moment. We need to combine two kinds of practice: cool practices to chill out in the storms of neurotic karma, and warm practices that keep the heart open in hell, because we will all suffer from compassion fatigue. It is almost impossible, in a world of nightmare, to keep on hoping, and to find the energy to go on loving, without the warm heart practices. Like a bird that can fly on two wings, we need the cool practices for times when we become hysterical and need to taste the truth of divine being, and we need the warm practices when we need energy. By marrying these sacred practices of peace and passion at the deepest depths, the masculine-feminine sacred androgyne is born.

The second law feathers into the first. In a time as devastating as ours, I have found that only one thing works at all moments, and that is to keep steady awareness of our divine and deathless identity. All of us have to go on a very profound journey, not simply to read about our divine identity, nor to taste it in the occasional moment of bliss, but to steadily be in touch with that indestructible soul that is our immortal reality. Knowing that the core of what we are cannot die makes us fearless in all situations.

-§-
Private pursuit of spiritual experience is absolutely not enough when the world is burning to death.
-§-

The third law, I cannot emphasize strongly enough: Know that evil is real. The demonic is here, and it will avail itself of your shadow side, acting through what I call the anti-Christ energies. Evil is not a poetic metaphor. I have met it, and I have been wounded by it. Love and evil are in a profound cosmic war, a mystery of antagonism that has a divine meaning we can only learn by becoming discriminating, by being realistic about our own addictions, and by understanding the amazing power of this darkness. Jesus said, "Be wise as serpents and innocent as doves." Becoming a mystical activist will arouse tremendous antagonism from that darkness. Terrible things will manifest to try and unnerve you. If you don't know this, you will be defeated. But if you know that this is an occult war and the most deadly game imaginable—and that you have to stay steady in your calling, and deeply at peace within your divine identity—then you will be strong.

The fourth law is a very subtle one. It has involved and tormented all of us at different moments. This law is a response to the question, "What do we do with anger?" The patriarchal religions have an interest in us not getting angry. They have told us that anger is an absolute obscenity and that we must get rid of it. That, of course, keeps us obedient slaves.

If unleashed, anger can blind us and lead us into hatred. Yet where are we without the power of outrage? In this world at this moment, millions of us ought to be absolutely speechless with outrage at what is being done in our name. But if we are so outraged that we are blinded by hatred, then the power that outrage can give us, rather than being a transfiguring energy, becomes a dirty, corrupt, damaging energy. So the fourth law is that you must awaken your outrage, face your outrage, and master your outrage by purifying your heart. You must constantly ensure, through deep sacred practice, that your outrage doesn't get sidetracked into hatred of others. To do that, we enact our outrage before God, offer our outrage to God, and beg the divine force to take that outrage and transform it into the living sacred fire of sacred passion. Outrage transfigured is the gold that is alchemized from the black, swirling, boiling power of anger. That sacred passion, when mobilized in the service of activism, makes you tireless, undaunted, extravagantly wild and unstoppable.

-§-

When the dark spears your heart open, the horror and the heartbreak and the pain turns you into a helpless babbler before the awe and majesty and terror of God.

-§-

The fifth law is absolutely central to the great Christian, Hindu and Buddhist teachings on action. Very simply, it is this: You must learn to give up the fruits of action to the divine. You do not act with a private agenda, followed by despair when your agenda is not enacted. You act from a love of God, for God, giving yourself selflessly up to God, and offering your actions to God as a sacrifice of divine love. If you can do that, what you do and what you say will have miraculous effects because it is not you who are doing it anymore. You are like a feather floating on the breath of God, a pen held in the hand of God. You have died to yourself; the God that loves the world is using you for God's inscrutable and mysterious purposes. If you are still acting from the ego you can be defeated. But if you're standing in the Self nothing can defeat you, not even endless defeat.

The sixth law has to do with ferocity. When somebody has the guts to stand in front of us, and rage like the lion on behalf of the lion in each of us, they are not assassinating us; they are trying to raise us from the dead. That ferocity is the fiercest and most gorgeous kind of love. We recognize it when it's in the room. I recognize it in the living Christ. I recognized it one incredible evening when the Dalai Lama finally lost his smile because he was so overcome with grief. He stood before his audience and said,

"When will you wake up to what is happening to my people?" He didn't do it to hurt or humiliate people, he did it to appeal to their hearts, to wake them up. So the sixth law is this: As a mystical activist, act with deep love and compassion, with a total commitment to non-violence. It may not always be possible, but we need to steep our whole being in satyagraha and soul force, to act from that deepest place so the truth of the divine nature can constantly flame out and inspire.

I cannot emphasize the seventh law enough. It is this: None of us can do it alone. I cannot do my work without my husband and my great spiritual helper and warrior Ellia who is an incredible mystic and healer and wild woman. I cannot do my work without the help of Rumi, Jesus, without the help of all the beings on whose lives I imperfectly model my life. None of us can do it alone. We have to reach out to all of the people who share our concern. We have to pool our resources, become brothers and sisters, give up our egos, give up our private organizations, open our hearts, and work together.

-§-
Evil is not a poetic metaphor. I have met it, and I have been wounded by it. Love and evil are in a profound cosmic war.
-§-

When all is chaotic and burning and terrible, there are three main ways that I reconnect with the source of divine love. The first, and simplest, is this: When I breathe, I imagine breathing in the living golden light of the mother's alchemical radiance. That golden light goes to the ends of my toes, to the top of my head, and into every cell of my entire body until I imagine myself glowing like a molten ingot. I then hold the breath until I can feel that gold light in every pore of my body. I then release the breath, and with it, all my fatigue, all my sadness, all my rage, all my desolation. Do this several times, for five or six minutes, and you will be recharged by peace and power.

The second way I retune with the source of love is by saying the Hail Mary very slowly and calmly while focusing my mind on an image of the Virgin that I love and hold dear. If you do not have a relationship with the Virgin, then choose another divine figure and see her very clearly in her most radiant and divine aspect. Saturate your every cell with devotion. The power will come, and the peace will come.

Another wonderful exercise is to lie on the floor and imagine a black, powerful magnet, about seven inches below the ground. Imagine that black magnet literally pulling out of your body, heart, mind and soul, all the stress and pain you are feeling. Imagine all the different worries and doubts and sufferings looking like little black needles. They're dragged out of you and into that black magnet. I conceive of that black magnet as the secret Kali, birthing us into generosity. Then imagine a light figure of the divine mother in exactly the same shape as your own body, about two feet above you, radiating your whole body with golden light. You are being worked on in this exercise both by the immanent mother, the black magnet below the ground, and by the transcendent mother saturating your whole body with deep healing power. It helps to say your preferred name for the divine mother in your heart, opening your whole being up for healing.

-§-

In this world at this moment, millions of us ought to be absolutely speechless with outrage at what is being done in our name.

-§-

Staying attuned to love in these ways is absolutely essential to being a mystical activist. Simple, powerful practices constantly re-attune you to the source. The simpler the practices are, the more they can be done in the hurly-burly of everyday life. Keep re-aligning yourself in these ways, and fuse your deepest mysticism with the most radical and brave action you are capable of. In this way you will help birth the new humanity that is appearing in blood and pus and shattered fragments of buildings and unutterable torment through the birth canal of the end of a world.

Ram Dass: Coming Down from the Mountain

When I asked my guru, how do I get enlightened? He said, "Feed everybody." Recently, I attended the Rainbow Gathering in Northern California. There were kitchens all over the place, giving away free food, taking that commandment literally. I could see that the free food made its mark on the awareness of the people present.

At the Gathering, we witnessed two remarkable things: family, and freedom from institutions. This both reflected the past, like a medieval village, and reflected the future, in the quality of the way people were being with each other. In that consciousness, I felt a foretaste of future evolution.

There is a universal tradition of people who complete the path of meditation, who transcend their intellects, open their hearts, and come into tune with that from which the universe flows. Such beings are sages, enlightened realized, free, children of God. They are God people.

Such unbounded spacious awareness contains an intense love of God, equanimity, compassion, and wisdom. In it there is openness and harmony with the whole universe. Beings whose awareness is free enter into the ocean of love that has no beginning or end—love that is clear like a diamond, flowing like the ocean, passionate as the height of the sexual act, and soft like the caress of the wind.

The absence of identity with personal ego means that the being is free, is pure compassion, pure love, pure awareness. For such a being, everything is in the moment. There is a richness in which past, present and future all co-exist. You cannot say of a moment of full awareness that

Ram Dass is one of the cultural icons of our age. In the nineteen sixties, he studied psychology in collaboration with Aldous Huxley, Timothy Leary, Allen Ginsberg, and other early experimenters with LSD. In India in 1967 he met his spiritual teacher Neem Karoli Baba, and wrote *Be Here Now* (Three Rivers, 1971), which has over one million copies in print. For decades, he pursued devotional yoga from several wisdom traditions, and taught widely, until in February 1997 a stroke left him partially paralyzed. His most recent book is *Paths to God: Living the Baghvad Gita* (Harmony, 2004). His web site is www.RamDassTapes.org. Photo courtesy of Lisa Law.

something is not present, nor can you say that something stands out. You can focus on one thing or another, or on the emptiness of the form, or on the many planes within form. The focus of a totally free being is guided by the need of the moment, by the karma of the individual he or she is with. For such a being, life is a constant unfolding. No need to think about what to do. It's all intuitive. It's as simple as the innocence and freshness that a young child experiences. Only in this silence—the silence that lies behind thought—can one hear the symphony of the universe, can one hear the whisper of the Word, can one approach the innate temple wherein dwells the soul.

The moment is timeless. But within timelessness there is time. The moment is spaceless. But within the undifferentiated boundaries of infinite space lies form, with its demarcations. There is clarity, so that everything is discrete and can be seen clearly if one focuses. There is liberation; there is perfect faith; no fear of change, no clinging to the moment. The moment is enough. The next moment is enough also. And the judgment of "enough" is gone—choiceless awareness.

-§-

There is a universal tradition of people who complete the path of meditation, who transcend their intellects, open their hearts, and come into tune with that from which the universe flows.

-§-

Many of the people at the Rainbow Gathering traveled a long distance to be there. By making that choice, they are making a pitch for freedom. I get the sense of Fierce Grace operating in our world. We all need such grace. Our individual karmas got us born into a frightened world. Each country is its citizenry. To have a peaceful country, each of us needs to become a peaceful person. Lack of inner peace, lack of the security of surrender to the universe, is the root of all our problems. When we bring our inner peace down from the mountain and return to the outer world, we contribute that peace to our society.

That return completes the cycle. It is this cycle which brings the spirit to Earth and allows the divine to feed once again the hopes and aspirations, the barely sensed possibility, that exists in each human being. This is the way of the bodhisattva, the maggid, the shayk, the enlightened soul, the saint.

We have in America little appreciation, less experience, and no models for this ultimate journey. This final path is reflected in Christ's forty days in the desert, by the many years of intense spiritual work which Gautama Buddha underwent before enlightenment, by the years in which the great saint Swami Nityananda sat in a tree like a monkey, living close to the edge of insanity, or by Ananda Mayee Ma, who roamed about lost to self and family in trance. Asia has innumerable stories of these few beings who made such a fierce journey—a journey that can only be made if you are propelled by an inner fire, a yearning and pull for liberation that is so powerful there is no way to deny it.

I see politics as heart to heart. I tell people to not be satisfied with their leaders until they find a representative of the heart. We need to apply ourselves to being peaceful, compassionate and loving. And we need to spread that from heart to heart. My guru spread it from his heart to my heart and I've spread it as much as I can to other hearts. We can find leaders who speak, from the heart, to the deeper being.

-§-

Only in this silence—the silence that lies behind thought—can one hear the symphony of the universe.

-§-

I don't ask about the future because I don't think we're supposed to know the future. My guru said, "Be like Gandhi." And Gandhi said, "My life is my message." That is how we all need to live.

Marsha Covington: Spiritual Alchemy

Earth is heavy. She is polluted. Darkness envelops her down to her bones. How did she get this way?

Spiritual history suggests that Earth began as a shining orb of alabaster-like substance. The ancient Greek "myth of the ages," as well as Hindu, Jewish, Zoroastrian and Indian traditions each tell the story of a once-radiant Mother Earth. According to these accounts, the first people who lived here were so filled with light that they didn't wear the dense "meat bodies" we now wear but wore bodies made of a filigree-like substance. These people lived peaceful lives, because they understood that the light that filled their bodies was the same light that had created the Earth and all the gifts they enjoyed. This era of purity, in which people didn't even know how to be prideful or hurtful, was a time the ancients wistfully look back upon as the Golden Age.

Indian Vedic philosophy repeats this view of our past. The first age, called a "yuga," was a perfect, beatific Golden Age filled with justice, happiness and prosperity. People lived by the divine plan and led exemplary lives. But, according to each of these ancient traditions, the people in the early Golden Ages lost their light by turning to thoughts that were less than pure. Succeeding ages, which the Greeks called the Silver, Bronze and Iron Ages, were marked by regression, as people observed less and less of the moral code and vice and evil increased. People began to allow hatred and impure feelings into the world. Ultimately when these feelings were acted out in murder and war, the Earth became dense like iron and was plunged into horrid darkness.

A student of the Theosophical tradition for twenty-five years, Marsha Covington, Ed.D., is president and founder of New Wisdom University, a modern mystery school dedicated to sharing the esoteric teachings that have been guarded in secret libraries around the globe. In addition to courses on the path of initiation and spiritual leadership, Marsha teaches Saint Germain's Pure Joy System of spiritual alchemy to transmute physical and psychological burdens. Marsha also serves as a guest lecturer and adjunct instructor in the communication arts and adult learning for universities and private organizations. More information at www.newwisdomuniversity.com.

During the final Iron Age, what the Hindus call the "Kali Yuga," society reached an extreme point of disintegration. According to the *Vishnu Purana* (IV, 24), the Kali Yuga "Is the only age in which property alone confers social rank; wealth becomes the only motive of the virtues, passion and lust the only bonds between the married, falsehood and deception the first condition of success in life, sexuality the sole means of enjoyment, while external, merely ritualistic religion is confused with spirituality."

For several thousand years now, according to both Greek and Hindu traditions, the Earth has been in the midst of the Iron Age, or Kali Yuga. The one blessing of the final Dark Age, according to most traditions, is that it leads ultimately to the re-establishment of the Golden Age, as a revolution of light finally brings peace and wholeness once again.

I am one of a generation of idealists who came to this life determined to bring a new Golden Age to the Earth. Perhaps we felt the impetus of the coming new millennium that we knew would be focused on Aquarian qualities of love and harmony among diverse factions. All my life I have known that if we could only find a way to help people understand what is needed, we could effect a mighty change and set the Earth back on her course.

-§-
Hindu, Jewish, Zoroastrian and Indian traditions each tell the story of a once-radiant Mother Earth.
-§-

Mircea Eliade, author of *The Myth of the Eternal Return,* comments on this longing to return Earth to a Golden Age. This compelling theme reveals an intense desire to go back to "the perfection of beginnings," a time when "the divine or semi-divine beings were active on Earth." We yearn to recover the "active presence of the gods" and to live in the world as it was in its original, pristine state.

Gregg Braden, in *Awakening to Zero Point,* claims that we have already entered into this time of new beginnings. He says that we are all going through a "collective initiation," and we are aware of the changes this is bringing us. "Almost universally, everyone feels it. Something has changed. Something feels different now, during these days. Everyone feels a shift on some level to some degree. The tension of tumultuous change.... Some individuals feel it rippling throughout every cell in their body.... Others are experiencing a new kind of confusion, as if nothing in their lives really fits any longer." Braden calls this "The Shift of the Ages." He says, "The time of The Shift marks our completion of a paradigm that has perpetuated the illusion of separation between ourselves and the creative forces of our world, and the birth of a new paradigm allowing the recognition of the oneness of all life."[1]

We may be shifting into a new time, but over the last several decades things have become worse rather than better. Today we face a crisis as our dear Mother Earth has become weighed down with pollutants both physical and spiritual. We realize that we must alleviate her burdens before it is too late. The good news is that we are living in a time when new spiritual and material tools are available to help us deal with the many issues we face. In my work as an author and teacher of what I call the "new wisdom," I share special knowledge previously guarded in secret societies and schools in both the East and the West. This knowledge was revealed by a small band of Himalayan adepts—the Indian Mahatmas El Morya and Koot Hoomi, together with the Western adept Saint Germain—and others. Together with their amanuensis Helena P. Blavatsky these masters founded the Theosophical Society in 1875 and have continued this work through various groups throughout the twentieth century.

The keys to this ancient wisdom were first published in an esoteric work called *The Secret Doctrine.* This book is a meditation on the transformation of life—the return of life to its original pristine state. Thanks to the work of Professor Jagannath Upadhyaya of Benares Sanskrit University and David and Nancy Reigle in the United States, we now know that *The Secret Doctrine* is a translation and interpretation of the Kalachakra Tantra, the most highly regarded esoteric teaching in Tibet. The Tibetans call this book "the Teaching of the Golden Age" and recognize it as the original source for the Wisdom Tradition, the universal religion that was practiced in the first Golden Age societies on Earth. Echoing the wisdom of the new sciences that clearly point to undivided wholeness as the fundamental property of the cosmos, Blavatsky wrote, "Every atom of the universe is permeated with the Universal Intelligence, from the latent spark in the mineral up to the quasi-divine light in man's brain."[2]

-§-

If we could only find a way to help people understand what is needed, we could effect a mighty change and set the Earth back on her course.

-§-

The ancient sages were aware of a wonderful truth that our own scientists are just beginning to discover: everything on Earth is made up of particles of energy. This energy is the same intelligent light that the sages say created our vast universe in the beginning. It comes streaming into Earth through her people, all natural things and the atmosphere all day, every day. Each of us has access to it as it descends first in waves and then, once it becomes the focus of our awareness, becomes billions of points of light and is distributed as fuel to every atom. It is with these tiny little suns that we create our individual worlds and contribute to the grace—or the demise—of our precious planet. Physicist Fred Alan Wolf, in *Mind into Matter,* explained the process this way: "Electrons can be imagined best as 'events with attributes,' rather than as objects with properties. The electron, in other words, is a construct of human thought."[3]

All of our thoughts and feelings are stamped with our unique pattern. The sages teach that each of us has a pattern, like a fingerprint, that is stamped on every erg of energy we use. So as we use this pure intelligent light, it goes out to make happen whatever we intended, and then returns to us. But on the way it picks up more energy like itself due to the law of attraction—"like attracts like." So when we intend something particularly good, like sending blessings to our children, our little electrons will go out, deliver our message of love, and return to us more full of this quality because they will magnetize to themselves more of this love.

What evidence do we have that this occurs? Have you ever been depressed and felt like you just got more depressed as the day or week went on? Have you ever become full-to-overwhelmed with negativity until you did something to change the pattern? This is caused by this law of magnetism—like attracts like.

Our energies get stored in our body and in places like the subconscious and unconscious mind. It's like we have a whole library there full of the records of everything we have seen, touched, said and felt. But we can't see it. This incredibly rich library is in the basement of our consciousness. Even though these are our very own creations, we forget about them because they are "sub"—below—consciousness. Negative energy can build up there, making us feel heavy.

-§-
The sages teach that each of us has a pattern, like a fingerprint, that is stamped on every erg of energy we use.
-§-

In *Looking In Seeing Out,* physicist Menas Kafatos reminds us: "Everything in the unconscious belongs to us, and yet we do not want others to see it. We want to forget it. Therefore we suppress it and do not allow it to come up. The content of the unconscious mind strives for expression, but the conscious mind prevents this."[4]

Caroline Myss talks about this weight that slows us down. In her seminar "Fundamentals of Spiritual Alchemy" she equates "weight" with having to "wait." All our unfinished business—our creations that didn't come out quite right—our "shadow parts"—are like lead to us. Our weight (the accumulation of our negative energy, or karma) causes us to be slower to change than we would be if we didn't have so much of our energy tied up in negative thoughts and feelings.

The science of spiritual alchemy is our key to changing this lead into gold. It allows us to take our pent-up energy and move it back into form to use again for another, better creation; changing the lead—the darkness in ourselves and our world—into gold, spiritually speaking. When we become spiritual alchemists our job is to free our energies from unwanted patterns so that they can be returned again to their original light momentum. But the practice is a tough one. "We are terrified," says Myss, "to think how fast our lives would change if we gave up our lead. It can be scary because our life can change very fast. So we say, 'I will keep some of my lead so that my life won't change that quickly.'"

Ultimately we realize that life is a laboratory for the creation—and recreation—of ourselves. What formula do we need to melt down this lead?

One of the Himalayan adepts who worked with Blavatsky, Saint Germain, was famous for his mastery in using an alchemical formula he had learned while in India and Tibet that gave him the power to transmute negatively qualified energy within the body and even in material objects, returning them to their original purity.

Saint Germain made a name for himself as an alchemist during the seventeenth and eighteenth centuries in Europe. Frederick the Great called him "A man whom no one has been able to understand." And in a letter to Fredrick II of Prussia, Voltaire called him "the man who never dies and who knows everything." Many European notables, in their diaries and letters, as well as newspapers, reported that he retained his youthful appearance decade after decade, that he possessed a rare knowledge of chemistry and the natural sciences, and that he had a high level of ability in the arts of the adepts.

Madame de Pompadour's *Memoirs* recounts a story about one evening she and King Louis XV of France spent with Saint Germain at Versailles. On this occasion Saint Germain was discoursing with the King and Madame about some of his secrets for removing flaws from diamonds. The king sent for a diamond of moderate size that had a flaw in it. "This diamond is worth 6,000 livres to me in this condition," said the king, but it would be worth 10,000 without the flaw. Will you undertake to enable me to make a profit of 4,000?" Saint Germain took the diamond, and a month later returned the diamond to the king without the flaw. Louis XV sent it to his jeweler, who became quite excited and proclaimed that it was now worth 9,600 livres.

Saint Germain was mentor to many of the mystics and members of Europe's secret societies such as the Rosicrucians and Masons, and scientists of his time including Franz Mesmer. Only one manuscript remains containing any of his teachings to his numerous disciples and students. This work, which is in the possession of the Bibliotheque de Troyes in France is, is called *La Tres Sainte Trinosophie (Most Holy Threefold Wisdom);* it is a cipher manuscript (not easily understood) that teaches what Manly P. Hall calls "soul-chemistry," or Kabalistic alchemy. In it Saint Germain prophesies the approach of a new age and the introduction of a new humanity with new cycles of opportunity. This work is considered the most precious manuscript of occultism in the Western tradition.

When he was performing miracles in Europe Saint Germain used a secret formula that he had learned during his long sojourn in Asia for the purpose of freeing electronic energy of negative or imperfect patterns. He refers to this formula as the "violet consuming flame." It uses the quality of freedom inherent in violet light to free electrons of their negative patterns so that this energy can be used again for another round of experimentation.

Violet is the seventh color in the spectrum that emerges when pure white light is projected through a prism. Traditionally seven is known to represent the quality of freedom and the transition between the physical and spiritual planes. It is also the color with the highest vibration—vibrating at 731 trillion times per second. Used in healing, violet is known as a purifier and balancer. It is calming, inspiring and spiritual. Leonardo da Vinci said, "The power of meditation can be ten times greater under violet light falling through the stained glass window of a quiet church."[5]

Violet flame practice is like taking a bath in liquid light. It involves visualizing scintillating energies in various shades of violet, pink, purple and lavender moving in the atmosphere like flames moving through space. Into these flames we place an image of whatever we would like to cleanse, and we watch as these violet flames purify our object or pattern of negative qualities. The practice is further enhanced when we add the power of prayer and ask for forgiveness for any part we or others had in creating the negatives. As we do this, we can say an affirmation Saint Germain has recommended for this practice: "I AM a being of violet fire. I AM the purity God desires."[6]

The term "I am" indicates that the best part of us—the part of us that is divine—is affirming this action. "Fire" means the pure, unqualified energy of creation, which we in the West call "spirit."

Saint Germain teaches that the violet flame can transmute anything negative that is sitting in our conscious mind, our subconscious, or our body. When it becomes active in us, the violet fire sweeps into these areas and acts like a solvent, dissolving the negatives and restoring energy to its original purity. The violet flame can combine with any substance, whether electronic or material.

Today, thousands of people use the violet flame not only in their spiritual meditations but in their healing practices. The violet flame is being used by psychologists, Reiki therapists, chiropractors, music therapists and many other practitioners to help with a host of problems like diabetes, cancer, anxiety and depression. A Google search reveals over 180,000 resources and articles posted on the Internet dealing with the violet flame.

My friend Karen who has a healing practice teaches all her clients to use the violet flame before she will agree to give them ongoing treatments. "I suggest that everyone who comes to me should give violet flame mantras every day in the morning and evening and especially whenever they have a crisis. I ask them to clear their emotions, psychology and their karma as much as they can before they come for a treatment. When the person can use the violet flame to clear the debris from the unconscious—the emotional energy—the body is much more able to heal itself."

Karen says that when a violet flame meditation is used in the morning, it will clear anything that happened while we were sleeping, like the energy we feel after an uncomfortable dream. "At night I suggest that people specifically visualize the violet action around everything they experienced during the day to transmute any mistakes they made. These times of cleansing are just as important as the other things we do like brushing our teeth or taking a shower before going to bed. I teach my clients to use the violet flame like a scrub to clean their emotional body."

Karen tells the following story to illustrate how healers work with the violet flame:

"I had not seen Roger for a year when he called to report blood in his stool. I learned that he had been experiencing some challenging times in his finances and family life. Roger had been feeling burdened, fearful and angry that all these personal issues were affecting his physical health. By using kinesthetic testing procedures, I was able to discern that the source of the problem was his feelings about his life. He liked his job, but wasn't providing enough for his family. His wife and friends were constantly telling him what to do and where to look for work. He and his wife have always had different views about life and spiritual matters. He felt everyone was against him. Roger had prayed but nothing had happened. Then he got angry with God. Even though he knew better, he let his emotions get the best of him.

"I explained to Roger that his negative feelings had been building up for quite awhile, putting a burden on his immune system. Each thought and feeling of inadequacy, doubt, fear or anger had resulted in the release of toxins into his body, eventually blocking the flow of energy. The free space between his atoms and electrons had become polluted and dense until, in his case, the large intestine area had weakened.

"Together we focused the transmutative energy of the violet flame to break down and remove the toxins and blocks throughout Roger's body. I taught him how to picture his organs and the large intestinal area filled with violet flame instead of the toxins from the negative emotions he had been carrying. We sent out the intention that his cells would return to their normal strength. And we gave thanks knowing that it would be done.

"I gave Roger a protocol for using the violet flame and warned that he might still experience the bleeding from time to time, especially when under stress. For a few days all was well, but by the end of the week the bleeding returned. Again I helped him apply his violet flame practice and the bleeding subsided. One more time, about a week later when Roger experienced difficulties with his marriage, the bleeding returned. Once again we applied the violet flame in the same protocol as before. Since that time Roger has not reported any bleeding."

The Dalai Lama also teaches on the importance of cleansing negative aspects of ourselves: "We are continuously under the control of negative emotions and thoughts. And as long as we are under their control, our very existence is a form of suffering. This level of suffering pervades our lives, sending us round and round in vicious circles of negative emotions and nonvirtuous actions… This pervasive suffering is most profound. It permeates all aspects of life."[7] William Blake said that, "Energy is eternal delight." The science of taking one's imperfections and relieving them of their weight results in electrons that are happier and therefore a body and emotions that can feel real joy.

I begin each day by asking my higher self, which I call my "I AM Presence," to send violet flame into my body to clear out anything that may have accumulated in my emotions or may have come up from my subconscious overnight. I invite you to try this exercise. Start by asking Saint Germain and his violet flame angels to bring the violet flame into your body and spiritual centers and to clear your world of debris you no longer want. Then begin saying Saint Germain's mantra slowly and clearly out loud: "I AM a being of violet fire. I AM the purity God desires."

-§-
We are continuously under the control of negative emotions and thoughts. And as long as we are under their control, our very existence is a form of suffering.
-§-

Visualize your heart, body, and whole aura being filled with violet energy in the form of tiny flames. See them moving with each word as they encounter the dense substance you wish to be rid of. See the flames begin to expand and blaze and whirl and grow hotter. You may begin to feel actual heat in the area of your heart or elsewhere in your body. Don't be concerned. It is a gentle action and will eventually turn to coolness when the debris has been transmuted.

I have noticed that the violet flame can impact your life in many ways by giving you:

- A greater sense of freedom from negative thoughts and feelings that can weigh you down
- More determination to focus on important things
- A feeling of lightness as you transmute your karma
- Love, joy, buoyancy and bliss
- More closeness to your higher self
- Greater spiritual mastery
- More synchronicity—even miracles—in your life

In addition, as an alchemist in the laboratory of your personal world, you become a blessing to others.

The feeling and thought you should have while practicing the violet flame is one of forgiveness—wanting to be forgiven for any misdeeds, and forgiving anyone who may have caused you pain. Do the mantra for five to fifteen minutes, or longer, and feel the pure joy that life was intended to be.

Many spiritual traditions teach that true liberation can only come to one who has acted to liberate others. And the reverse is also true: whatever we do for others we also do for ourselves.

I once participated in an experiment with several hundred people in Los Angeles. We held a prayer vigil over the New Year's holiday and used the violet flame to clear away the potential for accidents and violence that typically result on a big party night. The next day the astonished newspapers reported *a completely accident-free New Year holiday in Los Angeles that year.*

I recall a Buddhist tale about a small bird that lived near a vast jungle. A terrible fire whipped though the jungle one day, killing many trees and animals. When they saw the wildfire coming, all the birds in the jungle flew away to safety. But this little bird, heartbroken, couldn't bear to leave and let the fire destroy her home. There was a river close by, so she filled her little beak with water and flew over the fire, dropping her tiny drops of water to quench the blaze. She continued doing this day and night, determined to eradicate the fire that was destroying her world. Looking down, the heavenly gods took note of the intent and determination of this little bird. Moved with compassion, they began to shed tears. These tears became a powerful flow of water that soon extinguished the flames.

-§-

True liberation can only come to one who has acted to liberate others.

-§-

The salvation of Mother Earth can seem just as daunting. But we who care for our dear planet need to use spiritual practices we know like the violet flame, visualizations, and mantras to heal her. We may despair, wondering how one person can affect any real change. But all the great sages have known what our science now confirms: our intentions do matter, and our passionately held desires can make a tremendous difference. And each negative we transmute from ourselves will make a difference in the world. Collectively we can do this.

Kai Jakoma: Undefining the World

13

In the immortal words of Firesign Theater, "Everything you know is wrong." Our primary disease is our addiction to intellectual knowing. We need to undefine the world and live by our experiential knowing to be in relation to reality. Only by giving up all of our ideas, beliefs, values, morals, ethics, hopes, dreams, agendas, preferences—need I go on?—can we survive...because all those things are static lists or pictures that we're trying to get reality, and ourselves, to conform to.

Bingo! Right there begins the war. You want peace on earth? Stop fighting reality. Stop trying to become something other than what you are right now. Surrender all causes. You will become more effectively you—and reality will become more intimate—than you can ever imagine. Our survival is not dependent on our actions. Our survival is dependent on our willingness to die, to surrender, to give up trying to manage anything and everything. Only by dying can we survive. We are the ones who are killing us. We have to sacrifice ourselves to save ourselves. Boy, I sure love a good paradox, don't you?

What's this "dying" I'm talking about, huh? All we have to do is form new relationships to everything. That's all. All the old relationships were based on either our conditioning or our responses to our conditioning, in which case they're not in relationship to reality. We've been living in a fantasy world. That world and the identity connected to it must go away for us to find reality. That's what I mean by death.

Kai Jakoma has studied everything from geology, computer science and 3D computer animation; to philosophy, comparative religions and consciousness studies; to fine art, music theory and modern dance; to holistic health, somatic therapy and dance therapy. He is a writer, artist, musician, poet and companion to people on their journey toward their authentic selves. He is currently most interested and involved in the process of our recovery from Western civilization and the re-integration of our animal awareness into our everyday lives. His evolving web presence can be found at www.kaijakoma.com. Photo courtesy of Art Bock.

"But I don't want to die," I hear you saying. That's right. The you that's afraid of dying is the you that's disconnected from the flow of reality. It's the false you, the tame you, the domesticated you. It's the mask you wear so that you can manage the people around you so they'll accept you. The rest of you isn't afraid of dying. Yes, your mask has kept that you safe, but it's also kept you trussed up like a veal cow. Sure, the veal are nice and cozy and comfy in those tiny stalls—but they can hardly stand on their own two feet. Oops. I mean four feet.

-§-
"Everything you know is wrong."
—Firesign Theater
-§-

The only way to get out of our tiny stalls is to leave the managed world behind and go remember how to live like wild animals in the real world. Say goodbye to Kansas, Toto. The recent movie, "The Matrix," is a superbly crafted story of what it's like to extract ourselves from our conditioned lives and wake up to "the desert of the real," as Morpheus calls it.

What We Must Pretend

To be a member of my society (specifically American), I must pretend many things (and thanks to Kira Ohina for her help in compiling this list). I must pretend that:

I'm in control.

I'm well-adjusted.

I'm happy.

I care.

I'm important, I matter.

I'm not important, I don't matter.

I like it here and want to stay—at all costs.

What we're doing works.

I don't know that there's something very disturbing going on here.

I know what's happening.

I don't know what's happening.

I'm getting my needs met.

I don't have needs.

I'm not at war.

I'm not in pain, depressed, enraged, overwhelmed, angry, sad, exhausted, confused and/or despairing.

I'm ashamed of my pain, depression, hatred, anger, rage, etc.

My pain is not important.

We don't long for each other.

We're civilized.

We're better than nature.

There's nothing wrong with my family.

Repressed sexuality and anger are not driving our interactions and ways of being in the world.

There's no trustable self: my appetites are untrustworthy, the ways I experience the world are wrong, someone knows better than I do how to live my life.

Recovering from Western Civilization

Our undomesticated selves, the animal aspects of us, are always in the flow, always aware of what's happening, always aware of how life is moving through us and the world around us. As animals, we're content to respond according to how life moves—it's our inherent, natural state, the simple basis of our being. To be in control, the brain needs to choose to go against the flow of life and choose to shut up, or drown out, the rest of the being's awareness and contentment. This is the crux of our disease—individually and globally. And what does our beloved capitalism teach us? Ways to convince people that spending their money is more satisfying than simply being in relationship with reality.

-§-
Our undomesticated selves, the animal aspects of us, are always in the flow, always aware of what's happening, always aware of how life is moving through us.
-§-

If we become content animals, our brain, our society and our economy are no longer in control. I'm not talking about becoming content with the way things are, but becoming content with simply following where the movement of life calls us in any moment, whether that be violent or calm, fierce or compassionate, foolish or wise, sacred or profane, doing or being. Since there's really only one organism that exists, when we dethrone our egos we free ourselves up to be moved by the inherent movement of the being-at-large. The being we call "existence" is perfectly capable of moving everything in the direction it needs to be moved in. It doesn't need the interfering "help" of our puny, blind, arrogant, self-serving, two-year-old minds. What we call our "desire to do something" is merely our small consciousness becoming aware of the movement of life through us. Just because we're aware of what life is doing doesn't mean that we need to do anything about it. This is not football. Put your hands in the air and back away from the ball.

So how do we become content animals? We sacrifice ourselves to the great god-beast reality. We lay ourselves down on the altar of each moment and beg the great raven of death to tear holes in us so that our effort can bleed out onto the ground. We walk through the veils of our defense mechanisms, manipulation strategies and diversion tactics. We forget what we were taught. We shift the focus of our attention from thinking the world to sensing the world. We undefine ourselves and the world and allow our knowledge of reality to arise from our moment-by-moment experience instead of the semantic boxes we strive to force it into.

This process happens along a continuum of transformation. Here are some of the key threads involved in the process:

• Our focus and trust shift from the words and reasonings in our minds to the feelings and impulses in our bodies. These feelings and impulses evoke in us the sensory imagery of our inherent language—archetypes, dreams, daydreams, gut feelings, hunches, visions, hallucinations, rites of passage and other spiritual experiences. These are all examples of our inherent language. Our unconscious is actually the vast majority of our consciousness.

• Our relationship to reality changes from one of self-importance and anthropocentrism to one of humility, perspective, respect, and humor. We shift from seeing our civilization as huge and nature as tiny to seeing nature as huge and our civilization as tiny.

-§-
We lay ourselves down on the altar of each moment and beg the great raven of death to tear holes in us so that our effort can bleed out onto the ground.
-§-

• Will or surrender—how do we know when to do which? I think the interesting part of this one is that recovering ourselves from our conditioning can take a lot of attention *and* effort, whereas becoming the fullness of ourselves requires a lack of both attention and effort. There were many, many times in the midst of my recovery when I could find no way to tell if will or surrender was appropriate for the situation at hand. What a lovely way to engender humility, don't you think?

• Our relationship to the divine shifts from looking like a tiny flame that we've kept alive through all the dark, windy and desolate times to looking like a tiny chink in the wall of a small brick hut we built to keep out the blindingly all-encompassing fire of the divine so that our tiny ego could survive this long and keep us alive to recover ourselves.

• The shift in our relationship to reality opens a doorway onto a new experience of reality with new laws of nature. Phenomena that we used to see as rare, momentous omens become the everyday laws of nature that we come to rely on and ignore as much as we do gravity. That means that the novel and spectacular become secondhand and banal. Of course you're in the right place at the right time...all the time. Of course things work out magically according to some grand design...all the time.

• Our awareness of power moves from an external focus (authority figures), to self-focus (self-empowerment), to the being-at-large-focus (no one really has any power at all).

• The motivation for our actions shifts from being the resultant edicts of our mind's reasoning to the sense of rightness about a particular choice regardless of any reasoning.

Undefining the world is a blast. It's incredibly liberating. It's like creatively playing your way out of a prison you don't even know you're in while everyone around you is frozen in time. Here's an example of what I mean: about ten years ago I suddenly realized that I only had six categories that any relationship with a woman could fit into: acquaintance with no attraction, acquaintance with some attraction, friend with no attraction, friend with some attraction, lover and ex-lover. Since everything in existence is always changing, every moment in every relationship with every woman is a whole world in its own. The reality that I was neglecting was that each moment with any woman is a unique relationship.

-§-
Our unconscious is actually the vast majority of our consciousness.
-§-

It didn't take me long to realize that limiting this perspective to my relationships with women was absurd and that every moment with every person is a delectable new world of delicious wonders, bitter and sweet, brackish and rejuvenating, familiar and foreign. Geez. No wonder people stop paying attention. It's really difficult to support the economy that pretends to run the world when you're deliriously involved with those around you in the present moment.

What God Is

Presumptuous, aren't I? Our concept of God is merely our sensing of the overarching consciousness of the being that we're all a part of. It's like we're the muscles in the fingers of reality. When we turn our attention to the overarching consciousness of the being that encompasses all of reality, we're awe-struck at the brilliantly pulsing magnificence of it. We prostrate ourselves before it. It is our God. Yet it's just the consciousness of reality going about its business.

From it we experience directives to behave in certain ways. For example, the being decides to raise its finger. Messages are sent to the muscles that move the finger bones. We're the muscles of reality. It's the natural functioning state of everything to comply with the impulses from the being-at-large. We don't comply under our own power; it's our default state. The only power we really have is to go against the movement of life. Going with reality takes no choosing and no effort. This is the essence of free will, Satan's rebellion, our fall from grace, and the savage barbarism of our civilization.

Reality's overarching consciousness is the comforting presence that nourishes us all. Being able to experience one's connection to the whole kit and caboodle is like resting in our mother's arms. Being able to sense the being's awareness of us lets us know that we're not alone. God, meet humanity. Humanity, meet God. Welcome to the simplicity of reality.

Prehistoric man didn't live in constant battle with the forces of nature. Prehistoric man didn't "know" any better than to live in constant harmony with the forces of nature. Remember? We lived in the Garden of Eden until we knew the difference between good and bad. Prehistoric man was an animal with all of his animal faculties at the ready.

Life is like a river—flowing through and around us, knowing exactly where it's going and how to get there. Each of us is afloat in this river. How do we respond to the fact that we're afloat in a river that's always moving? How do we respond to the direction and force of the movement in any moment? How do we respond to the fact that there's a capricious river constantly flowing through us and that who we are is always changing?

Inner peace is not generated by the qualities of life's movements. It's generated from the qualities of our relationships to life's movements.

-§-
We shift from seeing our civilization as huge and nature as tiny to seeing nature as huge and our civilization as tiny.
-§-

When my ego is cut off from the rest of my being's inherent connection to the flow of movement, it wants to cling to anything that looks solid and stationary. Hence, it tends to gravitate toward any of the large boulders, here and there, that stick up out of the water—career, spouse, home, retirement account—whatever we think we know.

Now, anyone who's spent any time frolicking in a river knows that the first rule of engagement is to avoid the rocks because the force of the water against them can seriously damage you and/or maroon you. The safest way to float down a river is in a relaxed sitting position, with your legs stretched out in front of you to help you bounce off any rocks you might encounter. My ego doesn't care about this. It wants to know what's going on. It wants to be in control. It wants to know that everything is safe and stable. Sometimes I have to bring out the big guns: "Put your hands in the air and float away from the rock."

Practicing Trusting Life

It's possible, and quite engaging, to be very creative in coming up with ways that we can practice trusting life. For example, once we enter the unpredictable realms of traffic or mass transit we often find ourselves at the mercy of reality. How could we use these situations to cultivate our trust in life?

Usually, when we think we're late, we tend to look at our watches or clocks periodically whether there's anything we can do to change the rate of our progress or not. There's no sense in doing this and all it usually does is make us more uptight, so why not just cover our car clocks or watches? This way, every time we reflexively look at the clock we'll see the trickster sticking its tongue out at us, saying, "Oh no you don't!"

-§-

Our relationship to the divine shifts from looking like a tiny flame [in] the dark... to looking like a tiny chink in the wall... we built to keep out the blindingly all-encompassing fire of the divine.

-§-

Do everything you can on your end to be on time and then practice trusting life to take care of the rest—without you paying attention to how it's proceeding or worrying about it. Find things to do while you're in the hands of traffic. Make up a song. Read a book. Make up some poetry to describe the moment. Search for the square root of life. Just let life deal with getting you where you need to be at the appropriate time. And remember that the appropriate time may be something other than the expected time. For example, when I'm late, I often find that the people I was meeting are also late and that we rendezvous at "just the right time" for all concerned.

What Is Radical Trust?

- Living in the current moment without trying to make sure the future is going to be okay.
- Not expecting the world, people or oneself to be any different than they currently are.
- Making choices based on how the world and oneself feels rather than on what one's mind imagines, thinks or decides. If it feels right to do it, then do it. If it doesn't feel right to do it, then don't.
- Following one's own innate sense of reality rather than conforming oneself to someone else's view of reality, even one's culture's.
- Allowing oneself to be moved by life rather than manipulating life. Trusting that reality knows much more about where we're going than we ever can. Gladly following life's impulses without knowing where they're leading or why. Not needing to know why something feels right or doesn't feel right.
- Being able to sense how everything that happens is intimately intertwined in a mysterious way unfathomable to us. Being able to sense that everything makes sense even though it doesn't make sense. Seeing everything as trustable regardless of how it looks.

- Trust is acceptance of unity.
- Trust is integration and integrity.
- Fear cuts off trust and divides things up.
- Fear is the isolation of the constructed reality from the natural reality, the perceptual filter from the energy flow, the somewhat self-aware monitoring station from the rest of the being.
- My small self is afraid of not being in control.
- My large self knows that control just creates problems.
- Why do I want to fight the flow?
- Life works in strange ways, but it works—when we let it.
- There are no mistakes.
- Everything is trustable.
- Life gives us everything we need so we can do what it expects us to do.
- What does life expect us to do?
- What do we need it to provide so that we can do it?
- How do we recognize when it's being provided and what shape it's being offered in?

Practicing Intellectual Release Technique

Let's take a concept from modern dance, Release Technique, and apply it to the intellect. Let's say that Release Technique is about using as little effort as possible to accomplish a movement, using only the muscles necessary and allowing all the other ones to remain in a released state.

How could we practice this with how we think instead of how we move? How might our lives be different?

-§-
Every moment with every person is a delectable new world of delicious wonders, bitter and sweet, brackish and rejuvenating, familiar and foreign.
-§-

There's a similar concept in the realm of philosophy, Occam's Razor, or the *law of economy*. It states that the simplest explanation is the preferred one. I like to think of it as a razor I use to cut away the fat, the ex-traneous stuff.

How would it look if we used such a razor on our belief systems, on the stories that others tell us or we tell ourselves about the world and how it works? How much of my belief system us just fluff? How much of it is actually related to my experience of what is actually happening in reality?

How might our lives be different? How little can we use our minds and still go about our daily business? If my current way of life is any indication, not much at all. But that's just me. How much of your thinking is extraneous, erroneous, or distracting?

How Do We Live Radical Trust?

• Keep a watchful eye for self-importance and anthropocentrism. Any aspect of our life or belief system that's centered around us, individually or as a species, is suspect—eternal life, having power over reality, the transmigration of the soul, our preferences, or capitalizing our names.

• Become aware of how we make up lots of stories about reality and about our lives. How can we become more aware of the difference between our experience and what we do with our experience, what we make it mean?

• Shift our focus from believing our mind's stories, reasonings and justifications to how our interaction with the world feels in our body/being and how we feel moved to act. Learn how to wait for the right time. Pay attention to our motivations for action and clean up our involvements with reality so that we can be congruent with the movement of life. In other words, get out of the way—let go of resistance and attachment.

• Allow ourselves to conceive that the natural state of reality is for everything to interrelate more magically than we could design or even imagine. Allow ourselves to let go of our "control" of our life and trust that the being-at-large is moving our selves and those around us in the ways that life needs us to move for the good of the whole.

-§-

Life works in strange ways, but it works—when we let it.

-§-

• Be willing to understand how the being-at-large will never put us in a situation without giving us the resources to deal with it. Not because we're special, but because we're nothing. It's not we who are living life. Life is living us. We're just somewhat self-aware and tend to be fascinated with what we can do—how we can mess with things.

Teach Your Children Well

Besides the fact that the planet is just fine and can "heal" itself without our help, we can engender a more balanced and healthy planet and lifestyle by reorganizing our civilization. Human civilization has been organized around power for the few and manipulation of the many for millennia. "It is only by taming the wild human that we can put it to work to make us rich and powerful," we have believed. How can we create an economy and civilization based on cooperation and the movement of life through and around all of us instead?

Many things will have to go, of course. Civilization as a whole has to go through the kind of death and rebirth that we each have to go through individually for something truly authentic and connected to reality to arise. "Because we can" must be seen as the justification only a diseased person, social group or nation would use. We must relinquish our addictions to what I call the Toy Impulse—the seductiveness of playing with things that our economy dangles in front of our faces. The realm of science will have to become aware of its own limitations and fundamentalism.

-§-
It's not we who are living life. Life is living us.
-§-

Our concept of time and the reasons we structure it the way we do (for efficient production) will need to dissolve. Expecting any of us to live our lives by the alarm clock, the bell and the time card is extremely unrealistic and the implementation of it is one of the most violent things we do to ourselves without realizing it. It will take a while for each of us to get used to being kind with ourselves in the simplest of ways.

We'll have to stop compulsively trying to fix things that look wrong to our limited perspectives. How arrogant is it of us to think that we can tell when reality is working or not when our perspective is like that of an ant, relative to the being-at-large?

Most of all, we will have to shift from trusting our manipulation of reality with our reasoning to trusting life, the being-at-large, to organically move everything for the good of the whole. We will have to trust the organic process and timing of reality over our own preferences, ideas, beliefs, and reasonings. We'll have to wean ourselves of the illusion of safety and become familiar with the way of the fool—following the call of life, regardless of where it leads, regardless of what it looks like.

We have to begin teaching our children basic life skills according to a realistic paradigm:

- Teach them body awareness (as we've come to know it through such things as martial arts, meditation, yoga, massage and bodywork, somatic therapies and dance-related modalities).
- Teach them that the best course is always to follow themselves, not their minds, and that reasoning can justify anything and is therefore suspect.
- We need to encourage them to allow their beliefs to follow from their experience and not the other way around.
- Teach them to have perspective on their beliefs—to be aware of their relationships with them.
- Instill in them the value of cooperation over competition and that there is never an opponent or an enemy, that we are always all in this together.

- Show them how anything we consider evil is just the result of pain, disconnection and lack of respect—on everyone's part.

This is by no means a complete list. We will have to form completely new relationships with our children, as with everything else, both individually and globally. The reorganization of our civilization will be as catastrophic, demoralizing, humiliating, depressing and utterly transformative as is any death, as is any recovery from brainwashing, as is any hero or heroine's quest for the meaning of life. Perhaps we will finally become human.

-§-
We'll have to wean ourselves of the illusion of safety and become familiar with the way of the fool—following the call of life, regardless of where it leads.
-§-

The Simplicity Of It All

Electrical impulses and chemical interactions are experienced as waves of movement. Waves of movement are experienced as desire. The being inherently moves in the direction required of it for the balanced functioning of the whole—without the conscious mind being involved in the decision-making process, except possibly as a data consultant. With perspective, humility, flexibility and the willingness to recognize and comply, we can allow the natural state of wholeness to rebalance itself in our lives and on every other level of organization of reality around us and inside us.

Marshall Vian Summers:

The Great Turning Point

I would like to lead you further into this mystery today, the mystery of who you are, why you are here and where you are going—the mystery of purpose. Perhaps you have begun this mysterious journey and now we encounter each other in this place, this rendezvous point, a place where the road ends and the wilderness begins.

The Uncharted Territory

What I am about to say will lead you into uncharted territory. It may change your life. Ask yourself, "Am I ready to take this next step?"

I'm going to speak to you in mystical terms now. Perhaps you know this language. It is the language of this uncharted territory. Here we leave the world of concepts and intellect and enter a world of deeper understanding and recognition. Prepare yourself then. Prepare your inner vision. Prepare your inner listening. Become still inside so that you and I can stay connected through this experience. This is how deeper communication occurs. This will enable me to show you a way.

Deeper Inclinations

The deeper inclinations that you have been feeling throughout your life are signs that something greater is stirring within you. You who are drawn to discover what these deeper inclinations really mean are at the beginning of responding to the mystery of purpose. Purpose generates

Marshall Vian Summers is a dynamic teacher and inspired writer, providing a new awareness that humankind is not alone in the universe. He points to a deep understanding of humanity's spiritual reality and about our destiny within the greater community of intelligent life in the universe. In 1975, Marshall ended his career as a special educator for the blind. He later began teaching the principles and practices of inner knowing, and he has written a trilogy of books on the subject. Marshall lives in seclusion with his wife in the Rocky Mountains. He can be found on the web at www.greatercommunity.org.

meaning, and meaning is what we search for in all things. Yet what is greater purpose and what steps can you take to find it?

The idea that greater purpose exists is a confirmation that your true inclination towards spiritual development and understanding is real. However, spiritual development must eventually lead to something real in the world. It cannot merely be a personal quest. It cannot be self-indulgent. It is not about your personal enlightenment. Your deeper inclinations must lead you to something valid: a participation, a role, a service, an ability that is truly needed by the world. You have a unique gift to give to the world. Yet God would not waste your gift by giving it only to you, and it will never be realized until it is given to others. It will only remain a potential within you.

Self-Knowledge

Greater purpose is what you are looking for. It is within you. You have brought it with you into the world. It is like a secret cargo that you carry. It lives within your Self-Knowledge, the deeper Spiritual Mind that God has given you to guide and protect you in your journey in the world.

-§-
Mystery is where we have come from. Everything that is lasting comes from mystery.
-§-

To discover and to contribute the gift that is yours to give, you must first respond to this knowledge within you and over time have this Knowledge become your foundation. Within your personal mind, the mind that judges, evaluates, compares, hopes and fears, you will not be able to figure this out. Your ideas and beliefs cannot account for it. It must come from deeper within you.

You are not of one mind about your reason for being here. You are in conflict concerning your identity, your direction and your purpose. This conflict permeates all levels of your conscious mind, but it does not affect your Self-Knowledge, the deeper mind within you.

Your Knowledge is beyond error. It is the God-seed within you. It is higher truth within you. This is something you can finally trust. With Knowledge as your foundation, your true power, abilities and direction will return to you. This is the great reunion. This is what the world is waiting for—your power and abilities dedicated to a greater purpose.

Knowledge reaches you in mysterious ways. It is like water seeping through the soil. It finds the path of least resistance. It reaches down to the roots and nourishes. It does not filter in a uniform manner. If your mind, like soil, has been loosened so that it is aerated and opened, then the truth, like water, may enter more easily and nourish you more immediately.

Intuition and insight are the outermost expressions of Knowledge, yet they are but the snowflakes before the storm. They are signs that something greater is coming and you must prepare. Heed these signs. Watch for them. Listen for them. Feel them. Follow them. Yet don't make any conclusions yet. Just know that something is building. Knowledge is telling you that you must prepare to set out in a new direction. And only you will know what this may mean.

Higher Purpose

It is not enough for me to give a definition of higher purpose and to say your purpose is to forgive the world, or your purpose is to serve the world, or your purpose is to be one with God, or your purpose is to finally love yourself completely and to learn to love others. For your purpose contains all of these things. Yet it is really about something else.

The knowledge of your purpose is stored within your Self-Knowledge, like a treasure buried beneath the soil of your mind. You cannot find it on your own. You need great assistance. You cannot find it alone because in truth you are not alone. You are more than an individual. You are part of something greater.

-§-

To travel in the wilderness, you can't take everything with you. You need only what is essential now.

-§-

However, if you are ambivalent concerning this discovery, then you will not seek for it in earnest. You will be in conflict—part of you wanting it, part of you not wanting it. At this moment, you may not be wholehearted regarding this because your mind and your life are full of your plans, goals and obligations. As a result, the discovery of your purpose takes time because it takes time to wholeheartedly desire it and to be free to find it.

The Journey

Purpose is a discovery and a journey. It is born of disappointment with your life as it is, disillusionment with the world as it is—and a deep need to fulfill what you came here to do. To make this journey, however, you are going to have to give some things up. You need to lighten your load. To travel in the wilderness, you can't take everything with you. You need only what is essential now. You will have to leave some good people behind. They cannot take this journey with you because in truth this is not their journey. They are going in a different direction.

The First Great Gate

Here you are going to have to choose what you are going to follow within yourself. You cannot have it all. This is the first great gate. This is the great stopping place. This is where many people give up the journey. This is where many people walk out on themselves and their deeper inclinations. This is where people consign themselves to a life of compromise. This is where purpose dies and the needs of the world go unfulfilled.

The Calling

The mystery of purpose calls to you from beyond this gate. Will you pass through this gate? If you do, then you have entered the realm where the activation of Knowledge can truly occur. Once you are in the clear, Knowledge begins to have a more direct influence upon your conscious mind. You begin to seek quiet and solitude instead of stimulation. You begin to see, feel and know things that would have escaped your attention before. You look for real honesty in your communication with others. You remember insights you had long ago which now have real relevance. You are finally becoming free to be yourself again.

Being Reshaped

This is a long journey and there are more gates to pass through, more stopping places. At each one, you will have to choose between your growing experience of Knowledge and where it's taking you and those expectations, ideas and relationships that are holding you back.

As you pass through each gate, you relinquish more of your control to Knowledge and the mystery of purpose within you as your life is being reshaped. Here you are going from being a person who was primarily concerned with serving yourself and your ideas to becoming someone who has the power, capacity and grace to serve something far greater.

Relationships of Destiny

Greater relationships can come to you now as your life becomes unencumbered and begins to open up. These are not mere friends. They are individuals who hold the key to your destiny here, a destiny they share with you, and who are necessary participants in the realization of your greater purpose and contribution. These are relationships of destiny and you must prepare for them.

Living With the Question

Over the years, people have often told me what they think their purpose is. "It is my purpose to be in this relationship for now"; "It is my purpose to be living here"; "It is my purpose to travel around the world"; "It is my purpose to pursue this career." Listen for these declarations in yourself and in others. They are almost always premature. These may only be incremental movements. You have a long way to go. Your thirst for Knowledge and truth must be greater than these self-validating, self-selected definitions. Live with the question of your purpose unanswered. In truth, you can't define your purpose. It defines you in its own time and in its own way.

The Great Breaking Point

What I am speaking of is your calling in the world. This is when you reach the great breaking point where what you want, what you know and what the world requires of you finally converge. It is like an explosion. Energy long pent up is finally released. This is power, but it is power with a purpose. It is here to do something.

Seeing and Knowing

After this great breaking point, then you will begin to know specifically what you are to do in the world. You will *know* it. You will finally recognize it. And you will think, "I have always had this feeling. Why didn't I know this sooner?" You did not know it sooner because you could not accept it. You could not act upon it. You could not give yourself to it wholeheartedly.

The Turning Point

Those who have reached this point know that the truth about their purpose in life is more important than anything else—comfort, security, acknowledgment, love or money. They are becoming wholehearted in their desire for this calling and in their desire for Knowledge. This is a turning point. Now something important can really begin to happen.

Remember, Knowledge is your spiritual reality. It is bigger than this world. It accounts for far more than this one time and place. You cannot see the entire universe from where you are standing. Just like the fish in the sea cannot perceive the stars above or what is occurring in the landscapes beyond their realm, the world is like a sea and you are within it now. But Knowledge connects you with all of it.

-§-
Live with the question of your purpose unanswered. In truth, you can't define your purpose. It defines you in its own time and in its own way.
-§-

You must satisfy and complete each step towards this great turning point. You cannot skip ahead, thinking that you know what you are doing. The truth is, most of the time you won't know what you are doing. Other people will expect you to explain what is happening. But it is ineffable. If they are not on such a journey themselves, they will not understand. You are undergoing a great transition. In essence, you are shifting the center of authority within yourself.

Readiness

Your purpose will not arise until you are truly ready for it and until the conditions are right. You are not in a position to assess your readiness. The Mystery will determine that. Your task now is to take the next step that is in front of you.

To be successful, you must take each step without idealism, without ambition, without presumptuous ideas about the way God is, the way God works in the world and the way life is. These ideas can lead you astray. They are only ideas based on expectations and hope.

You must learn what your true responsibilities are here. You cannot determine your destiny in this life because you do not know where you are going or where you have come from. That is the Mystery. Yet you must manage your internal and external affairs to a very large degree. In this you are empowered. You are like the captain of your ship. Your thoughts and feelings are your crew. The ship is your body. You are meant to be the captain of the ship, but you do not yet know what the ship carries deep within its hold or what its ultimate destination is. Assuming this leadership over your thinking and behavior is one of your primary steps. You must be able to responsibly focus your mind and energy at each step along the way in order to ultimately do something important in the world.

The Great Attraction

What is this spiritual purpose that is so mysterious? It is a great attraction within you. When you have reached the point of realizing that it may be more desirable than self-fulfillment and your former attempts at self-gratification, then it begins to assert an attraction. It always had this attraction, yet it was misconstrued as something else. Now you begin to realize that this sense of purpose you have had all your life, however denied or neglected, is something to seriously consider and to honor.

Look at your purpose in terms of stages. This is much better, for stages involve action and an understanding that things grow in stages. This approach also tends to separate the dreamers from the doers—those who merely wish to entertain themselves with high ideals from those who actually set out to live a life that they know is possible, but which they cannot yet define.

Carrying Knowledge Within

Everyone carries Knowledge. If it is reaching its activation point, you cannot stop it. It will assert increasing influence. It will lead you towards new experiences. It will reshape your point of view as you proceed along. It will speak of things that people around you will never consider or find interesting.

As Knowledge becomes more potent within you and begins to emerge more powerfully, it begins to assert greater and greater power through you and within you. When this happens, you will see that you had been living according to ideas, but now there is something working within you. You may call it your Higher Self or God or something else, but this again is merely a classification process. In truth, it is beyond words. Your Higher Self is not a greater individual. It is part of a group. That is why it saves you from your isolation.

The Homecoming

Deep within you, you now feel that you have found something. You have found yourself. You finally feel at home in the world. This feeling of "Home" is a very important experience. When you meet those individuals who are destined to be a part of your greater purpose, you will have this experience of "home." Your relationship will not merely be about the sharing of ideas and interests. It will not be about the satisfaction of desires. It is far greater than this. You may say, "I feel at home with these people. I can't explain it."

What I am talking of here is satisfaction leading to greater satisfaction—wholeness leading to greater wholeness. To experience this, you will learn as you proceed that certain lines of thinking and certain activities strengthen your experience of Knowledge and others weaken it. This leads to ongoing choosing and development. This is what your daily life gives you.

Insights

Recall a time you absolutely *knew* something—something beyond your preferences and fears and your ideas in the moment. You just *knew* something. What a contrast this insight was to all of the thinking, all the worrying, all the anxiety, all the anticipation, all the excitement, all the questioning and all of the anger and frustration. Wait for these times of knowing. Recognize them. Call for them.

Decisions

On your journey, you must also make important decisions. How can you know you are making the right decision? Decision-making can take a lot of energy. Deliberation and ambivalence take time. To conserve your energy and to stay on course, if you find that you must take a position, then take a position. Yet if you do not have to take a position, then wait until you know. The Mystery gives you both opportunities. Both are very important. One requires determined action. The other requires patience and restraint. These abilities must be cultivated. That is why you have decisions that you must make immediately and you have decisions that can wait. Can you make a decision and hold to it, regardless of what everyone else says? On the other hand, can you *wait* to make a decision until everything settles down within you so that you can see clearly? These are necessary skills.

Stability

You have to be a greater person than you are today to carry Knowledge and to live a greater purpose. That is why you must develop yourself as a person—your physical ability, your emotional stability, your mental framework, your activities, your discernment in the world, many things. The Mystery reclaims; it does not destroy. But it must set things in order, both within you and around you. If your life is constrained or compromised, you will not be able to proceed.

The Mystery of Purpose

Knowledge is with you. It is a power. It is a force. It is a presence. It holds the mystery and the meaning of your purpose. It is the most powerful force in the universe, yet it has the humility and the simplicity to open your heart and the hearts of others. Knowledge is pervasive. It is the mysterious force that moves everything towards the fulfillment of its purpose in life. Without fanfare, without great show, Knowledge affects everything, but in an unseen way.

-§-

Can you wait to make a decision until everything settles down within you so that you can see clearly?

-§-

You came into the world with the Knowledge of who you are, who you must meet and what you must accomplish. It is time now to find this Knowledge and begin to live it. This is the mystery of your purpose, a mystery that you share with all others who are in the world with you at this critical time in history. Many more people now must respond to the mystery of their purpose. This is the great need of our world.

A Prayer and a Blessing

Before we leave this place on the edge of the wilderness let us conclude our time together with a prayer and a blessing. Join me now in this prayer:

Let me, then, be the recipient of Knowledge. Let me, then, embody Knowledge. Let me, then, learn to be an expression of Knowledge. Let my mind be illuminated. Let my body be invigorated. Let my relationships be balanced and harmonized. And let the way open before me, for I am ready to begin.

And here is a blessing:

May the mystery of your purpose emerge within you. May you be blessed to receive it and have the strength to follow it, wherever it may take you. May the world call out of you the gift that you have been sent here to give. And may your life be an inspiration that leaves a legacy for others who follow.

-§-
May the world call out of you the gift that you have been sent here to give.
-§-

Part Four

Beyond the Scientific Horizon

Larry Dossey: Non-Local Consciousness and the Revolution in Medicine

My wife Barbara and I recently visited one of the largest hospitals in Manhattan to talk about new research studies showing the healing effects of prayer. Among the assembled doctors, nurses, and other staff was a rabbi. Employed full time by the hospice unit to pray with patients, he also acted as minister to the staff. When I visited the hospice later that day, the rabbi took me aside. "I've just got to get one thing straight with you," he said. "Are you claiming that prayer actually *works?*"

Many people—even ministers and priests—believe that prayer provides little more than mental comfort. Like the rabbi, they see it as simply a psychological intervention, and nothing more. New research directly confronts this belief, and shows that consciousness, prayer, and intention are powerfully and literally creative.

Physicians are even more shocked than the rabbi when they see the results of these studies. Prayer, as an effective treatment, is an outrageous notion for most of the medical establishment, since no accepted theory exists to explain this phenomenon. Studies of distant healing and remote intercessory prayer demonstrate that, when a loving, empathic, compassionate intention, formed in the mind and held in the heart, is directed as prayer, a powerful healing effect is produced. Prayer works even if the person being prayed for hasn't a clue that the prayer is taking place. Some 150 studies have now been conducted that support this general idea.

Larry Dossey, M.D., is a physician of internal medicine. He is an eloquent advocate for anchoring complementary medicine in a model that is scientifically based, yet also answers to humankind's inner spiritual needs. He was a battalion surgeon in Vietnam, and chief of staff at Medical City Dallas Hospital. He has lectured all over the world, including the Mayo Clinic, Harvard, Johns Hopkins, Cornell, and numerous major universities. Among his many books are *The Power of Premonitions* (2007) and *The Extraordinary Healing Power of Ordinary Things* (2009). He is executive editor of *Explore: The Journal of Science and Healing*. Photo by Athi Mara Magadi.

Throughout recent history, our culture has believed that spirituality is an inward state, with little impact on the outside world. We think of spirituality as a private matter. Today, that perspective is being radically challenged by these studies. Science, the most powerful metaphor in our culture, is validating the power of consciousness to shift material form, and demonstrating that healing starts in consciousness. This is a breathtaking discovery.

The most high-profile study is being conducted at Duke Medical Center, one of the most prestigious medical centers in the world. Dr. Mitchell Krucoff and Suzy Crater, his nurse research assistant, are studying the effect of intercessory prayer on patients admitted to Duke University's cardiovascular center with severe chest pain. These patients are due for a procedure known as cardiac catheterization and angioplasty, a procedure in which doctors mechanically dilate the obstructed coronary arteries.

-§-

Studies of distant healing and remote intercessory prayer demonstrate that…a powerful healing effect is produced.

-§-

When these patients arrive in Duke's emergency room, they are asked, "Do you want to be a patient in the prayer study?" Those that say, "Yes," are randomized. They either go to the group assigned prayer, or the group not assigned prayer. Both groups receive identical treatment. The first names of those who fall into the prayed-for group are farmed out via email to various groups around the world. Buddhists in Tibet and Nepal pray for them. Hindus in India pray for them. They receive prayer from a group of Jews in Jerusalem called Virtual Jerusalem. Cloistered Catholic nuns outside of Baltimore pray for these patients. Fundamentalist Christian churches in the mid-Atlantic states participate. Silent Unity, an arm of the Unity Church, is part of this effort.

Findings from this study published in the *American Heart Journal* show that the people who received intercessory prayer had 50% to 100% fewer side effects from these invasive cardiac procedures when compared with people who were not assigned prayer. This is what scientists call "big data": a huge effect. Preliminary results are so promising that the study has been expanded to nine major American hospitals.

Traditional indigenous cultures have much to tell us about this phenomenon, and about why our culture has been unable to act on environmental challenges. Authors such as Constance Grauds, whose book, *Jungle Medicine,* chronicles her studies with shamans in the Amazon, and Sandra Ingerman, who wrote *Soul Retrieval,* tell us what indigenous peoples know: that souls can fragment, and portions can be lost or clouded. In the shamanic traditions, one of the reasons that souls are said to become fragmented is deep-rooted fear and insecurity. Our politicians nowadays have made fear and insecurity an art form. One of the symptoms of soul loss is apathy, ennui, the inability to experience passion. Those words describe today's America. We can't muster the political will to handle these problems. I suspect that we're suffering culturally, nationally, from a horrible case of soul loss. Our souls are paying the price of our inability to act.

On the positive side, surveys consistently show that the majority of taxpayers are willing to spend more of their tax dollars to protect the environment. People are willing to act, and they form a huge reservoir of potential power that can be tapped. But just as the momentum for alternative medicine did not come from the top, neither will the change in environmental practices come from the top. The move toward alternative and integral medicine began at the grassroots level. We may well see a similar phenomenon beginning, a huge surge of environmental concern, emerging from the same source. Although we certainly could use national leadership to capitalize on the groundswell of grassroots interest, a strong collective thrust will bypass politicians and the bureaucracies in many an instance. The movement has already caught fire in certain areas, including Santa Fe, New Mexico, where I live, and other communities. Even in China, one of the most environmentally degraded countries on earth, a small but active environmental group exists. The Chinese government is beginning to respond. Hope begets hope, and we may soon reach a tipping point.

-§-

People who received intercessory prayer had 50% to 100% fewer side effects from these invasive cardiac procedures. This is what scientists call "big data": a huge effect.

-§-

Our national culture needs less a dramatic shift in our programs, private or public, than it needs a shift in consciousness. The programs that have been advanced during the last few years, notably the Kyoto Protocol, have had great difficulty gaining traction in the U.S. The problem is not only the actual physical pollutants unleashed by our activities, but also our unwillingness as a nation to muster the will to do anything about it. The problem is not a failure of programs; we have plenty of those. We have plenty of intelligence and ingenuity, but we are suffering a failure of will. We need to muster the will, the vision, and the initiative to dig in and do something. We're like a nation of anesthetized zombies, sleepwalkers, stuck in deep emotional mud, unable to find the vision to motivate ourselves.

Fundamental shifts are occurring in certain areas of science if one knows where to look for the indicators. They portend a huge transition in the way we see ourselves in terms of connectedness with the world. The area that excites me most, personally and professionally, is the evidence that our consciousness can make concrete changes in the world. Ancient wisdom held this to be true, but it is new to modern science. Many controlled clinical trials of distant healing make it quite clear that our thoughts, intentions and prayers can help heal the world. We can do this at a distance, we can do this volitionally, we can do this through our intentions and good wishes, and so we're not as helpless as we might think. These studies show clearly that we can change the state of the physical world by our thoughts, to say nothing of our actions. This opens up a huge new horizon of personal empowerment.

The studies in distant intentionality and healing fall into two different categories. One group, like the Duke University study, examines the restoration of bodily health. The other group studies fertility. If I were designing an ability through which consciousness could interact with the world, I'd select these two categories. What is environmental action if not an effort to heal the earth and increase its fertility? Studies in distant healing examine precisely those factors: Helping restore health in human beings (and sometimes other species), and increasing fertility.

-§-

We're suffering culturally, nationally, from a horrible case of soul loss.

-§-

One particular fertility study is very simple, and profoundly positive. Performed by Columbia Medical School in New York City, the study focused on women suffering from infertility. The triple blind study was designed so that the doctors and the patients involved didn't even know a study was going on. The subjects of this study were visiting a fertility clinic in Seoul, South Korea. The patients were undergoing a technique called in vitro fertilization and embryo transfer, in an attempt to have a baby.

The doctors at Columbia initiated this study, and didn't inform the doctors and patients in Korea that the study was in progress. They recruited people in Canada, Australia and the United States to pray for a successful pregnancy in the women in the experimental group. The women in the control group were not assigned prayer. The results were startling. The women who received the prayers had twice the successful pregnancy rate as the women who were in the control group. There is less than one chance in a thousand this result could be explained by ascribing it to chance.

As one of the most elegant studies that has been done in this field, the Columbia fertility experiment is profoundly important. It ought to raise the eyebrows of anyone who is interested in fertility, not just in women, but in the earth itself. Bernard Grad, at McGill University in Canada, is a pioneer in nonhuman studies, which I consider to be of Nobel quality and significance. He points out similar remarkable increases in the germination rate of seeds, which is another form of fertility, and the growth rate of plants and seedlings. The nonhuman studies are immensely important because they bypass so many of the objections of critics in this field, such as the placebo response.

Beginning in the 1980s, researchers began to examine the correlations between religious and spiritual conduct, and how long people lived and how healthy they were. Currently we have upwards of 1,200 studies that explore the relationship between religious practices, and health and longevity. This is a huge database. The results are not trivial. These studies show a consistent pattern. Those people who follow some sort of religious path (it doesn't seem to matter which one they pick) live, on average, seven to thirteen years longer than those who do not. They have a lower incidence of virtually every disease, including the major killers of our day such as heart disease and cancer. One of the reasons that medical schools have begun to take notice is because of such data. It is becoming clear to most scholars and academics in medicine that we are no longer justified in not speaking about this effect of religious and spiritual practices on health. There are few things that doctors can recommend to patients that add seven to thirteen years to their life expectancy. This is a huge effect. To withhold this information and advice from patients is unethical and may constitute medical malpractice.

-§-

The studies show clearly that we can change the state of the physical world by our thoughts, to say nothing of our actions.

-§-

The reasons for this effect are several. Living within a rich social network—which most religious people do—promotes health. A positive health effect also comes with having a sense of meaning and purpose in life. Religious people may pay more attention to diet, and may avoid excessive smoking and drinking. When you put all these factors together, the incremental effects are significant. But where disagreement with the biomedical model opens up is when we begin assert that prayer works in and of itself.

When I began to investigate this area in the mid-1980s, I found a survey by Dr. David Benor, an American-trained psychiatrist working in England. At that time, there were 131 controlled trials of spiritual healing in a variety of species. Most of these were not studying human beings. Some were. The studies mainly looked at the ability of people—intentionally, empathically, compassionately and prayerfully—to influence biological systems. Some studied the growth rate of bacteria, the replication rate of test tube organisms, the spread of yeast on petri dishes, the germination rate of seeds, and the growth rates of seedlings.

Roughly two-thirds of the cases showed statistically significant correlations in the outcomes of the experiments. Now fast forward to the present. If we confine our interest to just human studies, we can find nine major randomized controlled clinical trials of distant healing or intercessory prayer. Statistics from five of these studies show profoundly significant results. You cannot explain this according to chance. Religious affiliation doesn't appear to matter.

As a doctor considering these questions, you ask yourself, "If the science is this compelling, am I ethically justified in withholding prayer from my patients?" I got to the point where I said, "No, I'm not." It changed my life as a doctor, and changed my patients' lives as well. I began going into my office earlier each morning. I devised my own prayer ritual; I prayed for the patients I was about to see on hospital rounds, and for all the patients who would come to my office later that day. I kept up that prayer ritual until I left my practice. Many physicians have told me that they have had similar life experiences as they engage this dramatic and exciting body of information.

I define prayer as, "Communication with the Absolute." I invite everyone to define what this communication might be, and what the Absolute may be within the context of their own wisdom tradition. My personal prayer is non-directed. It doesn't ask for specific goals. I think that the universe and this planet is smart enough to take care of itself without any instructions from me. So I simply pray, daily, "May the best thing happen to this world." Each person can pray in the way that feels most authentic and genuine for him or her. Religious historian Huston Smith writes about what he calls, "the tug from in front." I feel as though I'm being tugged by something out there, attracting me toward it. I've always felt that way. The importance of one's inner environment, a person's spiritual life, has always seemed self-evident to me. Even when I first entered medical school, it seemed to me to be the most important aspect of healing.

-§-

People who follow some sort of religious path live, on average, seven to thirteen years longer than those who do not.

-§-

The effectiveness of prayer and intention shown by these studies demonstrates to us that our society doesn't have to wait on intractable politicians and corporations to do something about the problems facing our world. We want to bring politicians and institutions along with us. But in the meantime we don't have to sit on our hands. We can put our own thoughts and will to work right now.

Yet I feel a sense of urgency about this transition. I do not believe that time is on our side. While we can rejoice that healing has become a legitimate source of study, we still need to be advancing as fast as we can. About a year before he died, I asked the late great physicist David Bohm if he thought we were going to survive without destroying the earth's environment. He pondered for a moment and said, "Yes, Larry, I think we will—barely."

I think we will squeak by. But we don't want to just barely make it. We need to do better than having to fall into the gutter before becoming motivated. Our society clearly has the understanding and the technologies to initiate a new Manhattan Project to rescue our environment. The technology to meet these tests is already available. I attend the Bioneers conference regularly, and I come away astonished at the solutions that are already in place. We need to incorporate them rapidly into our global culture. This is not complicated. For what we're spending annually in Iraq, we could underwrite these projects and have money left over. What is needed is will and vision. We need to find a source of vitality, and leadership to implement the obvious solutions.

Science can be a spiritual path. If used wisely, technology can be used for healing rather than destruction. Today, ninety of the 125 medical schools in the U.S. have courses devoted to exploring the links between spirituality and health. Ten years ago there were only three. This is a landmark development. It is an historic transition.

Medicine is on the threshold of a profound change. It is recognizing that emotions, feelings, and intentions are as much of the healing process as drugs and surgery. This realization is humanizing medicine, not just from a patient's point of view, but from the doctor's point of view. It is not fulfilling, as a doctor, to practice medicine as if people are just physical machines. The whole ambiance of the medical encounter is shifting. As I talk to young students now coming out of medical schools, they hold these values as self-evident. The medical profession has gone from rejecting prayer as "unscientific" to believing in it as received wisdom.

-§-

Our society clearly has the understanding and the technologies to initiate a new Manhattan Project to rescue our environment.

-§-

In 1998, the association of American Medical Colleges, to which all U.S. medical schools belong, drafted a resolution requiring all students be able to take a spiritual history from patients, and demonstrate an understanding that spirituality is important in the clinical encounter. In 1997, the Joint Commission on Accreditation of Health Care Institutions mandated that all their members—some 19,000 clinics and hospitals—have a mechanism in place to take a spiritual history from every patient who comes through the door. Most don't do this diligently yet, but this policy expresses an awareness that spirituality is important. While it may be a formality today, it the next twenty years it will become integral to the practice of medicine.

The most profound change in medicine in the future may have nothing to do with diseases getting better more quickly, or people living longer. They flow from the enormous spiritual implications of these studies, which clearly show that there's some quality or aspect of consciousness that operates beyond the body. This goes a long way toward validating the old idea of the soul. Some quality of who we are is infinite in space and time, and does not perish with the death of the body. This implication dwarfs whatever contribution these studies make toward healing. This is the greatest story of hope for human beings: the most essential part of who you are cannot die.

Today, the beginning assumption of medicine is tragedy—we all get sick, and eventually die, no matter what the doctor does. This is "time-based" medicine, and everyone's time runs out sooner or later. Tomorrow, the beginning assumption of medicine will be immortality—what I call "Eternity Medicine." The new medicine assumes that the most essential part of who we are is immortal. It doesn't have to be repaired or acquired. It's factory issue original equipment. You don't have to develop it or create it. It's the hard drive, and it can't crash. Realizing this deep in your heart is the essence of spiritual work. The antidote to soul loss, then, is the restoration of soul. In William Wordsworth's immortal words in his great poem, Tintern Abbey, he says:

-§-
Some quality of who we are is infinite in space and time, and does not perish with the death of the body.
-§-

And I have felt a presence that disturbs me with the joy of elevated thought

A sense sublime of something far more deeply interfused

whose dwelling is the light of the setting suns

And the round ocean of the living air,

And the blue sky

And in the mind of man

A motion and a spirit that impels all thinking things

all objects of all thought

and rolls through all things

This presence that so enraptured Wordsworth constantly rolls through the human heart. The medical profession is now looking inside the human heart, and this is leading to a great rethinking. Spirituality is returning to modern medicine. Health care professionals steeped in Eternity Medicine approach their patients knowing that their most essential self is immortal, eternal, infinite.

Spirituality, for me, is that sense of connectedness with an absolute and transcendent power beyond the individual self and ego. Whatever name you use for that presence and that power—God, the Great Spirit, Jehovah, the Goddess, Allah, the universe, overwhelming beauty and logic and order—that for you is spirituality. It is not the same as religion. Religion is simply ritualized spirituality. It has to do with those traditional behaviors such as attending worship services, reading sacred texts, and observing codes of conduct. Religion often includes a sense of the spiritual. Some people can be spiritual without being at all religious, and people can certainly be religious without having a shred of spirituality. People can be both or neither.

Whatever name we use for spirit, we are going to have to come up with a non-local picture of consciousness to accommodate the phenomena these studies point to. If you're going to think non-locally, here's what you've invented. You've come up with a picture of consciousness that has certain characteristics including being omnipresent, eternal and immortal. The most majestic contribution these studies make is to clearly show that there is some quality of consciousness that is unconfinable to specific points in space such as the brain, or specific points in time such as the present. There are certain operations of consciousness such as those we see in distant healing and prayer, to which the categories of space and time simply do not apply. The new physics teaches us that "non-local" is just a fancy word for "infinite." We have discovered a non-local or infinite quality of consciousness flowing from these studies. They reveal that there's some quality to who we are that's immortal. These studies are indirect evidence for the existence of the Soul, something that isn't born, doesn't die, and does not disappear with the death of the brain and body.

-§-
There are certain operations of consciousness such as those we see in distant healing and prayer, to which the categories of space and time simply do not apply.
-§-

This is not a new idea. Irwin Schrödinger, a great quantum physicist who was awarded the Nobel Prize for his Schrödinger wave equations, said, "Mind—by its very nature—is a singular entity. I should say the overall number of minds is just one." His reasoning went like this: If there is some factor of consciousness that is non-local or infinite, that means you can't put it into a box, and wall it off from all other minds. In some dimension, minds come together to form what he called the one mind; what our ancestors used to refer to as the universal mind. The poet William Butler Yeats said, "The borders of our minds are ever shifting, and many minds can flow into one another, and create or reveal a single mind, a single energy."

Barry Sears: Simple Solutions for Global Wellness

I believe that we may be witnessing the de-evolution of the human species. That's the bad news. The good news is that we can correct our course, in as little as thirty days, if we choose. How do I reach this startling conclusion? The evidence is clear as we look back through the development of human beings, what made us what we are, and the options that will shape our future. Diet has an enormous effect on behavior, and it can change our collective future worldwide.

There are some thirty million species on earth. What gave *Homo sapiens* the ability to become the dominant species? What made us so special? It certainly wasn't our physical skills.

If we go back 150,000 years, genetic modeling now allows us to trace every human being on the face of the earth today to a very small African tribe. This group probably numbered about 1,000 individuals, certainly no greater than 5,000. How did this one small tribe of Africans, and their descendants, come to dominate the world?

You have three options, and all of them are compatible with the genetic evidence saying that we all come from the same genetic stock. Option One: God put Adam and Eve in the East African Rift Valley. That theory is consistent with the genetic information.

Option Two: Aliens from outer space came and interbred with our pre-human ancestors. That too would be consistent with our genetic information.

Barry Sears, Ph.D. is a leading authority on the control of hormonal responses through food. A former research scientist at the Boston University School of Medicine and the Massachusetts Institute of Technology, he continues his research today through biotechnology company Sears Labs. Dr. Sears has been a frequent guest on many national programs such as *20/20, Today, Good Morning America, CBS Morning News, CNN,* and *MSNBC.* More than 4 million hardcover copies of books, including *The Zone* (HarperCollins, 1999), *The Anti-Aging Zone* (William Morrow, 1998), and *The Omega Rx Zone* (Avon, 2004) have been sold in the United States. *The Zone* has been translated into 22 languages.

The third option, and the most plausible, is that our ancestors in that small group of Africans blundered onto brain food by pure luck. This has nothing to do with Darwinian evolution based on natural selection. This is Lamarckian evolution, based on the luck of the draw.

The geology of the East African Rift Valley in ancient times created large lakes that provided an environment ideal for the growth of algae. The people living on the shores of those lakes didn't eat the algae directly. The algae were the main food for shellfish, and the human beings ate the shellfish that washed ashore. Their powers extended to cracking the shells in order to get to the meat inside. That meat contained large amounts of Omega-3 fatty acids. This food gave this one small group of Africans a significant advantage over all the other tribes and species.

-§-
When somebody has low blood sugar, what's the last thing on their minds? Politeness. That's what happens when you don't stabilize blood sugar to the brain.
-§-

Over the next 50,000 years their numbers built up. Then, about 100,000 years ago, groups of this larger population left Africa and meandered throughout the world. Through all their wanderings, they always stayed close to the seashore, with its supplies of shellfish.

The breakthrough in human dominance in evolution occurred about 40,000 years ago, when out of nowhere our species developed new tool-making abilities. Religion appeared. We developed art. Where did these major accomplishments come from?

That time frame corresponds almost exactly with the point when humankind learned to fish. This allowed us to obtain even higher levels of Omega-3 fatty acids than we'd previously absorbed from shellfish. There's a very strong argument for saying that these higher intakes gave us sufficient brain power to dominate the world.

If that's true, then the converse is also true. What if you take Omega-3 fatty acids out of the human diet? Will you see a significant drop in brain power?

The answer is that you do. But not for the first generation. There's still enough reserve capacity present to maintain the same level of brain function for a while. By the second and third generations, however, severe neurological deficits manifest themselves.

Brain power made humans dominant in the world. Brain power is highly dependent on our diet. There are two things we need in order for our brains to work at peak efficiency. One: A stable supply of blood glucose. That's the only fuel the brain can use. Two: An ongoing supply of these long-chain Omega-3 fatty acids. That's why your grandmother called fish oil "brain food."

If we want to maximize our human potential, we have to make our diet compatible with our genetic makeup. That genetic makeup is dependent upon stabilizing blood sugar for optimum brain function, which means stabilizing insulin, and finding adequate levels of long-chain Omega-3 fatty acids for optimal brain output.

If either of those begin to slip, the things that make us human begin to erode. For example, one of the things that we like to think of as a hallmark of being human is acting with civility. But when somebody has low blood sugar, what's the last thing on their minds? Politeness. That's what happens when you don't stabilize blood sugar to the brain. Yet you can rectify that blood sugar deficiency rapidly.

On the other hand, this very subtle and insidious decrease of the supply of Omega-3 fatty acids to the brain begins to short-circuit all the key factors that gave us our evolutionary advantage.

We have two major problems facing the world. One, we have too many people. We're competing for resources. Thomas Malthus was correct, but 200 years ahead of his time. We're outstripping the capacity of our food supply to provide us with nutrients that are in concordance with our genes. Our population is exceeding our production of the nutrients consistent with optimal hormonal function.

-§-
If we in America in fifteen or twenty years have not changed the way we eat, our country, as rich as it is, will be bankrupt.
-§-

There's no hard science to tell us precisely when this point might occur, but my sense is a time frame of ten to fifteen years. For example, if we in America in fifteen or twenty years have not changed the way we eat, our country, as rich as it is, will be bankrupt. The medical costs we incur will drive us under.

A more ominous aspect of our plight is that, if fish oil is the thing that makes us human, we're doing everything in our power to drive the agent, the ingredient, to extinction. There's enough fish oil right now for the next fifteen years. But from that time on, there'll be a bifurcation of society into two groups: Those who have adequate access to fish oil, and those who do not.

Can we use biotechnology to make fish oil? Possibly. We can make mutant algaes, but they're very expensive. And they're not very efficient at producing long-chain fatty acids.

Can we farm fish? It takes two pounds of natural fish to make one pound of farmed fish. And farmed fish are much worse for you than natural fish. All the contaminants we've thrown into the environment—things like mercury, dioxins, PCBs, and flame retardants—all wind up in the food chain, concentrated in fish oil. To grow farm-raised salmon, you have to feed them fish oil, otherwise they will not grow. When you feed them crude fish oil, you're feeding them high concentrations of these contaminants, which they further distill into even higher concentrations. Farm fish are much richer than wild fish in these contaminants, which are known carcinogens and neurotoxins. The government presents us with a Hobson's Choice. On the one hand, it says, "Eat fish, they're healthy." On the other hand it says, "Don't eat fish, they're contaminated." They're right on both counts.

Vegetarian fish like tilapia, which are being harvested increasingly as populations of carnivorous fish decrease, have less toxins. But they have low amounts of fat, and therefore low amounts of fatty acids. They're a good source of protein, but not a very good source of brain food. So supplements are the best source at this point.

Omega-3 fatty acids aren't just important to the brain. These nutrients are vitally important to the body's ability to control inflammation.

When you step back and view medicine as a whole, you see that much of its focus is on controlling inflammation. Every chronic disease we fear—heart disease, cancer, Alzheimer's—is an inflammatory disease. Even the aging process is inextricably tied to inflammation.

-§-
Things we want out of life—better health, better physical performance, better mental acuity, longevity, better emotional stability—are all controlled by our hormones.
-§-

Can we get away from this problem by taking anti-inflammatory drugs for the rest of our lives? Unfortunately not. When taken long term, anti-inflammatory drugs cause immune suppression, osteoporosis, and death. What's the alternative? What's out there in nature that has powerful anti-inflammatory properties without side effects? It again turns out to be fish oil.

Malthus was right, but wrong. He was right to ask the question, "Are we outstripping our capacity?" but he was wrong about the cause. Our problem is not a lack of calories, but a lack of the nutrients that control our hormonal responses. Things we want out of life—better health, better physical performance, better mental acuity, longevity, better emotional stability—are all controlled by our hormones. We control our bodies' production of those hormones by the food we eat. But the availability of the nutrients crucial to controlling those hormonal responses is growing scarcer by the moment. For many centuries, the basic human problem was staving off outright starvation. But today, for the first time in history, we have more overweight people on the face of the earth than malnourished people.

This has not been caused by any genetic change. What has changed in a major way is the methods we use for processing food. Today, the cheapest forms of calories are refined vegetable oils and refined sugars.

Twinkies are the cheapest source of calories. While we can feed our growing population, we can't feed them right.

These are now global dilemmas. They are far more frightening for the future of mankind than global warming, because the changes can take place very quickly, within one or two generations. Yet we have the technology and the power to reverse them if we choose to. The question is, do we have the political will?

Science allows us to discriminate between different possibilities. Science says, "Every human came from a small group of Africans." We have three possibilities that give rise to the same output: aliens, Adam and Eve, or brain food. The first two, we can't do anything to reverse. The third possibility gives us the option of reversing the process.

A recent study took kids who had Attention Deficit Disorder (ADD) and gave them fish oil instead of Ritalin "(EFA [Essential Fatty Acids] Supplementation in Children with Inattention, Hyperactivity and Other Disruptive Behaviors," *Lipids* magazine, September 2003). Their behavior normalized. It took about 30 days. I'm conducting a study at Harvard Medical School using higher doses of fish oil, because we've seen that within about six weeks, children don't just become better; they become superkids. Kids with ADD have learned a variety of tricks to try to help themselves cope with the world. Once you solve their basic problem, their need for these behaviors diminishes.

-§-
Today, for the first time in history, we have more overweight people on the face of the earth than malnourished people.
-§-

Hormones are the key to our future, and food is the key to our hormones. If we make the right choices of food, we can see significant changes in our society at every level within a matter of months. To make the world a better place, we need to feed the world right.

We have too many people on the face of the earth to supply them all with sufficient quantities of animal protein. We need renewable sources of protein, and the best renewable source turns out to be soybeans. One of my books, *The Soy Zone,* says, "Here's the answer. If we want to have six billion people on the face of the earth, we can do it if we make good use of renewable vegetarian sources of protein." But you need adequate amounts, like any drug. If you give a placebo dose of the drug, it doesn't work. If you administer adequate amounts, it works every time.

The other dilemma is that soy doesn't provide fish oil. We may have enough basic fish stocks at the moment, if we use them sustainably. But right now we're hunting fish to extinction.

The fish oil used in clinical studies comes from "trash" fish. These are species like sardines and anchovies, not the varieties you find on the menu in a five-star restaurant. These species are not under intense cultivation. But the time will soon come when supplies of even these abundant varieties start to decrease. When we deplete one fish stock, we start overfishing another. Our technology is so sophisticated that fish can run but they can't hide. The nutrients that made us human may well be disappearing from the face of the planet. When they're gone, they're gone. And when they're gone, we're not far behind. It won't happen in my lifetime, but it will probably happen in my children's lifetime. That doesn't mean the human race will disappear, but we'll evolve into a new form, similar to Jaba the Hutt, both in demeanor and physical appearance.

With sustainable sources of protein, and sustainable sources of fish oil, you can take the most impoverished people in the world, and, in just six months, dramatically change their future. I know it can be done. The question is, "Will it be done?" The kinds of studies I've been doing, and referencing in my books, point the way for governments and policy-makers.

-§-

We need renewable sources of protein, and the best renewable source turns out to be soybeans.

-§-

In Mexico, governments have embraced this technology much more than in the United States. Mexico has the benefit of not having lots of money to throw at the problem. Mexicans have to find ways of solving their health problems that are more innovative than buying yet more drugs.

A number of state governments in Mexico have endorsed the Zone diet and Zone supplements. They've witnessed significant improvements in health among people following this regimen. After seeing the data, two of the twenty-eight state governments in Mexico have endorsed the program for all their residents. Zone products are dispensed through physicians who have their own Zone Centers. They're making food the primary drug to improve the health of their people.

You have to set a hormonal baseline for your body. It's like building a house. You can either build it on a concrete foundation, or on sand. The one on concrete will have a longer life-span. The more you control the hormones in the body through the food you eat, the less drugs, if any, you need to maintain a state of wellness. This is my clarion call. Our society treats medicine as a discipline for treating disease. But the days of the magic pill are over. Penicillin was a magnificent exception: one bug, one pill, game over. But its success mislead us into taking the same approach for other diseases; what we now have instead is chronic, multi-factorial diseases. All that conventional medicine can do is treat the symptoms of these diseases.

The focus of our medical endeavors needs to shift, from treating the symptoms of chronic disease, to maintaining wellness as long as possible.

How do we define wellness? Medicine can provide standards for wellness; one very useful one is the degree of inflammation you have in your body, as measured by blood samples.

Inflammation as an indicator of wellness is a growing measure in the medical world, at least at the highest levels. Whatever technology controls inflammation will command the high ground of medicine in the twenty-first century. All the drug companies are looking for new, remarkable, powerful anti-inflammatory drugs. I believe we've already found them: one is fish oil, the other is the Zone diet.

How can the Zone diet be anti-inflammatory? Fish oils are anti-inflammatory by a direct interaction. There's a group of hormones called eicosanoids that control the inflammatory process. The more fish oil you consume, the less inflammation you have. If we ask questions like, "Who are the longest-lived people in the world today," or, "Who are the people with the longest health-span?" (health-span equals life-span minus years of disability), or "Who has the lowest rates of heart disease," or, "Who has the lowest rates of depression," or, "Which nation seems to have the most civil society," the answer in every case ought to be the Japanese.

-§-

With sustainable sources of protein, and sustainable sources of fish oil, you can take the most impoverished people in the world, and—in just six months—dramatically change their future.

-§-

By contrast, who are the most warlike people in the world today? Which nation is filled with factions that love to fight for the sake of fighting? This prize might go to the Afghanis. You don't see a whole lot of fish oil consumed in landlocked Afghanistan.

There are two fatty acids in the blood that server as markers of inflammation. One is called arachidonic acid. It's the building block of all the pro-inflammatory eicosanoids. The other fatty acid is called eicopentaenoic acid. It is the building block of all the anti-inflammatory eicosanoids. The ratio of these two fatty acids gives us an anti-inflammatory goal to aim for. You don't want this ratio too high, you don't want it too low. If you keep it within a certain range, you control inflammation. And if you control inflammation, you take a giant step toward improving world health and world civility. All of a sudden, much of the complexity of medicine can be reduced to the balance between these two fatty acids in the blood.

Americans are not only the fattest people on the face of the earth, they're probably the most inflamed. The average ratio of these two fatty acids in the Japanese population is about 1.5. In Americans, it's about 12. In kids with attention deficit disorder, it's between 40 and 50. For kids in the ghetto, the ratio is closer to 100. They don't have a chance.

Yet within thirty days we can change their prospects. It takes up to thirty days to build up sufficient levels of fatty acids in a depleted body. There are sixty trillion cells in your body. Each of them can make eicosanoids. It takes some time to build fatty acids in all of those sixty trillion cells.

Sugary snack foods also provide a drug solution to low blood sugar. From that standpoint, they are very effective drugs. If you have low blood sugar, you are self-medicating when you eat a sugary snack. You say, "I feel better." You're going to pay a price an hour and a half later, but it solves your problem right now. It's a lot cheaper to eat a Krispy Kreme than inject some glucose into the bloodstream.

How do we compete with Krispy Kremes? We have to provide attractive yet healthy alternatives to convenience foods. They have to look like junk food, they have to taste like junk food, but they have to be hormonally correct. They have to allow us to control our hormonal responses, and supply adequate levels of fish oil.

-§-

The more you control the hormones in the body through the food you eat, the less drugs, if any, you need to maintain a state of wellness.

-§-

Food technology is the modern battleground. It got us into this unhealthy mess. It can get us out. How can it solve the problem within thirty days? It can provide alternative products: ice cream, candy bars, milkshakes. Hormonally correct snack foods in these packages can be a training wheel. After eating them, consumers say, "I feel better." Once we've set up that stable hormonal baseline, we educate and train them into achieving the same feel-good results by adjusting the composition of their daily meals.

Our studies of kids with ADD have shown that they need very large amounts of fish oil to bring their blood ratios down to the single digits. How do we deliver large amounts of fish oil? We put it into milkshakes. My background is in drug delivery. Drug delivery works best when you make it easy for the patient to comply. You have to get their hormones stabilized first. If those hormones are unstabilized, all the admonitions, all the education, all the evidence, will go in one ear and out the other. It's a self-reinforcing problem.

Fish oil also raises levels of serotonin. Serotonin can be thought of as a morality hormone. The line between savage and compassionate behavior is a thin one. The less serotonin in the body, the thinner the line. Fish oil is one of the few drugs that can raise both serotonin and dopamine, the hormone in the brain that produces a sense of well-being, and of focus. Fish oil is so effective in these clinical studies because it treats not only ADD—lack of focus; it simultaneously treats depression with serotonin.

In *Zone Perfect Meals in Minutes,* I demonstrate that it's fast and easy to make Zone meals. Once people try it, they discover they like it. If you can keep your hormones in balance, life will be very good. Let them fall out of the Zone, and it becomes much tougher than it needs to be.

Once you try this method for as little as seven days, it becomes so self-evidently gratifying that no further argument is required. Human nature says, "Keep doing whatever feels good." That's why if you get a person into that Zone for a little while, they not only say, "I feel good," but they also say, "I feel so much worse when I'm out of the Zone." Human nature becomes your greatest ally, because we want to feel good all of the time.

-§-

The focus of our medical endeavors needs to shift, from treating the symptoms of chronic disease, to maintaining wellness as long as possible.

-§-

The scientific data supporting this approach is clear. It's now a matter of marketing. It's like a political campaign; we're competing for the hearts and minds of human beings, saying, "Here's the way to a better life."

Philosophy and religion give you rules for living a civil life. When you stabilize your hormones, all those injunctions about doing good make sense. People who've learned to keep inflammation under control can live the longest, healthiest and most moral lives. They can lead civil lives, lives that make the world around them a better place.

Bruce Lipton:

The Ching and I: Bio-Political Musings of a Transformed Scientist

17

The global crisis precipitated by the events of September 11, 2001 was a turning point for Western civilization. The tragedy served as a wake-up call, alerting us to the fact that our way of life is wreaking havoc in the global community and our survival is now in question. Another much-less heard, but no less important wake-up call about our survival was sounded at the same time by a community of concerned biologists. The scientists warned that the rapid disappearance of a wide variety of species has catapulted us deep into the sixth mass extinction to hit the planet since the origin of life. Unlike the first five such massive die-offs, attributed to extraterrestrial sources such as comets, the current wave of extinctions is due to a source much closer to home: humans. The September 11 tragedy and the disturbing rate at which species are disappearing on this planet are crises that should force us to pause and reconsider the path upon which our culture has embarked.

By their very nature, crises are harbingers of change, so when I started pondering these wake-up calls, I turned to the *I Ching,* the "Book of Changes." This ancient Chinese divination manual offers insight into the fundamental questions that have perplexed human beings since their arrival on this planet. I was particularly drawn to the I Ching hexagram for "the Returning" (#24), first introduced to me by Fritjof Capra in his influential book, *The Turning Point.* The Returning symbol offers three pronouncements: 1. After a time of decay comes the turning point. 2. The powerful light that has been banished returns. 3. There is movement, but it is not brought about by force.

Bruce Lipton, Ph.D. is an internationally recognized authority in bridging science and spirit. A cell biologist by training, he taught Anatomy at the University of Virginia, and later performed pioneering studies at Stanford University's School of Medicine. He has been a guest speaker on dozens of TV and radio shows, as well as keynote presenter for national conferences. His breakthrough studies on the cell membrane presaged the new science of Epigenetics, and made him a leading voice of the new biology. He is the author of the best-selling books *The Biology of Belief* and *Spontaneous Evolution;* see www.brucelipton.com.

These three ancient pronouncements offer valuable insights into our current social and political crises. But before we launch into that discussion, I'd like to tell you how my life as a "transformed" scientist began in order to set a context for why I turned to an "unscientific" oracle like the *I Ching* for understanding and direction about the fix we find ourselves in today.

As a cellular biologist, my work has always been driven by the desire to understand the nature of life. I will never forget the first time I used an electron microscope in graduate school. The large control console of the microscope resembled the instrument panels of a Boeing 747. It was filled with switches, illuminated gauges and multicolored indicator lamps. Large tentacle-like arrays of thick power cords, water hoses and vacuum lines radiated from the base of the microscope like tap roots at the trunk of a tree. The sound of clanking vacuum pumps and the whir of refrigerated water recirculators filled the air. For all I knew, I had just walked on to the command deck of the U.S.S. Enterprise. Apparently, it was Captain Kirk's day off, for sitting at the console was my cell biology professor. I watched attentively as my mentor began the elaborate procedure of introducing a tissue specimen into the high-vacuum chamber of the electron microscope. Finally, he began increasing the magnification of the tissue specimen, one step at a time: first 100X, then 1,000X, then 10,000X. When we hit warp drive, the cells were magnified to over 100,000 times their original size.

-§-

The door opened for me to become as comfortable consulting the *I Ching* as I am consulting the latest issue of *The Journal of Cell Biology!*

-§-

It was indeed Star Trek, but rather than entering outer space we were going into deep inner space where "no man has gone before." One moment I was observing a miniature cell and seconds later I was flying deep into its molecular architecture. I knew that buried within the *cytoarchitecture* of the cell were clues that would provide insight into the mysteries of life. Throughout graduate school, postdoctoral research and into my career as a medical school professor, my waking hours were consumed by explorations into the molecular anatomy of the cell.

Though my exploration of the "secrets of life" led to a successful research career studying cloned stem cells grown in tissue culture, I eventually ran afoul of the scientific establishment because the results of my research forced me to question the dogmas on which cell biologists and other life scientists base their work. I refer to these dogmas as the "Three Assumptions of the Apocalypse" because I do not believe human civilization will survive unless we turn away from these false beliefs. Specifically, I rejected these three assumptions: 1) genes control biology; 2) evolution is a random process driven by a struggle for the survival of the fittest; and, 3) life can be understood by only studying the physical parts of the body.

My feeling that these three assumptions were wrong was so strong that I left university life to study independently. Five years after leaving academia I experienced a moment of profound insight while pondering the lessons acquired in my own research and in astonishing new insights of leading edge cell science. With a start, I realized that the control mechanism for each individual cell—and by extension our bodies, which are made up of trillions of cells—is the cell's membrane: the boundary between the cell's body and the environment. While the membrane is the "mechanism," the environment *controls* its activities. Signals, i.e., information from the environment, engage membrane "switches" that activate the very movements that characterize life. The individuality of each human is distinguishable by a unique set of membrane "antennas," or self-receptors, displayed on their cells' membranes. By their nature, membrane receptors resonate with and "download" complementary environmental signals.

Then it struck me: my physical "self" is resonating with an environmental "self." The environmental "self" (i.e., information) is separate from and outlasts our mortal "self." In other words, we are immortal, just as spiritual sages have told us for thousands of years. In that instant, I was "transformed" from an agnostic scientist mired in the physical world into a spiritual scientist who considers the nonvisible, spiritual side of life with as much passion as I consider the physical, visible world. In that same instant, the door opened for me to become as comfortable consulting the *I Ching* as I am consulting the latest issue of *The Journal of Cell Biology!*

Indeed, the three pronouncements of the Returning hexagram offer us profound and valuable insight for these troubled times.

1. After a time of decay comes the turning point.

Among all of the world's cultures, there is a "history," or—to be more accurate—a mythology, about the existence of a former utopian era, similar to the Garden of Eden described in Judeo-Christian scriptures. Each culture describes a "decay," a falling-out with Nature, wherein mankind is essentially banished from that perfect world.

In the West, our falling out with Nature occurred when people began to perceive themselves as separate from the world in which they lived. In the earliest stages after the "fall," people held that their fates were in the hands of immaterial spirits, forces that they tried to appease in order to secure a good life. The ancient Greek, Roman and Egyptian polytheists believed in a panoply of gods who "controlled" their universe. By honoring and following the wishes of these gods, citizens could expect to have rewards in life. Those who shunned the ways of the deities were destined to pay for their transgressions through lives punctuated with personal tragedies.

The more recent evolution of Judeo-Christianity simplified the worship process by coalescing all of the gods into one almighty God and codifying His "laws" into scripture, so that all could understand what is required to receive the reward of a good life. In the new religion, spirituality was no longer associated with the planet, for God and His servants reigned over Earth from a distant, celestial throne. The Church of Rome claimed to be the chosen intercessor between God and humankind—its "truths" *infallible* because they were directly acquired from and mandated by God. The Church stressed Genesis's version of a "six day" course of evolution in which Adam and Eve were created separately from the rest of Nature. Human beings came to believe that our "special" moment of creation allows us to exploit our environment in any way we deem serves us.

Not only did religious philosophy disconnect us from Nature, that same philosophy also destroyed any notion that Nature is an ally of humanity. The Church emphasized a mistrust and fear of Nature, warning its followers that the material world is fraught with danger and is an impediment to spiritual fulfillment. The Church did, however, honor the Earth's majestic beauty as the grand design of God. In fact, the spiritually-based science of that time, Natural Theology, was premised on the principle that "the living word of God was to be found in Nature." Cleric-scientists studied the relationships among the elements that comprised His garden so that we would be better able to live in harmony with God.

However, the Church didn't want these cleric-scientists to dig too deep into the mysteries of Nature. Puzzling phenomena were not studied. Instead, they were dismissed as "mysteries of faith." God, and *only* God could understand the great mysteries. In fact, these mysteries were so out of bounds for human consideration, that the Church made it a sin to study them. For example, the Church declared the internal workings of the human body off-limits—banning Christians from even looking inside a body. Consequently, only Muslims and Jews were physicians, because their religious philosophies did not conflict with studying human anatomy and physiology.

The Church suppressed the advancement of scientific research for a very specific, self-serving motive. The Church ruled on the basis of the power afforded by "infallible" knowledge. If science ventured into the "unknown" and came back with answers that the Church did not possess, it would obviously compromise their claim of power. To avoid that pesky problem, people who offered truths other than those endorsed by the Church were declared heretics and subsequently punished according to the decrees of the Inquisition.

But over time, the Scientific Revolution toppled the Church's claim to infallibility. That revolution was launched in 1543 when Nicolas Copernicus published his discovery that the Earth was not the center of the Universe as was thought by the scientist-theologians of the day. The fact that the Earth actually revolved around the sun, and that the sun itself was not the center of the universe, undermined the teachings of the "infallible" Church. The "infallible" Church was revealed to be fallible indeed.

As modern science evolved, it offered a radically new philosophy about the nature of life and our relationship to the universe. The new philosophy was built on scientific truths that were verified through accurate observation and measurements of physical world phenomena. Science officially ignored the putative influences of a spiritual realm, because they were not amenable to scientific analysis. Consequently, civilization's search for Great Truths resulted in an adversarial relationship between science, which preoccupied itself with the physical realm, and religion, which focused on the spiritual plane.

While man's relationship with the earth and the environment did not prosper under the leadership of the Church, it has degenerated still further under the leadership of modern science to such an extreme point that we now find ourselves in a life-threatening global crisis. Modern science did not deny the existence of a God. It simply believed that God created the physical universe, and once that was done, He stepped back and let the mechanism run its own course. With the Hand of God out of the way, mankind's domination and control over Nature became a central theme of the seventeenth-century worldview.

The influential Sir Francis Bacon, a renowned scientist, philosopher and barrister, defined a reality wherein "nature takes orders from man and works under his authority." *She* (Nature) was to be "put in constraints"; the aim of science was to "torture nature's secrets from her" so she can be "forced out of her natural state and squeezed and molded." It is not coincidence that in a patriarchal culture nature is a "female" to be controlled and even tortured by a "masculine" science. The metaphors employed by Bacon in his scientific writings are directly linked to his position as attorney general for King James I. In that capacity, Bacon employed the same terminology in his prosecution of witches that resulted in the torture and murder of millions of women.

Bacon's philosophy devalued Nature by considering her an unruly handmaiden of *man*kind who needed taming. But how would she be "controlled?" Historically, humans tried to intervene and shape Nature through dreams and prayer, practices that implied the human mind could influence the behavior of Nature. However, the power of mind and consciousness was completely discounted by Renee Descartes' claim that the mind and body were separate entities. According to the beliefs of that time, an immaterial essence, such as the mind, could not interact with, nor move, matter.

With God and the mind eliminated as potential sources that control life, Descartes resolved the question of control by suggesting the Universe was one giant machine. The planet, including its living organisms, represented mechanical automata: robots. Through the process of reductionism, i.e. taking the Universe apart and studying it piece by piece, it was assumed that modern science would acquire knowledge that would allow us to not only understand the "machine," but also to *control* and *clone* it.

In the competition between the Church and science for control of western civilization, Charles Darwin delivered the decisive blow in 1859 when he published the *Origin of Species.* Darwin's theory of evolution suggested that the traits that characterize an individual were passed from the parents to the offspring. Life then was controlled by material hereditary factors, which a child acquires via the chemistry of the egg and sperm, not from God. Darwin extended his ideas to further suggest that random variations of these hereditary factors created the diversity of Nature's species. The idea that humans came into existence through the happenstance of genetic variations removed the last link between God and the human experience. Human beings evolved by pure "chance," which by extension means: *without an underlying purpose for our existence.* The rules of the Church about how to comport one's life became superfluous in a world devoid of God's influence.

But Darwinism and neo-Darwinism, a refinement of his theory embraced by modern evolutionists, left humans without a moral compass. Evolutionary success is based on "the survival of the fittest in the struggle for existence." It's a dog-eat-dog world out there, and as long as you are the top dog, you need not be concerned about the others. The *end* of the struggle is survival. As for the means to that end, apparently anything goes. The goal is survival by *any means.* Rather than framing the character of our lives by the laws of morality, science suggests that we live our lives by the laws of the jungle!

These laws of the jungle have led the modern world to shift from spiritual aspirations to a war for material accumulation. The one with the most toys wins. Evolution theory essentially concludes that those who have more…deserve it. In the West, we have become inured to the fact that our cultural imperative, by its definition, creates a civilization that is distinguished by those "who have" and those "who have not." Everything in this world has a price; unfortunately, this includes people as well. The homeless, who represent losers of this Darwinian struggle, are an accepted and apparently not-too-disturbing consequence of our adherence to this way of thinking.

Darwinian philosophy assures us that in our struggle for life we are not responsible to anyone or anything, other than ourselves and our genes. We become miffed when the price of bananas goes up five cents, but ignore the fact that in some other country, the laborer who picked those bananas toiled in the field for ten hours only to earn a dollar or two. Though we may balk at the price of designer jeans, we will readily spend seventy dollars on a pair and not think twice about the child labor that was literally enslaved to manufacture them.

While we want to believe that we are good people and we desire to help the less fortunate, *we have not even owned the reality that our preoccupation with material success is the primary factor in creating those less fortunate we are trying to help.* The truth is, we are so concerned about what we want that we never enquire as to how we got it. Our greed is so sanitized and our image so polished, that we are totally unaware of the people we hurt and the earth that we destroy in securing the life we have been programmed to seek. Being disconnected from the world community and having had our heads in the sand for so long, we are actually surprised when we hear that enraged citizens in other countries are demonstrating against our global policies.

-§-
Our greed is so sanitized and our image so polished, that we are totally unaware of the people we hurt and the earth that we destroy in securing the life we have been programmed to seek.
-§-

The chasm between the haves and the have-nots in our world has created a disastrous biological situation. The imminent danger relates to an interesting characteristic built into all of Nature's living creatures: the *will to survive.* By some unknown mechanism, all organisms, from bacteria to humans, are "programmed" to make every effort to survive when they perceive their life is being challenged. If you chase a rat, it will do its best to survive by simply escaping your grasp. However, if you corner that rat and it has no way out, in spite of the odds against success, that rat will lunge in your face with every intention of taking you down. The "haves" have built fortresses to protect themselves from the ever-expanding population of "have-nots." Soon, the "fittest" will be surrounded by a sea of the downtrodden and their protective refuges will, in the end, become their prisons.

In addition to terrorizing the world's human population, our scientific "progress" has been terrorizing Mother Nature herself. Our motto "Better Living Through Chemistry" has led to our attempt to control Nature with innumerable drugs, fertilizers and pesticides. We have now come to realize that our indiscriminate use of "magic bullets" has polluted the environment and altered the balance of Nature.

Similarly, genetic engineering, which offered promises of redder tomatoes, clones of your favorite pet or child and the opportunity for perfect health, has fallen far short of its goals. Genetic engineers, though familiar with the molecular mechanics of the cell, have no familiarity with the fact that each organism is a unit of life delicately balanced in a dynamic network. Science has already established that designer genes in GMOs escape and readily transfer their engineered genes to native organisms, changing the face of the environment. Without a full awareness of the *communal complexity* of species interactions, the creation and introduction of genetically modified organisms into the environment becomes a threat to the vitality of the biosphere and by consequence, to human survival.

Humankind's efforts to control and dominate Nature with technology have consistently disrupted the complex web of Nature that fostered our evolution as a species. Western philosophy and technology have now brought human civilization to the brink of spontaneous combustion. As you sit on your porch and watch the sunset, note its spectacular color. The beauty in the sky reflects the pollution in the air. Yet spontaneous combustion is not inevitable. Instead, we are at the *turning point* that comes after the decay. We can—says the *I Ching*—find our way back to the Garden.

2. The powerful light that has been banished returns.

How do we turn away from the decay? This second pronouncement tells us that we must embrace the light, which I believe is the new scientific knowledge that unites the "truths" underlying all religions and opens the door to global peace. Over the last twenty years, this extraordinary new research has revealed that sacred dogmas embraced by biologists and other life scientists are false. When we topple these three "Assumptions of the Apocalypse," i.e., the notion that genes control biology, that evolution is a random, dog-eat-dog process, and that we can understand our bodies and our world by studying only physical phenomena, we can embrace the powerful light that will guide our way back to the Garden.

-§-

Far from solving the mysteries of life and disease, the Human Genome Project only deepened them.

-§-

Though the unraveling of the structure of genes by James Watson and Francis Crick in 1953 was a stunning intellectual achievement, it ironically helped set humanity on a path *away* from the knowledge that can set us free. Specifically, discovery of the double helix turned scientific attention inward, to the nucleus of the cell, rather than outward to the environment where I believe the movements that characterize life begin. Because scientists thought that Watson and Crick had unraveled the "secret of life," genes were elevated to the lofty position of controlling life, control that I believe lies outside the cell. That left us hapless human beings as victims, with no responsibility for the unfolding of our lives because we cannot select or exchange our genes.

In our refreshed role as victims, we then looked to science to deliver us from our shortcomings. The pharmaceutical industry motivated the public to invest in the Human Genome Project, an effort to catalogue each of the genes present in a human body. Armed with that information, drug companies would be able to use genetic engineering to heal our ills and enhance our favorite attributes, or so it was supposed. But when the results of the Human Genome Project were revealed in 2001, researchers were shocked by the fact that human beings only have 25,500 genes, not enough to explain why we are the complex creatures we pride ourselves on being. The primitive *Caenorhabditis* worm has a precisely patterned body comprised of exactly 969 cells and a simple brain of about 302 cells. However, it boasts 24,000 genes, only 1,500 fewer genes than the infinitely complex human body. Far from solving the mysteries of life and disease, the Human Genome Project only deepened them.

-§-
In dynamically changing environments, genes are switched on and off to enable organisms to continuously adapt and survive in their new surroundings.
-§-

Meanwhile, my desire to understand the control mechanisms of the cell led me away from the genes-containing nucleus to the cell membrane. Once thought to be a simple, extremely thin, jell-like barrier, powerful electron microscopes are revealing that the membrane is an impressive mediator between the *environment* and the cell. It is signals in the environment processed by the membrane, not genes, which launch the cellular activity that defines life.

Other leading-edge scientists have also uncovered cellular mechanisms that reveal that every living organism is engaged with the *environment* in a delicate "pas de deux," a French phrase meaning "an intricate relationship or activity involving two parties." It is only via this interaction that genes are turned on and off, making the notion that genes control biology not just outmoded, but clearly false. In dynamically changing environments, genes are switched on and off to enable organisms to continuously adapt and survive in their new surroundings. It is a biochemical fact that genes do not control their own activity nor the activity of any other system in the body.

New research is also toppling the notion that evolution is driven by a random, survival-of-the-fittest mechanism independent of the environment. Researchers have discovered that organisms as primitive as bacteria are capable of creating beneficial mutations so that they can better survive in their environments. Through a mechanism described as directed or adaptive mutations, organisms can *select* which genes they need to mutate. Actually, two kinds of genetic mutations exist: random and directed. Random mutations almost invariably lead to dysfunction, while "directed" mutations lead to adaptation and enhanced survival.

This is a far cry from Darwin's notion that evolution is propelled by random natural selection. So far, that when British geneticist John Cairns first introduced proof for adaptive mutations in 1988, his research—published in the prestigious journal *Nature*—provoked the wrath of the scientific establishment. An editorial in *Science* on Cairns' work was called "A Heresy In Evolutionary Biology." (Heresies? Dogmas? Yes, science has become the new religion!)

The new science reveals that organisms shape their genomes, and species evolve, as a direct consequence of their interactions with their environment. Recognizing the importance of the environment in evolution and in genetics leads us to a completely different understanding of the origins and purpose of life. Our existence is not a random accident, but a carefully choreographed event that takes into account the balance of the biosphere. We are ignoring our in-built stewardship of that biosphere by "going it alone," recklessly and radically changing our environment. Our hubris threatens our survival as surely as the heroes in Greek tragedies were undone by their arrogance. We were designed to complement our environment, not to lord over it. By radically changing our environment we risk a future where we will no longer fit. Instead of complementing our environment, we may completely undo its complex balance, causing it to collapse.

-§-
Leading-edge scientific research returns us to our aboriginal roots, which stressed the belief that humans are one with Nature.
-§-

Finally, quantum physics provides compelling evidence that our environment is made up both of forces that cannot be seen, as well as those that can be seen. Quantum physics shows us that the universe and all of its matter are actually made out of energy. Every physical object manifests its own unique, invisible force. While an atom appears as a physical particle, we now know that it is comprised of evanescent units of energy called quarks, which are themselves made up of smaller quanta of energy. Rocks, air, water and humans are all fields of energy that wear the cloak of matter, which makes the old, Descartian notion that the mind (energy) and body (matter) are separate an antiquated anachronism.

Taken together, leading-edge scientific research returns us to our aboriginal roots, which stressed the belief that humans are one with Nature. Aboriginal people recognize and honor the "spirits" of the air, the water, the rocks, the plants and animals, and most importantly, the spiritual nature of themselves. Fortunately, many of the lost traditions of our forefathers are still available in the few remaining aboriginals that inhabit our planet. Native Americans, African tribes, South American Indians and Australian Aborigines still hold the secrets of how to live in harmony with the planet. We should create an international project to honor these people and we should sit at their feet to learn their life-sustaining insights about the secrets of Nature. When we return to our aboriginal roots, "The powerful light that has been banished will return." I am not suggesting that we shed our technology, don loincloths and camp in the woods. I am instead suggesting that we *and* our technology must learn to live in harmony with our mother, our dear Earth.

3. There is movement, but it is not brought about by force.

The revolution in which the powerful light will return, the revolution that will bring this planet back from the brink of extinction, requires no violence. I know that you and I have been programmed to think that revolutions occur only with force, be it the guns at Lexington and Concord or the sharp blade of the French guillotine. But this revolution back to our aboriginal roots requires a change in beliefs, not soldiers armed with guns, and jets armed with smart bombs. Just as the *I Ching* says, there is movement, but it is not brought about by force.

-§-
The lessons of the new science, which I call the new Biology of Belief, teach us that we have the power to change ourselves, and our planet, using the power of our minds.
-§-

The lessons of the new science, which I call the new Biology of Belief, teach us that we have the power to change ourselves, and our planet, using the power of our minds. Quantum physics and the well-documented placebo effect, in which people who *believe* (falsely) that they are getting medicine heal their physical bodies, tell us that the mind (energy) can be *more* powerful than the body's chemical reactions. The new science revives the message of Christ, who told us that we could perform all the miracles He did if we believed: "Be ye transformed by the renewing of your mind."

Of course, you can't just snap your fingers or read a book to effect change. You have to undo the self-defeating and planet-defeating programming your parents (and their parents before them) inculcated into your subconscious mind. Once we learn to reprogram our powerful subconscious minds using the insights of energy-based mind-body techniques, the possibilities for change are limitless. Just because you grew up believing that revolutions have to be bloody, or that you are stuck with your genes, or that there is no need to worry about the poor and the homeless does not mean that any of it is true.

In fact the latest science tells us that all of those "truths" are false. Scientists now realize not only that innumerable species are disappearing at an alarming rate, but also that we share genes with those disappearing species. Given this sharing of genes, organisms can no longer be seen as disconnected entities—the wall between species has fallen just as surely as the Berlin Wall.

Throughout our history, religion and science have built a wall between humans and Nature, one false brick of belief at a time. Let us take down this false wall that we have been programmed to build. Let us realize that our fates are inextricably tied up with the fate of our global neighbors and all the species in this world. Let us change our beliefs and join with other like-minded revolutionaries to save our world from destruction. I know from the many people I meet in my travels that such change has already begun. We are already moving back to the Garden. We are, in the words of the *I Ching,* experiencing the Returning.

Henry Han: The Gray Zone

Don is a forty-five-year-old computer software engineer. He is 5′ 11″ and weighs 260 lbs., with a family history of heart disease and hypertension. His health has been on a downhill course for many years, and he is not sure how it all started. The last time he exercised was about three years ago and he lost control of his diet long before that. He has been smoking for thirty years. Over the years, he has mounted numerous attempts to reclaim his health, but for one reason or another, he always fails. Lately he has been feeling more sluggish both physically and mentally. He is compelled to eat bad foods to support his energy, yet feels worse after he does. He is frequently sleepy after meals. He depends on coffee to stay alert at work. Don has been overworked and quite stressed for the past three years. About two years ago, he started to feel pain in his chest, and sometimes his left arm aches. He went to his doctor and had a complete physical, which included blood work, an EKG, and a cardiac stress test. The doctor found nothing other than slightly elevated blood pressure and cholesterol levels for which he prescribed blood pressure and anti-cholesterol medication. The doctor said the chest pain was "just muscular, nothing to worry about." However, the chest pain and left arm discomfort have persisted. Don is not sure what to do at this point and feels completely helpless.

Kelly is a twenty-two-year-old assistant office manager. Her health problems began in her early teens. Her period has been very painful and irregular from the beginning, and she has severe acne. Increasingly prone to the common cold and flu, she is always slow to recover. Her "hay

Henry Han, O.M.D., is the co-author of *Ancient Herbs, Modern Medicine* (Bantam, 2003). He was born to a family of doctors in China in 1958, and received his formal medical training both in traditional Chinese medicine and western medicine from Beijing University of Chinese Medicine. He moved to the United States in 1985 and studied psychology and cognitive science. He has been in private medical practice since 1989 in Santa Barbara, California. He is currently writing the book: *The Gray Zone*, the first part of which is outlined in this chapter. Photo by David Muskraft.

fever," goes back as early as she can remember, and has become more severe over time. Kelly got married at age nineteen. Two years later, a painful divorce left her the sole parent of her one-year-old son. Her health deteriorated rapidly. Her periods stopped. She has frequent headaches, is full of anxiety, often cannot sleep, and goes in and out of depression. Frequent colds and flu require her to take multiple antibiotics. Her acne has gotten so bad that she won't look at herself in the mirror. Kelly has seen quite a number of doctors and specialists who have conducted extensive tests. The only thing that came up positive was a mild elevation of Candida in her system, for which Diflucan, a systemic oral anti-fungal medication, was prescribed. She has also been prescribed antidepressants, tranquilizers, sleeping pills and painkillers. Nothing seems to help. She calls in sick nearly as often as she shows up for work. Her supervisor has warned her that if she does not go on disability leave, she will be fired. But her doctors will not file disability forms because there are no "objective findings" to justify doing so.

-§-
The superior doctor treats people who are not diseased.[1]
—Yellow Emperor
-§-

Thomas is a fifty-nine-year-old associate director of a personnel department at a large public university. He tries to take good care of himself and is fairly fit, but for many years he has had fluctuating, nagging symptoms of bloating, a feeling of heaviness, loss of appetite at times, and irregular bowel movements, along with fatigue, hypersensitive skin, headaches, irritability and poor sleep. Lifestyle changes, such as a healthier diet and exercise, give him marginal relief but do not break the cycle. Overall, the symptoms seem to become worse with each passing year. This "condition" has cast a shadow over Thomas's life. While he is not debilitated, the symptoms make life a daily grind. Unable to find anything wrong, his doctors have given him "a clean bill of health."

What Is the Gray Zone?

What we are looking at in the stories of Don, Kelly and Thomas is "the Gray Zone": a ubiquitous yet generally overlooked area of compromised health. Even though Dan, Kelly and Thomas have not been diagnosed with a definite disease, clearly they are not healthy either. Very few people will disagree that health is not merely the absence of the disease. The gray zone therefore can be defined as *the area between the state of health and the state of disease.* In essence, the gray zone can be considered a state of imbalance.

The state of health, the gray zone, and the state of disease represent different spectrums or sections of a continuum. A disease is, for the most part, the accumulation and culmination of imbalances leading up to a crisis of health, even though the transition is rarely a linear process. One cannot "jump" from the state of health to the state of disease without first going through the transitional area of the gray zone. This is especially true with the vast majority of chronic and noncommunicable diseases. The only two notable exceptions are sudden injury, and acute infection.

Being in a state of disease does not preclude the coexistence of a gray zone. Don might be diagnosed with hypertension, hypercholesterolemia, and GERD (gastro-esophageal reflux disorder); Kelly might be diagnosed with amenorrhea, systemic candidiasis, recurrent sinus and upper respiratory infections. Yet these diagnoses do not cover all the phenomena or symptoms in either case. In other words, the gray zone exists independently of disease much more frequently than the other way around. The gray zone is the shadow of disease: wherever there is disease, a gray zone is attached to it.

The stories of Don, Kelly and Thomas demonstrate several different scenarios in the gray zone. The common denominator is that they all need help. Lifestyle adjustments or other self-healing methods may no longer be enough to reinstate their health.

Don's case has all the classic ingredients of a pending disaster: he is heading for a heart attack. What he needs to do in order to avert the outcome is generally known.

Kelly's case, on the other hand, is more complicated. There is no clear "road map" to help a physician navigate her treatment. Considerable problem-solving skills, creativity and determination are required on both the doctor's and the patient's part. Healing at multiple levels—physical, emotional and spiritual—must occur to restore her health. The severity of Kelly's condition justifies calling her "diseased" yet the specific disease is unknown.

Thomas's case is what many call "a weird condition" because of a high degree of uniqueness. This type of broad, idiosyncratic condition is by no means uncommon. Treating Thomas means, at least to some degree, entering uncharted territory. The solution will likely be found outside conventional modes of treatment.

-§-

The gray zone can be defined as *the area between the state of health and the state of disease.*

-§-

The gray zone is nothing new. At least as old as disease itself, it has been given various names in modern times: pre-disease, sub-clinical condition, the Third State, sub-optimal health, Chronic Fatigue, adrenal burnout, and Syndrome X. As a whole, however, the gray zone has been largely overlooked and in many cases ignored by our disease-focused and crisis-oriented health care system. People with gray zone conditions are frequently made to feel embarrassed, inadequate, or crazy. They may be labeled hypochondriacs. Indeed, one of the most striking phenomena of modern health care is that when a disease cannot be identified, the problem is dismissed, in spite of the fact that a real person is clearly suffering and in need of help.

Don, Kelly and Thomas are not isolated cases. According to the estimate by the World Health Organization (WHO), "Sub-optimal health" affects more than two-thirds of the world population. That's about three times the number of people diagnosed with diseases.[2] A Chinese study found over 48% people in the "pre-disease state" in the major Chinese metropolitan areas.[3] The Third National Health and Nutritional Examination Survey conducted between 1988-1994 for the U.S. population finds that 58% of U.S. adults can be labeled as diseased, based on just four criteria: elevated blood pressure, elevated blood cholesterol level, elevated fasting blood sugar level, and elevated weight.

-§-
One of the most striking phenomena of modern health care is that when a disease cannot be identified, the problem is dismissed, in spite of the fact that a real person is clearly suffering and in need of help.
-§-

The gray zone has fueled and given rise to a vast and booming supplements and nutriceuticals industry, especially in the Western world. Americans spent an estimated $16 billion in 2000 on dietary supplements—almost double the amount in 1994. A nationwide survey conducted by the American Dietetic Association finds that more than 80% of U.S. adults above the age of twenty-five take vitamin and mineral supplements and about 40% of them use herbal remedies.[4] These statistics prompt one to ask: Why do so many people look outside the conventional health care system for help?

In one way or another, sooner or later, the gray zone directly touches nearly everyone's life. A review of its history tells us much about the gray zone.

The History of Disease and the Gray Zone

Pre-Human Ancestor Era (about 2 million years ago). Humanity was still in the process of evolving to the ancestor of modern humans *(Homo sapiens)* amidst African tropical forests, and was fully embedded in an elaborate and self-regulating ecological system. Disease and humans (like disease and all animals) had an equilibrium—a compromised state of coexistence. This status quo extended all the way into the dim and remote past—until one day "some ingenious character" decided to walk out of the forest and venture into the more temperate North, leaving behind many of the bugs—pathogenic microorganisms—in his or her old food chain.[5]

Hunter-Gatherer Era (2 million–10,000 B.C.). This is perhaps the golden age of human health. Much of our biological character was shaped in this period. Humanity for the first time achieved a disequilibrium with its pathogens as it adapted to the new environment and became aggressive hunters and gatherers—a state of constant nomadic search for food. A high level of physical activity demanded that every individual be fit and strong in order to cover a wide terrain on a daily basis. They did not stay in one place long enough to pollute their water, air and surroundings. There was no need for them to build elaborate dwellings, which might attract pests and insects—everything they needed had to be carried. The largest threats to human health during this era were food shortages, traumas incurred in hunting, and violent confrontations between competing groups. Famine, due to the depletion of food sources, decimated the population countless times. In spite of this, the population grew slowly and steadily, punctuated by periodic explosive expansions usually sparked by the invention of a crucial biological capacity or the improvement of a tool- or weapon-making technology.

-§-

"Sub-optimal health" affects more than two-thirds of the world population. That's about three times the number of people diagnosed with diseases.

-§-

By no later than 1.5 million years ago, population expansion and territorial extension had taken early humans to nearly every corner of the Old World (the African and Eurasian continents). But the real acceleration came around 50,000 years ago with the emergence of the first humans, with fully modern features and a wide array of refined tools and weapons. Within 30 to 35 thousand years, these people had filled every habitable land (with the exception of a few small islands in the remoter oceans) on the face of the earth. Humans became the dominant global predator. They not only hunted most of the large animals to extinction in the New World, but also displaced and replaced all the other humans, such as Neanderthals, who had existed before them.

As the human population exploded, most of the food disappeared. Stone Age technology was stretched to its limit. Under this pressure, about 12,000 years ago, modern humans took an irreversible next step: producing their own food.

Agricultural Revolution Era (12,000 B.C.–1800 A.D.). In this era, humans no longer adapted passively to their environment, but vigorously began to manipulate it. Domesticating wild plants and animals made it possible to support many more people with relatively little resources or land. As a result, the population increased dramatically. Villages grew into towns, into small cities, into major cultural and economical centers. But the brilliance of human civilization had its dark side: environmental degradation, and, as a direct consequence, disease. There is little doubt that most human diseases (80–85%) were created by humans themselves during this period—though unintentionally, for the most part.[6, 7, 8]

It did not take long for large numbers of humans, residing in permanent dwellings, to foul up their environment. Their elaborated residences attracted mice, rats, houseflies, mosquitoes, fleas, lice and dust mites that quickly adapted to the new human conditions, becoming vectors or intermediate hosts of pathogenic microorganisms, passing disease-causing bugs back and forth with their human companions. The domesticated animals posed an even graver danger. According to historian William McNeil, humans share about 65 diseases with dogs, 50 with cattle, 46 with sheep and goats, 42 with pigs, 35 with horses, and 26 with poultry.[9] In fact, some of the deadliest pathogens originated with domesticated animals: smallpox in humansis thought to be the evolutionary adaptation of cowpox in cows; measles is most likely the creation of canine distemper.[10] Animals and humans alike discharged their bodily wastes into the water. Armies of pathogenic parasites found permanent residence inside the human body. The common practices of agriculture—land clearance by slash-and-burn preparation, flooding and tilling—brought humans into intimate contact with disease-carrying insects and worms. Agriculture and related activities so disrupted the delicate ecological balance that frequent proliferations of mosquitoes and rodents spread lethal diseases.[11, 12]

-§-
Humans share about 65 diseases with dogs, 50 with cattle, 46 with sheep and goats, 42 with pigs, 35 with horses, and 26 with poultry.
-§-

Another consequence of the agricultural revolution was to drastically narrow the variety of foods. Tied to the land, the human diet became restricted to the foods they grew. Humans are among a very few species that suffer critical nutrient deficiency diseases such as scurvy, a vitamin C deficiency syndrome. As medical historian Kenneth Kiple points out, considering the importance of vitamin C to metabolic process, it is "unlikely that an ability to synthesize it would be lost in evolution, unless it had been rendered superfluous—unnecessary because ascorbic acid (vitamin C) had been well supplied by the diet over hundreds of thousands of years."[13] The same logic applies to most other deficiency diseases.

For the first time in the history, humans began to be sickened by infectious agents, causing widespread disease: endemics, epidemics and pandemics. The mass and density of the human population became high enough to sustain highly virulent pathogens: syphilis, diphtheria, typhus, typhoid fever, measles, plague, smallpox, cholera, tuberculosis and influenza. A killer bug could ravage its way through one human cluster after another, then make its way back to the original population years later. Human populations across the world were stagnated or decimated for centuries by wave after wave of pestilent diseases. Bubonic plague, for example, had at least three major outbreaks. During the second cycle across Europe, it left 20 million Europeans dead between 1347 and 1350 A.D.[14] Smallpox, unleashed on the American Indians of the Aztec Empire, devastated 90% of the population, numbering millions, within weeks.[15] Indeed, at many crucial junctures of human history, disease at this scale has played an important role in altering the course of human destiny.[16]

In response to these brutal assaults, humans developed complicated immunities to protect themselves. Toward the end of this era, some of the most violent diseases diminished. Measles, for example, became primarily limited to a childhood disease instead of a deadly stalker of all humans,[17] and syphilis specialized as a sexually transmitted disease instead of a major killer.[18]

In a nutshell, during this period, human health was in a state of constant crises—a matter of life and death or catastrophe. Any gray zone concerns were naturally pushed aside.

The interplay between humans and disease-causing microbes throughout this era can be viewed as the "rebound" effect of the displaced equilibrium trying to regain balance. In other words, after being left behind by our ancestors, bugs have finally caught up with us—with a vengeance. This process continued to the next era until some extraordinary human creations shifted the balance, once again.

-§-
After being left behind by our ancestors, bugs have finally caught up with us—with a vengeance.
-§-

Industrial Revolution Era (1800–1950 A.D.). The advent of modern science from the Renaissance on gave rise to two powerful developments by the nineteenth century: first, technology allowed the creation of machines for mass production resulting in greatly accelerated environmental pollution and ecological degradation, and, second, the emergence of modern biomedicine.

Occupational diseases became a significant threat to human health during the nineteenth century: for example, the well-known black lung, brown lung and white lung diseases suffered by the coal, cotton textile and asbestos workers. There were also a wide range of heavy metal and industrial chemical poisonings.

Most significantly, some of the ancient but rare chronic diseases such as cancer, heart disease, diabetes, and Alzheimer's became common, especially towards the mid-twentieth century, taking center stage as the main human diseases.

In the meantime, western biomedicine led to improved public health measures—better sanitation and hygiene—as well as more effective medical interventions for life-threatening situations. Consequently, the human population increased steadily from about one billion around 1800 to 2.5 billion by 1950[19] in spite of continuing struggles with some of the old microbial nemeses, a host of newly emerging diseases, frequent social unrest, famine and war.

Toward the end of this era, however, humanity suddenly found itself catapulted to the future. The driving force: the invention of vaccines and antibiotics. For the first time since the dawn of civilization, humans gained an upper hand in their struggle for survival against disease-causing microbes, which culminated in the triumphant declaration by the WHO in 1976 that smallpox had been eraticated worldwide. The balance of power between microbes and humans had changed again, resulting in a new disequilibrium.

Post-Industrial and Information Revolution Era (1950 A.D.–current). The end of the World War II saw the creation of enormous manufacturing and chemistry industries that provided products, convenience and comfort in every sector of life. Widespread optimism promised "Better Living Through Chemistry." Little attention was paid to the danger lurking in the proliferation and glorification of technology.

Once set on a new course, things started to happen at a dazzling speed. The human population doubled within the next 37 years from 2.5 to 5 billion by 1987, then again increased by another one billion in 12 years, between 1987 and 1999.[20] To put this in perspective: human population did not reach one billion until about 1800 A.D., and it had taken some 6 million years of evolutionary history to get there. The impact of massive population growth affects every aspect of life—behavior, relationships, food, sense of well-being—at a speed that does not allow time for biological adaptation.

-§-

The impact of massive population growth affects every aspect of life—behavior, relationships, food, sense of well-being—at a speed that does not allow time for biological adaptation.

-§-

In retrospect, the overflowing optimism of 1969 was premature—in that year the U.S. Surgeon General told Congress, "We can now close the book on infectious diseases." Not only do many old diseases continue to hold on, some have made a comeback—plus we now are faced with a series of new, emerging infectious diseases, not to mention the increasingly worrisome phenomenon of antibiotic resistance. AIDS is now the leading killer in Africa, and has claimed over 20 million victims worldwide since its identification a quarter-century ago.[21] Several non-classic hemorrhaging fever viruses including Ebola and Hanta viruses, as well as the recent SARS virus, have also caused lethal outbreaks. Nearly every case reveals the cause of viral emergence to be man-made ecological disturbances.[22, 23] These diseases are the symptoms of a planet out of balance. One cannot help but wonder: Are we seeing another "rebound effect" of a displaced equilibrium between humans and germs?

On the other hand, chronic diseases have, for the first time, become the leading cause of human mortality. According the 2002 *World Health Report* by the WHO, chronic diseases now account for 60% of human deaths worldwide. The percentage is significantly higher in developed countries than in developing countries.

Ever since the onset of the industrial revolution, our sense of well-being has been gradually encroached upon. The shadow of disease—the gray zone—is spreading. As infectious diseases are reduced to a less dominant status, and fatal chronic diseases became manageable, the gray zone comes to the foreground as one of the primary factors affecting human health.

The Input of the Gray Zone

Environmental Influence. In 1992, in the *World Scientists' Warning To Humanity,* 1,700 of the world's leading scientists, including the majority of Nobel laureates in the sciences, issued a public appeal stating that "a great change in our stewardship of the earth and the life on it, is required, if vast human misery is to be avoided and our global home on this planet is not to be irretrievably mutilated." Few will argue that we are now well into a global environmental crisis as the result of population growth and industrialization. Environmental deterioration knows no boundary, and permeates our entire existence.

-§-
The human body's burden of man-made chemicals has become universal, affecting everyone, whether living in Greenland or the Himalayas.
-§-

World industrial production has increased 100-fold since 1900.[24] For the past 50 years, more than 80,000 new synthetic chemicals have been developed and released into the environment,[25] many in quantities of millions, even billions of pounds, per year.[26] This number increases by 1,500 annually as new chemicals are introduced into the market.[27] Only a very small fraction of these chemicals have been previously studied for their potential biological or human toxicity.[28]

Human activities have already transformed about 50% of the Earth's surface, with 10% of land degraded from forest or rangeland to desert.[29] There is a further degradation of the productive capacity of up to 25% of all agricultural land, representing the loss of an area equal to the size of China and India *combined.*[30] The loss of forest cover, since the agricultural revolution, has accelerated at an alarming rate. Deforestation causes soil erosion, flooding, reduced agricultural capacity, loss of biodiversity and climate changes.

In the past half-century, fossil fuel use has increased by 500%, and the number of automobiles has gone from 53 million to 520 million.[31] Carbon dioxide, the main greenhouse gas, has increased by 30% in the earth's atmosphere in the past 150 years, contributing to global warming,[32] and a cascade of environmental complications. Chlorofluorocarbons have caused significant damage to the earth's stratospheric ozone layer,[33] which provides a protective shield for us against the UV radiation from the sun. Man-made emissions of sulfur and nitrogen are producing acid rain, resulting significant agricultural crop damage and land degradation.[34]

The first widely acknowledged indication of the enormous scope of the biological impact of environmental pollution was the global decline of frogs and some species of bird populations. Biodiversity loss is proceeding at a startling rate and involves every phylum of plants or animals. If this trend continues, a quarter or more of today's species could become extinct in the next 50 years.

Many pollutants are not biodegradable—once released into the ecosystem, they accumulate in the environment and find their way into our bodies through the air, through our food and water intake, and through skin permeation. Studies have shown that the human body's burden of man-made chemicals has become universal, affecting everyone, whether living in Greenland or the Himalayas.[35] Moreover, some classes of highly toxic substances commonly found in pesticides, plastics, paints, dyes, deodorants, bleaching agents, refrigerants, wood preservers and cleaning solvents resist degradation and excretion. Consequently, these chemicals magnify in concentration as they move up the food chain. Humans, at the apex of the food chain, have amassed particularly high amounts—millions of times more than the level found in the air and soil.[36, 37] There are hundreds, if not thousands of chemicals detectable in the adipose (fatty) tissue of modern humans, as well as in their blood, milk, hair, breath, saliva and excrement.

-§-

The fatty tissues of Americans contains at least 700 synthetic chemicals that have not been chemically characterized.

-§-

People in industrialized societies typically take a greater share of this chemical burden. It is estimated that the fatty tissues of Americans contains at least 700 synthetic chemicals that have not been chemically characterized.[38] Results of the National Human Adipose Tissue Survey (NHATS) conducted by the U.S. Environmental Protection Agency (EPA) since 1976 show that, of the top 54 lipophilic chemicals tested and classified as dangerous substances, nine are found in 100% of the samples, all at a high level. Another nine chemicals are found in 91-98% of all samples, and two more in 83-87% of the samples.[39] Other studies testing human blood samples in the U.S. yield similar results.[40]

There is a growing body of scientific evidence showing that this toxic load in some individuals can lead to a variety of metabolic and systemic dysfunctions, and in some cases, "outright disease states." The systems most affected are the immune, neurological and endocrine systems; the dysfunctions of these systems can lead to cancers, immune suppression, autoimmunity, asthma, allergies, cognitive deficit, mood changes, neurological disorders, changes in libido, reproductive dysfunction, and glucose deregulation.[41]

In the case of cancer, for instance, the prevalence has increased significantly in the past 50 years. The difference clearly cannot be explained by aging in population alone. In fact, the children's cancer rate is among the fastest growing sectors.[42] Nor can the increase be attributed to smoking, as the rate is still higher after excluding the confounding factor from smoking. Furthermore, the cancer rate is higher for those born after 1940 than those born before, regardless of whether or not they smoke.[43]

The U.S. Department of Health and Human Services officially lists 228 substances as confirmed or suspected human carcinogens.[44] Over 90% of these are man-made; they had never been present in the human environment prior to the industrial revolution.

-§-
Modern agriculture can be defined as the process of using land to convert petroleum to food.
-§-

According to WHO's *The World Cancer Report 2000,* 10 million people are diagnosed with cancer globally each year, and the number of new cases is projected to increase to 15 million annually by 2020. Cancer kills more than 6.2 million people per year worldwide, with the highest mortality rates in Europe, North America and Oceania (Australia and New Zealand). The overall cancer mortality rate in the developed countries is more than twice as high as in the developing countries.[45] It is estimated that, in the United States, 1 in 2 men and 1 in 3 women will develop cancer at some point,[46] as opposed to the worldwide average of 12%.[47]

The pattern of global distribution of different types of cancer is also revealing: the leading cancers in affluent societies are mostly lung, breast, prostate and colorectal cancers, known to be more associated with environmental and lifestyle factors, whereas the relatively high proportions of liver, uterine, cervical and stomach cancers in developing countries are associated with chronic infections, i.e., hepatitis B virus, human papillomaviruses, and H-pylori bacteria, respectively.[48]

We know now that cancer development is a gradual, multi-step process. It has a protracted latent period before a clinical diagnosis can be made.[49] In other words, it has a wide gray zone. The same is applicable to all the other chronic diseases.

If we accept the premise that disease, especially chronic disease, cannot arise out of the blue, and we know that environmental pollutants can cause cancer, hormonal disruption, immune imbalance, neurological disorder and many other diseases, the question to ask is: what do they do to our day-to-day sense of well-being?

Dietary Changes. Food in the industrialized societies has undergone drastic changes in the past half a century, more than it had for the prior 4,500 years. The basic trend is mass production and alteration from food's natural state. Industrialized agriculture mushroomed after World War II, with widespread use of chemical and petrochemical fertilizers, pesticides, and herbicides for high yield and efficiency. The change may be caused indirectly by pressure of growing population, but it is for the most part driven by profit, as the small, traditional and independent farmers are gradually annexed or assimilated into big agribusiness corporations. It has been said that modern agriculture can be defined as the process of using land to convert petroleum to food.[50]

-§-
Lab tests, imaging studies, and physicals are designed to detect diseases, and most likely will only pick up abnormalities when something is grossly wrong.
-§-

At the same time, the post World War II era also saw the rise of giant livestock and meat-packing industries. Cattle farming for commercial purpose, for example, has turned the traditionally grass-grazing animals to high protein eaters, confined in densely packed feeding pens. The feed for the cattle includes mainly corn (genetically engineered in recent years), mixed with a small portion of hay and often leftover cattle flesh and bones from the meat processing and packing, laced with antibiotics and growth-promoting hormones.[51] Other ingredients added to the feed can include dead cats and dogs purchased from animal pound, other dead animal flesh such as horses, poultry, pigs, sheep and goats, as well as chicken manure.[52] It was reported that American cattle were eating about 2 billion pounds of animal proteins every year prior to 1996.[53] Animal proteins are inexpensive feed additives that can promote fast growth, but their inclusion is a risky practice. The FDA only began to prohibit dead cattle, sheep, goats, dogs and cats from being fed to cattle a few years ago due to the outbreak of mad cow disease, and the finding that the responsible pathogen can cross the species barrier to infect humans.

Mass production and processing of meats have completely reshaped American dietary patterns, turning meat, especially beef and chicken, from something of a luxury item on the dining table to a daily staple. The impact on public health cannot be overstated.

Parallel to the transformation of agricultural and livestock farming, the same forces also worked to spawn the immense food processing and fast food industries.

Food processing is a $500 billion industry in U.S. that puts approximately 10,000 new processed food products on the market every year.[54] In a typical supermarket, 70-80% of the foods are processed.[55] Processed foods typically contain higher amounts of saturated fats, refined sugar and carbohydrates, and salt. With high-temperature pasteurizing, dehydrating, freezing and canning, it is inevitable that critical food nutrients are lost. "Refining" is accomplished by removing vital, natural constituents from the food. In the case of refined carbohydrates, milling not only removes a grain's outer coating (the bran), but also its germ (the inner compartment of the grain and its reproductive package). What is left is the starchy endosperm, which has little to no nutritional value. Almost all the soluble fibers, proteins, as well as vitamins, minerals and enzymes that come naturally with the grain—and are necessary for its biochemical breakdown during digestion—are lost. It is estimated that up to 75% of American food intake is from refined foods.[56]

Chemically altering the food structure, in the case of hydrogenated or partially hydrogenated oils, links a hydrogen molecule onto the fatty acid chain, creating an artificial saturated fat. Hydrogenated or partially hydrogenated fats are converted to trans fatty acid in the human body and have been found to raise HDL, the bad cholesterol, and are thereby linked to heart disease, diabetes, hypertension, obesity and some cancers. Trans fats are commonly found in margarine, salad dressings, breakfast cereals and baked goods such as crackers, pastries and cookies.

-§-

"We are in the midst of a chronic disease epidemic of unparalleled proportions."
—Tommy Thompson, U.S. Secretary of Health and Human Services

-§-

There is no compelling reason for all this processing of food other than to extend its shelf life and retexturing the food for taste.

Moreover, food processing also involves a huge array of food additives, ranging from coloring to preservatives to limitless flavoring and texturing agents. These additives are usually present in small amounts, but according to Julie Miller Jones, the author of *Food Safety,* a typical American eats enough food additives to equal his or her body weight each year.[57] Even though most of the additives are not harmful to humans, some certainly are—especially BHA, BHT, sulfites, nitrites, nitrates, and bromates, to name a few.

Processed foods contribute a major share in the sharp rise of chronic diseases and obesity levels around the globe, according to a recently released report from the WHO.[58]

The fast food industry, on the other hand, first came onto the scene in early 1950s with a few hamburger and hot dog stands in Southern California. Today it not only fills every corner of American society, it is all over the world. McDonald's alone has 31,000 restaurants worldwide, with nearly 2,000 new ones opening up every year. An average American eats about 3 hamburgers and 4 servings of French fries every week. Nearly half of the money they spend on foods goes to the fast food restaurants—more than $110 billion a year.

Today more than a billion people worldwide are overweight, of whom at least 300 million are clinically obese, according to the WHO. Most of these people are from the developed counties.[59] In the United States obesity is reaching "epidemic proportions," according to Surgeon General David Satcher. More than 61% of adults and 14% of children are affected by obesity-related diseases, and some 300,000 die each year from health problems caused by obesity.

Worldwide, heart disease has become the number one killer in the developed countries, along with fast increase in the prevalen ce of high blood pressure, high cholesterol, stroke, diabetes, many kinds of cancers, all of which are attributable to the over-consumption of processed and fast foods. But what are these dietary factors doing to the human body, and to our sense of well-being, on a daily basis, before causing disease?

Stress. Stress in modern life has a very different quality from the life our ancestors once knew. It may not be as intense, but is much more constant and psychological, as opposed to spotty and physical in the past. According to modern research, it is this relentless quality of the stress that takes a toll on human health.[60] Our high-consumption lifestyle and the associated difficulties of sustaining it contribute to this stress.

-§-
A disease-care and crisis-oriented system, no matter how advanced, risks becoming so expensive in the future that few will be able to afford it.
-§-

Persistent, high-level stress has always been known to cause stomach ulcer, insomnia, anxiety, depression, headache, back pain, and elevated blood pressure which leads to heart disease and stroke. In recent years, the long-suspected connection between stress and immune suppression has been elucidated.[61] In addition, stress can lead to overeating, smoking and drinking, the health consequences of which are well-documented. Prolonged or severe stress has also been shown to damage memory cells in the brain and cause abnormal metabolic disorders. Stress is further implicated in accelerated aging, diabetes, rheumatoid arthritis and fibromyalgia.[62] The more researchers have learned, the clearer it has become that stress may be a thread tying together many illnesses that were previously thought to be unrelated. In the U.S., stress-related complaints account for two-thirds of family doctor visits and, according to the U.S. Centers for Disease Control and Prevention, half of the deaths to Americans under the age of 65.

Inactivity. According to a report released recently by the U.S. Centers for Disease Control and Prevention, a quarter of all American adults get virtually no exercise either at work or at home. Of the other three quarters who do some exercise, only 20% of them are considered be exercising adequately—with "vigorously" defined as 30 minutes a day, five times a week, and "moderately" defined as three times a week for 20 minutes.[63]

And this amount is still significantly below what the WHO recommends: one hour daily, five days a week.[64]

Aging. The aging of the general population in the developed countries doubtless has contributed to the rise of chronic diseases, widening the gray zone. Globally, in wealthy countries, the percentage of the population over the age of sixty-five has grown dramatically and will continue to do so. In the U.S., the number of people aged sixty-five years or older has increased elevenfold, from over 3 million to nearly 35 million, since 1900. This number is expected to double to 70 million people over the next 30 years.[65]

Side Effect of Medication. The great influx of chronic diseases and the aging population has created an enormous demand for pharmaceuticals. A recent study published in the *Journal of the American Medical Association* shows that among Americans over age sixty-five, more than 90% take at least one medication regularly. Nearly 50% take five or more medications. Of these patients, 5% experience an "adverse drug event"—harmful side effects beyond those considered normal and expected. Most of the side effects (73%) are not preventable, due to the inherent properties of the drugs, or interactions among medications. Of the side effects that occurred, 38% were serious, life-threatening, or fatal.

Constitutional Imbalance. Needless to say, it is difficult to achieve absolutely perfect health, perhaps impossible. Most people are born with a constitutional imbalance, which is not necessarily a problem if their lifestyle agrees with their constitution. In other words, we can rebalance the original imbalance, instead of aggravating it. Constitutional imbalances define a person's biological uniqueness. A light gray zone, this original imbalance interacts with environmental influences and lifestyle factors, and thereby can determine a person's health.

The Character of the Gray Zone

Reversible. The gray zone conditions, for the most part, are reversible. This is the most significant character of the gray zone and has tremendous implications for the prevention of disease.

Insidious. The gray zone conditions do not grab our full attention: the onset is rarely marked by a dramatic event. These conditions sneak up on you. That is the danger of the gray zone.

Encompassing. The way the gray zone causes health problems is not restricted to a specific organ—a lung problem, or a heart problem—in the traditional biomedical sense. The gray zone has an affinity to the "soft," all-encompassing bodily systems, such as immune, endocrine and neurological systems.

Individualistic. The gray zone is unique to each individual, unlike a disease, which is an independent, self-contained entity wherein individual differences are irrelevant. The diagnosis of a gray zone condition requires comprehensive assessment of the relationship between the individual and the risk or causal factors.

Subjective. It is often difficult to obtain objective test or exam findings to ascertain the existence of a gray zone condition. The reasons are twofold: first, many gray zone conditions may not have altered or damaged the body enough to produce detectable laboratory results. Secondly, lab tests, imaging studies, and physicals are designed to detect diseases, and most likely will only pick up abnormalities when something is grossly wrong. Precisely because of this, many doctors who treat gray zone conditions are often forced to look for the most sensitive tests possible, or try to "read between the lines" of a test result. It is, of course, possible that, as the gray zone gradually comes into the focus of health care, there will be new tests developed that are much more sensitive and sophisticated to register the gray zone information in the future. But until then, physicians and healers who deal with the gray zone must have the courage to accept data that may seem ambiguous and unscientific.

Conclusion

The gray zone will become, I believe, the focus of public health in the near future. The reason is simple. According to Tommy Thompson, U.S. Secretary of Health and Human Services, "We are in the midst of a chronic disease epidemic of unparalleled proportions."[66]

Treating gray zone conditions will require health care that is bioharmonious. Solving one problem by introducing another is simply not acceptable, and has to be regarded as a treatment failure. A patient of mine said it pointedly: "I've already tried allopathic medicine. Why would I want to replace one set of symptoms with another? I am not that sick." Furthermore, treatment of the gray zone conditions needs to be multifaceted and multileveled whenever possible, involving not only therapeutic intervention, dietary change and lifestyle modification, but also body, mind and spirit integration. And finally, treatment has to be individualized: treating each person as a unique individual is the surest way to maximize the treatment benefit and minimize side-effects.

The United States spends more on health care than any other country in the world. About 15% of our national resources are devoted to health care and medical research. Yet national health care insurance is in a deep financial crisis.[67] In 1980, the nation's health care costs were $245 billion—an average of $1,066 for each American. In 2001, the total health care bill is $1.4 trillion. This is an average of $5,035 for each American. If this trend holds, in 8 years from now, the total cost will reach over $2.8 trillion. The health care chief of the nation has said recently: "We cannot afford this escalating cost."[68] A disease-care and crisis-oriented system, no matter how advanced, risks becoming so expensive in the future that few will be able to afford it.

On the other hand, gray zone care is naturally low-tech, low-cost and low-risk. Shifting our health care focus to treating gray zone conditions is an intelligent choice that will allow a more balanced, sustainable health care—focused on quality of life and well-being—in the future.

NELSON KELLOGG: Wisdom Communities

The Crisis in Ourselves, in Our Culture

We are living out a crisis, you and I. The crisis I am speaking of is not that of the depredation of the planet, or the exploitation of entire peoples. The crisis is one of meaning and purpose, both individually and collectively. We need to be able to produce satisfying answers to such questions as: "What constitutes a good life?"; "What is the narrative of my own life?"; "How do I understand my linkage and responsibility to other human beings?" and, "Is there any meaning to be found in the succession of human generations on this planet?" If we cannot address such questions straightforwardly, without a smirk of irony, then what does it matter that we do anything in life beyond the immediate and the selfish?

For us living in First World, postmodern societies, the problem of meaning and purpose is particularly acute, and a lack of resolution can lead to apathy and eventual paralysis, preventing us from taking passionate action to relieve the other problems we must face. This is a most dire consequence, since it is we who also control the most resources that could be brought to bear on the grave economic and humanitarian injustices we currently tolerate, as well as the ecological injuries which are unsustainable. We need to become engaged in the world beyond self, but if we continue to avoid all questions of meaning as if they were antiquarian artifacts that have lost their relevance in our sophisticated culture, our efforts in these other realms of action will be half-hearted and short-lived.

Nelson Kellogg, Ph.D., is Professor of Interdisciplinary Studies in The Hutchins School of Liberal Studies at Sonoma State University. In this position, since 1991, he has been able to develop a suite of new courses, including "Space, Time, and Culture," "Machine as Metaphor," "Biography of a Community," "Utopias and Monocultures," and "Inventing the Protean Self." His doctorate, from Johns Hopkins University is in the History of Science, and he has been a fellow at the Smithsonian (National Museum of American History) and for IEEE (Institute of Electrical and Electronic Engineers). He is the author of *The Persistence of Visions.* Photo courtesy of Art Bock.

The human experiment is in far too great a flux for static dogmas to supply its solutions. Wisdom is dynamic and multi-vocal. As the French playwright Andre Gide, wrote, "We must believe those who say they are seeking the truth, and doubt those who say they have found it. "The crux of the postmodern dilemma was already detected, a half-century ago, by the German philosopher Martin Heidegger, and was discussed in a remarkably insightful address called a "Discourse on Thinking." Heidegger saw the problem as nothing less than a battle for the human soul. More specifically it is a battle for the awareness and conscious attention of individuals. What we are—and are to be—as human beings is inextricably tied to that which occupies our thoughts.

-§-
We continue to avoid all questions of meaning as if they were antiquarian artifacts that have lost their relevance in our sophisticated culture.
-§-

Heidegger posited two types of thinking: "calculative" and "meditative" thought. Calcula-tive thinking is practical and presentist; it is tactical and manipulative; it starts and stops with the production of material advantage for the calculating individual. Calculative thinking appends no larger meaning to its business than the immediate, and therefore makes little attempt at assigning value to thoughts and actions beyond the obvious monetary ones. Calculative thinking is that which, to an ever-increasing degree, earns us our livings.

Meditative thinking, by contrast, is patient with itself. It seeks deeper understanding, instead of material gain, as its reward. Meditative thinking occurs when the individual is sufficiently protected from that which is merely fad, merely random transience and superficiality. It is the wellspring of truly original insight as opposed to a simple rearranging of what is. It is the repose from which the individual can learn to embrace other beings distinct from one's self. Martin Heidegger's fear, already in 1955, was that the so-called modern societies ("postmodern" had yet to be invented as a term) were engaged in a "flight from thinking," meaning an overabundance of the calculative at the cost of the meditative.

An Example of Cultural Meaninglessness in Higher Education

To look with any sobriety at contemporary American society reveals that Heidegger's toxic revolution is nearly complete. In most sectors of higher education —the very center, one would hope, of meditative thinking—we instead see a flight from meditative thinking. "How is this course relevant to my major?" is a common refrain among undergraduates. Their parents push them to fix on their major as soon as possible and get a high-paying job in this sink-or-swim culture. Universities themselves aid and abet the very problem they sometimes bemoan.

If a young undergraduate were unfortunate enough to ask a real question of meaning (such as "What should I get from all this education?") of some professor in her major whom she admires, she would get either a calculative answer ("to get a respectable career…"), or be shunted off to either the philosophy department or to psychological counseling. The rise of professional career specialties and subspecialties during the last century was simply a mirror image of academic specialization. Even faculty within the same department don't know what the others are doing. Conversation within disciplines connects small numbers of academics from widely disparate locations, and is rule-bound to consider only minor changes to the disciplinary dogma.

-§-
What we are—and are to be—as human beings is inextricably tied to that which occupies our thoughts.
-§-

The very composition of campuses is likewise bizarre. A single campus may be the site for (beyond all the standard teaching departments) a huge variety of professional graduate schools, each providing its own certifications, a music conservatory, a narrowly-defined medical research lab, an economics think tank, and on and on. No thought or expectation is given to why these far-flung enterprises should be located on the same piece of ground, or, once in place, how they might converse with each other for the synthesis of greater, holistic understanding. To an overwhelming degree, there is no synthesis because there is no conversation. Conversation, except among one's closest peers, is seen as a distraction, as is teaching itself in a research institution. Why would a youngster go to such an institution to find answers to life's perennial questions? The answer, increasingly, is that they don't. They go instead to get trained, and to get a "leg up."

Information, Knowledge, and Wisdom

There are three categories of *knowing* that elucidate Heidegger's two categories of *thought:* 1. Information; 2. Knowledge, and; 3. Wisdom. Information may simply be data, or it may be data arranged to answer a specific question. Knowledge is more systematic, aggregating information across certain webs of questions, which we often define as disciplines. Wisdom is of a radically different nature. Wisdom, like meditative thinking, does not shun questions of meaning categorically, but embraces them. It uses conversations among knowledge systems to aid in answering questions of meaning. And it goes even further. It incorporates the insights provided by knowledge systems through the high art of empathy.

In the modern world of objective knowledge we have presumed that we could hold the world at arm's length, test it and observe it, and find solutions unsullied by such unreliable informants as aesthetics and emotions. No one denies the power of the purely empirical approach in limited areas and to limited degrees. However, wisdom, with its attendant empathy, can change our stance toward life in ways both qualitatively and quantitatively different from knowledge alone.

We can, for instance, calculate the progression of AIDS on the African continent, factoring in every possible knowledge system (e.g., agriculture, climatology and famine cycles, trade policies, social structures, and cultural values) beyond the etiology of the disease itself. However, the very same systematized information will yield radically different responses depending upon whether we consider the results of our investigations through the high art of empathy, or simply as applied knowledge of the most calculative sort. In the second path our choice of collective action may well be to do the least intervention possible that will at the same time isolate our own economy from the most dire ramifications. In the first path, we may choose a much greater involvement simply because we wish to reduce human suffering.

Stories, Meaning, Wisdom, and Community

We, in the United States, rightly congratulate ourselves for being the most ethnically, racially, and religiously diverse society in history. But our manifold pluralities may prove to be both our ultimate salvation, and also a source of our current crisis of meaning. This paradoxical quality is best understood through the theme of storytelling.

-§-

In the modern world of objective knowledge we have presumed that we could hold the world at arm's length, test it and observe it, and find solutions unsullied by such unreliable informants as aesthetics and emotions.

-§-

The psychologist Dan P. McAdams has illustrated quite brilliantly in his book, *The Stories We Live By,* that telling stories ranks among the most fundamentally human things we do. I can certainly attest to the validity of this claim through my own small, intimate sampling: my four-year-old twins (girl and boy). Their eagerness for hearing stories is only surpassed by their desire to tell them. While each has drifted into a motif of choice (without any promptings from their parents: "princesses" and "dinosaurs"), they eagerly launch, with great enthusiasm, into a game of "pretend" that can last a very long time. To be sure, the plotlines do not include much allusion, symbol, or metaphor. In the case of dinosaur stories, they (the dinosaurs) come in two basic varieties (good and bad), and much of the story simply involves naming all the characters to be involved on both sides of the equation, after which they all duke it out. But that is as it should be. With more biological and psychological growth, as well as simply more life experience behind them, these children will likely develop a taste for more complex and multifaceted stories. This is why our most timeless stories are often found in the world's ancient religions, where stories must accommodate an audience at many different levels.

However, McAdams goes further than reclaiming the place of storytelling in humanity's persistent attempt to understand the world in which it finds itself. He writes: "We are tellers of tales. We each seek to provide our scattered and often confusing experiences with a sense of coherence by arranging the episodes of our lives into stories. This is not the stuff of delusion or self-deception. We are not telling ourselves lies. Rather, through our personal myths, each of us discovers what is true and what is meaningful in life. In order to live well, with unity and purpose, we compose a heroic narrative of the self that illustrates essential truths about ourselves. Enduring human truths still reside primarily in myth, as they have done for centuries." In other words, stories can impart not just codes of conduct but essential meaning, both for the individual and for the larger community.

But what are we to do in a society that has myths from many different cultural traditions, and where plurality is often a code word for merely tolerating the other ("Live and let live—then leave me alone"), not for embracing the other as a gift? What are we to do in a society that has indoctrinated itself in the lie that material surrogates for meaning and purpose are all one needs to know about meaning and purpose? What are we to do in a society that so believes in empiricism as the only path of knowing that it has reduced the value of myth to be synonymous with blatant fabrication? What are we to do in a society with so many storied traditions present, but which can't see the forest of meaning for its fixation on a single, objective truth? What are we to do in a society saturated with news on a twenty-four-hour cycle, but with no coherence among the flashing images and reports?

-§-
What are we to do in a society that has indoctrinated itself in the lie that material surrogates for meaning and purpose are all one needs to know about meaning and purpose?
-§-

Empiricism in its many forms has deprived us the possibility of a spiritual foundation in our search for meaning. Our science-based technologies have developed attractive surrogates—in the form of electronic communications—that keep us company and keep us distracted. Our lives are so dominated by technologies of distraction that we can easily live for long periods without pondering a single question of meaning. They not only fill up our time, but they feed off our innate need for community.

Yet blaming our abandonment of meaning on science does far more harm than good. The sum total of scientific discoveries from the past four centuries is magnificent, and is undeniably one of the greatest accomplishments of the human intellect. We would do well to allow ourselves joy in the contemplation of scientific leaps of imagination, just as we afford ourselves joy in the majesty of timeless art, or of nature herself.

As we reassert the magic of stories in our lives, we cannot simply appropriate mythologies from other wisdom traditions at face value, just because they worked well for the original authors and audiences of those stories. We can embrace stories from other cultures and other times for the wisdoms they express, but we can't, by force of will, believe plot elements that may have been very believable in the original time and place of their telling. The underlying truths may remain as valid as they ever were, but we cannot coerce ourselves or others into believing narratives that are no longer believable. We cannot reject what we have learned to be true, without doing harm to ourselves.

What stories will serve us in providing ultimate meaning and purpose in our lives? Here postmodern society is in a place it has never been before. Even durable life stories can only work at all levels so long as the underlying context for how one composes that life remains reasonably constant. Suppose that a person has lived to middle age, for example, as a farmer with certain expectations for self and family and continuity. Suddenly, through some twist of events, that individual finds himself selling the farm, and, at a local junior college, retraining for a job in the information technology industry! That person's life story, at very many levels, must change for him to make sense of what he is doing.

-§-
Our lives are so dominated by technologies of distraction that we can easily live for long periods without pondering a single question of meaning.
-§-

We have seen something similar happening at intervals for entire cultures, but usually these intervals are widely spaced, coinciding with huge culture-wide shifts. These are the demarcations left by the great revolutions, including the agricultural revolution, the scientific revolution, the industrial revolution, the Darwinian revolution, or others that changed the answers to the big questions. These questions, including how the world came into being, how we as humans came about, what elements constitute a life well-lived, and what one might expect to happen as one aged, all these and others, once answered by likely and compelling stories for a particular time and place, could be expected to remain stable for many generations. However, sometime during the last century our workable mythologies diminished to the point where they could not retain their validity for even a generation. We now find ourselves with several options. We can reinvent our mythologies on a nearly continual basis; we can step back from exact particulars in our explanatory mythologies and compose more fluid and evocative stories; we can retreat into any one of many dogmatisms; or we can simply allow the lives we lead to become disconnected from and narratives of meaning and purpose, relying upon such relative metrics as the size of our bank accounts to tell us what is important and how we are doing. Unfortunately, the last two "solutions" seem to be the ones the societies of the globe are choosing.

There is one great prerequisite for us, as a species, to embody hope rather than despair. The adults in our society must unshackle the rising generations from the dead weight of monotonic calculative thinking, and the materialistic lifestyle of competition and isolation that pure calculative thinking supports. This idiotic presumption that human life is a zero-sum game, where everything that "counts" can be counted and that what you have comes only at my expense, is lethal to the encouragement of species-optimism, and it is a crime against humanity to force such a worldview upon our young. This is a dull and life-depriving narrative to live by, and we simply must do better if we are to survive as more than brute beasts. Every semester, at the university where I teach, I am shocked by the numbers of young people who have resigned themselves to the materialistic credo.

This unshackling must take place at every juncture of opportunity. Everyone who has either contact with or responsibility for the younger generations, whether as parents, teachers or mentors of any stripe, or simply members of the same communities, must provide better narratives for living than our consumerist culture insists upon.

-§-
As we reassert the magic of stories in our lives, we cannot simply appropriate mythologies from other wisdom traditions at face value.
-§-

One of the most elegant ways to foster generative narratives for living is through developing the elegant art of conversation. True conversation produces wisdoms unknown to us prior to embarking upon the conversation. Like wisdom itself, conversation is not dogmatic. It is accepting and patient and multi-vocal. I count myself as extremely fortunate in that my regular working life involves teaching young adults, and almost without exception I have been able to do this in the seminar format. This is where a number of individuals (usually thirteen to fifteen) sit around a table and hold directed conversations on a particular topic and set of readings. One of the most frequent responses from students is that this is the first time they were actually encouraged to share their own thoughts and opinions on anything. I wonder how many adults would respond similarly in the same situation.

We need the sorts of conversations, in all of our overlapping communities, that generate continually evolving narratives relevant to our lives. We can begin by constructing our own stories and telling them to people we are close to. We can listen attentively to the stories of others. There are few things the human psyche and soul crave more than to truly be heard by another in an accepting way. We must take care that we don't stifle the humanistic sharing of wisdom in a misguided attempt to avoid, for example, conflating church and state. We value our cultural plurality. But if we force the sharing of those pluralities to stop abruptly at the point where the narrative departs from a superficial telling of facts to a sharing of the depth of how that tradition or that mythology feels, we have done nothing to impart the depth of the other's experience. Finally, we must hold our colleges and universities to account more for how they inspire wisdom and less for how they distribute facts and techniques. Anyone applying for a job in the teaching professions ought to be able to answer the undergraduate who asks what she should be getting from "all this education." A prospective faculty member should have given this *substantial* thought, even if the post is to teach a very narrow range of discipline-based courses. That undergraduate's question ought to be part of a hiring interview.

-§-

One of the most elegant ways to foster generative narratives for living is through developing the elegant art of conversation.

-§-

Where will all these conversations lead? Who knows? There are as many conceptions of the endpoint of truth stories as there are humans to think about them. The notions for constructing these conversations within wisdom communities range from a tradition of handed-down story in oral transmission communities, to the rigid and doctrinaire interpretations of text-bound religions, to the intellectual approach of sampling from a "great books" bibliography, to the notion that the only constant is change, to the jaundiced view that nothing matters. And those who give time to meditative thinking concerning their own mythologies will probably find themselves making a journey through more than one of the truth stories by the time they reach middle age. The only truth story modality that I am confident is bankrupt is the declaration that nothing matters.

Perhaps we will find our durable wisdoms of the future in the same way that the Sufi poet Rumi did, who wrote:

> I have lived on the lip
> of insanity, wanting to know reasons,
> knocking on a door. It opens.
> I've been knocking from the inside!

In any case, the sharing of wisdom stories, however limited or quotidian they may sound, as we construct our own life stories, is essential, no matter what stage of life we inhabit. Perhaps the great story of our times will be that we sought out truths and wisdoms. And while doing this, even flailing around in the dark at times, we gave ourselves the meaning and purpose that come with that striving, and this gave us the hope and optimism to tackle all the other problems that threatened to bring an abrupt close to the human experiment. That would be wonderful.

Part Five

Carrying Change into Daily Life

Trathen Heckman:

Proactive Audacity: Daily Acts of Revolutionary Delight

"Let no one be discouraged by the belief that there is nothing that one man or one woman can do against the enormous array of the world's ills. It is from numberless diverse acts of courage and belief that human history is shaped. Each time a man stands up for an ideal, strikes out against injustice, or acts to improve the lot of others, he sends a tiny ripple of hope, and crossing each other from a million different centers of energy and daring, those ripples build a current which can sweep down the mightiest walls of oppression and resistance."

These words were spoken by Robert F. Kennedy over thirty years ago. At the same time, Martin Luther King, Jr. referred to the "fierce urgency of now" and articulated a need for "vigorous and positive action." Today, our social and ecological situation is even more extreme than when King and Kennedy were alive. Their questions still haunt us: How do we sustain vigorous and positive action? How do we weave proactive steps into our cultural story? How do we make this our work, our financial support, our daily life?

I watched both my parents, and plenty of others, die of a systemic sickness that is so widespread in our world, most folks don't want to—much less know how to—fully acknowledge it. Each day, as we uncover the many failings of a disconnected and mechanistic society that costs countless lives, another chance exposes itself to reclaim an action, to grow a relationship, to become more whole. Each act is another chance to speak stronger, louder and more loving truths. Each act is another chance to

Trathen Heckman is the founder of Daily Acts organization and *Ripples* journal. He is a former professional snowboarder and software engineer who now writes, teaches and organizes around reclaiming our personal and planetary richness. Trathen weaves Permaculture Design and Tai Chi into everything he can dream up and believes that by approaching people in entertaining ways, we inspire the engagement of hearts, minds and senses. He lives in the Dutch Bill Creek Watershed in Monte Rio, California where he enjoys Tai Chi toast, working to compost apathy and planting subversive seeds of conscious delight. Web address: www.daily-acts.org.

grow the unyielding power, hope, and focused positive action necessary to embrace and recreate the normalized insanity filling our daily lives.

While deconstructing our global malaise may seem daunting at first, it is not a heinous task to hide from—it is our Holy Grail, our sprawling, globalized awakening. *Buenos dias, compadres!* Now step away from the snooze button. It's time to better know how we're bound together. So set aside your Palm Pilot and the cultural map fastened to your mind. Ditch any version of valid that's too narrowly defined. Open up what you consider to be real. Get ready for some affirmations you can taste and feel.

One of the largest issues we face on a personal level is this disturbing blend of comfort, complacency and fear that consistently suffocates our humanity and puts our imaginations to sleep. The fierce urgency of now requires that we come to better understand our planetary interdependence. We can no longer afford to allow our lives to be systematically destroyed and trinketized by seemingly innocuous decisions built on lies. In our collective sleepy state, we've become convinced that beauty comes in catalogs and leather bucket seats and health comes in prescriptions, or packaged, hydrogenated treats.

-§-
Each act is another chance to grow the unyielding power, hope, and focused positive action necessary to embrace and recreate the normalized insanity filling our daily lives.
-§-

As our vital ties with the earth and each other have silently slipped away, the mystery, growth, and change our world hinges upon have become vaguely familiar props we navigate around. But nature is doing her best to arouse us, and our ability to move beyond this incessant conditioning is woven into the spirit of life. To access this spirit we need to reconnect our lives and redesign our culture, reinventing our relations with everything and everyone shaping the life we call home.

Each day, shortly after I wake, I walk into the garden and sit down on a little wooden stool cupping a hot gourd of tea. With a quiet mind before the programs, filters and agendas take hold, I close my eyes and call universes of intent in through my pores, stirring Tai Chi incantations into my tea and morning. I ask myself, the hillside, and the far reaches of life, "How do we gain the passion, persistence and internal emphasis needed to recreate this cultural impetus toward the desecration of life?"

Every day, the answer comes back the same: uncover, create and share more vibrant and juicy ways to fall madly, madly in love with this life. So when my insides tell me to rub my face in a patch of chamomile, do Tai Chi with my tea, speak out in a crowd or recite the virtues of local bean curd to a stranger in the frozen food aisle, I kindly oblige.

When we open ourselves wide and see what rises to the day, we feel the necessary spark of renewal and hope that lures a smile to our face and summons a softness to our limbs. This vital spark, aligned with the systemic thinking which consciously connects each aspect of our lives to the whole—to the seasons and cycles and the greater worth of our diverse culture and ecology—must be flamed into a blazing fire of conviction. Fritjof Capra, Ph.D. feeds and clarifies these connections in his discussions about learning to think in terms of context, patterns, networks, cycles, processes and energy flows and thus understand the principles of organization that ecosystems have evolved over billions of years to sustain the web of life.

Together, we can and must strengthen our individual and collective immunity with each breath, bite, thought, and daily act. Each conscious effort reaffirms that we are much wider than society's seams and its hyper-consumptive billboard themes. By recapturing the sanctity of our minutes, hours and common tasks, we gain the capacity to live and act with the proactive audacity necessary to nurture, respect and protect what is sacred. And it's all sacred.

-§-

In our collective sleepy state, we've become convinced that beauty comes in catalogs and leather bucket seats and health comes in prescriptions, or packaged, hydrogenated treats.

-§-

It will take every chuckle, every tear, every exalted and painful moment to become more fully human and live boundlessly in the face of transforming this human culture that from the simplest sweatshop purchase to the endless procession of wars, has sacrificed over 100 million fellow beings and countless other life forms in the past century alone. By embracing our humanity and hope in the face of such severe hurt, we begin to live whole lives and further realize how truly interwoven we are with all life. With the potent implications of our interrelatedness at hand, we gain the broad perspective needed to transform culture through all we do.

"A tall task," some say, and, "where are the Gandhi-Zen-Buddha-Willy Wonkas who are going to pull off this miraculous turnaround?" When supported and inspired, each of us can do what it takes to cultivate the Gandhi-like efforts life requires of us now. This deep-seated belief is at the heart of our work at Daily Acts, an organization dedicated to providing people with the inspiration, tools and opportunities to live richer lives by enriching life. We begin by embracing the impact of our actions as they ripple out into the world, seeing how each decision empowers us to further clarify and build our vision of the future. With this ground beneath us, we can cultivate the inextinguishable flame of intent necessary to rekindle and steward our spirit-fire, discovering the planetary interdependence at the heart of what it means to be alive in this time.

By cultivating the passion, persistence and internal strength required to engage the diverse ails sickening our world, we gain a greater capacity, and the emotional resilience to assimilate not only what is screwed up, but what our role is and what new reality can be. While the harsh realities that flash across our lives—war, poverty, environmental degradation—will not disappear all at once, we cannot let that stop us from taking our next bold act. As Goethe said, "Whatever you can do or dream you can, begin it. Boldness has genius, power and magic in it." There is no time to waste, waiting for that perfect moment to take action, or for someone more skilled to steer. *You have enormous power.* Super size your dreams, then focus, commit and lunge forward with your heart.

-§-
Super size your dreams, then focus, commit and lunge forward with your heart.
-§-

By sampling creative and diverse actions we access the inspiration lying dormant in our common deeds, incanting magic into more of our moments. When this is done in a context that understands the deep-seated relationship between personal and planetary wellness, we become powerful cultural reference points for a richer way of being. What follows is a smattering of simple but potent efforts and affirmations. Such daily acts allow us to reclaim our personal and collective loss of meaning, and grab hold of much-needed balance and connection. Here are 201 tasty ways to find, refine, and illuminate your emotional, mental, and booty space.

Accept Your Divine Luminosity

- Begin and end each day with a ritual that makes you feel whole.
- Suck in the morning air and eavesdrop on life waking up.
- Indulge in reverie.
- Be unduly hopeful.
- Bask in compassion.
- Know that when your intent is on life, universes align, paradigms collide and your insides come alive!
- Inoculate apathy and denial with inspired acts, and cups of sun tea.
- Embody the wisdom you carry inside. Redefine how you relate.
- Create more time and space for conversation, questions and consciousness to arise. Forage for enticing ways to reclaim self and community.
- Start a good living file. Fill it with potent images, quotes, articles and sources of delight.
- Redefine what you consider to be sublime.
- Rest and lie fallow. Conserve. Store. Gather strength and sow faith.
- Blow kisses to the stars and etch your deepest truths in the evening sky.

Discover the Fecund Wisdom in Nature's Systems

- Dissolve distinctions between life and where you reside. Erase limits that include in and outside.
- See the wisdom in life's renewal. Soak in the fresh scents wedded to the stillness following a shower.
- Synchronize your words, breath and flesh to the season's intent.
- Study, uncover and apply the natural patterns that shape all life. Observe how they occur in gardens, bodies and lives; spirals that shape galaxies, sunflowers, and sap, your blood and bones, and a pine tree's cones.
- Discover why a drop of water splatters like a sunburst, like seeds disperse.
- Lick the dewdrops from laden leaves. Notice their veins the same as their branches and roots. Nature's innate truths on display in the branching pattern of tributary veins distributing lifeblood through leaves, our bodies and the rivers of the earth.
- Perceive larger natural systems, patterns, and your part. Choose to redesign, with these rhythms in mind—your garden, your day, your world.
- Uncover the wisdom in indigenous knowledge, sacred geometry and permaculture.
- Compost food, emotional and life scraps. Let worms eat your garbage. Know that all waste is food. The problem is the solution in healing our planetary and personal pollution. Renew your relationships. Your language. Your views.
- Remember each time you step outside, life is here to remind you how to stay alive to the real inside you.

Scrub, Rub and Love your Pores

- Begin the morning with towel Chi Gung, Tai Chi toast and sacred tea. Physically embody your prayers, thanks, and awestruck moments.
- Stretch your moral fiber.
- Exercise the belief that each part of your day is alive and begging to be celebrated.
- Build richer neural and life pathways through the alchemy of transformed disarray.
- Scrub, rub and love your pores. Tai Chi them until they absorb more.

- Use your breath, senses, stretches, and each movement to uncover actions of the elevating kind. Resuscitate life.

Cherish Dirt

- Grab a handful and thank it for your existence.
- Plant berry bushes, fruit and shade trees, flowers and veggies.
- Feed your yard only organic ingredients.
- Mulch and perennialize your garden.
- Break out unneeded cement.
- Lie on your back and make earth angels.
- Place your ear to the land. Listen for any secrets she may share.
- Each day touch the earth with your bare feet and give thanks.

Produce More Food, Love and Life than You Consume

- Grow food, medicine and wonder in your front yard. Share it with neighbors and friends.
- Grow edible flowers. Put them in everything! Ingest bright vibrant sunshine.
- Grow your connection to life with inextinguishable intent. Give thanks and distill goodness when you think and breathe, the way bees pollinate flowers who fill their needs.
- Plant a seed. Watch it grow. Feel it renew you.
- Recreate and reinvent how you invest, what you manifest. Propagate life. Renovate yours.

Question Everything

- Question your ingredients: there's too much obedience to what's printed on the box, and too much faith in what's not.
- Is your life full of rich relationships with the world or of products, processes and resources consumed?
- How much energy did it take to produce, package and transport that? Is there a local alternative?
- Question an individually wrapped existence and disposable lifestyle.
- Question the strip malls blotting out our horizons and paving over our green spaces.

- Without acting from reverence, what could any size house or wardrobe ever offer?
- How might they degenerate or obscure what we really seek to be offered?
- How do you define profit?
- What leaves you feeling disfigured, hurt and less than whole?
- How can this be a source of food and hope?
- Whose laugh, smile or touch is a source of nourishment you're deficient in?
- Which people, acts, media sources and incantations will help you and life flourish?
- When was your last full breath?
- Were the stars out last night?
- What if life becomes our hobby, leisure and love; living it, knowing it, digging and smoothing the flow of it?

Get To Know

- Your neighbors, your dreams, your farmers, your coffee.
- The unaware decisions that inhibit your visions, your values, your investments, your world.
- The integrity of those who act on your behalf.
- The why of when your heart's at half mast.
- The true cost of dependence on a fossil fuel past.
- The joy of conscious acts amassed .
- A broader sense of self where there is no personal without planetary health, no individual without collective wealth.
- The pitfalls of blind obedience and the purchases filling your life.
- The lightness, the full rich and rightness of when you speak, think and write in full alignment with your heart of hearts.

Adorn Family and Friends With Love Not Stuff

- Live in elegant simplicity.
- Fill out comment cards.
- Buy items with less packaging. Buy Seasonal. Local. Organic. Fresh. Bulk. Recycled content toilet paper. Recycled content office supplies. Recycled content everything.

- Acquire reusable or recyclable containers.
- Support family farms, artisans and community merchants. When purchasing from afar, buy Fair Trade certified.
- Know the land and hands that grow your food and fill your needs. When you purchase and invest, globalize love and kinship, not greed.
- Diversify your diet. Try heirloom varieties.
- Uncover where your decisions could matter more. Put life values back into your to-do list: your dinners, credit cards, patio furniture, retirement accounts, baby clothes, and ice cream cones.
- Buy nothing for one day a week.
- Cast your vote with what you purchase and what you don't.
- Re-use print cartridges, glass containers, travel mugs, clothing, water, cast off things, smiles, laughter, hugs, hope, paper scraps, old clothes for rags, cloth grocery bags.
- Justify and buy less. Lobotomize your artificially implanted desire to accessorize.

Dare To Commit Acts of Staggering Generosity

- Find pleasure in being relentless with your actions and love.
- Better assimilate what's been shown, but make it your own.
- Share your story. Take the chance to say what you think others may already know. Be a beacon of boundless hope.
- Organize friends and families around discussions, book and article readings. Potluck. Plot love. Start a guest speaker series.
- Empower. Enrich. Enlist.
- Lovingly challenge blind pride. Seek out diverse voices and views.
- Speak out in a crowd.
- Exercise the lashes of your eyes, sharing winks of delight with strangers who pass by.
- Take your life love to the store and stage. Speak it on trains. Distribute conscious questions wrapped in smiles from the edge of airplane aisles.
- Each day uncover the countless opportunities for guerrilla acts of subversive delight.

- Gracefully seek out captive audiences who secretly wish to be engaged.
- Speak up for what you often avoid, ignore, and let go.
- Carry pens, notebooks, cameras, and other pocketsize tools of personal and planetary liberation.
- Take the chance, act, and weather what comes.
- Become the media. Write, record, and seek to share, wiggle your booty and rock life sustenance loud and clear.

Shizzam, hot damn. Can you imagine if we each enlisted a few more of those acts more often and shared them with others, and made copies and mailed them to friends and posted them on bulletin boards? We're talking a good living revolution. The greatest richness is not found through hyper-consumption—a newer this or shinier that. It is found in steadily renewing and stewarding the delight of our lives. One step, breath, and act at a time.

In developing a criterion that guides us toward healthy and mutually beneficial relations, Brock Dolman likens our situation to building a puzzle: "Begin with the corners, which shape life; the earth, air, water and fire we are made of." From here, the integrated common acts of our lives provide the lines.

-§-
The lever we wield to move the world is in each choice we make as our decisions reach into forests, factories, and families across the Earth.
-§-

By uncovering, refining and relating our unique story within the context of all the hidden faces and tales we are part of, we remake the world with each locally made, free-range, organic, fair trade and whole grain decision. If these are unfamiliar words, Google them up. They are symbols, standards and certifications, a portal to greater life connection, and healthy relations with people, land and much, much more.

To better know what is local to our lives by supporting those who sustain us is vitally rich. Embodied in our want and need of place is a fondness for our chunk of the world—with all its people, places and spirit-filled in-between bits. By seeking to better understand what this means, stewardship-minded and integrity-filled decisions become potent and enlivened.

Archimedes said, "Give me a place to stand and a lever long enough, and I will move the world." The only place any of us ever have to stand is in each of our daily acts. The lever we wield to move the world is in each choice we make as our decisions reach into forests, factories, and families across the Earth. By sharing these visions with greater focus, power, and pizzazz, we become the vibrant catalysts necessary to incite an unsinkable force of mindful-masses eager to eat, breathe and dream into being a more just world through each act of our lives.

Remember: in your body is the breath of Gandhi, the blood of dinosaurs and the tears of children fallen to sweatshop floors. We are always and forever connected to all life, all wisdom, all hurt and all strength. When more of our individual and collective daily actions are focused and functioning in unison to uphold the value of all life, we come into our power. When we think and act collectively, we are more than sentient strands of life, we are the sum total of its shine.

-§-

In your body is the breath of Gandhi, the blood of dinosaurs and the tears of children fallen to sweatshop floors.

-§-

With this as our basis for thought and action, we can better decide and define the proper dictates of this precious life divine. Albert Schweitzer said "the greatest discovery of any generation is that human beings can alter their lives by altering the attitudes of their minds." By now, it should be old news that our beliefs shape how we experience life. What is never old news is what we can imagine when we open our hearts and minds. And imagination will make miracles happen when we fully embrace and acknowledge that we are the world, inseparable from the seasons, intimately interwoven with the hydrologic and nutrient cycles that sustain all life, and utterly dependent on the air we share with trees, the lungs of the earth.

Did you ever hear the minister at a wedding tell those gathered, "Your job is to help this marriage work?" Just like that, we're hitched at the hip to each other through all we do; accountable to life and living our ideals in clear, conscientious, and ever more ass-kicking, extra-loving ways. As one, we stand stronger and live greater truths more often. Together forever our task is to make this life shine with abundant grace and style. So with these words, I thee wed.

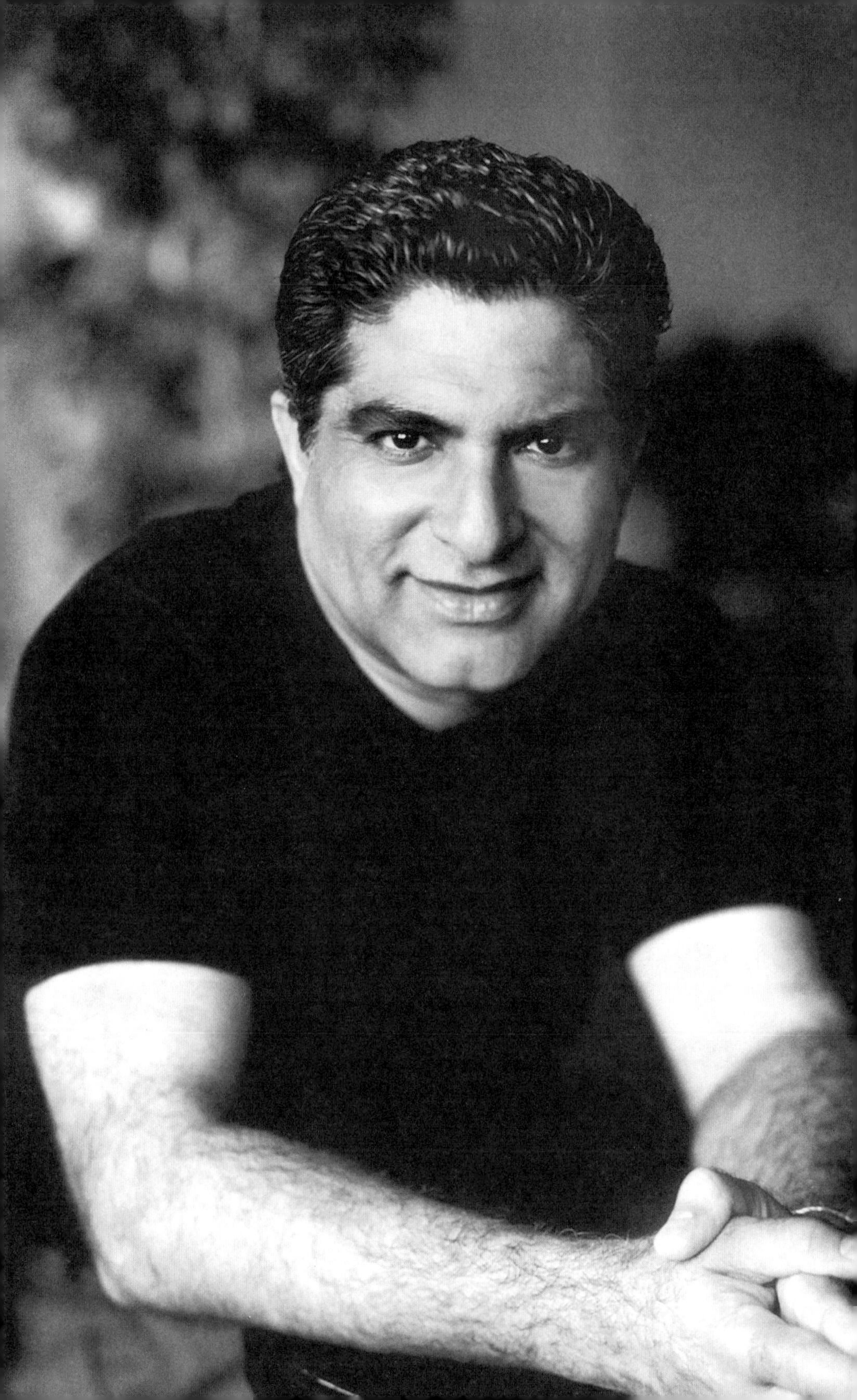

DEEPAK CHOPRA:

Heroes of Ordinary Life

Editor's Note: When great minds and hearts get together in dialog and sharing, the result is magical. The interview below with Richard Moss and Deepak Chopra is one such instance. As they discuss personal transformation, and, especially, signficant turning points in their own lives, you get a sense of how powerful teaching stems from powerful living. In addition to the interview below, an afterword by Richard Moss appears in the following chapter; his biographical information and photo also appear there.

Richard Moss: The words "personal transformation" are increasingly used in the community of people seeking psychological and spiritual healing and exploration, but there isn't general agreement on what the words mean. To some people it has to do with personal improvement. To others, like myself, it has to do with a fundamental transformation in the very structure of consciousness. What does personal transformation mean to you?

Deepak Chopra: I am glad you asked the question like you did, referring to the structure of consciousness. Like many people of my generation, I was exposed to *Vedanta* in India during my growing up years. We were brought up with a vocabulary that laid out a map for the transformation of consciousness. In that sense, what I say in this interview is not original at all.

When you study physics, you've got to learn the vocabulary that physicists use. The same is true if you want to understand the structure

Deepak Chopra, M.D., has written twenty-five books, which have been translated into thirty-five languages. He is also the author of more than one hundred audio- and videotape series, including five critically acclaimed programs on public television. In 1999 *Time* magazine selected Dr. Chopra as one of the Top 100 Icons and Heroes of the Century, describing him as "the poet-prophet of alternative medicine." Dr. Chopra currently serves as CEO and founder of The Chopra Center for Well Being in Carlsbad, California. For more information about his books and lectures you can visit his website at www.chopra.com.

of consciousness. People before us have traveled this road; they laid out a map and established a vocabulary. If you understand that vocabulary, you can understand what transformation of consciousness means. This is not the only vocabulary. Many vocabularies can be used to explore maps, and many maps can be used to get to the same place. If I am driving from Boston to New York, I use a road map; if I go by ship, I use another map; if I fly, I use yet another map. The maps explore certain types of territory, but they can all lead to the same destination.

I was brought up to think of transformation of consciousness in a certain sequential manner. I was told that consciousness has different states of awareness. Each state of awareness results in a certain kind of behavior for the human nervous system, and each state of consciousness creates its own physiology. It is not physiology that creates consciousness; rather consciousness uses the nervous system to create its own physiology. As a result of that physiology, your perception of your experience of the physical world is altered. What you behold with your physical eyes is a function of the state of awareness you are in, and as that state of awareness changes what you behold changes. Ken Wilber said, "We can see with the eyes of the flesh or we can see with the eyes of the mind or we can see with the eyes of the soul." Most of us, who have not explored the realms of experience of our consciousness, see with the eyes of the flesh and sometimes with the eyes of the mind, but never with the eyes of the soul. William Blake said so beautifully: "We are led to believe a lie when we see *with* and not *through* the eyes."

-§-
What you behold with your physical eyes is a function of the state of awareness you are in, and as that state of awareness changes what you behold changes.
-§-

In my spiritual indoctrination, from the earliest time of my life, I heard my parents and grandparents use the word *maya* for the artifacts of our perceptual experience. Every time they looked at the world they said, "This is maya." There was a deeper reality, which they referred to as *Brahma.* I became familiar with those words early in life, but it wasn't until many years later that I began to understand they weren't speaking metaphorically: they were speaking literally. As we shift from sleep to dreams to waking states of consciousness, reality shifts. Reality is infinitely flexible and subject to revision. I heard a phrase over and over early in childhood from the great sage Vasishtha, the incarnation of God himself. The great sage Vasishtha told his disciple Rama, "Infinite worlds come and go in the vast expanse of my consciousness; they are like moats of dust, dancing in a beam of light that's shining through a hole in my roof." Those words are beautiful, and I didn't realize until later that they were real; they were not a metaphor for reality. As our consciousness undergoes a structural change, reality shifts because reality is not some external thing. We are specks of awareness that project our own universe and then experience it.

Richard Moss: I am glad that you are talking about the origins of your work and early life. You are articulating a new way of understanding the Vedic and Vedantic tradition. If I take my life in comparison, I don't remember the richness of spirituality in my early life. In my life, and I think this is typical of many westerners, I didn't understand the lineage of my religion as a phenomenon for expression of consciousness. We don't understand the metaphors in Christianity or Judaism as maps or metaphors for deep states of consciousness. For myself, there was a deep sensitivity bordering on suffering which caused me to seek various disciplines and practices. At the age of thirty, I had a spontaneous experience that you could call a fundamental change of consciousness. For the first time, I begin to understand what the teachings from the Judeo-Christian lineage were about. I became hungrily interested in *Vedanta.* I read Shankara's *Crest Jewel of Discrimination,* and it made sense to me. I read Walt Whitman, and suddenly I was in the state of consciousness of the poet. I was transformed in a way. It seems self involved to discuss this, but it doesn't make sense to readers unless they understand that this isn't theory.

-§-
We can follow a lineage and a teaching, but at a certain place, we enter into mysterious territory that is beyond any teaching, beyond any teacher.
-§-

My perception of reality changed. I didn't know that at one level of consciousness you have one body, and when that level of consciousness is changed, you have another body. Yet my body changed, my capacity to perceive changed, my intuition and my energy changed. When a westerner comes to this lineage of teachings, most of the time we aren't coming because we want to change consciousness, but because we want to be happier, more successful, and want to escape suffering. It is the ego who wants these things, and it is the ego who generates the suffering. There is a fundamental paradox in how people come to spiritual work.

Deepak Chopra: You are right. You are one of those people who came from the need to alleviate suffering and found that the only way to do that was to go to a level which is beyond the ego, which gives birth to all suffering. Suffering brought you to a spiritual path. In many ways that is more credible than for someone like myself, who was brought up with the spiritual map being talked about all the time.

I, like you, went to medical school. I came to the west and got caught up in the rat race and stresses of a physician's life. It wasn't until I started the practice of meditation that those muffled learnings inside my consciousness from childhood returned and said, "This is what my parents and my grandparents were talking about." I went back to the same books I had seen in my house all the time, such as the *Crest Jewel of Discrimination* and the Upanishads. As consciousness began to slowly but definitely unfold these new experiences to me, I looked in books to find confirmation of what I was going through.

Richard Moss: In my late twenties, each morning I read one of the *Yoga Sutras of Pantanjali* and then meditated, watching my breathing. Then I again read from the *Yoga Sutras of Pantanjali.* I didn't understand the terminology, but into my subconscious came powerful images. One month before the major change of my life, a priest friend gave me the gospels. I had not read the gospels for many years. I re-read them and I found myself crying tears of recognition. Yet if I had tried to explain to my rational mind what was being affected, I would not have been able to convey it. When this change in my consciousness came, I found it difficult to pass through. I think this passage may be more difficult when there is no lineage to help you. Suddenly the gospels came to me, and I asked myself, "Who has lived this consciousness?" Strange as it would seem, having been raised as a Jew, it was clear to me that this was the Christ consciousness. Christ lived this. Immediately, inside myself, something eased. I won't say that I relaxed because the stress of the event was awesome for me, but I did know that others had been there before.

-§-
If you want to go beyond suffering, you have to experience it. We have to be intimate with our suffering.
-§-

The point I want to make is that we can follow a lineage and a teaching, but at a certain place, we enter into mysterious territory that is beyond any teaching, beyond any teacher. These teachings become powerful forces in our subconscious, but we enter something that no longer is attainable by our *effort.* I say this because most people confuse personal transformation with making a personal *effort* through spiritual practices and psychotherapy. These have profound value and can be helpful, depending on how we define personal transformation. Is it improvement? Is it elimination of certain kinds of negative or destructive patterns of behavior? Or is there something in evolution itself, something given by nature, that the sages talk about, that isn't necessarily the creation of a man's *effort,* but something we can come toward if we meditate or pray sincerely. What I call deep transformation isn't a *willed* process. In fact, it was after I gave up and surrendered inside myself, that the real change came, after I realized that my seeking was between me and whatever was real.

Deepak Chopra: Yes, I agree. Even meditation is never *willed;* it is a process of *surrender.* Most people confuse meditation with concentration, when it is the ability to let go of everything, including concentration. It is the ability to go beyond the thinking process, to transcend it. Exploring those realms of consciousness is a process of total and ultimate surrender.

The techniques and the disciplines are tools that help you go to a certain level where you can come to that place of surrender.

Every three months, I take four or five days and go into a silent retreat in some wilderness area, usually a rain forest or desert. About three years ago, I went to the rain forest of Costa Rica to be alone for three days. I didn't take books or writing material because that is not silence; that is having a conversation with the author. After one or two days, I got extremely restless. There was nothing I could do. The restlessness passed, and I experienced a profound silence. The day I was leaving, I went to the airport and stayed at the hotel. There was only one book in the room, the Bible. I read the Gospel of John and it was like reading Vedanta for me. I was familiar with every word—the word was made into flesh, I and my father are one, I am in you and you are in me, and greater works than these shall you do. I realized that Christ consciousness is what we are aspiring to and that Christ consciousness is a state of awareness that we go into. Christ wasn't about the crucifixion; he was about the resurrection and redemption. God-realized people are those who have achieved that state of Christ consciousness.

-§-

Do not judge yourself by the depth of what you can *teach*, but only by what you *live* in the ordinary, in the most benign parts of your life.

-§-

Richard Moss: I find that what limits a person's capacity for love or recognition is what they are afraid to feel. Wherever I go, whomever I talk with, their ability to stay in a marriage, to work consciously, to be without fear and to experience joy depends upon what they have the capacity to feel. I've found in my work you have to address suffering, and the Vedantic tradition suggests that if you use these tools, primarily meditation, you can avoid the necessity of engaging a certain kind of suffering.

Deepak Chopra: The authors of Vedanta, and the great teachers of the Upanishads did not have the karmic load that we have. Those problems that are so pertinent to us probably were not important to the great Rishis. Buddha said, "You know the Vedantas very well, but I have to talk to these people who are suffering and how should I do it?" One of the greatest teachings is that if you want to go beyond suffering, you have to experience it. A sutra that I remember well is that nothing should be clung to as *me* or *mine.* A long time ago, I started practicing that in my daily activity, attempting to keep that in my awareness, because reality is the universal being, and the rest is just a kind of a game. Yet, to get to that stage, you have to go through your suffering. If you don't experience it, if you run away from it or avoid it, suffering ultimately manifests the states of hostility, fear, guilt and depression, which are nothing other than not having addressed the suffering when it was taking place. Remembered pain is hostility and anger, anticipated pain is fear and anxiety, pain directed at yourself is guilt. The depletion of energy with all of the above is depression. We have to be intimate with our suffering—express it to ourselves, share it with other people, release our pain and surrender.

Richard Moss: This is the contribution of psychotherapies, even though they don't have a spiritual base. You have laid out this incredible map, but nobody can get to a state of cosmic consciousness if there is more truth in happiness and freedom and less truth in suffering. In other words, you used images of the flower and the sunset, but when you walk through a forest, there is glory in the dead trees lying on the ground as well. The cycle of life and death is part of the truth of life. You were talking about anxiety. Anxiety starts in the mind the moment there is a sense that I exist as a separate self and that I might not get something the separate self thinks it needs.

Deepak Chopra: In the end, it's all an artifact. That sense of a separate self is really an illusion because there is no separate self. It is easy to understand intellectually that what I call myself is a dynamic bundle of energy that is constantly transforming. I am not the same physical body that I was ten years ago, so I can't be my body. I am not the same mind that I was ten years ago; hopefully it is more mature, so I can't be my mind. I am not my emotional states because those come and go all the time. I am the witness of all that, and the witness of all that is not a person; it is a universal being and I am that universal being. Intellectually I can explain it, but experientially, if somebody meets me on the street and says, "You are a bloody fool," I suddenly start nursing my grievances. That is not me; that's my ego. This whole thing that I call myself is a bundle of memories and dreams and wishes I have created. By referring to myself through objects, I separate myself from my real inheritance, which is that I am a citizen of the cosmos.

Richard Moss: That someone on the street can insult you and you contract is part of the beauty of this world. The creature in us structures our activities to seek pleasure and avoid pain. What structures the average human mind is the pursuit of happiness and fulfillment through jobs, appearance, money, whom we marry and so on. A higher level of consciousness structures the mind through the desire for truth, for true understanding. You can meditate, and you can have glimpses of cosmic consciousness, but you have to turn into this world. You can't say to the world, "Oh, the world is *maya,* it's a lie." You turn to your wife or husband and discover how much pain you can cause in them, and you have to take responsibility for it. Or you feel yourself contract because you lose a job, and you realize that you are identified once again with this separate self. If the first part of the process is ascending to this wonderful state of unitive consciousness, the process is not complete until we bring that into every corner of our human experience—how we raise our children, how we live, how we care for each other. We will be provoked to contract. To the extent that we are insecure we will be provoked into seeking until, we begin to realize, I can't speak for myself because I still contract, but a deep place inside of me realizes that I am not that one who contracts.

Deepak Chopra: We have to go through it in order to transcend it. And there is no hurry; we have all of eternity to recognize who we really are. What's the big hurry? Whatever we are doing at this moment is from the level of awareness we are in, and in that sense, we all do the best we can. It's okay to desire; it is okay to get insulted. I am reminded of the prayer of St. Augustine in which he says, "Lord give me chastity, give me continence, but not just now."

-§-

In the end, what helps me most is to constantly experience gratitude for everything I have. As long as I keep my awareness in the experience of gratitude, the grace of God is there.

-§-

Richard Moss: I am going to ask you a personal question. When a voice of doubt arises within you, what does it say to you so that you get the chance to reexamine yourself?

Deepak Chopra: Doubt talks to me in the following way, "Deepak, are you so sure of yourself that you know you have created this map in your head? In fact, this may be a meaningless universe, maybe it's a speck of dust in the mindless void and you are a capricious anomaly in a sea of space; there is really nothing there. This is all your creation and your own imagination; we are freak accidents of nature…" When that doubt comes, I look at the beauty and the grandeur and the magnificence of everything around me, including my own physical body. The human body is the most marvelous, grand and mysterious thing. A psalm in the Bible says, "Behold, I am fearfully and wonderfully made." A human body can thank God, play a piano, kill germs, make a baby, and track the movement of stars. When I see this absolute beauty, my doubt goes away.

Richard Moss: You said there is no hurry, but you write so many books. Are you in a hurry?

Deepak Chopra: No. I have four or five books written now, waiting to be printed. My publisher said, "You've got a rage; you are cannibalizing yourself." Sometimes I feel this compulsive need to regurgitate every insight that I get. That is part of my addictive personality.

Richard Moss: That's interesting because years ago, early on, when I watched fantastic thoughts come in my mind, as I deepened in meditation, I said to myself, "I will not be a teacher when I meditate; I will not process information to give it to people when I meditate, because the identity of teacher or helper is too small, I know there is something more." For me, when that arises in meditation, I let that pass through, because that isn't who I am. I am more than a teacher.

Deepak Chopra: That requires a certain degree of maturity.

Richard Moss: One of my voices of doubt says, "Richard, when you are teaching, you are accessing energy by the focus of attention on you by the people." This lifts me to a different clarity, and it helps me stand above the tendency to identify with separate self or isolated self. So it says, "Do not judge yourself by the depth of what you can *teach,* but only by what you live in the ordinary, in the most benign parts of your life."

Deepak Chopra: Absolutely true. If you really want to know what somebody is like, speak to his wife.

Richard Moss: What would your wife say about you?

Deepak Chopra: She thinks I am a great intellect, but that I need to mature, that I am still trying to prove something to the world, and that I need to let go of that, and she is right. In the end, what helps me most is to constantly experience gratitude for everything I have, for the relationships I have. Gratitude always brings me to a place of peace. As long as I keep my awareness in the experience of gratitude, the grace of God is there.

Richard Moss: Birthing a New Culture

It is my feeling that the resurgence of ancient spiritual traditions like Vedanta, Buddhism and Kabbalah have real value for understanding and mastering our human nature. But we need to be discriminating about their limitations for the modern mind and modern situation. For one thing, Vedanta, as well as most meditative or contemplative traditions, were not just divinely inspired activities; they were also doubtless born out of suffering and helplessness. Most of human history was marked by human beings having relatively little empirical knowledge of the outside world and therefore little power to influence it. What was available to be explored that could leverage great power over suffering and toward accepting the general helplessness of early human life in the face of the vicissitudes of nature was the mind.

For the past five hundred years, scientific inquiry has given us unimagined power over nature and our physical circumstances. If the philosophies of India and the East profoundly examined levels of mind, they also encouraged a kind of passivity toward outer life. The contemporary challenge born of our scientific and technological successes is definitely not passivity. On the contrary, it is our helter skelter rush to exert control over everything which is now leading us to destroy the ecosystem upon which our lives depend. Against this modern situation, personal transformation becomes the most important work we can do. We must each learn what calls us to such potential for greatness and good, and to such potential for self-destructiveness. Personal transformation is more than a work about individual happiness or individual enlightenment. It is a

Richard Moss, M.D., received a Doctorate of Medicine in 1972 from New York Medical College. After a few years of general practice, he realized that he was called to serve life in another way. His work has been of value to countless individuals in many arenas of life and also has inspired changes of consciousness in healthcare, business and teaching organizations. He is the author of five books. Richard teaches in Europe, South America, and Australia, as well as in the United States. He lives with his wife Ariel in the foothills of the High Sierra in California. They have three grown children. Find him on the web at www.richardmoss.com.

work about becoming responsive to the evolutionary impulse, a movement from within Life itself that we must understand and obey if we are to continue to exist.

To imagine that Vedanta, even in a modern form, can hold the answers to these challenges is simplistic, naive and maybe dangerous. I think it seduces our egos into imagining that the answers already exist, that they have been attained in the past and all we have to do is follow the map. Of course, even to repeat the inner work that would enable the experiential confirmation of the map Deepak offered is an extremely arduous work. I doubt it can be done, for I believe that true transformation is, after all, a pathless path. In any case, I strongly feel that deep personal transformation must be a work immersed in a wide-ranging, broadly inclusive, contemporary and lived spiritual context and teaching. Crucial to this, I feel, is the birth of a new kind of community of exploration, a new quality of association of sincere individuals. Both Eastern mysticism and Western (or modern) science have the power to lead us to a vision of oneness, of the inter-connected wholeness of ourselves and all things, and we need this. This is the basic root of wisdom, the necessary under-pinning for a sane and healthy society. But bringing this vision into the world of social and cultural forms is a lived process that can never be predetermined. To me there is no one tradition, no special practices, no revelations of science that accomplish this. All are important, but every true teacher and every sincere student must reinvent the means anew. The dialogue must never cease, and it must go deeper. The call to transformation must burn forth from more and more nakedly exposed hearts and dedicated lives.

-§-
Bringing this vision into the world of social and cultural forms is a lived process. Every true teacher and every sincere student must reinvent the means anew.
-§-

Edward Viljoen: Every Problem a Prayer

Problems, according to Einstein, are not solved using the same level of consciousness that created them. Solutions require a change of perspective, a different way of thinking. With prayer, people of faith open themselves to new ways of thinking about problems. Through prayer we can develop an attitude of mind that is open to newness because prayer teaches us to appreciate different and higher levels of consciousness.

There are a number of reasons to pray. We pray sometimes as a celebration of what is present in our personal lives and in the world. Such prayers are appreciative and express thanksgiving or personal elation. Other times we might pray out of an awareness of what is absent in our personal lives and in the world. These prayers often address issues of our world such as the state of our environment, and may be imbued with a sense of sadness joined with a desire to have a solution.

Here we encounter a major distinction. According to my faith, when I am praying about a problem, I have to be careful not to bring the problem into the prayer. Through my prayer I have to cultivate the consciousness of a solution. I have to be cautious that my prayer sessions do not become concentrated worrying sessions, or moments focused purely on retelling the details of the matter. When I am praying a prayer of celebration or thanksgiving, I am usually praying from the consciousness of gratitude, so I don't face that dilemma of being distracted from my purpose. My attention is focused on the thought of celebration without distraction. I have to learn to develop the same focused attention when praying about

Rev. Edward Viljoen, D.D. is a dynamic and inspiring speaker, who has had a passion for spiritual understanding from a young age. During his tenure as senior minister, the Center for Spiritual Living, Santa Rosa, California, has grown to one of the largest churches in the San Francisco Bay Area, with groundbreaking lecture series's on prayer, creativity, and the world's major religions. He is also co-author with Rev. Joyce Duffala of *Seeing Good At Work* (DeVorss, 2004), a book that condenses perennial spiritual teachings into day-to-day exercises for greater peace and success in the workplace. You can find him at www.centerforspirituallivingsantarosa.org

the problems of my life. I practice adequately acknowledging the problem before I begin my prayer practice, by either writing it down, journaling about it, or stating it out loud. Then in the prayer, I have to turn from the problem and give my full focused and prayerful attention to an attitude of mind that is open to solution. Using whatever words or methods suit my faith, I practice entering a mind of receptivity to holiness.

Recently faced with a problem common to faith communities, our church Board of Trustees wrestled with inadequate parking spots at our facilities. We brainstormed strategies and solutions and considered building parking structures, valet parking and shuttles. At a pivotal point in our deliberation we realized that our thinking, while proactive and creative, was at the same level of consciousness that we used to create the parking crisis. We stopped our planning and agreed to turn in prayer to openness in thought, acknowledging that we in fact did not know the answer but trusted that one existed. The following day a benefactor, without forewarning and with no knowledge of our prayer practice, arranged to have the open lot adjacent to our property leveled and made ready for the parking spaces that our community so desperately needed.

-§-

When I am praying about a problem, I have to be careful not to bring the problem into the prayer.

-§-

This event instilled in me a resilience and courage to face the larger problems of life with hope. It has convinced me that I can do something about the issues I perceive as insurmountable. I think back to this event when I need to be reminded that the solution to the problems I face may be resolved in a way I have not yet imagined. Even those issues that because of their scope seem so overwhelming that they leave whole populations in a state of apathy now can be taken up in personal prayer. I am convinced that through prayer I can contribute something beneficial. Prayer allows me to break away from the sense of hopelessness I encounter when I try to understand the state of our environment and our species' impact on it. Prayer helps me trust that even though I do not know the answer, one does exist.

Without the strategy of prayer I might feel reluctant to listen to what seem to be unsolvable environmental problems. I might feel reticent to open to activism because I don't have enough understanding to properly evaluate the tactics proposed. I might feel resentful to having environmental problems forced into my attention and I might be disinclined to develop my understanding of the situation as a result. Prayer allows me to shift my perspective and open to new ways of thinking about problems by both acknowledging the immensity of the problem and turning toward a mindset of openness and inspiration. Prayer frequently has the effect of balancing my concerns and my hopes. Through praying about the environment, I have become willing to listen to information from many sides of the issue. Prayer has nurtured in me an ability to face ambiguous information with considerable more ease. Prayer has nurtured in me the willingness to challenge premature attachment to my own reflex thoughts. This has allowed me to celebrate the in environmental awareness, without feeling like I am avoiding the harsh reality of our grim challenges and earth's frailty.

The media scramble for the most sensational news in order to keep public's attention, and rarely report positive progress. Because of this, good news about our environment is underreported and the one-sided representation contributes to hopelessness and fear of the future. What if through prayer we effectively trained ourselves to value balanced reporting and solution-focused thinking? Would we influence the media to deliver a different product that would match our hunger for hope and possibilities? Would we hear more about trends such as India having more forests today than it had 50 years ago? Or other positive trends:

-§-
In the last fifty years, poverty has been reduced in most countries, more than it was reduced in the preceding five hundred years.
-§-

- The air in the developed world is becoming less polluted—not more.
- Starvation in developing countries is much less prevalent than it was a generation ago.
- Average daily waste per American has decreased by half a pound over the last five years.
- At the start of the last century, the average life expectancy in developed countries averaged some thirty years; today it's pushing seventy.
- In the last fifty years, poverty has been reduced in most countries, more than it was reduced in the preceding five hundred years.
- The air and water around us is, on the whole, becoming less, not more polluted.
- In 1970, 30% of the world's population had access to clean water; today, that figure is 80%.
- In developing nations in the last century, illiteracy has fallen from 75% to under 20% today.
- Not long ago, the chance that an infant would die was 1 in 2. Today, it is 1 in 20.

There is a lot to celebrate; but certainly not enough to be complacent. In my personal work, I have to be mindful about complacency. I can let my own eagerness for improvement lull me into a false sense of satisfaction when progress shows itself. When the international media focused on South Africa prior to the release of Nelson Mandela, many people talked to me in an informed way, and with genuine concern about the urgency for change. After Nelson Mandela was released there seemed to be a reduction in international coverage about the South African people's journey to recovery as the world sighed with relief that everything was now going to be okay. I noticed in the subsequent conversations I had about South Africa a diminishing interest in that country's challenges and a general surface understanding of what radical change the people of South Africa were facing.

What I didn't realize is this same sigh of relief at the first sign of progress can be experienced in matters of global importance as easily as it can in personal projects and goals. What makes a difference is that a project motivated by willpower and effort alone, requires sustained willpower and effort to maintain progress. Consider the number of people who at the first sign of improvement due to a diet or exercise regime fall back to previous habits and undo the good work.

-§-
Through prayer, I believe we can tap a source of solution-thinking that is not of the same consciousness that contributed to the world problems.
-§-

On the other hand, when a project or an action emerges from a change in consciousness, or a change in belief, then the actions and activities that follow are sustained by something bigger than willpower. For a project to begin in this mode, prayer is an essential component of the beginning strategy, eventually bringing me to the same crossroads as the Church parking challenge: continue with the same thinking that created the problem, or turn in prayer to an openness of thought with a willingness to be led into transforming ideas and choices. Our work in personal matters and in global matters is not so much to develop the willpower to change, but to change consciousness. Our work through prayer can be to foster openness in thought about, hunger, and pollution, our earth and so on. Through prayer, I believe we can tap a source of solution-thinking that is not of the same consciousness that contributed to the world problems.

The thinking that contributed to our environmental problem may be described as "separate thinking," thinking that promotes a belief that nature and humanity are separate and that human beings are on Earth to subdue and master nature, wrestling secrets from it, and surviving as best as possible until such time as humans are received into heaven, the final resting place. This old way of thinking and believing is not working. A different kind of thinking wants to emerge; the idea that all of life is made from one primordial source, one building block. This new thought is beginning to uncover our interdependence, our closeness, and our unity with all life. It will nurture a sense of holiness about creation and encourage a reverence for all of life. Rather than being a separate and temporary holding zone, our earth could become our cherished home.

A new thinking might lead us to revere how we are connected, through the air we breathe, through the planet we share, through the basic building blocks we are made of, and through the intelligence that creates us. When we see this connection, this oneness, then surely our actions will naturally fall into alignment with that awareness. Surely we will not only be inclined to value individual life, but also the role our species plays through the immense power we have to either conclude our existence disastrously, or to make a positive and creative difference in everything we give our focused loving attention to.

-§-
We need not wait for internal harmony before we can contribute to the world.
-§-

Prayer is a personal spiritual response to the global environmental crisis just as prayer is a response to personal challenges. Through prayer we learn to take care of, the personal structures of our life and to create harmony in our affairs. Then each one of us can begin to think outside our own personal survival, to the survival of our community, then of our country, then of our planet. We need not wait for internal harmony before we can contribute to the world outside of ourselves. They are parallel processes, co-existing with each other. Daily spiritual practice creates peace inside; selfless service and conscious social action creates peace outside. The one is dependent on the other and both are within our reach to accomplish.

Angie Grainger: The Shadow Side of Money

I will never forget that voice. It came from deep within me. The words were so calm, so firm, so knowing, so downright determined. All my patience had run out. Accepting any and all consequences, I rose to my feet. My insides grew thick with strength and I silently screamed an unequivocal "No!" that seemed to come straight from my bones. The fear that had crippled me for years vanished, and my body became the next string of silent words: Don't you ever touch my kids like that again! I grabbed his arm. Those dragon eyes zoomed in as his vicious rage transferred from the children to me. I didn't care. I felt like steel. Something within me had forever changed. He released my son, and turned toward me:

"How dare you disagree with me in front of the kids," he said, burning my face with fiery hate. I felt my chest rise and fall, my outer surroundings blur, as I reached into my deepest reservoir of strength. Time slowed. Calmly, I began to see, to witness—for the first time. I lay on the floor with the weight of his body on mine, the grip of his fingers encasing my neck, his soul completely lost. But this time it was different. The help I had been seeking was beginning to show up, for I was not afraid. I began to hear. I began to listen. My ears tuned into my daughter's scream. At the same time, I heard my son's calm voice: "Dad, let her go. Dad, Dad.... Let her go, Dad."

In that moment, I knew that my life would never be the same again. I had made a decision from somewhere in my core to take responsibility for

Angie M. Grainger, CPA/PFS, CFP®, and Founder of RETHINK Money Coaching, Inc., promotes the RETHINK corporate mission of changing social norms around money and being at peace. Her $1-a-Day solutions help people understand critical elements of money to gain lasting improvement in their financial lives. She has over 20 years experience in the financial industries, is a graduate of Sonoma State University, and has her Master's in Taxation & Financial Planning from Golden Gate University. By increasing financial literacy efforts and bringing regional prosperity, Angie has become a leader in her industry and her community. www.RETHINKmoneycoaching.com.

my life, my actions, and the consequences that ensued. I was done. That deep decision changed my life forever.

Sitting in front of Project Sanctuary in my old Chevy sedan, the back seat piled high with all my clothes, my tears suddenly ceased. In a moment of pure peace, I realized that I had no other place to go. And it didn't matter at all. What mattered was being honest with myself.

Be True to Yourself and Speak Your Truth

The inability or unwillingness to be honest with ourselves, to look squarely at how we live day-to-day, causes us harm. Dishonesty, and its companion, denial, may be the most prevalent weapon of mass destruction known to humankind.

Whether in an individual, family, business, or government, where denial takes root and begins to grow, so does destruction. Living dishonestly creates a self-perpetuating system. Being the one who stands up and says, "Enough!" is difficult, because it constitutes a threat to the others involved. When one person begins to speak up about something that is not right, it requires others to either look at their part, or work even harder to keep things the same. Facing reality and accepting the consequences of our actions doesn't feel good—at least not at first. When the fear of taking that hard, honest look at ourselves blinds us, it becomes easier to continue behaving badly despite horrific consequences. Unaware of the effect this has on others, our natural morals and values collapse.

-§-

Dishonesty, and its companion, denial, may be the most prevalent weapon of mass destruction known to humankind.

-§-

This dynamic is rampant in our current economy. When an individual, an Enron executive for example, lives a life beyond his means, he must seek ways to get more—more money, more status, more respect—in order to gain a sense of peace. This distortion is carried into the corporate world when he brings his attitude into his job. Now at work, his eyes look for ways to create money to keep up: for himself and for the extension of himself that is his business. The business takes on the characteristics of selfishness and greed while falsely seeking that sense of peace. This dishonesty, denial, greed, and self-interest brought about the collapse of Enron. Individuals made day-to-day decisions based on personal gain, rather than the greater good for our society. One misguided act lead to another. No one stepped up to say, "No, this is not right," and eventually some employees' sense of right and wrong got so distorted that energy traders could not even see the destructiveness of their behavior. They saw only the excitement of bonuses earned and targets met. They joked about the prices that grannies in California must be paying for their electricity, and were unmoved by an entire state facing rolling blackouts. Even though their conversations were being recorded, they were so out of touch with reality that they perceived nothing wrong with their comments. No one stood up and declared, "Enough!"

The World Sees Our Actions, Not Our Intentions

Waking up ethically means recognizing that, as an individual, a business, or a nation, we have a responsibility to live accountably. In the aftermath of the Enron scandal and the disintegration of Enron's auditor Arthur Andersen, the accounting industry has been forced to take a stand for practicing integrity rather than simply talking about it. The California Society of CPAs is spearheading a movement to promote education in financial literacy, and in aligning our actions with our values. Accounting firms are taking the lead in practicing business with integrity. *The Journal of Accountancy* (July 2004) notes, "It's one thing to talk about integrity; it's another for people to believe leaders practice integrity and to buy into the idea that ethics in business and the integrity of business are quintessential success factors."

This not only applies to business; it applies to you and me. To be successful as a society and to live accountably, we need to be completely willing to accept the consequences of our choices. Your family may choose to buy a huge, gas-guzzling SUV. Your bottom line will suffer as you make higher payments and face large gas bills. But when your neighbors do the same thing—and SUVs today account for about half of U.S. car purchases—suddenly the country as a whole is sucking up more oil, and forcing petroleum prices and supplies to the forefront of government policy. Our national fiscal crisis is a reflection of individual financial behavior. How willing are you to accept the consequences of the way you use money? What are the consequences of huge debt loads and over-consumption on your family, your community, your nation, and your planet?

-§-

Being the one who stands up and says, "Enough!" is difficult, because it constitutes a threat to the others involved.

-§-

Release the Attachment to Desire and Suffering Disintegrates

Becoming neutral to desire is essential in order to shift our perspective on money and move in the direction of financial integrity. As we take steps in the direction of greater behavioral awareness, desire will pull us into an emotional tug of war. That urge to buy, shop, spend, get, and fulfill is strong, and deeply ingrained. When we cannot stiffen our resolve and say "No," we talk ourselves into that next new thing—and the financial consequences. Saying "No" to short-term desires in order to build long-term fulfillment requires objectivity and discipline.

When I began to rebuild my life after my marriage crumbled, I was determined to teach my kids, by example, that there was another way to live. I set out to be the person I hoped they might become. Never in my wildest dreams had I imagined that leaving my husband would result in being separated from my children. Night after night, I cried, my heart and belly feeling ripped open by the knowledge that my two teenagers were living with the insane blend of addiction, poverty and violence that was my husband's life. With no phone and no address, his addiction took him to the bottom of the barrel: bankruptcy, homelessness, and jail.

-§-
Deep personal satisfaction may be subtle and immeasurable, and is certainly less exciting than a new Hummer, but it comes with a more enduring reward.
-§-

In the beat-up Chevy pickup camper he called home, our two kids and he—along with a large Golden Retriever—made the fairground parking lot their residence.

Determined to construct a poverty-to-prosperity template for my kids, I set out to find myself a good career. As soon as possible, I bought a three-bedroom home, upgraded my furnishings, and created a rich, picture-perfect lifestyle.

It didn't matter to the mortgage industry whether or not I could afford the house payment, or whether I was slipping into financial self-sabotage. What mattered was my credit score, my job history, and a few financial ratios. It didn't matter to me that I depleted my savings and "charged a little" on my credit cards to get my new home in order. I knew that I'd get increases in pay in the future, and that the money would "work itself out." What mattered to me was the fantasy life I was creating. I felt good anticipating the arrival of my kids. I felt like a good mom. I was certain that once I'd bought all the right stuff, my children would want to come and live with me. So I did.

And they didn't. They chose to stay with their dad, living out of the back of his truck. I could not understand their choice. What I did begin to understand, however, was this: my expectations of what money could bring me were totally off-base.

Spend Time, Not Money

Commercialism feeds on emotional dissatisfaction. In a world such as ours, the deep need for kinship and community is displaced by artificial wants. The latest style of clothing, newest gadget, and/or other novelty of urban life subdues our dissatisfaction, but not for long. The thrill of that latest purchase quickly fades, but the deeper emotional need is not met. Our feeling of emptiness grows and with it, our debt. Albeit unconscious for the most part, this self-sabotage breeds another layer of discontent: guilt. In *Rich Dad Poor Dad* (Warner Business Books, 2000), author Robert Kiyosaki writes, "Guilt is worse than greed. For guilt robs the body of its soul."

Debt is a vicious cycle—a self-constructed prison—we have grown accustomed to and come to accept. High speed spending sacrifices the more human aspects of our experience in the name of a dead-end game. In *Sabbath,* Wayne Muller says, "People who have a lot of money and no time, we call 'rich,' and people who have a great deal of time but no money, we call 'poor.'" Our society places more importance on money than on time. We keep moving faster and faster, in the hope of obtaining financial success. But somewhere along the line, we have lost touch with what truly makes for a satisfying life. As Muller points out, "even an innocent deer becomes a life or death threat at high speed."

In order to rediscover our true values, we need to slow down. Only then can we be moved by a higher purpose. Last year, I decided to look honestly at how I spend my money. I made a list of the things that are important to me and ranked them from highest to lowest priority. Then I made a second list of all the things I spend money on. I ranked that list according to the percent they take up of my monthly budget. To my life-changing surprise, the lists were completely inverted. Both shocked and sad, I was forced to see that I was spending the most on the things I valued least. Nearly 70% of what I earned went to pay my house payment. On my three highest values—spirituality, family and friends—combined, I spent less than 5% of my earnings.

-§-

In order to rediscover our true values, we need to slow down.

-§-

Integrity Comes When Our Actions and Our Values Are Aligned

Financial illiteracy is a growing national problem. Our education system does not teach people how to manage money in a responsible way. Research shows that forty-four percent of Americans live above their means, and sixty percent carry credit card debt in excess of $4,000 each month. Average credit card debt per household rose to $8,562 in 2002, up from $2,985 in 1990. Over 1.6 million families filed for bankruptcy in 2003. On average, the American family spends $1.22 for every dollar it earns. How long can this last?

College freshmen get an average of eight credit card offers their first week of school. Is it any wonder university administrators report that students are more likely to drop out of school due to credit card debt than academic failure?

The American Institute of Certified Public Accountants (AICPA) is beginning to address this problem. Programs like Jump$tart and Youth Business Week teach comprehensive business and money management skills to students in grades K-12. Jump$tart brings basic financial skills into classroom curriculums, while Youth Business Week offers a week-long intensive business and fiscal immersion program to teenagers. The CalCPA's Dollars and Sense program brings a panel of CPA experts to town hall meetings hosted by legislators to help improve their constituents' financial literacy. California Governor Schwarzenegger has acknowledged the importance of our financial future by proclaiming April as "Financial Literacy Month," and states, "by increasing Californians' fiscal knowledge, we contribute to personal financial stability and strengthen the economic climate in our state."

-§-

On my three highest values—spirituality, family and friends—combined, I spent less than five percent of my earnings.

-§-

In *The Soul of Money,* Lynne Twist speaks of overspending as, "the logical response if you fear there's not enough, but the idea of 'more is better' drives a competitive culture of accumulation, acquisition, and greed that only heightens fears and quickens the pace of the race.... When we buy into the premise that more is better, we can never arrive. Wherever we are, it is not enough because more is always better.

During the Industrial Age, people worked for many years in a single job. Upon retirement, they could count on a pension for support through the golden years. But the economy has changed, and our financial acumen has not kept up. Personal finance, retirement planning, income replacement, 401Ks, electronic banking, debit and credit management, is far more complex than even twenty years ago. It is up to each individual to learn fiscal accountability and responsibility because no system exists to teach these basic skills.

Now, in the Information Age, our income structure has shifted. The average American will change careers three times in the course of his or her working life. For women, the financial responsibilities are vastly different. Responsible for starting 70% of all new businesses, women receive only about half as much Social Security income upon retirement as men. Eighty-eight percent of men can expect a pension upon retirement, but only 47% of women will enjoy this benefit. Working for thirty years at a stable job is no longer the norm. Decreased pensions and Social Security will not support most people through their elder years, yet relatively few have a plan to supplement retirement income. The average Social Security benefit in 2003 was $895 per month. Almost one-third of retirees now rely on Social Security for 90% or more of their retirement income, and almost 20% rely on the program for all their retirement income. About half of the retired persons in this country live on annual incomes of between $10,000-

11,000 per year. Is this annual salary going to fulfill your retirement needs? Could you live on this today?

We Have Enough

When I came face to face with the truth that the family I craved could not be bought with material things, the pain in my heart broke me open. I had spent beyond my means in pursuit of a dream, hoping my family could be reunited. Maintaining an empty household left me little room to breathe, and did nothing to ease the emptiness inside me. I had been trying to buy my family back. Facing that hurt as much as having failed. But that pain propelled me forward. I had to learn to be responsible with money and detach from my desires. Today, I know that money is not family, money is not love, money is not comfort, and money does not give me security. Today, my actions are based on this simple reality: money is money. As a close friend and mentor consistently reminds me: It is not healthy to deny reality and live in the hope that things will change.

-§-

Students are more likely to drop out of school due to credit card debt than academic failure.

-§-

Sitting at a desk piled high with papers, my associate and I listen to our client through a speakerphone. We look at each other and silently shake our heads in a familiar way while Sam stammers, "Well, um…." Each time we ask about the shortfall in his company, his response is the same. Then we ask, "What is your plan to get you where you want to be?" The conversation flips back on automatic. I feel like I am hearing track number three on the "Don't ask. Don't tell" audio CD. Sam replies, "Well, things are turning around now. I just need to get through the next few months. Things are different this year." When we ask what makes him think so, track number six begins to play. Sam doesn't really want to face reality. In three months time, his company will not have enough cash to pay the payroll and bills. If he doesn't implement a plan for the shortfalls now, he will once again have to take money from his portfolio account to float his business. If Sam could face the difficult truth, he would be propelled to make needed changes. But denial keeps him from seeing the bigger picture and formulating a plan. The company needs to bring in fifteen new customers to get back in the black. The pressure cooker of the real situation would force a strategy to rise up which could make that business expansion happen. But Sam keeps his rose-colored glasses firmly in place. He fritters away his precious time on the things he likes to do—working in the shop, searching for special fixtures, and on Fridays, going fishing.

As accountants, we see this with alarming regularity. Business owners avoid the difficult questions, "Can you afford to retire? How much do you need? Are your personal finances in order?" Without full knowledge of their financial situation, decisions are made on the basis of faith and hope. Desperate to avoid drowning, they paddle farther away from the boat. By the time they wake up, the boat has disappeared on the horizon. As trusted advisors, we do our best to help. But year after year, we have the same conversations, and see few people make the necessary changes. Fear, embarrassment, and guilt keep the impasse in place. Refusal to look honestly at the bottom line sits like a heavy sewer lid on a deep well of fiscal denial.

For the fourth time in a year, Sam poured money from his retirement account into the business saying, "I'll get it back in a few months." But the company already owes him nearly half his retirement account. Without a solid business plan, his bank will likely cancel his notes. Sam's unsustainable business practices will affect his personal financial future for many years to come. But he does not connect his choices with the fulfillment of his goals to keep his home, provide his children with an education, and support his wife through their retirement years. Their entire lifestyle sits precariously on the edge: "Will we be able to do it?"

Sam's awareness of his responsibility to others is even further removed. His employees, creditors, shareholders, and the larger business community all have something at stake.

-§-

When I came face to face with the truth that the family I craved could not be bought with material things, the pain in my heart broke me open.

-§-

Experienced accountants and financial planners see and feel the disappointment their clients face when they move toward retirement and are confronted with the reality of their financial situation. Many have spent their entire lives building a business in the hope of transferring it to their children. But the business goes in the red and begins to hemorrhage all their cash. They can't even afford to retire, much less fulfill their dreams. It is heartbreaking.

Becoming fiscally responsible means learning to say "No" and look ahead. Honestly evaluating how your financial picture will look ten to twenty years from now is the best antidote to denial. In addition to lack of education, denial builds from fear. Fear keeps people stuck in a pattern that extracts a tremendous cost. Peace of mind stays elusively out of reach.

Release the Addiction To Passion and Desire

What defines an addiction is being unable to stop. An addict feels the instant rush, and the chemistry of pleasure races through the bloodstream. Relief is the reward. A sense of peace allows us to rest in a moment of bliss. The chase is over, for the moment. But before long, the calm subsides and the chase begins again. Something bigger, faster, and more luxurious looms on the horizon of desire, luring us toward the next big buy. The arc of tension and anxiety builds as the withdrawal sets in and is once again relieved in that moment of bliss. The addictive cycle blinds the addict to the effect of his or her behavior on others. The ability to care for or act in regard to others is lost in the sole focus on getting the next high at all costs.

Once You Admit, You Begin To Have Choice

By slowing down we create the necessary space to recognize our *deeper needs*—the ones longing to be met outside the addictive cycle. The pain of breaking the cycle is temporary. We learn to live with discomfort, knowing it will pass. In the space that opens with acceptance, new decisions can be made. A commitment to living with integrity can be built step by tender step. The process is like growing new limbs—whether we're talking about cocaine addiction, or overspending. It is an act of courage and strength to embrace reality on its own terms rather than on our fantasy terms.

Once the choice has been made to spend responsibly, we begin making changes through disciplined practice. Making a personal commitment to financial health is no small step. Making a slow start is wise. Finding that deeper strength and making a true commitment to yourself that says, "enough!" fosters the likelihood of long-term success. Pay attention to the consequences of each decision and live with the greatest good for all in mind. Find the commitment that is right for you, the one that goes "clunk" in your heart, and stick to it. Then begin with a few simple tools and practice them on a daily basis. Master the small things. Here are a few initial steps to take:

-§-
It is an act of courage and strength to embrace reality on its own terms rather than on our fantasy terms.
-§-

- Listen To Your Words. How do you talk about money? What are you telling your children? Listen carefully to your self-talk about money.
- Watch How You Handle Money. What are your habits with money? When do you pay your bills? Do you carry cash? Do you carry it in your wallet, or crumpled in your pocket?
- Reveal Your Financial Self. Talk to someone about your relationship with money. Be honest with how much you have, how you struggle, what you want and what you love.
- Order Your Finances. Keep your cash tidy. Organize a system to pay bills, track deposits, and balance your checkbook.
- Know Your Financial Picture. Prepare monthly financial statements. Know how much money and debt you have.
- Chart Your Progress. Draw a picture or graph of your financial path from your first encounter with money. Recognize your progress, and your setbacks.

- Discover Your True Values. Compare your values to your spending. Do they align?

Once these fundamentals are in place, you can begin to plan for the future. As you begin to master the basics, you can reach out for more advanced money management skills: financial planning, investing, retirement planning, tithing, and philanthropy. A long-term healthy financial future is built on a solid foundation of integrity, responsibility, and accountability that must be carefully and intentionally laid.

I have less money now then I ever had, but I have a long-term plan based on my true values to grow my financial future. I practice my new financial habits on a daily basis, treating myself with respect when I slip into old ideas. Careful discernment guides my spending habits and I continue to learn how my actions contribute to the financial state of my community and nation. The joy I experience today comes from loving, respectful relationships with my children, and even with my ex-husband. Tears well up when my son calls to ask about credit cards, or the expense of a new apartment. When my daughter inquires about stock prices, I feel proud to know that she sees me as a good example of fiscal responsibility.

-§-

Find the commitment that is right for you, the one that goes "clunk" in your heart, and stick to it.

-§-

Our nation, our world, is a reflection of how we act as individuals on a day-to-day basis. In order for us to achieve national and global peace around money—practicing generosity, kindness, abundance, and financial freedom—we must each master these qualities in our own financial lives. Mastery comes from discipline. Discipline is a consistent, dedicated, committed practice. As we are disciplined in our personal financial lives, we become masters of financial integrity and that translates into financial freedom.

We Create Tomorrow through Self-Mastery Today

In *The Millionaire's Course,* Marc Allen shares his daily mantra, "in an easy and relaxed manner, in a healthy and positive way, in its own perfect time, for the highest good of all." This highlights the importance of relaxing while we change. Will you create financial peace by slowing down, and just being with how you are? *Being* a master of money and *being* at peace? Becoming financially free takes time. When we relax, time is on our side. Begin to look at the values behind your financial choices and bring your use of money to a higher level.

Dawson Church: Personal Disarmament

There are two types of eccentrics that I particularly adore. One is the activist. I'm sure you know one too; someone who is perpetually protesting whatever government does, no matter what it is. Perpetually grieving the state of the planet. Perpetually outraged by the scandal of the day. Seeing conspiracies everywhere. Given half a chance, pinning you in a corner to regale you with dark tales of sinister conspiracies. Even though usually broke, always giving money to worthy causes. Beset by a helpless sense of being unable to change any of the problems.

The other type is the mystic. These are the people who you see doing perfect poses in the yoga class, displaying a casual ability to bend their bodies to the most extreme degees of flexibility. You see them buying the most organic of foods in the health food store. You see them pinning up notices about meditation classes, and talking in very quiet tones. They have a stillness about them so intense that you feel as though a hearty laugh might tear them in two.

I outraged an activist friend recently; let's call him Art the Activist. He lives in Sebastopol, California, and he's always traveling to march in the latest protest—by carpool or bus, of course. My offense lay in calling that general region the International Headquarters of the Impotent Activist. Sebastopol is a quaint and charming little town. As you drive into downtown, a sign greets you naming its sister cities all over the globe, and announcing that Sebastopol is a nuclear-free zone. I can just picture the mushroom cloud as it drifts North from San Francisco. It notices the sign,

Dawson Church, PhD, is an award-winning author whose best-selling book, *The Genie in Your Genes,* (www.YourGeniusGene.com) has been hailed as a breakthrough in the field of epigenetics. He has published numerous scientific papers, with a focus on the remarkable self-healing mechanisms now emerging at the intersection of emotion and gene expression. He applies these breakthroughs to health and athletic performance through EFT Universe.com, one of the largest alternative medicine sites on the web. www.EFTuniverse.com.

coughs apologetically, and murmurs, "Er…sorry. I think I'll just detour a few miles East."

Art dates Yolanda the Yogini, who is a mystic. She once lived as a celibate nun on an ashram for nine years, but now contents herself with meditating for four hours each day. She ekes out a living as a yoga teacher, renting a room in a communal house. She is fragile, beautiful, otherworldly, pure, and soft-spoken. Even her cat is a vegan, and insists upon eating only sustainably grown, fair farming practice, triple-washed, non GMO, locally produced, organic foods.

The rust on the back of Art's Volkswagen van is held in place primarily by bumper stickers. Among the many messages displayed are these: Good Planets are Hard to Find; Compassionate Objector; Wage Peace; Thank Goddess; Practice Impeachment; We Are Spiritual Beings on a Human Path; Free Tibet, and You Can't Take Sides Because the World Is Round. While Yolanda runs from the world to her peaceful meadow of serenity, Art fumes. It is much easier for him to project his demons onto the screen of "the people in power" than it is for him (completely out of power) to deal with the demons that hold the floor of his own inner parliament.

-§-

That is why the master can be wise; her perceptions are not clouded by the swirls of emotional attachment that pull the student off his path.

-§-

As I sit in my little publishing office, cranking out words by night and by day, I grapple with this question: What am I doing to radically alter the fatal direction in which our civilization is traveling? What actions can I take that spring from the pure heart of the Great Spirit that sees the whole unfolding picture, rather than the hopeless flailings of the limited human mind—which sees only a fragmentary blur? What does it mean to work on my own personal growth and enlightenment, even while the world as we know it totters on the brink of ecological, economic and political disaster? What effect does the work I am doing within the confines of my own consciousness each moment have on the world outside? Am I as powerless as Art; have I abandoned the outer world like Yolanda?

Each morning, after reading an inspirational scripture, I sit in meditation. I feel a sense of stillness and connection with the universal whole that provides an anchor to my entire day. But I cannot afford simply to sit in a smug tower of meditative bliss while the planet burns, and gaze upon the ashes with a benign smile. We cannot afford to marginalize ourselves with marginal issues like painting nuclear-free signs while genocide engulfs the Caucasus, while Nigerian women wade in the toxic runoff from a power plant in order to gather the sludge to make soap, while hundreds of species are vanishing into the dark abyss of extinction every hour.

I know, from reading their words and meeting some of them, that great spiritual masters are detached. Students bring to them their great worries and personal problems, and the masters answer from a perspective of calm equanimity. The master is not swayed by all the problems and turmoil that so trouble the student. The master maintains an inner calm despite the turbulence of life. That is why the master can be wise; her perceptions are not clouded by the swirls of emotional attachment that pull the student off his path. The master sees the path to true change because her consciousness is unclouded.

We can't always affect our external circumstances, or directly change the course of history. Yet we can always change our internal emotional climate, and that changes everything. When our hearts relax, we are subsequently more able to approach the challenge of daily life in a more rational way.

A poor farmer came to the Buddha for help with his problems. He told the Buddha about the wilting of his crop. The Buddha said, "I can't help you with that problem." Disappointed, the farmer told the great teacher about his shrewish wife. "I have no advice for you about that one either," said the Buddha. The farmer poured out all his problems, eighty-three of them to be exact, but the Buddha could help with none of them. The exasperated farmer exclaimed, "Well what good are you if you can't help me with any of my problems?"

"I can help you with your eight-fourth problem," the Buddha responded.

"What problem is that?" asked the farmer.

The sage responded: "Your eighty-fourth problem is craving release from your other eighty-three problems."

-§-
We can always change our internal emotional climate, and that changes everything.
-§-

The farmer looked baffled, so the Buddha elaborated. "We all have about eighty-three problems," he explained. Sometimes we solve one of them, or two or three. But new ones always arise to take their places. Every person, rich or poor, old or young, has about eighty-three problems. Being content—in the midst of them—being at peace inside, despite the imperfections of the world, is the heart of spiritual work. That's the only problem I can truly solve."

This story points to one of the great paradoxes of life. Only action that springs from an undisturbed well of inner peace can pierce to the heart of a problem. When you solve the eighty-fourth problem, you see the other eighty-three in a new and transformative light. Inner peace must come first, then enlightened and compassionate social action can follow. Social action that stems from helpless emotional outrage and flailing intellectual confusion cannot truly succeed.

Defusing your inner triggers solves your eighty-fourth problem, so that you can then look upon the other eighty-three with equanimity. In a calm state, you are much better able to deal with both your personal issues and global ones. When opportunities for social change present themselves, inner calm allows us to notice them and be available to them. We have to be effective in the world. Yet we need inner peace as well. This is detachment. But it is also effective. It is passionate detachment.

What are your eighty-three problems? I'm sure you have as little trouble listing them as the farmer had telling them to the Buddha. Which one of them most disturbs your own inner peace? Which problems reliably make you crazy? Who in your life triggers you the most? Is it your wife or husband? When your child throws herself into your arms, do you clench up? Do you have an employee who makes you wince? Does a screaming baby make your skin crawl? Do you cringe when your wife or husband picks up the TV remote? Are you embarrased when you see a friend crying? Do you quickly change the subject when a co-worker pays you a compliment?

-§-

When opportunities for social change present themselves, inner calm allows us to notice them and be available to them.

-§-

Mastering our own reactivity to these people and situations is the absolute key to peace in ourselves, in our families, in our countries, and in our world. Our first life-work is to notice who we react to the most, who pulls us out of calmness and into reactivity, and defuse that trigger. Until we master this vital skill, we are toxic bombs, continually primed to detonate whenever faced with the right stimulus. We can be disarmed—but only by ourselves, by our own choice. Dealing with our own triggering is a practical contribution you can make to global peace each and every day.

Here's a test to discover if you're dumping your mushroom cloud into the nuclear-free zone of your neighbor's consciousness. Any kind of an edge, any charge, any sense of urgency in your feelings, indicates that you're triggered.

When a bell-ringer strikes a bell, every other bell in the vicinity tuned to the same frequency vibrates as well, even though they have not been struck. The ringing bell is the external trigger; the feelings of upset or urgency inside of you are the resonant echoes. Getting this distinction right between what is actually happening in the real world, the trigger, and what is happening inside you, the emotional upheaval, is the key to solving the eighty-fourth problem.

It's easy to believe that the person or situation out there "caused" your distress. Something happened, and you feel bad. Therefore, we believe, the something that happened caused us to feel bad.

But this is rarely the case. Your nemesis Harry may say something callous, cruel, harsh and unkind to you, and you may feel angry and upset. It's easy to point to Harry's harsh words as the "cause" of your upset. But they are not. The real cause is the Inner Harry right inside your own head, resonating in perfect frequency with the words spoken by the Outer Harry. When you've disarmed the inner Harry, when you've healed, soothed and silenced your vicious inner critic, then the words that spiteful Outer Harry says to you have no emotional impact. Outer Harry can then say the meanest things, and there's no bell to ring inside your own heart in resonance. That is how the master stays calm despite the outrages of the outer world. She has defused the frequencies inside herself that resonate with the outrages of the world.

When you aren't emotionally jangled by what Outer Harry says, then you don't need to react to him. You don't feel hurt. You don't need to take revenge on him. You don't need to defend yourself, or point out how wrong he is. You stay cool and collected—maybe even cool enough to notice how much pain Harry must be in for him to speak to another human being that way. Maybe cool enough for that noticing to lead to compassion, allowing you to laugh and say, "Gee, Harry, you must be having a bad day. What's up with you?" Perhaps Harry hasn't been heard for years, and been stewing unnoticed in a toxic brew of his own anger and frustration. Maybe your compassionate response will open a door for him to be able to share his pain. Maybe it won't. You're whole, either way, and you haven't contributed to the sum of pain in the world. You haven't tried to take care of Harry's pain. You've taken care of your own pain in an act of enlightened selfishness. Yet once your own pain is gone, you are able to offer compassion to Old Dirty Harry.

When someone does or says something that sets your teeth on edge, and you feel upset, nothing is wrong. In fact, something is very right. A part of your psyche has presented itself for your examination in order to be healed. If you feel uncomfortable, angry, or upset, give thanks! A part of your subconscious that has been split off, suffering in the dark, has come to you to be embraced, loved, and integrated into the whole of your being. Having the feeling come up is a gift from God, because it gives you access to your unhealed material so that you can heal it. Your anger doesn't come up when Outer Harry yells at you in order for you to be able to nuke him back. Your anger comes up at that time saying, "Hey, here I am, presenting myself to be healed." If you pause, and reach within, focusing on yourself rather than on counterattacking Harry, then you have a sudden priceless moment in which to heal yourself and your old wounded pattern.

If, when we're triggered, we look at ourselves, then we seize that opportunity to heal. If—instead—we look at the other, blaming and projecting, then our opportunity to heal is lost, and the wound festers on; in Shakespeare's words, we "but skin and film the ulcerous place, whilst rank corruption, mining all within, infects unseen." Eckhart Tolle suggests that we be at least as interested in our own reaction as in the person who caused that reaction. In the second before you react, if you can catch yourself, and redirect your enquiry to your own feelings, you suddenly have healing within your grasp. Mastering that instant of reactivity is key.

Curbing our own reactivity may sound simple. In fact, it may be the hardest challenge we ever take on. It makes stopping logging in the rainforest—"cutting out the lungs of the Earth," as David Brower phrased it—seem easy. Stopping North Korea or Israel from making more bombs might seem like a more reasonable goal. Try intervening in your own reactive patterns for a day, and you'll find out!

-§-

The collective reactivity of a nation of individually reactive people is very dangerous to the world.

-§-

We can't physically remove the triggers from the thousands of old Soviet warheads in Russia, which the Western powers have been disarming at a shamefully desultory pace. But every day, we can pull the triggers off our own reactive bombs.

We saw America rush reactively into a senseless war with Iraq in 2003. While people blame George Bush, anyone who read the newspapers at that time will recall a jingoistic rush to judgment by the whole country, including virtually all stripes of public opinion, all the media, the Congress and all the organs of government. The verdict of the nation to go to war was virtually unanimous. To my shame, I went along with the tide. After a couple of months of harboring uneasy misgivings, I eventually thought that I must be the only crazy person on the block, since every commentator and neighbor seemed to believe in the rightness of going to war. Eventually I thought, "Every voice is for this war, even the most distinguished of our opposition leaders. Perhaps it really is right." It wasn't. It was a seductive group psychosis. That's what reactivity looks like on a national scale. The collective reactivity of a nation of individually reactive people is very dangerous to the world. In most regions of the world, polls reveal that citizens regard U.S. President George Bush as a greater threat to world peace than North Korea or Osama bin Laden.

Changing our individual reactive patterns is difficult. Very, very difficult. We have spent a lifetime engraving neural pathways in our brains. Taking all that wiring and rewiring it is very difficult. Especially since it's on automatic. That's why the many books, tapes and classes on personal growth and change don't work in the real world. It's easy to be loving in a seminar, or while reading a relationship book. But when Dirty Harry's in your face, the old patterns immediately take over. They're very familiar, your body's used to feeling this way, and anything else feels strange in your body. And the feelings come up so quickly that you can't stop them. So how do you find the Pause button, so that you have even a fifty-fifty chance of changing your old reactive patterns?

What to do?

Here are a few very simple yet valuable ways to stop the clock before you lash out reactively.

The first comes from Thomas Jefferson. He said, "If you're angry, count to ten before replying. If very angry, count to one hundred." The reason that a quarter-millennium-old piece of advice still works is that any pause at all interrupts our automatic patterns. It gives the flare of anger time to cool. It disables the reactive pattern before it expresses itself in angry words that, once spoken, can never be unspoken.

The second is to breathe. Shifting your attention to the breath breaks the cycle of reactivity. Take a few deep breaths, and your desire to retaliate against the person who has triggered you will dissipate. Lionel, my eldest son, learned this in preschool: "Breathe out the bad stuff, breathe in the good stuff." Perhaps nothing else he ever learned in school has been as important.

The third is to tap the end points of the energy meridians of your body a few times with a finger. There are thirteen of them, and the process takes under a minute. Yet I have repeatedly seen people go from bubbling anger to utter calm in moments using this technique. It's like hitting the reset button on your emotional body. You can find complete instructions on how to do this at www.emofree.com; you will be amazed at the instant results you will experience if you use this method of defusing yourself.

The fourth is to meditate daily. Starting your day this way gives you a foundation of peace. It is like filling up your reservoir; when you face an arid world, its challenges do not find you dry if you have tapped into the great reserve of spirit upon waking.

The fifth is to be fully present in your body. When you're triggered, shift your attention to notice what you feel physically, and exactly where. Fully feel how your body feels. Often, the reason we jump on poor old Harry is that we can't deal with the cauldron inside us. We jump out of our bodies and into Harry's face to escape the huge emotional burst we're feeling. So staying in your bones, feeling what you feel, keeps our attention in the one place it can do the work of healing: within.

Any technique you can use to bring yourself back to consciousness, bring you back into the present moment, is going to break the cycle of reacitivity. Getting emotionally triggered and feeling hot and upset isn't a signal to talk or lash back. It's a signal to grow. The bigger your feeling of upset, the bigger the signal your psyche is giving you to grow. Experiment until you find your own method of disarming yourself, something that works for you. Practice it until you're so good that nothing can shake you. Become the master of your own emotions.

It doesn't take a change in 51% of the people in a culture to shift a culture. It takes only a very small percentage changing to change a culture. One of the most striking and amazing experiences I had was being in Central Park, New York, on June 12, 1982. Perhaps half a million people gathered that day to protest the martial policies of the government of U.S. President Ronald Reagan, who was locked in a testoterone-laden alpha male staredown with Soviet Premier Yuri Andropov.

We forget, today, that a whole generation lived with a very real and concrete possibility of imminent nuclear annihilation. The U.S. was developing neutron bombs, parodied as able to kill people but avoid damaging property. Europe was outraged by U.S. proposals to deploy them there. A powerful new missile with the Orwellian name of the Peacekeeper was in development. Both sides rattled their sabres, and neither blinked.

The huge peace rally was covered by all the major television networks. Then the talk show commentators interviewed U.S. Secretary of State George Shultz. With a face graved in stone, his lips barely moving, he said, in effect, "Such protests will have absolutely no effect on American government policy." We had failed—or so we thought.

Within a year, the world gaped in blank astonishment as Ronald Reagan made a complete U-turn. He didn't just start paying lip service to disarmament. He didn't even merely start focusing on the issue. He went the whole way, declaring nuclear arms reduction the primary goal of American foreign policy and his presidency. Suddenly the values of June 12 became the values of a nation. It was a defining moment in Western civilization, and four billion people began to breathe a little more easily as the threat of a nuclear showdown receded. The actions of a few people can have a disproportionate influence on the whole.

-§-
Start with yourself, and the world will follow.
-§-

Imagine, with me, three actually and genuinely peaceful nations. Imagine if most of the individuals in the United States, Great Britain and South Africa, to pick some names, every day and in every human interaction, consistently practiced disarming their own attacking thoughts and creating peace. Imagine all the mystics of all three nations providing a national reservoir of connection with the Great Spirit. Imagine all the activists of all three nations joining together to spread goodwill, and to find non-adversarial solutions to society's problems. Imagine those bells of thought being rung millions of times by millions of people each day, setting up a resonant frequency to every other peaceful person in the world.

Let's do that. Let's become the first nation in which every citizen thinks, projects, and practices peace. Start with yourself, and the world will follow.

Part Six

Shifting Cultural Values

Daryl Hannah: Living Consistent With Your Values

My awakening to responsibility for our world began when I was about ten years old. My uncle, an Academy Award-winning cinematographer, sat me down and told me about nuclear power, something that I had never heard of before. I was horrified. I couldn't believe that we as a species were creating waste from nuclear power plants that had a half-life of hundreds of thousands of years. I also couldn't believe that our tax dollars were being put to such use. I was absolutely appalled. When I started working in the movies at the age of eleven, I got my first paycheck. I immediately went into my dad's office and told him that I refused to pay part of it in taxes because I didn't want the money going toward war or toward nuclear power. My dad responded that I would go to jail for that belief, and I said, "That's okay." That's where my awakening began, and it is still happening as my awareness grows.

It manifested even more personally the following year. Suddenly, I was not able to disassociate my food from the creatures that I was eating. So at a relatively early age, I became a vegetarian. After that, my idea of living my life harmlessly and well kept expanding. I realized that all my concerns—about the cleanliness of our air and water, about the health of our soil, about the preservation of our natural resources, and the protection of people who are being exploited—all have the same roots. Humanitarian and environmental concerns are one and the same. I've never been someone who can pick one specific cause, and make that the only thing I work for. They're all notes of the same song; it's all connected. I really love this quote from Francis Thompson:

Daryl Hannah is an accomplished actress and producer. After graduating from the University of Southern California School of Theatre, she studied drama at Chicago's Goodman Theater. Her breakout role was the gymnastic android in the movie *Blade Runner* (1982) starring opposite Harrison Ford. She portrayed a mermaid in *Splash* (1984) and went on to star in *Steel Magnolias* and many other movies. At the Berlin Film Festival in 1994, she won the Best Short award for a movie she directed and produced entitled *The Last Supper*. She is currently involved in several new movie projects. Photo by Sandrine Weinstein.

Thou canst not stir a flower
Without troubling of a star.

As an actor, I've had a hard time figuring out the most effective things I can do personally, aside from giving money to organizations that I believe in. A musician can go out and play a concert and raise money and awareness in a big way. What comparable gift can an actor offer?

I have decided that the best thing I can do is to make sure that, in every area of my life, I am actually living by my own ideals and principles. My home was built with green materials. We salvaged a barn that was being torn down to make way for a post office. The barn was built from exquisitely beautiful old wood, giant lengths of good, solid board. You can't buy anything like it new because we don't have old growth forests anymore. I did a lot of research about different types of green insulation materials, about non-toxic paint, and about gray water system. I equipped the house with solar power; it has a backup generator that runs on biodiesel.

-§-
Humanitarian and environmental concerns are one and the same.
-§-

I also pick all-organic ingredients in my food, and use non-toxic products in my house. I am actually living within my belief system. And that's really important to me, because, in a sense, the strongest effect you can have is a personal one. When people come to my house, they witness that this lifestyle isn't just nice in the abstract. Everything actually works well, and it's beautiful. Even those who want lavish lifestyles can still employ green and harmless methods and materials. You can still have a refrigerator and have earth-friendly values. You can keep nearly all the amenities that people assume you have to give up in order to live in harmony with nature.

Another choice that many people can make is the vehicle they drive. I drive a 1983 diesel El Camino. I drove from Southern to Northern California on about twenty gallons of recycled french-fry grease. Our society is realizing that there's a limit to our reserves of fossil fuels, and that it's very wrong to go to war and incur the wrath of the world to steal oil. We have other options. Even Detroit is starting to realize this. Family-sized hybrid cars are starting to be sold. The demand for new, low-impact vehicles is going through the roof. In the foreseeable future, all the auto manufacturers will be making them because once consumers change the way they consume, big business is right behind them.

I'm moving into a new phase in which I'm focusing on getting the information that supports these choices out to a great many people. The world is open to it at last.

My manager is the kind of person who has never concerned himself with any cause like the environment. However, his dog began getting sick repeatedly, and developing tumors. He couldn't figure out why. Then he realized that he was using chlorine cleaners on his floors, and the fumes were affecting the dog. He began using a non-toxic cleaner, and his dog hasn't had a problem since. It made him think about what he could do for his own health, and the health of his wife and kids. Many families have a member who has cancer, or know a family that has been touched by cancer. This is causing us to consider the toxins that surround us and that we've been ingesting.

It may take a difficult experience to wake people up to the wonderful alternatives that are now available. My effort now is to make sure that the information we need is easily available, to assist us in making good choices. It's getting easier to find the best alternatives, to discover what really works. The formula is pretty simple: what's good for the planet is also what's healthiest for humans. So I recommend we choose organic everything, buy local produce, eat organic food, and eliminate toxic cleaning products from our homes. The harmless ones work just as well, smell better, and are good for you.

Americans are raised to be short-sighted, and to look just at what we need now—not the price of our needs in the long term. We are going to have to learn to be a different kind of consumer. Big business isn't going to take us there, but big business will follow once they see the huge market for natural products. It's already happening: suddenly, Heinz is marketing an organic ketchup. There are even organic versions of the silliest foods, like potato chips and Cheese Curls. People are coming around.

-§-
The formula is pretty simple: what's good for the planet is also what's healthiest for humans.
-§-

On this planet we have one, and only one, beautiful, magical, karmic set of circumstances. We have this unique atmosphere, water and soil, and all these wonderful fellow creatures. Let's keep it going, rather than turning downward in a drawn-out spiral. Do we really want fish genes in our tomatoes? Are square tomatoes a good idea? I don't think so. This direction doesn't make sense to anyone who understands the situation. We have a great struggle before us, but we're all in it together. We have excellent tools, and alternatives to our destructive path. I'm excited to be one of millions of people actively making a contribution to a green and growing future.

Gay Hendricks: Bedroom Wars Meet Bosnian Wars

There's a great fundamental issue facing the world. It will make Earth much more—or much less—liveable. That issue is personal responsibility. In my work as a clinical psychologist, working with several thousand individuals and couples, I have noticed that it is a human habit to step into feeling like a victim. From that position, we blame other people or systems for our problems, instead of taking personal responsibility for fixing them.

Avoidance of personal responsibility is not just a habit; it's an addiction, just like a chemical addiction. Novelist James Michener, during a car trip through Afghanistan in 1949, happened to visit a village where a woman had just been stoned to death for adultery. It was obvious to him that the villagers were having a drug experience. They were elated all day after the stoning. That elation comes from the glee of affixing blame, from a powerful hit of that drug. Then, as the drug wore off, the villagers slid into a powerful, community-wide depression. For a couple of days, they were barely able to move. Their internal biochemistry changed completely during and after the stoning.

At the moment when you step out of personal responsibility and into the victim position, pointing the finger of blame, you relieve yourself of the awesome ecstasy of actually taking responsibility. It's the natural organic ecstasy that arises from standing in a fully co-creative position with the universe itself. When you step into blame, you relieve yourself of having to open up the circuitry in yourself to feel that ecstasy. That's the fundamental developmental problem we face at this stage of evolution:

Gay Hendricks, Ph.D., is the author and co-author of twenty-five books in conscious relationship, conscious business, and body-mind transformation. Included are such enduring bestsellers as *Conscious Loving* (Bantam, 1992), *Conscious Breathing* (Bantam, 1995), and *Conscious Living* (HarperSanFrancisco, 2001). Before founding his own institute, he was Professor of Counseling at the University of Colorado. Over the twenty-four years of their relationship, he and his wife Kathlyn have raised two children, accumulated a million frequent flyer miles and appeared on more than 500 radio and television programs. You can see him on the web at www.hendricks.com.

We're opening up the wiring that allows us to feel organic ecstasy for longer and longer periods of time. At present, most people can't sustain that state, so they slip back into a dangerous addiction to blame. In the body, the moment when the blame is assigned feels like a gleeful, "Gotcha!"

In its extreme form, this habit produces fundamentalism. People who have been programmed to live in that state of finger-pointing since they could walk, who have never had any other opportunity, think that this experience of glee is what life is all about. It can cause them to overlook the physical reality of flying a plane into a building and killing themselves, along with thousands of innocent people. It was a dangerous state centuries ago, when human beings had only rocks to throw at each other. Today, it's much more dangerous because human beings have rockets to throw at each other.

-§-

When we try new behavior and our biochemistry changes, it feels uncomfortable at first. Moving to new states of experience may feel foreign to our bodies.

-§-

Once we're accustomed to a certain chemical state inside of ourselves, we tend to feel comfortable with that even if it's attached to obviously dysfunctional behavior. When we try new behavior and our biochemistry changes, it feels uncomfortable at first. Moving to new states of experience may feel foreign to our bodies.

In recent years I've dived down deep to find out what the real issues are that drive the behavior of fundamentalism. I would occasionally see a couple in my office who behaved this way. One marriage stands out because both partners were Ph.D.s who had written brilliant scholarly papers. But when either of them encountered anything they perceived as a threat, their understanding flew out the window and they immediately became Stone Age fundamentalists, convinced that they *knew* that the other person was wrong.

It is extraordinarily important to understand the real fear underneath all of this. If you look around the world, you'll see that one of the big fears that drives conflicts is the fear of being left behind. Societies are *afraid* of being left behind even if they aren't actually *being* left behind.

Historically, human beings were left behind in very physical ways, such as watching a line of camels in the desert walking away from you because you were ill or old or unwanted. Or, you might be abandoned by your tribe because you were the wrong color or had too many toes.

In today's world the issue takes the form of a *conceptual* getting left behind. I've seen the radical Iraqi cleric Muktadr al-Sadr on television. He's a classic case of a fundamentalist who thinks he's right, who is convinced he knows who the enemy is. He has no compunction about blaming Jews and Westerners for the plight of his followers.

As al-Sadr walked through the street and across my television screen, about fifty of his followers strode behind him. Their body language proclaimed that these were people who couldn't do anything useful in the modern world. They didn't know how to drive a car, operate a computer, run a farm, manufacture goods, or otherwise make a positive contribution to their society. The best idea they could come up with, springing from that fear of getting left behind, was to keep other people from going too far ahead.

If you've given up and decided that you're not going to be able to support your family well, or have a good life yourself, there aren't too many options left. One option is to try to mess up the game for other people, so that nobody else is having a good time either, so that everybody else is as scared as you are. One of the fundamental, unconscious purposes of terrorism is to make sure that the rest of the population is as scared as the terrorist is.

-§-
One of the fundamental, unconscious purposes of terrorism is to make sure that the rest of the population is as scared as the terrorist is.
-§-

Healing starts from opening up this territory in yourself. That means acknowledging it; looking at ways in which *you* have that same feeling. Your action begins to open up a contagious field of awareness of that issue. This is an important thing we can all do. By looking at some of the deeper emotional issues that drive societal problems, people can begin to speak about them publicly. For example, instead of having a meeting between Palestinians and Jews in Israel that turns into a shouting match followed by a suicide bomber, the two sides might talk about their common fears of being left behind, rather than projecting them onto each other.

Here's a question that social groups can start with: What can we do to make sure that our children don't have to live in the same kind of fear that we live in?

The first issue that needs to be addressed with a group is the same issue couples have, and that is: Are you willing to make a commitment to solving this problem? The moment you ask that question, the most typical response is, "Well, yes, I'd be committed if she was." Then the couple needs an hour and a half to work through that issue.

At some point in the process, both people bond and turn on the therapist. I tell my therapy students that those are the only times you're worth what you're getting paid. When both members of the couple turn to you and say, "Hey, what the hell are you suggesting here? Are you suggesting that it's not his fault?" it's always a sweaty moment. Yet it's the moment when transformation can actually occur. Once you're through that barrier, the possibility opens up of both people taking responsibility and getting out of the field of blame.

A few years back, I was helping facilitate resolution between different factions in Bosnia: the Serbian Christians and the Bosnian Muslims. There were about sixty people in the group. I asked this basic question: Are you willing to resolve this issue between you? One of the men stood up and said, "This is not an issue that can be resolved, because it started in 1389."

He talked about 1389 like it was yesterday. And in a way it was, because these people had kept alive the source of this dispute between them through careful inoculation of each generation for *six hundred years!* That's a *major* commitment to not solving a problem.

The first problem you have to confront, whether you have a married couple or a room full of Bosnians, is despair that the problem is not solvable. That despair is always accompanied by about fifteen levels of justification for why it's not solvable, along with fifteen more levels of explanation about why it's the other person's fault. This despair has to aired in the service of resolving the problem.

When both sides make a commitment to resolving the issue, 90% of the work is done. Once you get to a place of genuine commitment, you have stepped into a co-creative role with not only the other side, but with the universe itself.

-§-

What can we do to make sure that our children don't have to live in the same kind of fear that we live in?

-§-

The breakthrough with the Serbs and Croats shows the power of belief to either destroy or heal. There were no physical differences between them; one wasn't brown and the other pink. The differences were on the conceptual level. When that set of concepts and beliefs changed, healing was suddenly possible. Both Serbs and Croats let go of their belief that there was an insurmountable barrier between them. The shift was displayed in the form of people looking at others and saying, "I had never really thought of you before as a human being. It never occurred to me that you love your children, too."

When you commit to resolving an issue, you step out of the state of consciousness called blame. When you do that, you automatically step into responsibility. There are several levels of responsibility. Junior level responsibility is going from blame to being willing to consider what you're contributing to this problem. Senior level responsibility is being so impeccably clear that human beings are responsible for themselves that you create a space in which it's possible for other people to step into that understanding. You have to train yourself to do that. If you don't, then the moment you get hungry or angry or tired or lonely, you start projecting blame onto other people.

At some point, some extremely visible person is going to take responsibility for his or her actions, and it will affect the world. I can feel the ripple of energy building up to this. I don't know who or where it will be, but I sense a big space of listening for that call. To get a sense of what this might look like, roll the clock back to the moment, during the Watergate scandal, when Richard Nixon said, "I am not a crook."

Imagine if instead he had said something like this: "People who work for me got discovered breaking into the Democratic National Committee headquarters. While I didn't know the details of this action, I certainly knew that a lot of shady things had been going on, and I didn't do anything to stop them. And because this has come to light so publicly, I'm looking inside myself and I find a very sleazy streak in me. I'm beginning to wonder about how to heal that in myself, because as I tune in to it, I see it's been there as long as I've been here. Since you all voted for me, I think you ought to do the same thing, because I wouldn't have been elected with this sleazy streak if it didn't match something in you. So let's all use this as an opportunity to look inside and find where we're out of integrity with ourselves, where we've stopped telling the truth to ourselves, and where we think of ourselves as victims. Let's see if we can use this whole situation to learn something that can heal a lot of the divisions in this country."

-§-

The first problem you have to confront, whether you have a married couple or a room full of Bosnians, is despair that the problem is not solvable.

-§-

That kind of moment could change history. We haven't seen such a moment yet, though there have been glimpses of it. It's a very difficult thing to do because it requires a rare level of emotional maturity.

If I were addressing the U.N. General Assembly with my most profound word of advice, I'd probably ask just one question: "Would you be willing to stay completely out of blaming anyone else for the next year, and instead make a sincere commitment to resolving all the issues we confront?"

I've asked that question of literally thousands of people, many of whom had gone to great lengths to come to me and were paying me very large sums of money. Even with those high stakes, 99 times out of 100 the person goes into the default position of blame *immediately,* just upon hearing that question. Weaning ourselves from that stance takes patience, repetition and skill.

Do you want to be right or be happy? I invite you to make that tiny choice that is actually a huge choice. You only have to do it once, and the whole field changes. After that it's a matter of practice. It's like the first time you ride a bicycle. You wobble for ten feet then fall over. You get back on and master riding twenty feet. The first time you stay upright is the moment everything changes. Mastering personal responsibility involves the same learning curve. After a while you feel great when you do it, and miserable when you don't.

Wherever you see the tendency in yourself to default to blame, you have identified the exact place that needs healing. Healing for yourself comes when you take 100% impeccable responsibility for yourself; healing for the planet comes when you create a space for other people to take 100% impeccable responsibility as well. Do it yourself, and you will have a contagious effect on those around you.

Duane Elgin: Reprogramming the Global Neural Network

The Mind-Body Challenge of Civilizations

Over the past several decades, countless books, tapes, and self-help workshops have been developed that focus on the critical connection between our mental and physical well-being. The connection between mind and body is now broadly recognized. For example, the Internet search engine Google, gives well over a million responses for the phrase "mind-body." Many people bring a daily awareness of the mind-body connection to their personal health. Unfortunately, this important wisdom from the personal realm has not been applied with equal effectiveness when it comes to our mind-body health as a nation.

Stated simply, here is the mind-body challenge that I see at a social level: I believe that the collective mind of our society is manifested primarily through the mass media. In other words, the mass media is the most direct and visible expression of our social brain or collective mental functioning as civilizations. In the U.S. 99% of all homes have a TV set and the average person watches nearly four hours per day. Television has become our primary window onto the world and the mirror in which we see ourselves. Most people in the U.S. get most of their news about the world from television. Like it or not, television has become the central nervous system of modern society. When we turn on the television set and search through the channels, we are literally moving through the stream of consciousness of a civilization. We all swim in this electronic ocean and it has a powerful influence on our collective well-being. Just as our mental

Duane Elgin, MBA, M.A., is an author, speaker, evolutionary activist, and Internet entrepreneur. Author of *Voluntary Simplicity* (Perennial Currents, 1998), *Promise Ahead* (Perennial Currents, 2001) and *Awakening Earth* (Morrow, 1993), he is a former senior social scientist at SRI International, where he coauthored numerous studies on the long-range future for the Environmental Protection Agency, the president's science advisor, and the National Science Foundation. Prior to SRI, Elgin worked as a senior staff member for the National Commission on Population Growth and the American Future. Find him on the web at www.awakeningearth.org.

habits impact the physical health of individuals, so too can our collective mental habits that are manifested through the mass media impact every aspect of the health of civilizations.

At this pivotal time in human evolution, it is vitally important that the mass media and its messages serve our psychological and spiritual health and not distort our collective intelligence, imagination, and evolution. However, the collective mind of our consumer society is dominated by the profit-making interests of the mass media and, with profits as the primary guide, our social mind-set is moving out of touch with the real world. To illustrate, in the past generation in the U.S., divorce rates have doubled, teen suicide rates have tripled, a number of crime rates have quadrupled, and there is an epidemic of obesity. At a global level, physical evidence of ill-health includes global warming with increasingly powerful storms, the extinction of a vast number of plant and animal species, and the rapid depletion of critical resources such as fresh water and cheap oil. In short, the American dream advertised so profusely in today's mass media is fast becoming the world's nightmare. The bottom line is this: If we are to build a sustainable and compassionate future, it will require corresponding changes in our social mind-set—and the messages and images of "success" and the "good life" that are portrayed through the mass media.

-§-
At this pivotal time in human evolution, it is vitally important that the mass media and its messages serve our psychological and spiritual health.
-§-

For the past thirty years, I've been exploring the process of "awakening" at a civilizational scale and I have concluded that the mass media is the primary carrier of our collective "thought stream." In turn, how we use the mass media can foster either collective greed and fear—or collective awakening and compassion. For the individual, awakening involves developing a capacity for reflective consciousness; paying attention to the flow of thoughts and feelings as we move through life. Similarly, for a civilization, awakening involves developing a capacity for reflective consciousness at the scale of the entire society, and the ability to examine our collective thoughts and feelings as we move through our social evolution. With awakening, a conscious civilization will not consume media so passively but will be more purposefully engaged in directing the media's attention in ways that serve the health of the social mind.

What is required for the mass media to serve our collective awakening? After several decades of organizing, I've concluded that the basic challenge is with us as citizens. For example, most citizens are ignorant of the fact that television broadcasters that use the public's airwaves (ABC, CBS, NBC, and Fox) have a strict legal responsibility to serve the public interest of the community before their own profits. Currently, most people complain passively about the media, not recognizing that we have the legal right and the affirmative obligation to hold the media accountable for serving the public interest and the health of our collective mind. However, with a new "politics of collective consciousness" we could mobilize electronic town meetings and other forms of dialogue to come together as communities in order to transform the heart of the media—broadcast television.

A Menu of Perspectives

Here are five different ways of framing the issue of the mass media and the mental health of civilizations.

1) Our evolutionary challenge is to see that the mass media is manufacturing desire, and this is creating a psychology of mass consumption that cannot be sustained. By programming television primarily for commercial success, the mind-set of our civilization is simultaneously being programmed for ecological failure. Rather than awakening the public to the challenge of sustainability, the television industry is distracting us from this critical concern. Instead of educating for a workable future over the long run, the television industry is promoting consumption in the short run. The average person sees roughly 25,000 commercials a year. These are more than ads for a product; they are also advertisements for a consumerist lifestyle and the attitudes and values that support that lifestyle. As we move into a new era where the challenge is to live sustainably, we need new programming that reflects the new realities.

-§-

By programming television primarily for commercial success, the mind-set of our civilization is simultaneously being programmed for ecological failure.

-§-

Psychologist Carl Jung said that schizophrenia is a condition in which "the dream becomes the reality." Has the American dream of a consumerist lifestyle become our primary reality? Is this manufactured reality increasingly out of touch with the reality of nature and our soulful existence? Are we building the foundation of our global consciousness literally upon a schizophrenic base? Are we implanting a deep, and unnecessary, conflict into the structure of our collective psyche? The American people (and much of the rest of the world exposed to American television) are being placed in an impossible double-bind: the mass media that dominates our consciousness tells us to buy ever more while our ecological concern for the planet inclines us to consume ever less. We are literally creating a schizophrenic civilization that is divided against itself.

2) Our evolutionary challenge is transforming the lack of reflective consciousness in the media. The media does not hold a mirror up to itself. The last taboo topic on television is television itself and its own practices, ethics, and priorities. Never do we see the cameras turned around to look back and investigate how the television system is doing its job. Television turns a blind eye to itself and thereby is able to hide many of its practices and policies that are so detrimental. Reflective consciousness is healing for the individual, and can be healing for the media that is the social brain of our civilization.

3) Our evolutionary challenge is to see what is missing from the mass media. The media focuses on sensational events and personal conflicts and generally fails to report on the really big stories of our time. In turn, if we don't hear regularly televised reports about climate change, species-extinction, resource depletion, and so on, then the general public will assume that these areas are not yet critical. However, just because the mass media ignores urgent trends does not mean it will conveniently cease to exist. These largely ignored but immensely powerful trends are, in this generation, forever changing the Earth as a natural system and social system.

4) Our evolutionary challenge is the lack of love being communicated through our primary tools of mass communication. Our global future depends on love—which blossoms when there is mutual understanding; which develops when there is authentic and meaningful communication; which builds upon a foundation of mutual respect. Therefore, we need to bring a loving consciousness into the mass media if we are to have a future that is sustainable and compassionate. If the mass media fails to actively cultivate qualities of empathy, mutual understanding, and communication and, instead, fosters a callous disregard for life (with mindless violence and exploitative sex), then, we will create a self-fulfilling reality of suffering. The challenge is to discover ways of using the mass media that nourish, strengthen and enrich the life of the individual soul and our capacity for collective service.

5) Our evolutionary challenge is that we are not cultivating healthy "factors of social enlightenment" via the mass media. Applying insights from meditative traditions, a healthy "social brain" will be characterized by qualities such as mindfulness, equanimity, and concentration. For example:

• Mindfulness—Is the broadcast media being used to foster awareness of the condition of the larger world, or are the mass media largely oblivious to the big picture, inattentive to critical trends, and unmindful of where the world is headed?

• Concentration—Is the mass media being used to mobilize public attention and focus on critical choices that need our attention? Or is it used to distract the public so that we cannot focus our societal attention on critical concerns? Are we able to cut through the turbulence of our social chatter and distraction and, with penetrating attention, bring a steady focus to concerns vital to our future?

• Equanimity—Is the mass media reactive, wildly thrashing our societal attention about? Or does the media remain relatively calm and steady in the midst of social turbulence, chaos, distress? Instead of being thrown off balance, are we able, as a society, to remain steadily present and responsive?

Just as these qualities or factors can be cultivated by an individual, so too can they be cultivated by an entire civilization. These are vitally important factors of social awakening and they may well determine whether civilizations will be able to respond successfully to the global ecological crisis rapidly closing in around us.

There are multiple ways of framing the mind-body connection between our mass media and our social body. Nothing short of our evolutionary intelligence as a civilization is being tested as we work to build a mature and compassionate social mind that is in alignment with creating a healthy and sustainable social body.

Transforming Our Social Mind

We have seen that, although the power of positive visualization is widely recognized in the realm of individual mind-body medicine, we have been slow to apply this wisdom to the healing of our social mind-body. As a society, we have yet to appreciate the power of the collective self-images that are presented in the social mirror of the media. Whatever they may be, the persistent self-images that we present to ourselves through the mass media set into motion a self-fulfilling process of realization. Looking ahead, this means that we cannot consciously build a positive future that we have not first collectively imagined. We are a visual species. When we can see it, we can become it and build it.

-§-
Nothing short of our evolutionary intelligence as a civilization is being tested as we work to build a mature and compassionate social mind.
-§-

Here is just one example of the kind of television programming that I believe could stir public consciousness into authentic reflection about how we are using our collective mind. To balance the aggressive onslaught of consumer commercials, alternative commercials that I call *"Earthvisions,"* could be developed. Produced by non-profit organizations and local community groups working in partnership with local television stations, *Earthvisions* could be thirty-second mini-stories portraying some aspect of a sustainable and meaningful future. They could be low in cost and high in creativity, and done with playfulness, compassion, and humor. They could focus on humankind's connection with the web of life, or on positive visions of the future from the perspective of future generations, or on awakening an appreciation of nature and sustainability. In my opinion, the public would be delighted with these refreshing perspectives. Once underway, a virtual avalanche of Earthvisions could emerge from communities around the world and be shared over the Internet. Other media—such as public access TV, newspapers, radio, and specialty publications—could be used to enrich the dialogue.

We could also develop a rich array of programming beyond thirty-second spots. For instance, television comedies could offer a humorous look at everyday life in a sustainable society such as the challenges of living in an "eco-village community." Television news-magazine shows could be developed that focus in-depth on themes pertaining to a sustainable future and our evolutionary journey as a human family. Dramas could explore the deeper tensions and larger opportunities that families and communities may encounter as we begin designing ourselves into nature and a promising future. Viewer feedback forums could enable local communities to give regular feedback to television broadcasters regarding programming that truly serves the public interest.

By bringing inspiring stories, positive self-images, and hopeful visions of the future into the mass media, we simultaneously bring those healing visions into the collective mind of our civilization. Healing our collective mind-body connection requires a new and far more conscious relationship between the public and the mass media. Transforming our relationship with the mass media is far more than a matter of taste; it is essential for the success of our evolutionary journey as an awakening species.

-§-
How can communities "take back" the public airwaves for the purposes of mature visioning and the exploration of a more promising future?
-§-

If we are to heal our mass media, then it requires that we ask difficult but immensely important questions: Is the mass media creating a level of desire for consumption around the world that cannot be sustained? If media-generated desires cannot be sustained, then how will those who are left out respond? How well does the "media mind-set" of consumerism fit the reality of our changing world? Does our use of the mass media accurately reflect our evolutionary intelligence as a species? Is the mass media's focus on consumerism diverting our cultural attention, dumbing-down humanity's self-image, and holding back our social evolution? What is a more positive and elevated view of humanity's potentials? How might the mass media nourish and strengthen our culture and enable us to cope with unprecedented ecological, social, and spiritual challenges? How can communities "take back" the public airwaves for the purposes of mature visioning and the exploration of a more promising future?

This is an inquiry into the most practical and direct expression of our collective consciousness in our everyday lives. The quality of our shared, social attention is the most precious resource that we possess as a society. Instead of taking our collective consciousness for granted as an unchangeable given, our responsibility is to inspect, explore, and call forth the most healthy qualities of consciousness that we can muster. To place the health of our shared consciousness on our social agenda requires us to stand back from unconscious immersion in our collective mind-set and recognize our capacity to evolve our civilizational consciousness. Because we have never before had the ability to consciously evolve our collective consciousness, this is an unfamiliar territory for everyone—citizens, political leaders, media managers, educators, and more. Nonetheless, healing the mass media from its narrow and shallow view of the world may be one of the most decisive factors in determining whether we will be successful in building a sustainable and compassionate future for ourselves as a species.

Neriah Lothamer: The New Chivalry

As I climb to the crest of the hill, the deep blue sky opens out over a lush green valley. Birds fly around my head and swoop down to drink from the gently flowing river at the valley's floor. The air is clean, filled with shifting fragrances of wildflowers. I find the shade of a large tree inviting, sit on the soft lush grass and lean against its trunk, looking out over the beautiful valley.

People in colorful costumes dance and sing, parading through a grassy meadow near the river. Sprinkled along the path are numerous tepees, yurts, geodesic domes, Bedouin tents, and brightly colored canopies. I see people of all races: Tibetans, Hindus, Native Americans, Africans, Europeans, Asians, and indigenous people—a truly international celebration. This beautiful, colorful display of humanity's diverse spiritual cultures parading together strikes a thrilling cord in the depths of my being.

Musicians and drummers blend diverse textures and heavenly harmonies. Like angelic conductors, they inspire other voices to naturally join in and sing along. Dancers parade with colorful banners, flags, costumes, and streaming ribbons. Brightly colored kites and balloons fill the air with festive anticipation. Baton twirlers, clowns, stilt-walkers, and giant puppets gesture for all to join in the joyful throng. With painted faces and fancy costumes, a procession of dancing children cheer with delight as they enter the parade. Smiling, happy people are everywhere.

Neriah Lothamer, who since 1967 has produced, promoted, and recorded alternative culture events, is a cultural archivist and visionary activist. His background includes Catholic seminary, training in Neurolinguistic Programming, Nonviolent Communication and Ericksonian hypnosis. He has facilitated encounter groups, consensus communities, Rainbow gatherings, rock and roll shows, and alternative festivals. His activist experiences include the Kent State University strikes, the Black Hills Alliance, resistance to the relocation of the Hopi-Dineh tribes, the Headwaters Alliance, and the Medical Marijuana initiatives. Details: www.NeriahLothamer.com.

As she enters a huge, circular meadow, the old Native American woman who is leading the parade blows a conch. The low deep sound trumpets long and loud down the valley. A chorus of echoing conch shells reply from the surrounding hills. Holding a bundle of smoking sage, the old woman circles the meadow four times chanting a prayer. Then she walks to the center of the circle and raises a long-stemmed pipe covered with medicine feathers high above her head, pointing to the sky. A group of people carry a large wooden pole to the spot where she stands in the center of the meadow. Beautifully bedecked with ribbons and feathers, the pole has been carved with religious symbols and words of peace from many different cultures. More people come, carrying rocks to stack around the base of the pole and secure it upright.

The parade enters, celebrants circle around the edges of the meadow until the space is filled with thousands. The drumming reaches a crescendo. The crowd roars. Then, all become silent and everyone sits down. The elder woman remains standing, looking at the top of the pole, holding her pipe aloft. Silently, she moves the pipe in prayer to the seven sacred directions. When she finishes her invocation, she places the pipe at the foot of the pole and sits down next to it in silence.

A peaceful quiet pervades the meadow. People are rapt in prayer. Minutes become hours as the silence deepens; a profound state of collective reverence is reached. When the sun is at high noon, a low humming sound begins. The hum grows and grows and for twenty minutes, thousands of voices join in a powerful, harmonious hum that finally bursts into a climax of hoops, hollers and alleluias. Musicians and drummers resume their lively jubilee. People stroll, talk, and dance, serenaded by the spontaneous orchestra. As the afternoon grows late, an early dinner is brought out, another prayer is shared, and all sit down in concentric circles to communion at the meal.

As I look over the surrounding hills, I see the graceful movement of a beautiful woman dancing through the forest. Her dance is fluid, effortless and utterly natural as she drifts through the trees. Entranced by her grace, I watch for awhile, enjoying the delight her dance inspires in my heart and mind. Several minutes pass before I realize this angel is not simply dancing her joy: she is picking up litter! I am so inspired that I joyfully pick up trash wherever go throughout the rest of my day.

Everyone I meet bears a welcoming smile. Folks hauling food and supplies on their backs smile with beaming awareness. Latrine diggers, wood choppers, and kitchen crews work happily in service of community needs. Circles of people cluster around, sharing healing techniques, stories and visions, and speaking their highest hopes and dreams. Volunteers are first entertained and then enlisted by a colorful cast of characters. Community health and safety needs are portrayed in a theatrical, artful display. A tangible spirit of cooperation makes taking care of basic community needs natural and easy with plenty of time left over for teaching, learning, playing, enjoying, appreciating, trading, creating, storytelling, entertaining, healing, and praying together.

Is this a utopian dream? Or is it a peace-lover's futuristic fantasy?

The events herein described are neither fiction, nor fantasy. They are an aggregate of actual experiences I have had over the past thirty-two years. The events did not spring out of imagination, but out of personal experience. When common sense in the midst of these experiences demanded that I function in a responsible way, I could and did. I cooked, changed diapers, dug latrines, chopped wood, and put out forest fires. All this often without electricity or automobiles, and in the company of thousands of others. I am not describing an alternate universe, although such gatherings are certainly an alternate reality to the common everyday world we call life in these United States.

-§-

Common sense is the radar that helps us navigate without getting sunk by hidden dangers under the surface.

-§-

I have attended many such events. Along with the exhilaration of gathering together—the awe of sharing community alternatives, the inspiration of evolving a whole new human social system—comes a tremendous amount of work. The work involves much more than manual labor; it involves the hard work of communication. How do 20,000 people with children survive as a cohesive community in the wilds? Group coordination is required, as are many agreements about how to keep our food and water safe for consumption, our women and children clear of danger. Learning how to keep the peace is essential. And all it takes, oddly enough, are two things humans possess in ample supply: common sense and imagination.

Common sense says, people are just people; we all have basic needs. Take care of basic human needs and the rest is up to individual free will. Common sense also tells us that one person's freedom ends where it deprives another of his or her freedom. But we need imagination to apply common sense at large gatherings. And we need common sense to temper imagination. We need the ability to perceive reality without the blinding veil of mental concepts that also makes good use of the gut feelings that come through our solar plexus. Common sense is the radar that helps us navigate without getting sunk by hidden dangers under the surface.

In many ways, the gatherings described above can be seen as a collaborative experiment in right-imagination or "right mindfulness" as taught by the Buddha. These events have shown me what is possible for humanity. By combining common sense and imagination we can live in harmony. We can evolve systems that care for our basic human needs by applying our collective imagination tempered with common sense. To do this we share a code of ethics that comes from our prayers to bring the peace of Heaven on Earth, and that code of ethics comes from the Code of Life.

The Code of Life is in our DNA, in our blood, in our cells. Expressed in the highest values humans share in common, the Code of Life defines the ways of the physical universe: the parameters and principles by which matter and energy manifest. These principles have evolved human consciousness; they completely compose, support, and sustain human consciousness. They are fundamental truths of the universe that existed before humans, and will continue when humans are gone.

The human heart pulses through an alliance of forces that rule stars as well as atoms, forces that create complex human organisms and develop within them a capacity for consciousness. Whether conceived as deities or "the one true god" by human definition, these forces are everywhere, in everything. The principles they enforce permeate our experience: physical, mental, emotional, and spiritual. Evolution meets humanity head-on with these principles, challenging us to recycle our traditional values and beliefs.

-§-
The human heart pulses through an alliance of forces that rule stars as well as atoms.
-§-

Although humanity's moral and ethical codes have their roots in history, the current values of humanity are in a vast transition. Our twenty-first century world is an ever-accelerating whirlwind of change. Mayan prophecies suggest an exponential acceleration in human evolution at this time. Humans are discovering more in all dimensions because of this accelerated growth of knowledge and technology, a phenomenon we must understand as both internal and external.

Julian Huxley said, "In mankind, evolution is conscious of itself." What if the goal of evolution is the consciousness possible in the human cerebral cortex? What if our consciousness-of-self is what gives evolution the resource to achieve spiritual awareness? Pierre Teilhard De Chardin believed the conscious unification of spirit and matter to be the purpose of evolution. He suggested humans are not only capable of this consciousness individually, but also collectively. "It is the Spirit of Evolution which, suppressing the spirit of egoism, is of its own right springing to new life in our hearts, and in such a way as to counteract those elements in the forces of collectivization which are poisonous to life." De Chardin suggested that the human capacity to gather information and to reflect upon ourselves, individually and collectively, creates a collective consciousness that will eventually lead individuals to see themselves as a cell in the collective body of humanity.

Silenced by the Church for his radical views, De Chardin wrote letters which were passed around underground and eventually published. The "mystical body of Christ" and the "second coming" or "parousia" as

De Chardin called it, are all the same thing. He believed the second coming meant individual enlightenment and awareness of the Christ within, coupled with an awareness of the same Christ in others, in humanity as a whole, and in all life on Earth. Teilhard de Chardin's mystical understanding of evolution shows Western mystics how to embrace evolutionary theory as something spiritual rather than materialistic. The transformation of the world is the same as the transformation of each person—and changes are crucial and profound in both. We are evolution conscious of itself, evolution seeking fusion of spirit and matter. This understanding ennobles our spirit, and transforms the context in which we live.

It is July 4, 2004. Twenty thousand people sit silently in a forest meadow for the annual prayer gathering. The silence is awesome. Birds sing in the trees. The breeze of early morning rises through the grass. A profound stillness begins to envelope my heart, but I am struggling with anger. Two old friends sit near me in the circle, the very two my anger has grudged throughout the last year. I judge them for betraying the trust of friendship and being malicious. I feel like hitting, hurting, berating, screaming, and yes, even that old feeling inside of wanting to kill haunts me as I try to pray. I am suddenly aware that my struggle is exactly what humanity, as a whole, needs to heal to bring peace to the world.

-§-

We are evolution conscious of itself, evolution seeking fusion of spirit and matter.

-§-

I know I am responsible for my experience, and that blame does not serve anyone. I begin to accept reality. I feel an opening in my heart, the light of peace relaxing me. I am aware that in oneness is diversity and within divinity is all possibility. I remember my commitment to revere the divine in everyone. I let go of judgments, realizing that discernment is more appropriate. This is helping me accept and love my friends despite my dislike of their behavioral choices which have shown me I need to stay safely out of range.

I begin to imagine integrity as a code of ethics. Evolutionary forces seem to coalesce with my prayers in this meadow. I feel human, archetypal and spiritual currents moving between the people in the circle and all across this planet. My turbulent emotions calm down and I feel peace again.

Evolution has met something new in the human cerebral cortex: imagination. Every law, rule, religion, belief, and value originates in the imagination of the human mind. Through human imagination and human belief, evolution deals its hand. People who lived a hundred years ago would have been stunned into disbelief if a time travel machine allowed them to drop in on your typical day. How shocked might we be if the same time machine could afford us a glimpse of what will be a hundred years hence? Imagining this, I see two clear scenarios, both of which demand a better code of conduct for humanity.

The first scenario is apocalyptic, wherein the world is almost destroyed and human life takes a giant evolutionary step backward. The second scenario is the utopian vision: humanity working in natural harmony with each other and the Earth. Innumerable scenarios exist between these extremes, but all point out the need for a better code—one that diverts our current path toward global suicide.

This is not the first time in human history the demand for a code of honor has been felt. A similar demand brought forward a code of decency and respect known as Chivalry at a time when armored men on tall warhorses could hack up anyone standing in their way. To kill and ride out of town with whatever they could claim was all too easy. Men would plunder, pillage, rape, burn, murder, scorn, torture, and enslave in the name of "might is right." Chivalry emerged to extol the merits of using force judiciously and only to defend oneself and the helpless. As a set of principles to which a man could aspire, it refined men's behavior and defined Knighthood, a societal position of honor.

-§-
Involution evolves and evolution involves. As we process our inner experience, we become more involved in the collective human experience.
-§-

The emerging code of humanity likewise requires we summon chivalrous refinements of character, such as gallantry, courtesy, and respectful attention to women and children. The new code is different in many ways to Chivalry, however, and must be designed for our time. Blind obedience to any church is no more appropriate than blind obedience to a liege lord. Devotion to divinity within each person is preferable to blind obedience to organized religion. This is a radical change we would do well to recognize, for it is a radical change in our understanding of the Code of Life. Compelled by the evolutionary forces of fusion, humanity must reject the divisionary and separatist aspects of religion. Respect and tolerance for all religions is now required. This revolution in our thinking, attitudes, and beliefs is the result of humanity reflecting on the historical abuses by and of religions. Propelled by the urge toward unification which is motivating us to live more harmoniously, humanity must now use imagination to find religious tolerance, rather than continue the "holy wars."

Involution evolves and evolution involves. As we process our inner experience, we become more involved in the collective human experience. Involvement happens through awareness gained through reflection on our collective experience. Imagination allows us to consider our options. Without imagination, we have no choice but to keep repeating the same mistakes. Imagination is evolution's way of using the human cerebral cortex to achieve the prime directive of conscious unity. Imagination empowers consciousness to reflect upon what has yet to be experienced and made manifest.

Evolution meets imagination with common sense. Without common sense as a reality check, imagination would run off on any number of tangents. Common sense not only means common to all but accessible to all. This is why the new code is based on the Code of Life. The Code of Life can be found everywhere and its principles are recognized by all Creation.

The New Chivalry reveals how to communicate; how to speak and listen with respect and attention; it shows us the heart of consensus. Communication can solve any problem. Consensus, and the circumspect point of view it brings, allows communities to get needed support to solve their problems. This takes time to learn, but the "how to" of communicating clearly and learning to listen with compassionate consideration is essential to this emerging code.

The New Chivalry reveals the way of peaceful nonviolence. It shows how to achieve peace and nonviolence in words and deeds. It shows how to start with ourselves and create a peaceful life experience. It identifies the problem areas needing attention that bring distress and turmoil within us, the exact problem areas that erupt violently in our language and behavior toward others. It does all this by revealing the natural love in our heart, the affection which inspires our respect and consideration for others.

-§-
Humanity must reject the divisionary and separatist aspects of religion.
-§-

Through love, the code reveals how we can experience ourselves and our world in a healthy, happy, and harmonious manner. When we love someone enough to learn not to hit them angrily, not to threaten them, not to sexually abuse them, and not to yell at them; then we feel like changing. Unless we really feel the love within us, we will not change our harmful behaviors.

To love God by praying before statues is easy compared to loving God in people. The devotion required to see God in each person and in all things is challenging, and stretches the soul to embrace what is hardest to accept. When we revere the essential "Buddha nature" in even the most unenlightened; we can accept that our own evil exists within the omnipresence of God. To deny evil is to empower it. When we face evil in ourselves and in others, we loosen its stronghold. Facing evil can only be done by simultaneously facing divinity. It is the divinity within us, struggling with the bestial values and beliefs of our ancestors, that can imagine new ways to ensure survival now.

We, as the human part of evolution, must learn to control our childish tyrannical behavior before we destroy ourselves. In the Pathwork lectures, Eva Pierrakos said, "Humanity has now left behind infancy and childhood. It is just about coming through its adolescence, but is not yet a mature, adult entity." Humanity is changing its values, seeking more mature freedoms, and learning about self-responsibility and partnership. As a species, we are at war with ourselves, divided by contradictory views, confused by philosophical and cultural splits. As Pierrakos points out, "The organism which, in perfection, could and will function harmoniously, in union with itself, must be at war with itself as long as it is divided within by unrealistic concepts, wrong conclusions, self-centered and infantile pursuits, limited outlooks, lack of concern, subjectivity and unfairness due to blind, isolating tendencies…the individual human body, soul, and spirit is identical with the body, soul and spirit of humanity as a whole." According to Pierrakos, the abuses of humanity, of our collective past, need to be healed as well as each one's personal past. Humanity must consciously examine the ugliest memories it has sealed behind denial.

To enter into this global self-examination means accepting that history has been rewritten by each conquering culture to show their version of the facts. To do this we must be willing to see our favorite superstitions revealed as just that: superstition, not fact.

-§-
As a species, we are at war with ourselves, divided by contradictory views, confused by philosophical and cultural splits.
-§-

Awareness is now demanded by mama evolution, an awareness which both takes responsibility for the past and looks to the future. When we wake up in an auto going downhill out of control with no one in the driver's seat; pointing the finger of blame, or trying to escape will not work. Times like this demand fast action and force us to mature, first by recognizing that we have the ability to respond and second, by choosing to respond with swift, decisive action.

The only way I know to feel responsibility is to tune into love; love for myself, divinity, humanity, those dear to me, and Life on Earth. Love is not lust or selfish pleasure. It is an experience that reaches into my soul, stretches deep into my body, and erupts in my heart with tears of bliss. Love makes me feel like saving the world.

The challenge to all humanity is to love more than ever now. This love is not the "gimme" type of love, but a giving that spontaneously springs from the heart. This love needs no forcing, coaxing, cajoling, or manipulation. This love knows no fear. This love accepts the challenge of bringing true and lasting peace among the nations. This love rolls up its shirtsleeves and exuberantly exclaims, "We can do it!"

Humanity is not you or me; humanity is we. Humanity is not divisive, but inclusive. We all share in this adventure—within each of us is the source that manifested this moment in time and space. Humanity is a parade of diversity we all walk in, as well as a parade of resources we all check out in time. Human nature is humanity's nature, it is "our" nature. This human nature is parading now toward changing values. This human nature is you and I and everyone else lifting our eyes toward those banners that lead the parade, and saying in our hearts with them:

"We are the sources of all movements, the mothers of all gatherings, and the creators of all religions. We have spawned the visionary Bohemian rhapsody of love, freedom, and beauty throughout the world. We bring joy everywhere with our entertaining way of enlightening everything on our path."

"We have opened the hearts of children who seek the truth about Life and Earth and Spirit. We have shown them how to follow Spirit where it leads and to give thanks for what we can share together. We have brought the elders of the ancient ones to speak to our children and we carry their teachings everywhere we go. The Mayan calendar, the Hopi prophecies, the legends of indigenous Americans, Revelations; all these tell of and prove our existence. We are here now to point to the light in each and every human, we invoke its activation; we beseech and coax and cajole and urge it to come forward in all its brightness, and shine."

-§-

The challenge to all humanity is to love more than ever now.

-§-

"We are the drummers, the artists, the musicians, the feeders of the poor and homeless, the gypsies, the eccentric and colorfully dressed, the monks and priestesses, the goddesses and the highest of the holy laborers. We can leap in divine bliss as we dance through our lives. We are the result of humanity's deepest prayers, we are the children of light and peace and love."

"Love, and the oneness it pulses with, is our heart beating with the eternal prime directive of evolution. We are pointing to this Light of Love, and inviting humanity to join in the greatest miracle of love that has ever happened: Peace on Earth."

Now we begin to express the love of which humanity is really capable, Love incarnate.

Patricia Sun: The Evolutionary Leap

The human race is in the midst of an evolutionary leap. The evolutionary leap is characterized primarily by a capacity to perceive in a new way. This capacity is so unique to our past experience that it produces something of a crisis in the world. It is interesting that the ancient Chinese ideograph for crisis is the combination of opportunity and danger. We are beginning to face the dangers, but we need to understand the wondrous opportunities that await us.

"The technological and scientific advances primarily characterized by Einstein's physics brought us not only the atom bomb with its capacity to annihilate the world, and the ability to put satellites in space for total communication on the planet, it has actually set us up so that we must learn to love one another. Learning to communicate, to feel one another, and to understand the other person's reality and experience creates an almost miraculous expansion of the whole.

"This vision of the evolutionary leap is in almost every religion, every political situation. Every political vision and goal cares for this moment when we really fulfill our potential and our abilities. I don't think it's an accident that we use only one-tenth of our brains and that all human beings feel that it should be different—it should be better. Through our personal commitment to heal ourselves, to be open when it is difficult, to heal fear wherever we find it, we make room for genuine trust—which will lead to the common sense and wonderfulness of peace."

Patricia Sun is a communication expert and philosopher whose insights are ahead of her time. Her pioneering work has supported and seeded many individuals in the human potential and spiritual movement over the last three decades. She is the Director of ICU, Institute of Communication for Understanding, and has her own daily radio show "Connections with Patricia Sun"; her workshops, audiotapes and conferences appear in over forty-nine countries. As well as doing private consulting, she has lectured everywhere from the FBI to Stanford Medical School to the United Nations, and her work can be found on the web at www.PatriciaSun.com.

These were my opening words when I met with the Soviet Women's Committee in Moscow in May 1985.

These women—prominent doctors, lawyers, magazine editors, and the first woman astronaut—in response to this brief statement, embraced me with a reverence and genuine respect that their counterparts in America would probably not have offered in a similar situation.

During my apolitical peace travels in Russia, whenever I saw fear of Americans in the eyes of the people—especially elderly women—it hurt me deeply. I would look into their eyes with as much love as I could hold, and say in Russian, "Peace and Friendship." The women would fall into my arms and sob, overwhelmed by relief and hope. This happened many, many times. They would pat my face tenderly as grief, fear and relief—and then gratitude—flowed from them. I shall never forget those women. What a remarkable counterpoint to what Americans felt about the Soviets at a time when both nations were immersed in the fear-driven relations of the Cold War.

As an historical event and personal experience for those of us who lived through it, the fall of the Iron Curtain teaches us a great deal about how to swing wide the door to pioneering outcomes in the wider world. By staying open, we allow something new and more honest to happen within ourselves as individuals and as nations. That change restructures how we perceive situations—and therefore, how we communicate with each other. It changes the solutions that we can create. It changes the outcome.

Former Soviet President Gorbachev chose the guiding principles of *perestroika,* which means "restructuring," and *glasnost,* which means "openness," to help the Soviet Union through a massive transition. He led an amazing bloodless coup and a complete transition for his country without exercising the totalitarian option. Instead, he allowed for relations to stay open in the midst of turmoil. That type of earnest openness is the very prerequisite that *creates a new possibility* where it would not otherwise emerge. Gorbachev created an environment of safety and tolerance that midwifed the transformation of a huge country—without force, without control or domination, and without bloodshed. His earnest respect for the means created an opening for greater liberty.

The Evolutionary Leap

The enormous changes we are seeing in the outer world are part of an evolutionary leap our species is in the process of making. Part of this evolutionary leap involves a change in the way our brains work and in what we can perceive. We are a very young species—so new we are not finished yet. We are evolving the latent potential of our brain to become a transcendent whole brain. The two hemispheres have a potential of synergy that we barely use, but which is released by healing old defense mechanisms. We respect and own the power of paradox, by using logic and intuition together as we think, perceive and solve problems. This new style of thinking is humanity maturing as a species.

Old-style thinking is characterized by cause and effect, blame and judgment, black or white, good or bad, "you did or you didn't" attitudes. The old style of thinking is reductionistic and leaves little or no room for the *process and the discovery of new insight,* which is all life, really, is. In reality, we seldom have black or white, or even shades of gray, but an endless myriad of colors varying in shade, tone and hue.

I was ten years old when I learned that we use only 10% of the brain. "Why would nature do that?" I asked myself. "Nature is never wasteful. It can't be true." Over time, I began to see that this condition was symptomatic of a stage in our development. All the things I was trying to figure out came into sharper focus. Why do people suffer? Why do they lie to one another? Why do they hurt each other? Why do parents refuse to understand their children? Why are teachers so ineffective? Why do men and women fear each other? Why don't doctors seem to know what they are doing? The answer came to me: "We're just not finished yet." There is more to come.

What's In the Way?

A primary difficulty in our current stage of development is that we block empathy. This natural human capacity has been significantly shut down through many generations of immaturity compounded by injury, which creates denial—a defensive inability to recognize and remember the consequences of our actions. We keep making the same mistakes, because the solution for our unprocessed awareness is to convert the pain into invented demons, and to blame; projecting our own feelings onto others. Each generation has its own version of "things that go bump in the night," the devils and witches we must fight. The fear of women escalated to mass psychosis and murder in Europe in the Middle Ages. Today, we project our fears onto political opponents, other races, and other religions—causing conflicts and wars. We wage them with increasingly monstrous weapons of mass destruction, ones that kill massive groups of people as though they were things; in the process we poison our Earth as well. Avoiding self-awareness—and instead projecting—is a fatal thinking dysfunction.

-§-

We are a very young species—so new we are not finished yet.

-§-

We are faced with more of a psychological and developmental crisis than a political or religious one. This situation is also an opportunity, in that it requires us to acquire a whole new capacity to perceive, in order to heal ourselves. Healing is characterized, primarily, by being willing to be honest and look at ourselves, and—here is the jumping-off point for the leap—to self-correct while allowing inspiration to guide our choices.

Our species has a unique power: the capacity to *choose* to be self-aware; *and then* to choose to consciously align with that which is greater and good. We have the free will to choose to self-correct. It is this choice that enables us to heal the past—all the conditioned programming that doesn't work. This is how we evolve *ourselves;* it is the process of evolution in creative action. It actually is a change in the way the brain works.

The new way of seeing cannot afford to be judgmental. That doesn't mean you can't have judgments. The distinction is worthwhile drawing here. Good judgment, the ability to observe and discern and sense into what is happening is vital, of course. Good judgment moves and changes as we gain information. That is very different than the solidified, simplistic, black-or-white, either-or, hyperjudgmental approach characteristic of immature, old-style thinking.

Old-Style Thinking

All kinds of fundamentalism typify old-style thinking. The more scared people get, the more "only" they become. This "thinking dysfunction" is then injected into religion, politics, sex, and family dynamics. "My way," or "our way," becomes "the only way." Situations become more and more polarized, it boils down to "us or them," and the polarity escalates. The blinders come up, and knowledge and intelligence diminishes.

Righteous intensity can be like a drug. At first, taking the drug makes a person feel better. Being "right" simplifies things and we feel good, for after all, we are right. A simple choice between black and white makes us feel secure, as though we now have things figured out. But it doesn't produce connection with the other, so resolution is not reached. This makes people even more angry with the "other who must be to blame" for it not working. Projections abound!

This immature thinking process can't bear to see its own shadow. Mistakes and limitations, which may seem humiliating, are displaced by immature defense mechanisms and blaming the "other." This keeps people busy, distracted and in survival mode so they need not look at themselves.

New-Style Thinking

What we learn as we grow and mature—both individually and collectively—is that life is not black-or-white simple. As we grow more mature, we see that—in truth—reality is moving and changing all the time. Nothing in the universe is static. This realization causes us to reach into ourselves for a deeper dimension of knowing awareness, one that is soft and open enough to tell us what is good—in a moment. Looking for healthy goodness is what matters; this is the mature intuitive mind in action.

I call it my "soft mind" because this gentle state isn't grasping. It feels soft. It is intuitive, feeling, nonverbal, receptive, filled with metaphor and imagery, and the capacity to love. From my soft mind, I don't have expectations, but am filled with optimistic open expectancy for something good. It is more powerful to be good than to be right—the difference is distinct and brings about a profound shift in context. The essence of creativity, spirituality, and even genius, emerges, opening the door to thoughts and solutions which never were before.

Human beings have an immature logical mind and an immature intuitive mind. The immature logical mind involves us in win-lose thinking and tangles us up in the worst sin of all: the promotion of fear, in order to gain power. The immature intuitive mind generates images of these fears.

-§-
War represents a failure of humankind's intelligence.
-§-

But there is another dimension to our intelligence. We might call it the receptive; the yin force; the softness that conquers the hard, the gentleness that releases resistance. To paraphrase Lao Tzu: "The power of 'yielding' to overcome the resistant is a fact known by all, yet utilized by none." This is also what Jesus taught: "Love your enemy; turn the other cheek." And the great commandment Jesus gave, "Love one another even as I have loved you," is a pure expression of the power of receptive compassion. It literally changes how your brain works.

The characteristic of mature logic is to keep accurate track of facts *and* not be judgmental. Mature intuitive mind is characterized by inspiration; mature logic by honesty. Together they create integrity, which is the next level of humanness.

The way we find the highest form of our intuition—our higher minded genius where healing, music, art, science, and creativity of all sorts comes from—is by accessing the highest frequency we can, where we can receive the most helpful, the most beautiful knowledge and information—this is inspiration. In my life and work, I have found that the most compelling and most consistent touchstone opening us to this dimension is to seek to be inspired. The most mature among us live to inspire others.

War represents a failure of humankind's intelligence. Terrorism and war are horrible escalating standoffs. They are indicative of old-style thinking, where one injury promotes a retaliating injury twice as big.

Everybody is hurt, stubbornly "right," and unsatisfied, fuming and killing and harming as they try to conquer or get back at each other. This clumsy, deadly thinking style usually only ends when there is so much exhaustion and destruction that people cannot move. Someone has to give up and start life over. Then the other group is said to "win."

Now we have another option. We have intelligence. We have a maturing capacity that is part of the crisis of this moment—globally and personally. The danger of now is that we have the power to annihilate ourselves and poison the planet. And the opportunity we have is this: we could choose to grow up and create heaven on earth.

People keep talking about destruction as unthinkable. Yet we think about it constantly. We are, in fact, suffocating in destruction, real and grossly imagined, in our newspaper headlines, in our television and in our films.

The unthinkable is to *truly* do what Jesus and Buddha said: Love your enemies. The unthinkable is to look inward and see your part and correct *you*. The unthinkable is to open to inspiration and have compassion for the person who is harming you. That does not mean letting harm continue with no feedback or action. The key is to give feedback that isn't filled with hate. As a 5,000-year-old Chinese proverb says, "You become what you resist." Politically and culturally, this simply means: justice and love for all the sides—including yours.

-§-
This is how you transform the world: you transform the piece of the world you are sitting in.
-§-

Here is our work. It is to not to be fake, and *look like* we are caring. It is to not be self-righteous and need attention, but rather to be self-reflective and self-correcting. To find the good will within is to be mature. This is what Jesus and Buddha taught: The power of compassion for yourself and for others. It is the kingdom of heaven.

If we are to grow and to heal ourselves and the planet, we must work on ourselves wherever we are—in whatever relationship, work situation, family dynamic, or world pursuit we are engaged. Wherever you find yourself, especially when stuck, try to find a way to meet life in an inspired way. Be grateful regardless of circumstances. This is how you transform the world: you transform the piece of the world you are sitting in. To actually do it is the creation of the evolutionary leap.

Taking the Leap Within Yourself

Evil is "live" spelled backwards. At the source of evil lies an anti-life fear. The fear of being wrong is insidious, debilitating, and almost universal. With mature intelligence, we can see that what unravels and dissipates fear is love. Love is not an appearance, or a performance in the name of love; it is the feeling of love. Love, truly and deeply felt, is a transcendent power. As long as we stay intellectually stuck and stubborn about being right, we live at the appearance level. We collectively don't realize that it's much more powerful to be loving, and that it is our choice to cultivate it.

If we allow ourselves to use the intuitive mind at a more mature level, it will give us images that begin to speak right to our very core when we see something "off." We will naturally want to heal, and we will intuitively receive antidotes to fear and stuck places that we can feel and act from. Our first internal questions then become: "How can I heal that? How can I neutralize fear or hate? What can I do to touch that? What do I need to understand—to see differently and to understand the other?" This type of question sets a different tone and a new requirement, raising the bar on our intelligence. In wonderful and unexpected ways, powerful and creative solutions are generated. When we do the emotional work, everything shifts.

-§-
Love, truly and deeply felt, is a transcendent power.
-§-

We also give our powers of logic a new request. We give our intuition a new request. In so doing, we restructure the software of our mind; this builds a greater interface between left and right brain. We increase our capacity to think, perceive, and feel how empathy can find new and deeper solutions. Intuition becomes a natural function of intelligence, just as vision is a natural function of perception. Clairvoyance—clear seeing—and extrasensory perception are not a big deal. They are part of our native intelligence. But we must mature to make room for it, and allow it to influence us. In this period of development, an important marker is that we become more free and more transparent. We grow up.

What awaits us is an experience of harmony, which is far more encompassing than what we now know. All of nature is like a great symphony: it is connected. This is the new dimension we humans are about to break into. The secret of breaking into it, in my experience, is a willingness to have a consistent, fair self-observer.

Enlightenment is not a static place you land. It is not about having no problems: it is about trusting the problem. Trust that the problem is part of a flow of creation and that it is an opportunity for you to handle it differently. As Buckminster Fuller said, "God invented people to solve problems. And when you're good at it, he gives you more."

Observe what you do that's harmful and try to rectify it, first in the privacy of your own mind, and then in the sphere of "other." That is being a grown-up. I believe that this reflection plus making amends is what has made Alcoholics Anoymous so successful. People create addictions to distract themselves from the suffering they feel because they cannot forgive themselves for what they've done wrong—and wrongs that have been done to them. The thinking style and the judgmental, deadlocked mind-trap of the addict is intolerable. The need to escape self-judgment becomes paramount because the state of mind and body is so painful. Drugs and other addictions offer numbness.

The solution is to feel and use the energy of hurt to claim new insight and actions. This breaks the syndrome of violation and denial. This is the step that has people look at themselves. They feel the grief and make amends, while staying open to God or goodness for inspiration. This process opens the door of that destructive mental prison. The key to the lock is turning inward, to being honest with good will. It is first a realization and then a conscious choice—one we must choose again and again. This is how we create the evolutionary leap. There is no way out except growing up. When we do it is our choice.

-§-

Trust that the problem is part of a flow of creation and that it is an opportunity for you to handle it differently.

-§-

Here's a powerful exercise you can use to support and create this evolutionary shift: From this moment forward, consider that everyone you meet can read your mind.

When I suggest this to a room full of people, the whole room goes silent. People hold their breath. Then a little laughter breaks the breath-holding seriousness. But the practice is profound. Try it for an hour. Then try it for an afternoon. This exercise can rewrite the software of the logical mind. It teaches the mind to self-correct the logical filter, which can then evolve out of controlling behavior for the sake of appearances to a deeper, far more authentic earnestness. Most importantly, you will begin to gain conscious awareness of how much you deceive yourself. As self-deception becomes more transparent, you lift the defensive veil and see. This is freedom. The biggest empowerment to our freedom is a mind free to be honest.

We are pioneers, learning what goodness is from an internal experience. We are maturing, developmentally, into an understanding of the difference between being "right" and having good information. We are discovering how to live from a deeper place of truth and knowing. When you live this way, congruence radiates out of your voice and out of your body, the net effect of which opens the doors of perception in both you and others. We begin to experience time, cause and effect, and need, in a whole new way. We become more relaxed. We see the bigger picture of life. The two hemispheres of our brains work together. More synchronicity happens, more magical serendipity, and more of a sense that we are part of a bigger flow.

The next leap in our evolution hinges on this newly developing capacity. Abraham Lincoln foreshadowed this leap when he said to Congress in 1862: "The dogmas of the quiet past are inadequate to the stormy present.

The occasion is piled high with difficulty, and we must rise—with the occasion. As our case is new, so we must think anew, and act anew. We must dis-enthrall ourselves, and then we shall save our country.

"Fellow-citizens, *we* cannot escape history.

"We shall nobly save, or meanly lose, the last best hope of earth. Other means may succeed; this could not fail. The way is plain, peaceful, generous, just—a way which, if followed, the world will forever applaud, and God must forever bless."

Jean Shinoda Bolen: Women's Circles Ripple into Peace

The original Mother's Day proclamation was written by Julia Ward Howe in 1870. It did not announce a day to honor mothers with cards, flowers, and candy. It announced a day for the mothers of the world to come together in sufficient numbers to bring about peace.

In the proclamation, Howe wrote:

"Our sons shall not be taken from us to unlearn all that we have been able to teach them of charity, mercy and patience. We women of one country will be too tender of those of another country to allow our sons to be trained to injure theirs.

"Let women now leave all that may be left of home for a great and earnest day of counsel. Let us meet first, as women, to bewail and commemorate the dead. And then solemnly take counsel with each other as to the means, whereby the great human family can live in peace."

And she proposed:

"In the name of womanhood and humanity, I earnestly ask that a general congress of women without limit of nationality may be appointed and held at some place deemed most convenient. And the point of it is to promote the alliance of different nationalities, the amicable settlement of international questions and to bring about the great and general interest of peace."

What is missing from the global conversation about peace is what women as a gender instinctively know. In touch with their vulnerability

Jean Shinoda Bolen, M.D., is a psychiatrist, Jungian analyst, clinical professor of psychiatry at the University of California San Francisco, a Distinguished Life Fellow of the American Psychiatric Association, and the 2002 recipient of "Pioneers in Arts, Sciences, and the Soul of Healing Award" from the Institute for Health and Healing. She is a former board member of the Ms. Foundation for Women, and the author of *The Tao of Psychology* (25th Anniversary Edition, 2004), *Goddesses in Everywoman* (20th Anniversary Edition, 2004), *Crossing to Avalon* (10th Anniversary Edition, 2004), and many other books. Full information at www.jeanbolen.com.

and strength, women can speak from the feminine principle of interconnectedness, nurturing, and compassion. Only now, at this crucial historical time when humanity has the power to destroy life on Earth, has there also been a generation of women who can speak for feminine values.

Because of the women's movement, women in great numbers have had opportunities, responsibilities, experiences and choices beyond those of any generation ever. The women's movement grew out of a peaceful revolutionary idea: that women are equal to men, and that something called patriarchy exists, something that can now be named. Patriarchy is a hierarchal social, political, and religious structure in which those higher in the hierarchy can exercise power over those below.

The symbols of the grail and the wounded fisher king are powerful metaphors for this crucial historic turning point. The king has a wound that will not heal, and his kingdom is a wasteland. Wounded in his genitals, the king lacks generativity, creativity and vitality; nothing grows in his kingdom. While the wasteland is—figuratively—spiritual, social, and psychological terrain, we also note that there are ecological wastelands—and know that the whole earth could be turned into a literal wasteland by a nuclear holocaust. In the grail legend, the king can only be healed by the grail—a mysterious, numinous object, usually thought of as a chalice (a shape which is a feminine symbol) that is always carried by a woman. The healing, sacred grail disappeared from the world of long ago, and is symbolic of the sacred feminine, which is carried by women.

-§-
What is missing from the global conversation about peace is what women as a gender instinctively know.
-§-

Shifting into metaphor allows us to speak in a language that is understood by the psyche or the soul. This is important, because the energy needed to empower us today is spiritual. By connecting at a soul level with each other, we find a place of commonality that is spiritual rather than religious. Religion at the moment is very divisive. Violence between countries, between peoples, and within families is a symptom of an unbalanced society in which hierarchy and expressing power over others is the ruling principle. We have mostly men in power, or women who identify with power, making all the major decisions that concern humanity's fate.

The grail legends revolve around the missing chalice that has disappeared and must be found. The power of this metaphor lies not in what it presents to the logical mind—which is almost always in critical, analytical mode—but in how it speaks to the soul. The soul elements in us understand the feelings, images, and poetic impressions of myth, and learn by absorbing them inwardly. In a psychological and spiritual sense, the wasteland is the psyche without the feminine principle. The grail that disappeared is the sacred feminine—a reverence for Earth, and for life on this Earth. The quest is to find the grail, in order to heal the wounded fisher king and regenerate the wasteland.

My thesis is this: for the grail to be returned to the world, women must find it in their own psyches and experience, and bring it into their part of patriarchy. The desert landscape of the wasteland calls out for the feminine principle. At the deepest level of the planet, it is calling us—she is calling us—to gather the women. There is an awareness somewhere within the psyche that we need to bring the sacred feminine back into consciousness because that is what could heal the wasteland of dominator politics and the potential of destroying the planet. The interest in fiction best-sellers such as Dan Brown's *The Da Vinci Code,* and before that, Marion Zimmer Bradley's *The Mists of Avalon,* point to this awareness.

The dominator culture begins with the sense that men, since Adam, have dominion over everything by divine right. Religious fundamentalists begin with the belief that men were created in the image of God, and are therefore superior to women and all other living things. The egalitarian perspective of the women's movement challenged male superiority. The generation that comprised the women's movement and those baby boomers who were the direct beneficiaries know how much the world changed for women as a result. There are close to fifty million American women over age fifty who can recall or have a sense of what the world was like for women before that time.

-§-

By connecting at a soul level with each other, we find a place of commonality that is spiritual rather than religious.

-§-

The fundamentalist men of all three monotheistic religions emphasize obedience to hierarchy and dominion over women, while creating crusades and jihads against each other. On a global level, fundamentalism creates fratricidal wars such as in Rwanda, and the Middle East. All over the world, people who have lived next to each other for generations—in the Balkans for example, the Serbs, Croatians, Albanians, Moslem and Christians—harbor hate and vengeance. Men who, in the name of honor, kill sisters and daughters for losing their virginity; men who incite war to gain more power or more territory; men who send young men to die—these are today's wounded fisher kings. They are unable to feel, and are therefore unable to care if soldiers are mere children, or if innocent noncombatants are killed.

Mothers do not see their twenty-year-old sons as warriors. They don't have the appalling team mentality about war that keeps score in body counts and how much land is gained. Patriarchy fixates on power. For balance to be restored, women must be heard.

Women gathering together in groups and telling the truth of their lives can actually change the world. That is what led to the women's movement. In the movement itself, women did what they were personally motivated to do, once they understood how patriarchy had defined and limited them. Those who wanted to be activists and march in demonstrations did so. Those who wanted to write and put together anthologies to influence women who weren't in consciousness-raising groups did so. Women lawyers who wanted to fight in court did so. Women who wanted to challenge access to education and jobs did so. It was not a hierarchical movement. It came through loosely organized groups of women that supported the women in them to do whatever they felt motivated to do. As a result, enormous social change came about. The stuff of ordinary life—what women can do, how they are in relationships—changed. Today, from housewife to astronaut, a woman can do just about anything, except be a Roman Catholic priest.

The transformative power of women gathering together is a historical fact—and it is also an energy field. Biologist Rupert Sheldrake introduced the idea of morphic fields and discussed how people change. Once a critical mass of people changes their behavior, attitude, or perception, behavior that was previously resisted becomes what is naturally done. Women's right to vote is an example. C. G. Jung's collective unconscious is identical to Sheldrake's morphic field for our species. Once we start to embody a pattern that exists as a latent potential or archetype (such as a circle of women), we tap into a source that energizes our actions.

-§-
The grail that disappeared is the sacred feminine—a reverence for Earth, and for life on this Earth.
-§-

Sheldrake adds another active dimension to Jung's concept. In his model, the energy of the archetypal or morphic field runs in two directions, from the field and back to the field. Every new women's circle that forms increases the ease of others forming, by adding to the field. When there is a critical mass, the circle will enter human consciousness as a natural way for people to be together, even in institutions.

In my book *The Millionth Circle* (Conari/Red Wheel, 1999), I envisioned women's circles with a spiritual center as the means to change the women in them and change the world, and to heal the women in them and heal the world. The "millionth circle" is a metaphoric number, the circle that tips the scales when added to all the others. It creates a critical mass to bring the sacred feminine into human consciousness. It is a spiritual evolutionary change that comes, once again, through small groups of women—as did the social and political changes made by the women's movement.

That book was like a seed packet, which led many women to start a circle, or to transform an existing group into a circle with a sacred center. It inspired the formation of an organization, The Millionth Circle Initiative (www.millionthcircle.org). Its members in turn helped organize Gather the Women congresses, first in San Francisco in 2003 and then in Dallas in 2004. Kathe Schaaf, the first president of Gather the Women (www.gatherthewomen.org) saw the possibility of "Six Congresses on Six continents in 2006" as a lead-in to a fifth Women's World Conference. The experience of being in a circle with a sacred center leads to the formation of new circles. Circles proliferate like strawberry runners, as the idea takes root in new locations.

I recently had the pleasure of meeting Elana Rozenman, an orthodox Jew from Israel who comes to Marin County regularly to see her aging mother. Every time she comes for a visit, Elana invites women who know of her peace work to come together in a circle and do a walking meditation in Muir Woods. Imagine the contrast between walking through the tranquil beauty of the ancient redwood trees in Muir Woods and walking on a street in parts of Israel today.

Elana is part of an interfaith women's group in Jerusalem that includes Christian, Muslim, and Jewish women. The women don't talk about religion when they meet in their circle. They talk about their lives and difficulties, and the common hope for peace that they carry. I found Elena's story particularly instructive. A number of years ago, her teenage son was walking along the street when a terrorist bomb went off. Although he got some 200 pieces of shrapnel in his body, her son lived. A little girl walking along on the same street was hit by just one piece of shrapnel, and she died. Elana came away from that experience with a profound realization that she could not allow her life to be dictated by fear. Walking out into the world is a risk. Some will be killed, and others will live. Mothers who don't turn into haters know that a Palestinian mother who loses a child and an Israeli mother who loses a child suffer the same heartbreak. Both live under stress.

-§-

The fundamentalist men of all three monotheistic religions emphasize obedience to hierarchy and dominion over women, while creating crusades and jihads against each other.

-§-

Women react to stress very differently than men. It has always been assumed that the genders react the same way to stress. But a recent study by the University of California at Los Angeles has turned up some surprising results. It shows that women have a "tend and befriend" reaction to stress, in contrast to the "flight or fight" response of the typical male. Women tend to talk to each other and share their feelings in order to reduce stress. As they do so, the levels of oxytocin—the maternal bonding hormone—in their blood increase. In contrast, men under stress are likely to either withdraw or become more aggressive, with a corresponding increase in adrenaline—the flight or fight hormone. Testosterone enhances an adrenaline response. In another interesting and relevant research study of testosterone levels, the top male had the highest level, until he lost his position to another man. After that, his testosterone level decreased. In a hierarchy of power, which is the structure that underlies patriarchy, dominance by one means submission by the others.

One of the longest running unresolved conflicts in the world is in the Middle East. It is an example of why women need to be involved in the peace process. Ariel Sharon and Yasser Arafat can't negotiate peace if their physiological model is dominance or submission, and their psychological intent is to humiliate the other rather than bringing peace to their suffering people.

By way of contrast, in the Iroquois Confederacy, women elders determined the priorities of the five Seneca nations. Women who had raised children and were beyond childbearing years were chosen by the people to form the women's council. It was up to these grandmothers to decide whether the nation would go to war. This decision—like all others—drew upon the preceding seven generations for direction—and considered the effect of the decision on the seven generations to come. If the consensus decision of the women's council was to go to war, they would pass the decision on to the men's council. The men would then decide among themselves who would be the war chief. Interesting to note, however, is the fact that it was the elder women who proposed the members of the men's council. Only elder women who had observed that generation of men from boyhood would know their character and strengths.

-§-

Women gathering together in groups and telling the truth of their lives can actually change the world.

-§-

I am optimistic. I think a window of opportunity exists in which patriarchy can be transformed into a balanced culture, through circles of women reaching a critical mass. The United Nations has passed resolutions that put into words aspirations that can lead to a world without war. One of these is the Universal Declaration of Human Rights. Another is U.N. Resolution 1325, sometimes referred to as the "Women, Peace and Security" resolution. It states that wherever there is violence in the world—whether at the level of domestic violence or international conflict—women need to be involved in the peace process.

Women, meeting in circles, with a spiritual center, tap into an archetypal field. It's as if they're clustered around a well, drawing water from an aquifer buried deep within the human psyche. Each woman and each circle finds wisdom and compassion at the center, and brings the feminine principle back into the world, bringing healing to the spiritual wasteland. Every woman is a potential grail carrier. She can take her experience of the sacred feminine back to her world of relationships and institutions.

The expression, "There is nothing so powerful as an idea whose time has come," describes the moment of achieving a critical mass. Peace can come to the world through the involvement of women. In growing numbers and influence, women are meeting in circles with a spiritual center. They are meeting in congresses and conferences, connecting though their hearts, and communicating through every available means, including the Internet. Women who are wise elders and effective activists, women who put the well-being of children first, women who speak as mothers and grandmothers, must all be heard. Through geometrical progression, becoming a critical mass, reaching a tipping point, women can embody and fulfill the Mother's Day proclamation. As Julia Ward Howe envisioned, women can "solemnly take counsel with each other as to the means, whereby the great human family can live in peace."

-§-

A Palestinian mother who loses a child and an Israeli mother who loses a child suffer the same heartbreak.

-§-

Part Seven

Earth Wisdom

Joan Borysenko: Putting the Soul Back in Medicine

Once upon a time, when the rays of the morning sun rose over peoples who were still hunters and gatherers, the clock of the bodymind was regulated by the magnetic forces of nature. By sun and moon, by cycles and seasons, by feasting and fasting.

The wise ones, known as healers or shamans, believed that illness was a result of being out of tune with the natural cycles. The disharmony, and the dis-ease which resulted from it, had different types of cures. There were powerful herbs which could rebalance the flow of energy which, in turn, determined physical function. Some cultures developed a large pharmacopia of active agents. Others, such as some of the Native American cultures, employed only a few plants. The shaman or medicine person dreamed which herb to use and invoked the specific healing quality required through prayer and ritual.

But the shamans were much more than intuitive pharmacologists. They were also intuitive psychologists. The patient was questioned about their life, their role in the tribe, their relationships and their dreams. Turbulent emotions could cause turbulence in the bodymind. The cure in this case was to correct the source of the emotional disbalance. In cases where the patient had been traumatized by grief, accident, heartbreak or abuse, it was not the energy body or the emotional body that required healing, but the soul.

Soul retrieval was a common medical treatment in which the shaman entered a state of non-ordinary reality similar to what people describe

Joan Borysenko, Ph.D., has a powerfully clear personal vision—to bring science, medicine, psychology and spirituality together in the service of healing. Her brilliance as a scientist, clinician and teacher have placed her on the leading edge of the mind-body revolution, and she has become a world-renowned spokesperson for this new approach to health, sharing her pioneering work with a gentle graciousness, enthusiasm and humility. She is the author of the best-seller *Minding the Body, Mending the Mind* (1987) and eight other books. This chapter appeared initially in the *Leifer Report,* and is used with permission of author and publisher.

during near-death experiences and mystical visions. In this state, the shaman tracked parts of the patient's soul that had been split off and lost as a result of trauma. The retrieved soul parts were then blown back into the patient's body through the heart and the top of the head and oftentimes a physical and emotional cure was achieved. Our modern psychology and psychiatry, in contrast, has a much poorer track record with post-traumatic stress disorder and the cure of dissociative disorders resulting from childhood physical abuse, sexual abuse or unusual trauma.

The soul of medicine itself has become fragmented. We have retained the pharmacology and refined the technical aspects of pathophysiology, diagnosis and treatment, but we have lost the emotional and spiritual components that can make healing a sacred art as well as a more effective science. Nearly two millennia ago, coincident with the spread of the Catholic Church to Europe, tremendous sociological and religious upheavals occurred which resulted in the stamping out of shamanic cultures. This in turn had a far-reaching effect on the development of medicine. Illness was viewed as evidence of sin, an idea that is poignantly considered in the old testament Book of Job. After all, if illness and misfortune are the result of offending God, then all you have to do is to be is very, very good and then you'll be safe. Or if you are beyond reproach, then all you have to do is get rid of the bad guys who are offending God. Enter the Crusades and the Inquisition.

-§-

The soul of medicine itself has become fragmented. We have retained the...technical aspects, but we have lost the emotional and spiritual components that can make healing a sacred art.

-§-

During the middle ages the Black Death killed one third of the population of Europe. A search for the sinners who must surely have caused it gave rise to a bloody chapter in the history of religious persecution. Entire villages of Jews were murdered and several million women were condemned as witches in the hope of defeating the plague. But when the plague continued to spread, religion ultimately lost its authority over illness and the age of science began. For an excellent review I heartily recommend Sacred Eyes, by psychologist and minister Robert Keck.

By the sixteenth century, modern science was being birthed by the famous triad of scientific reductionists—Francis Bacon, Renee Descartes and Isaac Newton—who succeeded in reducing nature to a machine devoid of soul or guiding intelligence. To their credit, they exorcised the toxic notion of disease as punishment by a peevish deity. But they also threw the baby out with the bathwater. Bacon's stated purpose was to subjugate nature altogether by desouling it. To take her by force and to "torture and vex" her into revealing her secrets so that mankind would have dominion over the earth—over life and death itself.

This is the thinking that underlies the rape and plunder of natural resources, the dehumanization of third world cultures, and the de-souling of modern medicine. It presumes a lack of organizing intelligence in the universe and since life is therefore not sacred, resources become expendable in the name of progress. Soul loss ultimately leads to amoral behavior- acts performed with oblivion to their eventual consequences. Were we, like our native predecessors, conditioned to assess the consequences of our health-care system seven generations into the future we would have to ask some very penetrating questions. Is it appropriate that the majority of monies spent on the medical care of any one individual are spent in the last few months of their life? Would they be better spent in prevention programs, or in early childhood education programs, or in parenting programs that would aid emotional wellbeing and therefore cut down on illness and suffering?

And what is a soul approach to an individual patient? Once again, it has to do with a macroscopic view that investigates the illness as part of a life, rather than as an isolated symptom. The physician who practices fragmented medicine and cures a symptom may actually compound the patient's problems. For example, a diuretic may decrease Mrs. Jones blood pressure, but if it is high because of an alcoholic husband, poor self-esteem and ruinous health habits has her physician healed her with a prescription or has he colluded to help her maintain a sick status quo? To be a healer, a physician needs to have a larger vision of the human being than is taught in most medical schools which pander to molecules while denigrating the emotional and spiritual aspects of life.

-§-
Soul loss ultimately leads to amoral behavior- acts performed with oblivion to their eventual consequences.
-§-

Part of the problem in medicine's loss of soul is that death is seen as unnatural, as the enemy, so that disproportionate resources are put into discouraging death as opposed to encouraging life. Let me tell you a story. My mother died in a Boston teaching hospital about five years ago, and overall, she had a wonderful quality of care. But on the last day of her life, as her heart and lungs and kidneys failed, she developed internal bleeding and was whisked off to nuclear medicine so that the source of the bleed could be determined. Why? Was it going to make a clinical difference? Four hours passed, and the family, which was gathered around her empty bed to say goodbye, started to get impatient and scared. Since I had worked in that hospital for a decade, they dispatched me to rescue her. I knew it wouldn't be easy. When I got down to nuclear medicine, she was still waiting on the gurney that had brought her down four hours before. I demanded her immediate release and the doctor was equally adamant about getting a diagnosis. My mother broke the stalemate by virtually resurrecting from near-death to give the doctor a dose of common sense, "A diagnosis. Is that all you need? I'm dying. That's your diagnosis." And with that, the doctor gave in.

Fortunately, we had time to say goodbye back in her room before she slipped into a last morphine-assisted sleep. My son Justin, who was twenty at the time, and I were at her bedside at about three in the morning. I was meditating when I had a vivid vision that seemed far more real than waking life. In the vision I was a pregnant mother giving birth and I was also the baby being born. As the baby, I was being propelled down a long, dark tunnel. And then I came out into the presence of the ineffable light that so many of my patients who have had near-death experiences describe. The light is omniscient, incomprehensibly loving, infinitely wise and perfectly forgiving. It feels like home. In the presence of the light, my relationship with my mother, which had been a difficult one, seemed perfect. I saw the lessons we had learned from one another and felt immense gratitude toward her. She had birthed me into this world, and I felt as though I had birthed her soul back out again.

-§-

Part of the problem in medicine's loss of soul is that death is seen as unnatural, as the enemy.

-§-

When I opened my eyes, Justin had a look of total awe on his face. He asked me if I could see the light in the room. When I said that I could, for indeed the whole room was glowing, Justin said, "Grandma is holding open the door to eternity to give us a glimpse." Justin felt that he had received a priceless gift, because he knew with certainty that we are not our bodies. We inhabit our bodies, but our souls are immortal. He wept as he told me that he would never be afraid of death again. The only type of death that is really worth fearing, after all, is a living death in which we fail to become ourselves because we get stuck in some one else's definition of who we should be.

Albert Camus wrote, "There is but one freedom, to put oneself right with death. After that everything is possible." When people visit their doctor, they might not be thinking in terms of their immortal souls, but most are looking for emotional and spiritual healing. They want to know they are worthy and lovable. They want to confess, to complain, to be forgiven, to make meaning of their lives. Clearly, this can't always be done in an eight-minute office visit. But compassion can be communicated, and when appropriate the patient can be referred to a therapist or clergyperson who can help them with the big questions that illness puts to us. "Who am I?," "What is the purpose of my life?" and "How can I profit from this illness as an opportunity to find greater freedom and happiness?"

Consumers are patently dissatisfied with a mechanistic medicine that denies its own soul and theirs. It's time we heed the symptoms indicating that our medical system is dangerously out of balance. Modern technology is marvelous and lifesaving, and if we can integrate it with the deep wisdom of the past then we can birth a medicine that exalts and nurtures life rather than one than is predicated on the fear of death.

Anthony Scheving & Geralyn Gendreau: Deep Empathy

A great awakening is happening within humanity. Our way of life is out of sync with the natural order and we are collectively waking up to that fact. Poised at the brink of another mass extinction, we can no longer ignore the Earth's alarm. Mother Nature is doing her best to wake us up. Daily she moans, begging us to expand our awareness, shaking us so we will consciously evolve. As Nina Simons said in her opening remarks at the 2004 Bioneers Conference: "We stand at a choice point. We face either an age of extinction or an age of restoration."

Three great opportunities appear before us as we begin to rub our mole-eyes open and commit ourselves to restoring the planet. The new paradigm is a threefold invitation: one, to embrace our world as a living, sacred habitat and learn to co-exist in harmony with nature; two, to experience and celebrate the power of imagination to ignite the collective human soul; and, three, to rejuvenate the body of Gaia and our own human flesh.

Neurobiology and quantum physics have now unveiled what poets and mystics have pointed to for ages. Alignment within the formerly disparate fields of science and spirituality now convincingly demonstrates that the fabric of reality is like a Gossamer web, woven by consciousness, to constellate "the real."

With masters degrees in both Art and Psychology, Anthony Scheving is a visionary artist and adept myth maker. After teaching design and technology at San Francisco State University for ten years, he straddled the worlds between corporate America and explorations in spirituality. He has since turned his interests to studies in imaginal psychology. Visit him at www.heartsoulvision.com.

Geralyn Gendreau is a licensed therapist, black-belt martial artist, and professional muse. A Pacific Rim yogini, she was initiated into the path of union by the Pacific Ocean rather than a guru. She is the originator of Animal Yoga, a "yoga of the Americas" that explores the realm of human being as an indigenous life form. Find her at www.awakenedlover.com.

Inspired afresh by quantum physics, a new paradigm is coming to the fore. The mainstream may not reflect it yet, but the stage is surely and beautifully set for the regeneration of culture. A culture that embraces the alchemy of mind may prove our saving grace. Aftab Omer, founder and president of the Institute for Imaginal Studies, clarifies the ace-role of culture when he says, "Culture is evolution's trump card."

Omer raises a deep question about the genesis of change and the role of cultural transformation, stating that: "There is a complex relationship between genetic, physiological, and cultural transformation—they are profoundly related. The appearance of agriculture and the appearance of writing are profound cultural discontinuities. Are these physiological transformations? Are these mutations? Or are these primarily cultural transformations? Recognizing that the three entail each other to some degree, my own hunch is that these are cultural transformations."

Could a collective awakening within humanity unfold such a sudden and radical transformation in culture? Perhaps, as Aftab Omer suggests, "we can live out the hypothesis and know its truth to the degree we are living it."

A Culture at the Breaking Point

The patriarchal push for reductionistic science crowned reason and logic while casting imagination and intuition outside the castle walls. This created a self-image for most of humanity of self as separate—an isolated, independent thinking machine. In essence, we got plugged into the matrix of civilization. So pathological is our addiction to the mechanistic view of reality, the human imagination came up with an analogy called "The Matrix" in the feature film by that name, wherein human beings are harvested as a natural resource by the artificial intelligence of machines.

-§-

The fabric of reality is like a Gossamer web, woven by consciousness, to constellate "the real."

-§-

So pervasive is our indoctrination, most of us have lost all sense of what a connected, interwoven, non-separate reality might be. When one individual suddenly breaks through the glass cage of separateness to the freedom of awake-awareness beyond, we call that person "enlightened"—or crazy—and set them apart as if they were different from the rest of us. Our notion of "the individual" has become so axiomatic we often cannot feel the effect we have on others, on the biosphere, or even on our own selves. The ego function that identifies self as a separate, individuated entity makes it easy to ignore genocide in far off nations, the pain of a neighbor next door, the degradation of our earthly environment, and even the nefarious ache of our own self-destructive habits.

Another world—one that has always been there, despite our inability to see—stretches out before us now. Quantum physics reveals a far more fluid, responsive and interactive world than that inhabited by the rational, separated self. Before quantum physics, we relied on poets, artists and mystics to show us the way, as can be seen in D. H. Lawrence's poem, Terra Incognita:

There are vast realms of consciousness still undreamed of vast ranges of experience, like the humming of unseen harps, we know nothing of, within us.

Poets and mystics hold much of the same ground as Shamanic peoples do, always aware of the fluid field of gorgeous, lace-like magic in which we all exist. The ancient wisdom of Tibet likewise recognizes the pliability of reality. While Tibetan monks refer to "seeds" in the mind, indigenous people move through a world full of "songs." Both notions make real the interactive realm wherein humans participate in a creative capacity, through aware will and imagination to influence the manifest physical world within the context of ritual and a relationship with the invisible.

-§-

When one individual suddenly breaks through the glass cage of separateness to the freedom of awake-awareness beyond, we call that person "enlightened"—or crazy.

-§-

Terra Firma and the Wet Clay of Consciousness

A large and lively crowd had gathered in the Bay View Room of San Francisco's Hyatt Regency Hotel. The audience was prepared to hear an eightfold path perspective on business practices to generate prosperity and personal wealth. What they weren't prepared for was a magic carpet ride.

"Potential and seeds," says Geshe Michael Roach after over twenty years of Tibetan monastic training, "This is all you need to know. Everything has the potential to be everything. You need to find the right seeds to put in your mind. Like gardening, it takes technique. Reach in, plant seeds in the Matrix, sit back and wait. Works for health, relationship anything we want." Roach predicts standard business practice in the twenty-first century will reflect this ancient wisdom from Tibet.

What if business schools stopped teaching the profit-machine mentality of how to build the base and pump up the corporate bottom line, and instead taught free-enterprise economics and marketing through mental seed control? The teaching may come from the Tibetan lamas, but the opportunity to hear in our culture is just beginning to dawn. And as a cultural groundswell, the new paradigm view of reality is a wave-form to behold.

So how do we plant seeds? What is our best gardening technique? According to Roach, and Tibetan wisdom, the first thing is harmony.

What collectively costs us the most in our day-by-day emotional-mental biosphere in the intimacy of our homes and around the globe—is when people don't get along. But where does the disharmony come from? Is it coming from out there? No. We see people fighting with each other because of something—a seed—in the mind. How did that seed get in the mind? Listen carefully. This is 2,500-year-old wisdom that has withstood the test of time: whenever you give something to someone, images are planted in the mind. "If you don't think so," says Geshe Michael, "go into a three-year retreat. After two years, every cartoon you ever heard, every movie you saw, they are playing in your mind. Everything you watched when you were a kid, it's there. Stored. If you're quiet for a year or two, they come back with a vengeance. No more! [you want to shout] No more loony toons!"

-§-
The songs in thehearts of the indigenous peoples have flowed through generations and resonate now as the voice of the ancestors.
-§-

Every time we do something, something kind, something cruel, or even something neutral, mirror images are planted in the mind. And then, those images play back, out of our consciousness. And that is what life becomes. Now here comes the crucial point, the one that sent the audience on a magic carpet ride. Says Geshe Michael, "You think there's a carpet on the floor, but you are throwing this carpet out ahead of yourself as you walk.... As you walk out of here, you feel the sensation of the carpet beneath your feet...and it is coming out of your mind. It's like throwing flagstones out ahead and then stepping on them. That's really what's happening. It's not as if there is a carpet here and we're stepping on it. It's that your mind is throwing ahead a carpet as you walk. It's very beautiful. If you get it, the rest of your life is fat city."

In fat city, the joke is on "ordinary" humans—"muggles" as they're called in Harry Potter's realm. We live in a fractal universe, as it turns out. All of life is a constant turning in on itself in the very process of birthing more of itself into being. Reality is an intricate play of mirror images. Everything we do to others plays back in reverse order. The more we understand this, the faster changes "out there" can happen. Change for the better comes with tuning in, getting in synch, and finding the resonant harmonic pattern that supports and sustains.

People Who Sing To the Earth

The songs in the hearts of the indigenous peoples have flowed through generations and resonate now as the voice of the ancestors. These songs, when used in ritual, allow access to non-ordinary time. Perhaps shamanic people have always known that the singing of the traditional songs in ritual has an integrative effect on the body-mind. They might not have conceived of it that way, but they undoubtedly valued the dance of communion. Ritual works synergistically with sensory, emotional, and cognitive centers of the brain to produce experience that is not limited by ordinary constructs. Aftab Omer describes it this way, "Ritual shifts imagination, and the triune brain works as a whole through imagination. The reptilian, old mammalian and new mammalian brains, can work as a unit because imagination is the amplifier and integrator...if you are working with imagination through ritual then you are also undoing the individual and collective disjunction, because the individual is experiencing within a collective field. When I think of the reptilian brain I think of R for reptilian and R for ritual. That's how deep ritual is in our nature. It's as much our nature as the reptilian brain."

Beyond the above-described effects, indigenous songs activate a quality of connectedness that is difficult to name. Many of the songs express respect and gratitude to all there is. This atmosphere of deep respect allows us to touch what D. H. Lawrence called "a marvelous rich world of contact and sheer fluid beauty." Like a new quantum physics toy, the magic carpet rolls out before us. We see it once again in this entry from the dream journal of Anthony Scheving, one of the authors of this chapter:

> "I am sitting in a circle of people. Across from me is a Shaman preparing for ceremony. He makes an incantation and ritual blessings. We all sit around chanting songs of the rain forest. The shaman has brought with him a fan made of leaves. He continues to sing and chant as he pats me on the top of the head with the fan. In a brief moment, I begin to growl and I notice that my toes and fingers have become like claws. My skin becomes translucent and I see that I am no longer just human, but also reptilian, tiger, baboon, human animal, and also alien.
>
> "As the Shaman walks back across the room to his place in the circle, I notice the floor has come alive. I see patterns of geometry and color move across the carpet. I feel a deep sadness that I have walked across this carpet so many times without noticing the magic. I return my focus to the circle and see a light glowing in its center. I see that our lives are a constant dance of waves of light and breath, waves turning inward and turning outward, receiving and sending love. Enlightenment is the awareness of the waves. Attunement with the waves is enlightened living."

What if a critical mass of human beings could suddenly grok that experience issues forth from seeds in the mind and songs in the heart? What innate potential would dawn on the erstwhile horizon of the new millennium? Perhaps the vision of an "awakened society" is not so far off.

Perhaps the advances of postmodern quantum understanding will comprise an undertow of sufficient strength to divert our Titanic culture from its current sink-or-swim, bow-sprit-aimed-at-disaster course.

In order to progress we best re-imagine our body-mind as a multi-dimensional, inter-relational organism dependent on the Mother Gaia for our sustenance. Implicit cultural assumptions portray a hierarchical arrangement of the human brain-mind, wherein the neocortex rules the limbic system, the limbic (old mammalian), rules the reptilian brain, and the reptilian rules the autonomic responses of the body. How would consciousness change if we began to re-imagine not only who, but what we are? To start on this journey, we might engage our imaginal potential and begin to embody and integrate more fully the creature-nature living within our body-mind.

-§-
To start on this journey, we might engage our imaginal potential and begin to embody and integrate more fully the creature-nature living within our body-mind.
-§-

In a chapter entitled "Animal Yoga" (from the manuscript *When I Became God's Lover* by Geralyn Gendreau), this idea is played out in creative non-fiction:

"When I first told Kelly I could turn myself into a toad, I was guilty of being just a little bit cocky. I grew up with three brothers, for god sakes, I had learned to boast big. It wasn't a flip fabrication. There was precedent for it. I'd already mastered snake. And my tiger was getting pretty darn convincing. It's easy enough; you should try it. Start out with snake. Lose your arms and legs. Just forget you have them and lie on your belly and writhe for a while. Pretty soon, snake memory will emerge from your medulla oblongata, that's the hindmost part of the brain at the top of the spinal cord. The reptilian experience will come to the fore if you stick with it long enough and try not to think. Rainforest music helps.

"This whole thing started out as a game. The more I played around with it, the more real it became. The snake, that is. I never took it too far, never bit anybody or wrapped myself around their neck or anything. Although one night, at Dancejam, I did miscalculate how long I could stay in the reptile mind before people would freak. One woman got so upset she had to leave. The following day, I heard through the grapevine she'd said to her lover, "That woman can change herself into a boa constrictor!" If only she had given me a minute to explain about the lucid daydream.

"Funny thing, daydreams. We don't take them as seriously as the dreams we have at night because we're wide-awake. What none of us has fully realized just yet is how starkly awake we can widely get."

Perhaps it is our responsibility as consciously evolving beings to embody the fierceness of the panther in our limbic system, the coldness of the lizard in our medulla oblongata, and to embrace these energies *with consciousness* instead of acting them out on a global scale. Rather than allow these biophysical forces to run us blindly as they do now, we would do well to recognize that basic creature functioning is hard-wired into our neurology.

When we actively participate in embodying the many facets that make each of us the diamond-like human animal we are, we begin to reconnect and feel more whole. Our place in the garden, and our intimate relationship with earth consciousness, is not foreign to our animal nature. The sounds of the forest—birds with their morning and evening prayer rituals, frogs and crickets chanting a rhythmic drone, the rushing sound of the streams, the rustling breezes high in the forest canopy—all play together in an elaborate biophysical orchestra of Gaia. But our civility has inhibited our ability to tune into and resonate with our mother planet. The ancient arts of yoga and Tai Chi have mimicked the poses of animals for centuries. Through such practices, human animals tune in to the cycles and songs, and prayers of the earth. For a modern-day yogi, such practices help us rediscover what we are—an indigenous life form within the body of Gaia.

-§-
Such practices help us rediscover what we are—an indigenous life form within the body of Gaia.
-§-

Relational Intelligence

With our indigenous soul nature revived, and the creative alchemy of mind and imagination activated, we are invited into a deeper level of personal and collective responsibility within our relational world. In *The End of Patriarchy and the Dawning of a Triune Society* (Amber Lotus, 1994), Claudio Naranjo writes:

> "We might say, simply (as I have throughout the years) that it is our incapacity for human relationship which supports our sick society and which has brought us to our crisis predicament. Anybody with a good grasp of dynamic psychology can conclude that it is our incapacity to love our neighbor, ourselves, and the highest values that militates against our sustaining truly brotherly relationships with those around us, and results in a sick society and a host of secondary problems."

Naranjo's unflinching distinction about the nature of our dilemma points toward an alarming deficit in postmodern life wherein *relational intimacies are not even considered an intelligence function.*

We have, as a species, been profoundly derailed when it comes to our relational world. With a primary focus on gaining mastery over physical reality, we have brought forward the enormous technological advances that now threaten our continued existence. Meanwhile, our relational reality has become a wasteland. Even within our religious and philosophical traditions, we have overlooked the intricacies of relationship with each other and with what indigenous people of the Americas call "all our relations." Sensitivity to these intricacies is a vital form of intelligence that, once activated, allows us to thrive instead of just survive. Our deeper need for relational continuity—for a felt-sense of bonded unity—must now come to the fore. The interrelatedness of all humanity, and of humanity with all of creation, must emerge as a living reality in our awareness.

-§-
If we recognize the few who break through as trailblazing pioneers instead of saviors, we might avoid the pitfall of setting them apart to be first idolized, and then crucified.
-§-

What if those individuals we consider "enlightened" have simply evolved a new, more sophisticated perceptual function? Perhaps the yogic state of "samadhi," the blossoming of the thousand-petalled lotus at the crown chakra, results when a switch is flipped within the endocrine glands that allows a higher-order capacity to "see" the larger whole of reality. Our attachment to the notion of individuality may very well prevent us from recognizing what is really happening when a person goes through the type of personal transformation and soul acceleration we affix with labels such as "enlightenment" and "self-realization." In the awakened state, we grok the quantum field in which we live and breathe. This type of transition might very well be the plan of evolution for all of us. If we recognize the few who break through as trailblazing pioneers instead of saviors, we might avoid the pitfall of setting them apart to be first idolized, and then crucified.

Respect and appreciation are the hallmarks of relationships that thrive. Resonance of heart is easier to achieve in a field of respect and deep care. Holding ground in that field allows us to grasp the tail, so to speak, of our own evolution—to wake up from the dream of separation and transform the dysfunctional archetypes currently playing out in the family of man. If we can muster the courage and presence to rescue ourselves, individually and collectively, from the tyranny of rejection and its downstream consequences—contempt, disrespect, and violence—our relational intelligence will grow swift and strong. So many aspects of each of us have been trapped in states of arrested development precisely because we lack a deep relational context, a fertile and honoring ground, in which our true nature might flower.

To open the heart and live deeply aware of one another and all of earth's inhabitants involves a clear and conscious leap. We escape the barbed-wire trap of our "person-constructs" and become like musical instruments in a grand, chaordic, exquisitely sensate orchestra conducted by that ever-loving trickster—the ineffable divine.

A Dialog With the Invisible

What we know of the world comes in through vibrational stimulation. Each of our sensory organs is attuned to different frequencies of vibration. Our senses and brain organize vibrations we call teal or magenta, tender or tough, pungent or fragrant, melodic or discordant. Over millions of years, vision evolved in the human species to be able to respond to the electromagnetic frequencies of light. Hearing, likewise, allows us to encounter and experience the frequencies of sound. Our senses of smell, taste, and touch, all bring sensation through different channels that register a world of spiraling particles and waves. We process, evaluate, reason, invent, re-invent and make-story in response to vibratory input, giving meaning to the ocean of never-ending particles and waves—giving it and us "intelligence."

-§-
We escape the barbed-wire trap of our "person-constructs" and become like musical instruments in a grand, chaordic, exquisitely sensate orchestra conducted by that ever-loving trickster—the ineffable divine.
-§-

A new intelligence function, a distinct emerging faculty, has been evolving in the human species over time. What we think of as "enlightenment" evidences this new capacity. A refined aptitude, this type of intelligence enables us to sense the unseen bonds that sustain every single irreducible integer of matter in the universe. This new, or latent, or evolving sense could be called "kaleido," from the Greek root meaning "with a beautiful form." Enlightenment, as a new way of sensing, encompasses the complex relationship of genetic, physiological, psychological, and cultural transformation. This can be seen in creative transformational communities operating in the borderlands at the periphery of mainstream culture (you know who you are). When all of our senses fuse and give birth to the faculty we are calling kaleido, we are able to directly, experientially encounter our bond with all that is.

Herein lies the great marriage. We are all wed to one another and the time to make a conscious leap into that depth of kinship is now. We marry this truth: we are incredibly vulnerable creatures, with neurological pathways conditioned to distort reality and make it difficult to re-enter the Eden that awaits our return. We can rise up from the ashes of our great demons—isolation and lack—and slay their companions, the dragons of gluttony and greed. Getting through the eye of the needle requires us to evolve a new capacity to sense ourselves as holographic organisms of consciousness. This sense can be learned when we engage active imagination and decide to consciously evolve.

Our kaleido capacity, which allows us to grok one another and our world, opens a door to deep empathy and natural ethical behavior because we suddenly simply know what to do. Human conduct, at the individual and collective level, either harmonizes with the natural order of the universe or creates disharmony. We can accelerate our own evolution, and quicken our kaleido capacity, by engaging in practices that increase our sensitivity to the vibration of our surrounding environment. Just as a musical instrument must be constantly tuned, so we must tune ourselves, attending to the ever-present harmony-inherent.

Quantum reality reveals the interdependence of everything. Once our kaleido-sense opens, we can no longer pretend that our actions and thoughts have no affect on others. Quantum physics becomes less theoretical and more experiential. We begin to play in a much wider field—a field of awe and wonder.

Constellations in the Social Interactive Field

A fascinating phenomenon that has been brought to light by the new physics is that matter exists primarily as empty space. Further discovery suggests that the solidity of form only really occurswhen two or more objects approach one anoter. This can be seen within our psychologyas well.

-§-

A new intelligence function, a distinct emerging faculty, has been evolving in the human species… "enlightenment" evidences this new capacity.

-§-

We all have relationships with certain others that cause us to constellate reactive patterns that don't show up in their absence. Certain relational dynamics activate poles of opposition when two or more enter the same space. When we become identified with constellations within the social interactive field, (this is me, that is you) relational dynamics can become so polarized that rifts, splits and degradation of the field can occur.

Those of us who are waking up and coming into greater awareness have a deep responsibility. The intricacies of relationship play out on many levels. Humans are multi-dimensional organisms of consciousness. Some of the play is in our chemistry, some in the realm of thoughts—which we now know are real things—and some in the quiet depths of the soul. If we feel slighted by someone's indifference or spite, we need to recognize in the moment, that we may be experiencing a collision of conditioned states. If our desire is to make contact and connect, we best develop fierce devotion because ours may be the only finesse that can penetrate that conditioning. First, we must deeply sense the other, not out of reaction or coercion but in an attempt to break the spell of disrespect. This may be what Jesus meant by love your enemies, and turn the other cheek. We go back to Anthony's dream:

"There are responsibilities to sitting in the circle. The Shaman is clearly the master and the maestro. He conducts the human orchestra, does not judge or chastise, but witnesses each in his or her song. When egos emerge discordant with the music, he gently charms and guides them toward harmony. He never struggles to control anyone, but coaxes the divinity out of each with his flute. He plays the wild song of emotions, psychic space, psychological space, ego, and air. Some songs sing of power and enormity—others of softness and intricacy."

When facing others in the social interactive field we do well to understand what kind of animals we are. If not alert, we can behave in a way to exactly provoke what we most fear. Or, if we have embodied and integrated our own primal instincts and triune brain, empathic attunement can help us sense what might be needed in the moment. If someone is barking at us, do we bark back? Or do we roll over and expose our soft underbelly? In a constant dance, we can shift in and out of identifying and dis-identifying with a multitude of subjective voices. The multiplicity gives us greater range, and makes available new options for meeting and facing others. When we see that we are part of a larger organism, not just an individualized identity, we recognize that it is in our own best interest, and the interest of the larger whole, to meet reactive subjectivity with acceptance. "Other" is, after all, part of our own body. This is the development of deep empathy.

-§-

Quantum physics becomes less theoretical and more experiential. We begin to play in a much wider field—a field of awe and wonder.

-§-

We have to bring all our will, courage, and vulnerability to moments of disharmony because that is when we can consciously evolve. I have to know that next time I am confronted with a reactive, conditioned response, in myself or in another, it requires every bit of my evolving intelligence to redirect the current and find a new way. The old stories of disharmony and strife, of humans not getting along, of humans dissociating from one another's plight, are stale seeds—storylines that lead to the "same old, same old." To sing a new song and plant our chosen seeds, we need to realize that the storylines are not necessarily of our own design. They have been planted in our mind, sown into our neural pathways by the countless conversations and human dramas of a dying, competitive culture that believes the war between the sexes, and all the other wars, are inevitable. Seeded in the ground of our being, the soap opera of separation has become all too real. Waking up means chucking the old storylines and writing a brand new script now. We can do it in the twinkle of an eye, as expressed in the following verse:

Motherground

by Geralyn Gendreau

There is a state, an awareness coming through
that is completely whole
and it opens the window to immortal bliss
to a flow of experience that is uninterrupted,
fully companioned
in every moment
by the Mother
of All That Is.

What we are
is what we've always been.
There's never been anything anywhere but God.
Take a look, see it inside you.
The light is there.
All it takes is one person
seeing it in another
for all of us to shine.

Marya Mann:

Quantum Kin: Creating Communities in the New Time

Enchanting masks of the Queen Witch Rangda are kept in the secret, innermost shrines of Balinese temples. They are only brought out on holy occasions to help restore balance to a tilting world. My first night in Bali, a friend picked me up and we drove to the outskirts of Denpasar at break-neck speed. Headed to a graveyard for a ceremonial meditation on the nature of existence, the drive itself was a meditation on sudden death. From her mythic abode on the most sacred volcano Gunung Agung, Rangda was due to descend and reveal her terrifying face.

I'd seen photos depicting Rangda's bulging eyes, her long stringy hair, her sharp nails and twisted fangs. Rangda, like her sisters Kali and Durga, is said to be so frightening, she scares away even the worst wickedness.

Although I knew Rangda to be a mythic creature, on that November night in 1985, with bats circling over my head inside the moist, murky cemetery, Rangda—or my anticipation of her—was more frightening than the cemetery itself. Thus began my first night on the island "where the gods spend their vacation." Amid gloomy gravestones and misshapen corpses awaiting cremation, as we watched for the "the evil one" to appear, I understood my first lesson from this elder culture: behind all that is visible, there is a more potent invisible realm.

Marya Mann, Ph.D., trained as a dancer, yogini, and poet in West Texas. A student of Joseph Campbell, Richard Freeman, Jean Houston, and Balinese, Haitian, and Native American Shamans, she choreographs dances for the multi-dimensional body and has brought sacred art traditions in the U. S., Bali, Australia, and the Solomon Islands. Dr. Mann teaches Yoga Dance, Quantum Leap Creativity, Mythic Theater, and Healing Movement, and performs with the musical group Moonshine. Writing fiction, theater, and film, her goal is "dancing for the world, laughing for love, and leaving a legacy of harmony." www.lotuslivingarts.org. Photo courtesy of Shari 'Star' Dewar.

Original Gifts

This is not exactly how I'd imagined myself unwinding from the eighteen-hour plane ride from San Francisco. Earlier that day, I had gone to have a coconut oil massage on the beach. Madé, the medicine woman, smoothed my jet lagged muscles with her gnarly brown hands. Her face, bronze and withered like a ginger root, bore a perpetual smile. Even with two missing teeth, she was beautiful, incandescent, overflowing with a natural glow of equanimity. In Bali, Madé explained, every woman who is older than you is called *Ibu,* or mother, and every man who is older is called *Bapak,* or father. In this way, love extends to kin, and yet reaches beyond kinship, into the total web of life. "In Bali, everyone is family," she said, "You'll be part of our family too."

Having learned bodywork from traditional Balinese shamans and medicine women, Madé transmitted ancient, sensuous knowledge through her fingers, knuckles, and palms. After the massage, we arranged red and purple flowers, green leaves, white rice, and betel nuts in palm leaf trays called *banten.* We carried these offerings to a stunning seaside temple, and prayed for a safe and fruitful journey. At the temple, I was surprised to meet up with friends of a religious scholar I'd met at the University of Colorado. "You want to come to cemetery," said Ketut. "You meet Rangda tonight. We have ceremony there. You will come?" He laughed a little luminous giggle, as if he already knew my answer. "Yes?"

-§-

"Humans, more than any other living form, invent themselves."
—Thomas Berry

-§-

I had traveled halfway around the world to dance, see theater, and enjoy the colorful displays of creative vision Bali is known for—I didn't want to miss a thing. Despite jet lag, I agreed to go. As we left the temple, Madé waved and said, *"Selamat Jalan!"* Peace on your journey.

On the way to the cemetery, Ketut said, "We must stand up to Rangda as warriors for Barong." Barong, he explained, was a ferocious yet lighthearted lion who embodies all that is good. On holy days in every temple on the island, Rangda and Barong, both beloved mythical creatures among the Balinese, play out the eternal battle between good and evil, and life and death. In between ceremonies, their sacred masks are kept in the village temples to magically protect the community from harm.

Going from a blissful, oceanic massage, to a dainty flower temple offering, to crouching in mud on a black night next to a tomb waiting for the personification of evil to appear, seemed somehow appropriate in Bali. The astonishing union of opposites and balancing of all the forces of life is what makes Balinese culture so intriguing. Small rituals, daily offerings, and grandiose ceremonies blend together in one of most profound sacred art traditions on the planet.

In the graveyard, bloodcurdling night sounds and putrid smells added to a tingling in my spine, but as far as I could tell, the real and fearful thoughts came only from my mind. Like a kitten, frightened by the sight of myself in a mirror, I found that no one else was there. My own fear of death—an evil feeling if ever there was one—was suddenly pointless, as were most of my fears. In the cemetery, several hours after our meditation began, Ketut said, "We face Rangda to face reality. That's all."

After facing death, evil, and annihilation by my own thoughts, my appreciation of truth, beauty, and goodness made a sharp ascent. Cleansed and empowered by our contemplation on life and death, light and dark, I had peeked through the curtain between us and thunder, this world and the next, and lived to tell about it.

Phil Cousineau wrote in *The Art of Pilgrimage,* "Everywhere, the way of the pilgrim is twofold, exterior and interior, the simultaneous movement of the feet and the soul through time as well as space." In Bali, together with feet and soul, the mind moves through multidimensional space too. One encounters gods and goddesses and learns to be more god-like inside. The desire for knowledge nudges something within us that is already divine. Having journeyed across the quantum field into the minds and hearts of people I had never met before, I was invited into their wisdom ways. Doors normally closed to foreigners opened easily, and I was included as kin.

The Balinese have a word for their uncanny perceptions of the subtle aspects of people, what is unspoken and unseen, yet moves at the speed of light. *Kaiket* (pronounced k_'-ye-ket) means, literally, "to be tied." An extraordinary word, it points to the Balinese belief that each person is tied from birth to luminous fields of energy that connect everything and extend in all directions. Like subatomic "massless particles" identified by quantum physicists, these invisible streamers of energy travel through space, mountains, people, animals, plants, and even planets. Carrying wisdom, language, and love, this impersonal medium is as malleable to our thoughts and our affections as warm honey is to the dip of a finger.

While some Balinese priests, priestesses, and shamans, or *balian,* have more experience and expertise with *kaiket,* and function as community healers, most Balinese have a mystical sensitivity that navigates easily on the rivers of kaiket. They learn at an early age to appease, celebrate, and connect with the vital life force which dances in invisible, indivisible streams, nourishing, stimulating, and informing us—if we pay attention.

In the Western world, we generally pay attention to just four directions, but the Balinese have a highly developed sense of direction and place. They recognize at least nine, and in some cases, eleven directions. Energies or vitalities—which the Balinese call gods and goddesses—reside in the North, South, East, and West. There are four more in the Northeast,

Southeast, Northwest, and Southwest. A ninth, the center called puseh, is the position of the observer. In the North of Bali, general agreement has it that up and down form two more important directions, bringing the total to eleven. One is surrounded in every direction by a multidimensional spirit percolating through all space, time, and matter. Because the Balinese are so intimately tied through this moving sea of energy, it becomes crucial to know where one is in space. Spatial relationships to the mountains, the sea, and each other, come alive. The Web of Life reaches from the underworld to the heavens, and is populated by mythical beings that penetrate all things.

Hindu scholar Gusti Ngurah, who translates original Sanskrit teachings into Balinese, Indonesian and English, laughed when I told him Rangda had appeared to me and my comrades. I met him the day after my visit to the cemetery. He implied that a fearless goddess like Rangda would never select such innocents as her opponents. The battle of good and evil, I was glad to learn, was fought on evenhanded terms.

-§-

Nature is a worldwide symbiosis of love, mutuality, and nurturance.

-§-

"Everything in nature exists in balance," he said. "But sometimes, the weather, outsiders, or chaotic spirits disrupt the natural order by getting entangled in the flow of harmonizing energies." Powerful *bhutas* and *kalas*—Earth demons, whose job is to create chaos and disarrange the universe—exist, and therefore, we can take nothing for granted. *Bhutas* are entropy personified, he explained. In contrast, *Sangyang Widhi Wasa,* the supreme Balinese oversoul, is the energetic pattern for goodness and natural harmony.

Later, as we walked through Tanah Lot, a temple that honors the guardian spirits of the sea, Bapak Gusti continued, "Ancestors also exist in space, but generally come to *Palinggih,* or spirit houses like these." He pointed to a carved throne two stories high. Sculpted by local stonemasons who consider their work an offering for the gods, the spirit house welcomes ancestral kin. Embellished with intricate spirals, swastikas, leaves, rivers, animals, tendrils, flowers and trees, the throne stands for balance between the various forces of nature. On a shelf above the steps, below a high tower, fresh frangipani flowers blended their aroma with spicy incense. Every inch of the shrine was a work of art.

Modern science keeps shifting its theories and metaphors to explain the quantum field. They tell us subatomic particles are not particles at all, but wave motions shifting into particle-hood, then shifting, just as quickly back into the wave-world. The basic stuff of the universe is an ever-creating medium, re-creating itself in ongoing, provocative play. If particles can be dualistic, so can science, art, and spirituality. The poetic understanding and rituals of Balinese culture reflect this. Bali itself is a work of art, a credit to the creative spirit inherent in every human being. Our secularized, mechanistic notions in the West turn us into human machines instead of human beings. The Balinese see the divine everywhere—not only in churches, temples, or mosques. The Balinese relate to each other and to nature with minuscule offerings no bigger than a thought, and with elaborate gifts that can take years to make.

Daily cycles of creation and gift-giving feed the air we breathe, sustaining a sense of abundance that goes beyond material goods. *Have we forgotten to honor the invisible, or Niskala side of nature?* I wondered. *Is that why our planet suffers? When we don't use our creative energy for good, the energy goes bad?* We are innately creative, continually in creative exchange with our environment. We breathe in oxygen produced by the oaks, aspens, and palm trees; the forests are fed by the carbon dioxide we exhale. Nature is a worldwide symbiosis of love, mutuality, and nurturance. We take in food, air and water to create blood, bone, and skin. We turn our emotions into thoughts and our thoughts into memories. We create all the time. But we're often unaware of how and what we're creating. Sometimes, without knowing it, we create pain, alienation, fear, and discontent.

Consciously aligning with our inborn creativity, we can become more responsible co-creators. We feel our kinship with the creative principle itself, flowing through the total Web of Life. We need not feel separate or alienated, for we are a member of the cosmic family as purely as every flower, star, and wave in the ocean. And we are just as necessary.

We belong here, and we each have original gifts to give to the universe.

In the New Time, there is no original sin, only original gifts. Once we face our fears, especially our fear of death, as Ketut showed me in the cemetery, we can bring forth our original gifts. We can do this for all our kin; and we're all quantum *kin.*

Natural Creativity, Kinship, and the Cycles of Nature

In Kintamani, a busload of commuters veers off a busy road in front of one of Bali's 22,000 temples. Dozens of pilgrims climb out, palm leaf and flower offerings in hand. They kneel before the spirit house. Incense is lit. As they pray, a priest sprinkles holy water, and gives them rice. They get back in the bus and leave. Three minutes have passed.

What a concept! Drive-by blessings. Drive-in confessionals. Drive-through churches. These petite temples couldn't be less like our modern steel, brick, and glass places of worship. They're open to the air, humble and mystical. There are no walls to make a prison or keep outsiders out. The light of spirit shines on all.

In the New Time, we are beginning to remember what indigenous societies all over the world have known. First, when we slow down, we have the space and time to let the good stuff catch up with us. And secondly, the good stuff is the life force, or soul, permeating all things.

Martin Prechtel, an advocate of the Mayan cosmology, says in *The Toe Bone and the Tooth,* "The only way to live in harmony with the natural and spiritual world is through nurturing the natural world." What we receive from the soul of the Earth, water, and air to make a living, he says, needs to be given back to the elements. "We need to create a relationship with what feeds us. What we have that nature doesn't is our voice and opposable thumbs! So with our hands we create offerings and with the voice we make prayers and songs. We can make a collective offering."

In his book, *Songlines,* Bruce Chatwin speaks of another indigenous culture, the Australian Koories, who go on Walkabout to sing into the landscape. In the time before time, in the Dreamtime, the Cosmic Soul, in the form of Ancient Ones, came to Earth to create "songlines," natural forms—rivers, trees, and mountains—that are like musical scores of celestial music. The natural world is sustained by the cyclical singing of human tribes on Walkabout. By traversing the ancient pathways or songlines where streams, valleys, and landforms were chanted to life by the Ancient Ones, Aborigines keep the world alive, awake, and resplendent with generosity toward our human and more-than-human kin.

-§-
When we slow down, we have the space and time to let the good stuff catch up with us.
-§-

Most indigenous people dialogue with the world of spirit as intimately as we might chat with a best friend. This ongoing communication gives them a profound sense of belonging, of being connected. In West Africa, there is a belief similar to Balinese *kaiket.* Instead of the Cartesian idea, *Cogito, ergo sum,* or "I think, therefore I am," West Africans say, "I belong, therefore I am." They, like the Balinese, trust that deep contact with each other, spirit, and the rhythms of nature upholds a palpable magic that can be directed toward health, well-being and abundance in the community.

Influenced by their Indonesian ancestors, by South Indian Hinduism, by North Indian Buddhism, and by ninth century Chinese and Malaysian traders, the Balinese have evolved an original, multi-dimensional cosmology called Bali Hinduism. The Balinese have always been quick to assimilate new ideas, incorporating those features they like and discarding others. They have open minds that have over millennia created an "elder culture," with much to teach us about living in harmony and living life as an offering.

When offerings of banana leaf, areca nut, and lime are made by groups of women for the gods, the very act of creating is an offering, a social event, part of the gift. What is given to spirit is made carefully, with as much attention to detail as possible. Francine Brinkgreve, author of *Offerings: The Ritual Art of Bali,* says, "Charming elements in an offering are sometimes hidden from human eyes, but not from the invisible powers for whom they are conscientiously made. The art of the offering goes beyond the beauty of the outwardly visible forms, for creativity and skill extends to many little details which are not directly visible."

Much human effort is involved in re-creating the fruits of the Earth into an element of worship. Rice might be dyed pink or blue, sculpted into cones or animal shapes, constructed into tree-like cones, assembled with flowers, and modeled into a geometric rendition of a six-foot-tall mandala. These edible arts are piled into delicate towers on the women's heads, then carried to the temple. Gods and goddesses receive their essence, and then the humans enjoy them as part of their feast.

Life feeds on life. Life creates life. Life leads to more life.

Making beautiful things for the presence of spirit heals, mollifies, and balances the forces of nature, maintaining the web of life by bringing people together, healing fractures in the social body, restoring friendliness, and affirming kinship and kindness to the community.

-§-

Aborigines keep the world alive, awake, and resplendent with generosity toward our human and more-than-human kin.

-§-

When a Balinese child is born, a spiritual board of directors, the *kanda empat,* or four siblings, comes along. These subtle siblings come into the body with the soul and stand guard in the womb, inhabiting the placenta, amniotic fluid, blood, and the *vernix caseosa.* In the last trimester, prayers are offered not only for the baby, but also for the *kanda empat,* which are imbued with tremendous spiritual power. During childbirth, the amniotic fluid "opens the door" for the baby to exit, the *vernix caseosa* and blood assist on each side, and the placenta pushes from behind. After birth, the placenta is washed and placed in a carved yellow coconut, wrapped in white cloth, and buried by the parents' front door. From that sacred spot, the child draws divine strength for years to come.

Once born, the *kanda empat* remain with the child throughout life. If heard, appeased, and celebrated, they help the child respond harmoniously to cosmic forces. One sibling guides on the physical plane, teaching how to digest food or make a house. Another helps the child emotionally, showing how to develop self-discipline or choose a mate. The third gives advice in the mental realm, helping with career and business decisions, while the fourth is a soul guide, who advises the individual in how to die properly. Given enormous respect, the *kanda empat* are addressed at every ceremony and are believed to have great powers of protection. A Balinese child is never alone. Even in the darkest night or the loneliest day, this spiritual board of directors is available for consultation.

As subtle but very real presences, the *kanda empat* nurture each and every Balinese person. In the West, we tend to look upon myth, and the mythic body, as preposterous fantasy. Joseph Campbell, however, once referred to myths as "facts of the mind." Mythic energies are just as real as matter; they simply exist in more subtle dimensions, in the *Niskala,* or unseen world. They may in fact be more powerful than the visible, or *Sekala,* reality we can see and feel. From the Balinese point of view, *Sekala* and *Niskala* interweave imperceptibly. Divine beings rise out of the watery depths, devas live in jungle-clad crevices, and gods and goddesses attend lavish ceremonies on high holy days. It is a busy spiritual world, filled with mystery, wonder, love, humor, and celebration—all designed to realize harmony, which is the most precious treasure on the one web of life.

-§-

Making beautiful things for the presence of spirit heals, mollifies, and balances the forces of nature, maintaining the web of life.

-§-

Offerings to the Web of Life

As the full moon rises, streams of people walk from the inner courtyard of the temple, cross an avenue of coconut palms, step over cobbled stones, and head toward the Javanese Sea. Women in sacred sashes carry bowls of fruit, flowers, and elaborate figurines on their heads. Men clothed in batik sarongs, white Nehru jackets, and white headdresses chat with their neighbors. Children and teens in colorful scarves and painted toenails hurry to the water's edge to catch the moon's first light on the lavender sea.

Full moon is a special time for Puja, for aligning with celestial dynamics in the Balinese world. When families and clans arrive on the white sand beach, a gamelan orchestra bursts open, a sonic flower in sudden bloom. Aromatic gifts and fabulous towers of rice, meat, and color are blessed by priests and priestesses chanting robust Sanskrit prayers. The moon casts a neon lavender glow on the Javanese Sea, shining a river of light across the water's surface to shore.

Bundles of clove and cinnamon incense are lit. Individual sticks are passed to each of the one thousand or so people sitting in casual rows along the undulating shoreline. Worshippers fix their incense sticks in the sand in front of them, near offerings of flower and rice. Offerings, representing the fruits of their labors, are given freely to the invisible generative forces. Sweeping their palms over the incense smoke, the Balinese cleanse all that has passed, all psychic debris, from their hands. Then they bring their hands over their heads into international prayer position to honor the one spirit.

When the temple priest or priestess, called a *Pemangku,* rings the temple bell, all in attendance point their purified hands toward the Earth, to honor all creation and their own bodies. Second, they bring their hands over the heart, to honor all people and the mind. Third, they bring their prayer hands over their heads again. In unison, they weave together lower, middle, and upper worlds.

As the incense smoke continues to wind its way upward, it carries prayers for abundance and peace to the heavens. Devotees place a red flower from their offering trays between their middle fingers, slowly wave the flowers over the incense and place their hands, palms together, above their heads. The red flower represents the power of the Creator, the vitality of Brahma, and is an offering for the effulgence of the entire Spiritual milieu. Then they move their praying hands to the forehead, thumbs touching the third eye between the eyebrows, and then to the heart. The next flower they select is yellow and represents Vishnu, the sustaining power of life. Waving it over the incense, they again move prayer hands through the three levels. Then they choose a white flower, for Shiva, the power that dissolves what is no longer needed, and move through the three prayer positions again.

Thousands of people reach down to their offering trays, lifting their offerings to the sky in perfect step, and with this simple acknowledgment of a higher purpose, the age-old choreography creates harmony. The waves, the mountains, the fish, the fire, can't help but notice. All the forces of life come into accord.

-§-

Mythic energies are just as real as matter; they simply exist in more subtle dimensions.

-§-

In the breezes undulating through the salty night air, the primal Creative Spirit lives. Ritually honored and thanked by the people, that spirit is poured in the form of holy water into the worshippers' waiting palms by temple *Pemangku* who circulate through the crowd. Three pours, three drinks, cleanse body, speech, and mind. A dab of sticky rice placed on the forehead or third eye "opens the mind." A dab on each temple "clears the vision," and a dab goes on the sternum, "to nourish the heart." The cycle is complete. The community has given to spirit, and spirit has returned the favor.

Mantra, music, dance, and art are the visible means by which humans contribute to the delight of spirit. Spirit responds by showering goodness, truth, and beauty upon the land in an ongoing creative cycle.

Making more and more beauty to maintain this cyclical pattern of nature is the purpose of life in Bali. Creativity nurtures the spiritual world and keeps the upper, middle and lower worlds in balance. Without conscious and continual creativity, the demonic aspects of life would gain the upper hand. Things would fall apart. Lines of *kaiket* would get tangled. People would wander without direction or purpose.

Masculine and feminine. High and low. Good and evil. In and out. Waking and dreaming. Seen and unseen. All the opposites must be balanced. Yet while these dualities are basic tenets of Balinese cosmology, it is the middle way, the addition of a third element, that creates ultimate concordance in the natural order of the universe.

-§-
Mantra, music, dance, and art are the visible means by which humans contribute to the delight of spirit.
-§-

Gusti told me that when Hindu Majapahit scholars arrived in Bali in the mid-14th century with teachings derived from the Upanishads, they brought with them the Trimurti, or "three shapes." Always willing to try a new way, indigenous Balinese saw that in their land of sharp contrasts, the duality of opposing forces could be philosophically resolved by synthesis into a trinity.

They built the Balinese temples, or *Pura,* to have three areas, the outer steps, the middle courtyard and the inner shrine. Like the human body, which has outer skin, middle muscles, and inner organs, the temple is a microcosm of the cosmos, which has outer, or visible elements, the magical in-between, and the inner, or invisible essence. Just as the body and the temple have upper, middle and lower aspects, so the entire cosmos has an upper world for high spirits, the middle world for humans and a lower world for demons. The principle of the threes is interwoven throughout Balinese cosmology, which reflect both spiritual and material patterns of life.

The most important triad in Bali is the Hindu trinity: *Brahma,* the creator; *Vishnu,* or *Wisnu,* the sustainer; and *Shiva,* or *Siwa* (pronounced S long-EWA), the destroyer or dissolver. Much like the Christian Father, Son, and Holy Spirit, or the Goddess tradition of Mother, Virgin, and Crone, the trinity represents three aspects of one indivisible whole. The cycles of life are in continual movement, creating and sustaining what is created, then dissolving and recreating itself. Different vitalities or aspects of the divine creative force represent these different movements, much as a symphony has diverse melodies at various points in the music.

In Bali, I often felt I was experiencing the higher notes of the celestial symphony, the uncommon unities and melodies lost to most of our world, but which the Balinese have preserved. It is sometimes said that Bali is more Indian than India, for many of the ancient devotional traditions were brought to Bali before they deteriorated in India. Rabindranath Tagore commented once that "Bali has taken the dance, and left India the ashes."

Of course these vital energies, or archetypes, can exist everywhere. They are part of a multidimensional latticework that flows throughout space, extending between and throughout our physical bodies as meridians, or electromagnetic pathways, and connecting us to the land, to spiritual presences, and each other. These streamers of energy, *kaiket,* can be broken, but they can also be woven together again.

Kaiket carries qualities we can affect through the power of our minds, through intention, thought and dreaming. The Balinese pray, not so much to ask for things, but to offer beautiful thoughts and wishes to the loom of life, to the presence of love, which always produces a response.

-§-
Every thought is a sacred trust, creating or destroying your original gifts, your best life dream.
-§-

Whether you believe this is true or not, you're right. Every thought is a sacred trust, creating or destroying your original gifts, your best life dream. Your every wish is eventually fulfilled.

Selamat Jalan. Peace on your journey.

John Easterling:
Living Treasure

Hunting for treasure and for lost cities of gold had been my full-time occupation for five years when the tunic came into my hands. A small, waist-length poncho from the Chimu period, it was the most spectacular artifact I had ever seen. When I held it in my hands, they immediately started to sweat.

I'd had a long-standing interest in pre-Columbian history and I was fascinated to find that much of the history of that era is accurate only by coincidence. Examining a pottery shard and retrofitting the demographics of a culture that disappeared over 500 years ago is speculative at best. We really know very little about those early civilizations. The mystery of Machu Picchu, the lost city of the Incas, and its mysterious Nazca lines—giant figures of spiders, birds and monkeys forming long runways that can only be seen from 3,000 feet in the air—had held me entranced since I was a boy. Evidence led me to believe that millions of people were living along that coast in ancient times. Even distant visitors were likely, as evidenced by head pots—small vessels made in the shape of a head—found from that period. I've seen head pots dated from 200 A.D. to 200 B.C. with features that look very much like the indigenous people who still live there today—but others that look Oriental; and still others with features that are distinctly Arabic.

I'd met the group of men conducting this particular dig through a pre-Columbian museum in Peru. Once they heard what I was doing, they invited me into their circle. Over ninety percent of the digs that were

An internationally recognized expert on environmental economics and natural healing modalities, Amazon John Easterling has twenty-five years experience exploring the Amazon as an entrepreneur and adventurer. A frequent guest on television and radio, his vision and leadership has helped secure the future of the rainforest as a concentrated repository of new chemistry and nutrition. Founded in 1990, Amazon Herb Company models ecological commerce, making life-saving botanicals available to a larger population, while providing resources at the village level for indigenous communities. Information at www.21stcenturyherbs.amazon herb.net.

going on in South America at the time were unofficial. It was real "Raiders of the Lost Ark" stuff, and we were about to unearth an important find.

The desert coast of Peru is dryer than the Sahara. When we found the mummy, it was so well preserved we could still see fingernails and hair. One of my comrades worked the tunic off the mummy. Having been involved with a number of pre-Inca, Chimu and Moche digs on the north coast of Peru, I knew this piece was special and felt an immediate attraction to it. These occasional treasure finds were always thrilling.

The Chimu textile we found on the mummy turned out to be significant from a historical standpoint because of the patterns drawn on the tunic. The step motif was most certainly Inca, but the color and pattern were clearly Chimu. A transitional piece between the two cultures, it was over 800 years old. I showed the artifact at the Merrin Gallery in New York City, and at the Smithsonian Institute. The curator for pre-Columbian textiles at the Smithsonian expressed interest in the piece, as did many collectors.

Each year in August, there is a show of pre-Columbian textiles in Santa Fe, New Mexico. That year, there was a great deal of talk about the Harmonic Convergence. It was 1987, and I had been in possession of the textile for five years. Whenever I would show the piece, as soon as I began to unroll it, my hands would start to sweat, and I would feel feverish.

-§-

Just as I had finished covering the fabric up—swoop!—a condor came out of nowhere and brushed my right shoulder with its talons.

-§-

While at the Santa Fe show that year, I had a number of offers to buy the Chimu piece. But every time someone made an offer, I would raise the price. I could not bring myself to sell the unusual textile. Finally, a light bulb came on in my head. It became clear to me that I should take the piece back to Peru and rebury it. I made a conscious decision to return it, and from that moment forward, the hand-sweating and other reactions I was having when handling the tunic never recurred.

I don't know what officials would have thought had I been caught smuggling a Peruvian artifact back into the country, but that is what I did. Unfortunately, the area where we found the mummy had been looted, so I could not return the tunic to the place it had been found. I stored it in Lima for almost a year before making a dedicated trip to rebury it.

The piece was too precious to put back in the ground just anywhere. I knew it was important to find a place with the right resonance, so I took the tunic with me to the highlands and several other places. In Tambo Machay, North of Cusco, where the old Incan empire was located, I found a beautiful area where water comes right out of the side of the mountain. The Inca had treated this as a sacred place where they would go for spiritual renewal. The area had the type of resonance I had been looking for to re-bury the artifact. I washed the textile in order to release whatever energies were trapped there, and to soak it so that it would decompose after having survived nearly a thousand years on the dry desert coast.

It was a perfectly clear day, and the bright, big blue sky high up in the Andes gave me the sense that I could see forever. As I climbed up the side of a very steep mountain, I could see women grazing their llamas on another hill across the valley. The hill was so steep that I had to lean into it, and I lay on the ground to keep from falling as I dug a hole with a small pick. I put the tunic into the ground and began to cover it with dirt. Just as I had finished covering the fabric up—swoop!—a condor came out of nowhere and brushed my right shoulder with its talons. I felt the claws sweep the side of my head and almost take my ear off. My hair blew back as the large raptor flew by. I lay into the hill and turned to watch it fly off, but nothing was there. I could see forever, and yet the condor was nowhere to be seen.

I came off the side of that hill feeling very light, as if a heavy load had been lifted from me. Things started shifting for me that very day. I had re-buried the tunic on a Saturday, flew back to the U.S. the following Wednesday, and within a week I had two offers on the table to buy my business, Raiders of the Lost Art. This was surprising to me, because it had been for sale for several months with no offers.

I sold my trading company for more than I had anticipated. As part of the deal, I spent the next three months with the new owners, showing them the ropes. Their interests lay more toward gemstones than artifacts, so I toured around Brazil and Uruguay with them, introducing them to my South American associates. Then we exhibited at a number of shows in the U.S., so I could introduce the new owners to customers and teach them how to display and sell the treasures. During those three months, I began to plan an extended trip to Nepal and the Far East.

It was to be my last weekend as a South American trader—the last day of the last gem show, down to the last hour. In another hour, I would be free to go. An adventurer at heart, I could hardly wait; this segment of my life was almost complete. A man walked up and began looking over the gems displayed on the table before me. We struck up a conversation about the lost cities of gold. We talked about the Nazca lines on the desert floor in Peru, a subject that had fascinated me since the age of eight. We talked about positive and negative energy and the different modes of transportation that might be made available by harnessing those energy potentials. We discussed a number of other topics of shared interest. Then the man left.

I thought nothing of it; gem shows attract a lot of interesting folks. But the man came back an hour later, as the show was closing down. He told me he'd never been to a gem show before, which was curious, because only gem dealers can get into that show. When he woke up that morning, he told me, he knew he had to go to the show to meet someone and deliver a message. He said he was sure that I was the person he'd been directed to speak to, and asked me to step aside with him for a moment. Once alone, he asked if I had ever thought about working in the area of health. I said, "Well, I run occasionally, and try to eat right. I have some special jungle herbs I eat, but—other than that—not really."

He said, "You will do something in the field of health that will affect the lives of millions of people. Would you accept that charge?"

Without thinking, I said, "Sure," and reached to shake his outstretched hand. He dropped a small crystal point into my hand and said, "You will be very busy and there will be many demands on your time, so remember to guard your own health." He then took three steps into the crowd and vanished.

On my way back to my home in Florida, I felt a compelling urge to telephone a friend named Nicole Maxwell. I wanted her to know I had just sold my business and would be going back to Bolivia and Peru one last time. Nicole and I had met many years earlier and she had helped me gain an early understanding of medicinal plants from the jungle.

-§-
He said, "You will do something in the field of health that will affect the lives of millions of people. Would you accept that charge?"
-§-

I had my first experience of the healing potential of wild jungle herbs in my twenties while exploring the Amazon. I was in an ongoing state of compromised health, functioning at about 50% of my normal capacity. My health problems had begun before my first trip to South America with a case of hepatitis, and were compounded later by a near-fatal bout with Rocky Mountain spotted fever.

My doctor had put me on a very restrictive recovery schedule for hepatitis. I did little but rest for a number of weeks. Once recovered, I began to feel strong again and took a job working with a survey crew in North Carolina. My first week on the job, we were surveying a thickly wooded area full of heavy grasses and infested with millions of ticks. We had to tape our pants to our shoes to prevent the ticks from crawling up our clothes. It was a long, hot, sweaty week. When we got our paychecks that Friday, the whole crew went down to the local bar for a cold one. It was 1972, I was in my twenties, and that ice cold beer just looked too good. My doctor had warned me that the damage to my liver caused by the hepatitis meant I could never drink again. Certain a lone beer couldn't hurt, I decided to drink just one.

By the time I got home that night, I was running a high fever. I had just read an article about a guy who died from Rocky Mountain spotted fever—there were seven cases in North Carolina that year, and four people died—so I called the hospital and described my symptoms. That is the last thing I remember about that day. When my brother found me, I was in a state of delirium, fussing around with ice cubes in the freezer in an attempt to keep my fever down. When I woke up in the hospital the following day, I could barely speak, or keep track of my thoughts through a single sentence. I became weaker and weaker. My mind became fixated on going over basic functions in math, reviewing subtraction and addition problems, and then scanning through every lesson I'd ever learned. Completely oblivious to what was going on outside me, I brought all of my attention to maintaining the basic functions of my body. It took all the strength I could bring to bear just to keep my breath moving and my heart pumping.

-§-
Sailing toward the bright moon through the deep peaceful darkness into the light, I was completely filled with joy. I realized that I was in the presence of God.
-§-

After what seemed a very long time maintaining this vigilance, I grew tired and began to think I would take a nap. I realized, however, that if I didn't consciously attend to keeping my breath and my heartbeat going, I would very soon be moving on. The body required that much supervision to keep it going. Releasing my attention would be a sure-fire exit strategy. I didn't see any other option, so I was willing to let go. As soon as I did, I found myself sailing across a vast lake that was black and oily and very placid. At the far side of the lake I saw a huge moon, shining as bright as any sun. Sailing toward the bright moon through the deep peaceful darkness into the light, I was completely filled with joy. I realized that I was in the presence of God—there was total forgiveness and pure love. All of the mysteries I'd been curious about and puzzled by for years—from the lost cities of the Inca to the Nazca lines in Peru—suddenly made sense. The total history of the South America scene I'd been steeped in all those years came to my awareness. All the pieces fit together in the most remarkable and beautiful way. I flew closer and closer to the light on the far side of the lake until I came to a choice point. I had to make a decision. Essentially, I was offered an option: stay here, or, go back—knowing that someday I would return to this place. The next thing I knew, I was back in my body, remembering to breathe and keep my heart beating. Reversing the sequence I'd gone through on my way out, I once again reviewed everything I'd learned in this body on the way back in. I came right back to basic math equations and tracking my thoughts to make a full sentence. Three days later, I was strong enough to leave, and I walked out of the hospital.

Shortly thereafter, I went back to college and finished my degree in Environmental Studies. Upon graduation, I sold my car and bought a ticket to Ecuador. Although I did not find the lost cities of gold and Inca treasure, I did buy highland textiles and handicrafts to bring back to the 'States. I sold those pieces almost immediately upon my return, and had enough money to buy another ticket to Ecuador.

To support my avocation of searching for lost cities, I developed a trading business focusing primarily on woven alpaca wool and handicrafts from Ecuador, Peru, and Bolivia. Over the years, I increased the scope of the business to include gemstones and mineral specimens from Brazil and Uruguay, as well as jungle artifacts such as carved monkey bones, blowguns, and ceramics.

During one of the trips I took down river on the Ucayali, the jungle was especially hot and steamy. The Amazon can seriously drain a person's energy when the weather gets that extreme. As I was still compromised from the hepatitis, my energy began to fade. The indigenous people I was staying with gave me some local herbs—Una de gato and Chanca Piedra—boiled into a tea. Upon drinking this tea, I began to feel changes taking place in my body. Within a few days I felt a big difference in my energy level. A few more days went by, and I found myself feeling better than I had felt in a long time. Soon I felt better than I had before getting sick. The mental acuity I'd lost came back, and I was as clear as ever. I felt a core strength and vitality like nothing I could remember, and I also felt at peace in my environment. I'd been going down to the Amazon jungle for years, searching through ruins, looking for ceramics and lost treasure, chopping my way through the rainforest with a machete. What I had never realized before was that the treasure of the Amazon was the Amazon itself. I now began to recognize it for what it was. With over 200,000 species of plants, the Amazon Rainforest is the densest concentration of life energy on our planet.

-§-
What I had never realized before was that the treasure of the Amazon was the Amazon itself.
-§-

I have Nicole Maxwell to thank for being a source of inspiration and encouraging me to pursue the healing potential of rainforest plants. Born to a privileged San Francisco family in the early 1900s, Nicole grew up with an independent pioneering spirit. She married and spent time traveling in Europe. But eventually, she left that life and went to South America to become a gun-toating, cigarette-smoking reporter in Bolivia. While hacking her way through the jungle with a machete one day, Nicole cut her arm quite badly. The arterial bleeding was so severe that she might have died before finding her way out of the jungle. But the Indians in the jungle helped her out by putting the sap from a Sangre de Drago tree into the open wound. The medicinal plant sealed the gash in her arm and healed it with very little scarring. That got Nicole's attention. She spent twenty years in the jungle studying rainforest botanicals. Eventually she wrote *Witch Doctor's Apprentice: Searching for Medicinal Plants in the Amazon,* which was published in 1965.

When I met Nicole and she began to share her knowledge of rainforest herbs and plants, it hit me that the real treasure of the region was far more precious than anyone could have imagined. The rainforest is a vast treasure trove, a natural pharmacy of healing botanicals.

When I telephoned Nicole after selling my business, she kept saying how much she would love to go back to South America again. She was eighty-three years old at the time, and living in Mississippi. I offered to take her with me for that final trip. On the plane, Nicole and I discussed at length the remarkable untapped resource of the living forest. With my mind free from my previous business, I began to wonder what could be done to tap into the healing potential of medicinal plants. During my stay in Peru, I ended up collecting a number of bags full of rainforest herbs, and returned with them.

Upon my return to Florida, I consulted with my chiropractor and another associate who works with bioenergetics and electro-dermal screening technology to evaluate the herbs. When looked at with these diagnostic technologies, we discovered we had a new inventory of raw material that had extraordinary healing potential. We began testing and formulating the herbs into extracts that would be easy for people to use and appreciate.

In 1990, eight months into the formulation stage, I formed the Amazon Herb Company.

As people began to experience the powerful positive benefits of these formulas, a demand was created for more wild herbs. I returned to the Shipibo communities, and asked the Indians to collect more herbs—first twenty kilos, then fifty kilos. They were amazed. People in the Amazon live in very small communities of thirty to a hundred people, in general. There are a few communities of four- or five hundred people and a rare large community of one- or two- thousand, but the groups are usually much smaller. As I began to ask for larger and larger quantities of jungle herbs, they said, "Wow, your people really like these herbs. How many people in your community?" I told them we have 270 million people in my community, and after their shock wore off, the light began to dawn.

Over time, the model of environmental and ecological exchange became more and more clear. It became apparent that we could establish ecological commerce that would provide a solution for many of the jungle tribes by giving them a place in the larger economy that would enable them to protect and preserve their precious lands. And, it would provide a remarkable solution to degenerative disease issues for people in the West.

Heart disease, stroke, cancer, and the many degenerative diseases common to Americans are not seen among rainforest people upriver in the Amazon basin. To deal with these problems, Western medicine relies heavily on pharmaceuticals—drugs that are themselves the fourth leading cause of death in the U.S. Last year, medical doctors wrote 2.8 billion prescriptions for the American people. That is close to ten prescriptions for each man, woman and child in the United States. Drugs are chemicals that are not biodegradable. These chemicals pass through people and what is not absorbed is excreted back into the environment, and eventually into the water table. The potential consequences of this we can only imagine.

Compare our habits to eating a diet of wild plants growing in virgin soil. Wild plants, by their very nature, are the strongest and most potent, having survived hundreds of years of ecological change and challenge. Being the most hardy of their species, they possess a unique composition, a higher density of nutrition than that of wimpy cultivated plants. The more remote native communities hunt and gather jungle food—forest plants, wild bananas and plantains, wild game and birds, and fish taken live from the rivers and lagoons. A few plants are cultivated: root crops like yucca—which is boiled or fried—serve as a staple, much like rice is in China. Even these plants are not put into tidy rows, but allowed to grow semi-wild in small fields.

I believe the exploration of the Amazon rainforest and the discoveries it yields will be recorded in history as one of the most dramatic stories of our century. I am confident of this because of two simple facts. The first is that degenerative disease is the leading cause of death in the modern world. The second is that the Amazon rainforest is the richest source of nutrients and life energy on our planet.

-§-
Heart disease, stroke, cancer, and the many degenerative diseases common to Americans are not seen among rainforest people.
-§-

Even with growing volumes of data proving the life-saving value of the living rainforest, its very existence continues to be threatened. Our planet's greatest treasure house is being chain sawed and poisoned. The biggest offenders are farming, lumbering interests, cattle ranching, mineral exploration, and oil drilling.

This picture of destruction and pollution is alarming, but it serves as a call to action to show the magnitude of the opportunity in front of us. By employing a proven model of environmental economics, we demonstrate that the rainforest is more valuable alive than dead. We can effect positive change. By purchasing sustainably harvested and renewable rainforest products, we help to protect the rainforest and support the native people's economy.

This was proven to me beyond a shadow of doubt in the Shipibo village of Shambo. I was in Shambo to consult with the curanderos and to collect plants. As I was bidding farewell to some of the elders, they led me to a counsel where other elders and the chief had assembled. They gave speeches for the next hour on how Amazon Herb Company had saved their village, which had been in a state of social and economic disintegration. To survive, they had even considered selling their pristine rainforest off to lumbering interests. Now that we are providing them resources for the sustainable and ecological harvesting of medicinal plants, they have an ongoing stream of revenue. They went on to say that their sense of dignity had returned because they could now make new choices about their own future.

I believe in freedom of choice. I used to think that perhaps we shouldn't mess with the natives living in harmony with the earth. I thought we should leave the forest people alone. Over time, it occurred to me that I held that view because it made me feel good, but it was not the view the people of the Amazon have of themselves. They have a very different vision. Like all people, they want to expand from where they are into the new. It was pure hypocrisy on my part to think that I knew what was best for them. In some cases, the indigenous people choose not to connect with the outside world, but most of the time they do. They want to be participants in the global community. Trade is a basic form of language. When you treat people with respect and offer a fair deal in an atmosphere of trust, relationships evolve. My role is to make options and choices available. What they choose is up to them. Like any population anywhere, some people are wise, thoughtful, creative and industrious, while others may be less so.

-§-

By employing a proven model of environmental economics, we demonstrate that the rainforest is more valuable alive than dead.

-§-

We work with several different communities that actively trade with us at different times; our greatest landmark victory to date involved the rainforest community of Porvenir. Located in Peru near the Rio Ucayali on a small tributary off a beautiful lagoon full of dolphins, Porvenir is an idyllic place. From a historical perspective, the idea of land ownership is a foreign concept to the native people. Today, however, the importance of having land rights and title has become clear. The rainforest is being threatened by lumber interests, farmers, and mineral and oil exploration. Loggers were moving into the territory of Porvenir. The community asked for our help and we were happy to assist. We worked with the elders, providing surveyors, engineers and legal assistance. We brought community representatives down river, and flew them to Iquitos to meet with government officials. This process was repeated many times, and the project took nearly three years to complete. In the end, a community of 150 people held the deed to thirteen thousand acres of idyllic rainforest land.

Our model of ecological commerce and rainforest preservation is now a proven model for a healthy future. Partnering with indigenous rainforest communities with a common vision and goal that provides incentives to support a healthy rainforest is a winning strategy that works. Imagine thousands of indigenous peoples secure in the knowing that their land is protected. Imagine an opportunity to better understand the largest, richest, most biologically diverse ecosystem on Earth. Imagine the benefits to all mankind with a more secure source of oxygen, clean air, botanicals, and phyto-nutrients that have the potential to reverse the frightening trend of degenerative disease. Imagine your body taking advantage of a new chemistry profile from wild plants that haven't been altered. Imagine what happens energetically when you ingest and become intimate with rainforest botanicals whose memory is all about harmony and balance. Imagine your heart, spleen, liver, lungs, thymus, and all your organs utilizing new nutritional materials they have never had available to work with before. Imagine a deeper appreciation for the most complex and yet fragile environment on Earth where new species of life are being identified every month. These are all benefits that will unfold many years into the future. Equally important, we are realizing these benefits now, in real time, today. The future has arrived.

-§-
Imagine your heart, spleen, liver, lungs, thymus, and all your organs utilizing new nutritional materials they have never had available to work with before.
-§-

Alberto Villoldo:

Homo Luminous: New Shamans of the West

Many prophesies in the indigenous world speak of this time in human history as a period of great transformation. In the medicine tradition of the Inca, legend tells of a great angel who looked into the future and saw that humanity would face an enormous task at the beginning of the twenty-first century. Extenuating circumstances in an extremely difficult and challenging time would require extraordinary effort to bring about peace and heal the heart of the world. "Who would like to volunteer?" the angel asked. Knowing we could make a difference, we jumped up and said, "Me!"

The legend brings to mind a scene in the movie "Lord of the Rings" when the dwarf says, "Small chance of success, certain death ahead? What are we waiting for!" Of course, our odds are better than those faced by the dwarf, but the problems humanity is facing are huge. It is no longer a matter of global warming or carbon emissions, but the possible collapse of the entire climate system—a catastrophe beyond imagination. At the human level, the distribution of water is a huge problem. Who owns the water? Can private interests own the water? And how do we distribute water to places that don't have it? The problems we face are vast and overwhelming. But the problem the Earth is facing is simple: do away with the parasite affecting it. The Earth has an immune system that recognizes what is toxic and will do what is necessary to eliminate it.

The indigenous peoples have a body of prophesy that says up to two-thirds of humanity will be eradicated in the next decade, between now and 2012. There is to be a tremendous culling of humanity because the

Alberto Villoldo, Ph.D., founder of The Four Winds Society, trained as a psychologist and medical anthropologist, and has investigated the traditions of the Andes and the Amazon for more than twenty-five years. He makes available a complex body of shamanic knowledge in an elegant and accessible manner. His book, *Shaman, Healer, Sage* (Harmony, 2000), was selected as book of the month by the One Spirit Book Club. Other books include *Dance of the Four Winds: Secrets of the Inca Medicine Wheel* (Destiny, 1996) and *Island of the Sun* (Destiny, 1994). He can be found on the web at www.thefourwinds.com.

Earth can no longer sustain this parasite humanity has become. But every crisis brings with it a marvelous opportunity and this is why we stood up and said, "Me!" Our work is to find new solutions, to develop sustainable ecological practices in commerce, business, and medicine. This is what we came to do.

I see the main problem as a spiritual one. They are not resource problems, but problems centered on human beliefs, the troublesome elements founded in our mythology. Our problematic mythology is collapsing all around us. It is a mythology that is predatory, that is abusive, that reaps the cream of the Earth—timber, water, topsoil—and passes the furtive costs onto future generations. The greedy, rapacious paradigms that pose humans as a dominator over nature are no longer sustainable.

One day, I was walking with a medicine woman and her husband deep in the Amazon. "Alberto, go across the clearing," they said. "Go back into the rain forest and see what happens." So I turned and went back into the forest. From all around me, the forest was full of song. The sounds of the macaws and the monkeys and the parrots from all around me were like an orchestra. I took the first step, second step, third step into the jungle. And then, the music stopped. The shamans came up to me and said, "See? The animals know that you've been kicked out of the garden. They know that you don't belong here."

-§-

A second element unique to Western culture is that we have practically the only mythology on the planet in which the masculine gives birth to the feminine.

-§-

Certain that all of nature could smell my underarm deodorant, my hairspray, my toothpaste, and my athlete's foot powder, I looked around for a way to cover up my scent. By the edge of the river, I came upon a couple of Indians cooking a boa on a spit. I asked them for the fat they had been collecting from the boa. Stripping down to my shorts, I smeared myself with boa fat, thinking that this would conceal my smell. I walked back into the rain forest. First step, the forest was full of song. Second step, the forest was full of song. Third step, and again, everything stopped—except for the flies; hundreds and hundreds of flies swarmed about me.

It took ten years of study with the indigenous people before I was able to walk through the rain forest and have it continue singing. No longer did the forest recognize me as someone who did not belong. I belonged in the garden again.

This reveals a great deal about our mythology. Mythology creates our beliefs and those beliefs inform our reality. In the West, we have the only mythology on the planet in which we are kicked out of the garden. Nobody else was cast out of the garden. The aborigines were not kicked out, the sub-Saharan Africans were not kicked out, the indigenous

Americans were not kicked out. These peoples were given the garden. They were stewards and the caretakers of the garden. We, on the other hand, were not only cast out, but as we are being cast out, a voice says, "and cursed is the Earth because of you," pointing to the woman. And to the man, condemning him to a life of hard work, "with the sweat of your brow you will take your fruit from the Earth and the Earth shall produce thorns and thistles for you." This is the original damnation. The Bible doesn't say, "and the Earth shall grow strawberries and mangoes and papayas for you." It says thorns and thistles. This is our mythology. From the beginning, we have had a hostile relationship with the feminine, with the Earth itself. And if we look still deeper, even before we were cast out of the garden, we learned on the seventh day of creation that all of the food on the planet belongs to us. The animals and the trees and the flowers were created for our pleasure and for our feeding as humans. Instead of putting us in a position of stewardship with all life on the planet, it puts us in the position of the consumer. The assumption is that all of the food on the Earth belongs to humans. It doesn't. The food on the Earth belongs to all living beings on the Earth.

A second element unique to Western culture is that we have practically the only mythology on the planet in which the masculine gives birth to the feminine. Eve is made from the rib of Adam. Nowhere else, except in Greek mythology, does this appear. As the ways of the feminine began to be lost, Zeus became the dominant god. In the early Greek mythologies, the goddess, the "creatrix" was predominant. As she began to be eclipsed by the masculine principle, Zeus became predominant. And though Zeus took the goddess Hera for his bride, she refused to submit to him. Thereafter, she was known in mythology as "the bitch" because you cannot repress the feminine without ill effect. Eventually, it becomes deadly for a culture and this is what has happened to us.

The paradigms of the West are the paradigms of the masculine. This is at the core of the problem. We have to break free of this mythology that sees the Earth as ours to consume and sees the feminine as damned. These mythologies express themselves in our economic, political, social, and educational systems. Even our medical practices are, by their very nature, hostile and aggressive. These paradigms hold that all the food and resources on the planet belong to us. Not to the other animals, not to the plants; it all belongs to us. We can rape, loot and pillage, we can spoil the Earth and postpone the price of cleanup to future generations. We have been in the grip of a mythology that has exhausted itself. Our economy, our political system, education, and even our relationship paradigms—all show signs of collapse. The old mythology has taken us as far as it can.

Now we must look for mythologies of sustainability, of collaborative relationships with the Earth. This new mythology has yet to emerge, but we have the traditions of the Earth Peoples to provide us with models of the kind of world our children's children can truly inhabit. The Earth People have an animistic relationship with all of life. Animism is practiced by people who believe they can speak to the rivers and to the trees and to the canyons and to the mountains and to God. This is what we were able to do before we were cast out of the garden. We were still in relationship with spirit and with the natural world. Spirit is actually talking to us all the time. But we, in the West, don't open our ears to hear. If we are to find that self that still walks with beauty on the Earth, that speaks to the rivers and to the trees and to God, and to whom the rivers and the trees and the voice of spirit talks back, we need a great kind of soul retrieval.

I embarked on my study in shamanism nearly thirty years ago as a result of my frustration with Western psychology and my inability to discover the workings of the mind. I spent twenty-five years, first as a medical anthropologist and psychologist, and then becoming a student of the shamans, immersing myself in the ways of the shaman. I began to study the techniques, methodologies and practices of the Earth peoples who have developed a body of knowledge for stepping beyond mind, for living mindfully, but outside the visceral grip of the mind.

-§-
The shaman believes that we live in a benign universe. We live in a collaborative universe that will actually go out of its way to conspire with you on your behalf.
-§-

My studies led me to South America, to the rain forest, to study with medicine men and women of the Amazon. These traditions were neglected by anthropologists and by students of religion because they had left no body of writing. Modern prejudice says that if you do not learn to read or write, you are illiterate and therefore, not intelligent. These traditions were dismissed, whereas students of religion and anthropology have been studying the other world traditions, ones that left the Vedas and the Sutras and the Koran and the Bible, for hundreds of years. The indigenous practices of the Americas were neglected because writing is largely absent. Only since Margaret Mead and the advent of experiential anthropology have we begun to discover the true wealth and beauty of the indigenous teachings of our land, of the Americas.

The shaman believes that we live in a benign universe. Evil exists, but only in the human heart. We live in a collaborative universe that will actually go out of its way to conspire with you on your behalf. But you have to be in proper relationship with it. In the medicine traditions, the shaman sees no difference between being killed by a microbe or killed by a jaguar. To us, one of them is an illness, and one is an accident, "Poor boy, he went to the river at dusk, and got eaten up." For the shaman, these two are identical. You have to be in proper relationship with microbes and with jaguars, otherwise they both begin to look at you as lunch. When you're not in proper relationship, the universe turns predatory. It begins to stalk you. When we come out of proper relationship, the universe becomes adversarial—we hit obstacle after obstacle—but when we are in proper relationship, it conspires on our behalf. The most unlikely possibilities line up to make things work for us. This is an essential aspect of the healing process in the medicine way: to come into proper relationship. Not to medicate, to treat, to intervene, but to come into proper relationship through an energetic process.

The shamans of the Americas understand that we have a luminous energy field that surrounds the physical body. It informs the physical body in a way similar to the energy fields of a magnet that organize iron filings on a piece of paper. In the paradigms of the West, we are intent on shuffling and moving the iron filings about, trying to change at the level of the physical. Shamans possess a body of ancient energy healing practices that move and shift at the level of the energetic—moving the magnet—and the physical body follows. The shaman works at the core, at the essential level, and healing happens.

The shamans discovered that time runs in figure eights, that it loops in wormholes back and forth. The way we can know that is by breaking free of the grip of time and experiencing infinity. The core healing practice of the medicine way—the illumination process—happens outside time, in infinity. It happens when we access a self that never entered the stream of time, that cannot be affected by disease, that cannot be touched by ill-health. Once having made contact with the infinite, we can re-inform who we are today. We can grow bodies that age differently, that heal differently, that die differently.

We are constantly challenged to face little deaths in our lives: who we once were, a relationship ending, loss of a loved one, a career, a cherished time in our lives. During transitions, we have time to reinvent ourselves. When we don't, a deadening happens. That deadening causes us to age instead of becoming the sage. If we go through these little deaths consciously, they become opportunities for new life. If we have the prerequisite courage, instead of being wounded by transitions we become inspired by them. How we respond to adversity turns us into courageous beings. Courage can come out of frustration, illness, or despair, sparked either by adversity or by the divine.

I remember when my daughter was thrown from a horse at age six. The horse stepped on her and ruptured her liver. She was very close to death for three days. I was in the Amazon at the time. Getting back to upstate New York was the longest journey of my life. When I arrived at the hospital, she was in the pediatric intensive care unit, hooked up to tubes and intravenous drips. We didn't know if she was going to make it. I sat beside her, crying, praying to God that she be saved. Suddenly an immense clarity came over me. My sadness disappeared and I spoke to her soul. Although she was unconscious, I said to her, "Sweetheart, I love you, and you have to make a choice if it's time for you to go or not. It's your choice. I love you. Your soul knows if your journey is done." Three minutes later, she regained consciousness. She chose Yes.

To go from victim to hero we go into the feminine, into the Earth, the mother, the great one. There is no way to make a personal journey without embracing the greater journey of the planet. The heroic stories are the stories of accepting that call to the hero's journey, accepting the calling to a destiny. While we all have a future, only a few have a destiny. A destiny is something you must make yourself available to by saying Yes—Yes to life, Yes to God, Yes to your own growth, Yes to your own spirit.

The medicine way is as contemporary today as it was 50,000 years ago. My mentor believed that the new shamans, the new caretakers of the Earth, would come from the West. We are the ones who can bring healing and transformation to our families, to our communities, and to the Earth. This is a critical time in history, a time for a reawakening of the Earth and of our own feminine. It is a time of tremendous transformation. All our old models are being reinvented, in every facet of society. And we are the change agents. That is what the shaman has always been. The shaman is a mapmaker. We need new mapmakers. Essential maps do not simply depict the territory; they guide the traveler through the territory. So we must make new maps to guide us.

-§-
My mentor believed that the new shamans, the new caretakers of the Earth, would come from the West.
-§-

The nature of the dialogue that shaman has with nature is one of life speaking to life, life connecting with life, life responding to a call and responding to life, to us. We call on four great archetypes: the serpent, the jaguar, the hummingbird and the condor. These are the four organizing principles in the medicine tradition. They are known by different names among the Hopi, among the Shashoni, among the Navajo, the Maya and the Inca. The important thing is not whether you call it the eagle or the buffalo. The important thing is that when you call that spirit, it comes. That is the shaman's agreement with spirit. Our agreement with spirit, that each and every one of us has made, is that when you call, spirit comes. Not 60% of the time, not 90% of the time, but 100% of the time.

Each of the four archetypes is the embodiment of an organizing principle in the universe, described in animistic fashion. Each one of the directions, East, West, North and South, represents one of the steps that the shaman must go through in order to become a man or woman of knowledge. The shaman differentiates between information and knowledge. Information is what we are flooded in every day. Knowledge is wisdom.

Information is knowing that water is two hydrogen atoms and one oxygen atom. Knowledge is being able to make it rain.

The shaman is a person of the percept, of perceptual traditions. In the West, we are people of the precept. We make precepts, laws, rules. We get the Ten Commandments. We elect legislators who make more rules. When the shamans want to change the world, they work at the level of the essential to bring about a shift in perception. By shifting perception, they dream the new world into being—and the world changes. That is our task, to dream with our eyes open.

-§-
Information is knowing that water is two hydrogen atoms and one oxygen atom. Knowledge is being able to make it rain.
-§-

Through this great transformation, a new human is emerging on the Earth. I call this new human "Homo Luminous." In the West, we believe evolution happens in between generations: maybe your children will be smarter and more handsome, maybe the indigo children will climb to the next rung on the evolutionary ladder. Shamanic traditions understand that evolution happens within generations. It is for us to take that quantum leap into who we are becoming. We can become Homo Luminous in our lifetime. This is our greatest task: to take that quantum leap individually. As we do it for ourselves, we do it for the entire planet. Each and every one of us, when we choose truth, when we choose life, when we choose light, we are transforming the world.still live there today—but others that look Oriental; and still others with features that are distinctly Arabic.

I'd met the group of men conducting this particular dig through a pre-Columbian museum in Peru. Once they heard what I was doing,

Notes and Sources

The editors of this book are indebted to the the authors who contributed their wisdom to the collection. Many of the chapters are the result of interviews conducted with the authors, either by telephone or in person, interspersed with notes from their public presentations, except where noted otherwise in the text or on the copyright page of this book.

The dates and places of the interviews are as follows: Andrew Harvey was interviewed in his home on August 18th, 2004, and his comments interspersed with those he made at the Prophet's conference in Palm Springs, California, in March 2004. Larry Dossey was interviewed in his office on April 14th, and his comments combined with those he made at the Prophet's conference in Palm Springs, California, in June 2004. Neale Donald Walsh was interviewed in his home Feb 24th, 2004. Barbara Marx Hubbard was interviewed in her office on July 14th, 2004. Daryl Hannah was interviewed at the Health and Harmony Festival, June 13th, 2004. Huston Smith was interviewed in his home on June 30, 2004 and his comments interspersed with those he made at Sonoma State University on May 8th, 2004. Barry Sears was interviewed in his office on January 27th, 2004. John Easterling was interviewed at his home on October 22nd, 2004. Ram Dass was interviewed in his home on September 25th, 2004, and his comments interspersed with those noted on the copyright page of this book. Patricia Sun was interviewed in her office on May 19th, 2004. Jean Shinoda Bolen was inerviewed at her home office on September 22nd, 2004. Debbie Ford was interviewed at her home on August 6th, 2004. Alberto Villoldo was interviewed at his home on May 15th, 2004, and his comments combined with those he made at the 2004 Prophet's Conference in Palm Springs, California. The book was copyedited by Melissa Mower (mbeem13@sonic.net), and typeset by Nan Sea Love, (www.NanSea Love.com).

CH 5 Gregory Bateson, *Steps to an Ecology of Mind.* San Francisco: Chandler Publishing, 1974. Reprint Edition, University of Chicago Press, 2000.

Sister Souljah, *No Disrespect.* New York: Vintage, 1994.

Heinz von Foerster, editor, *Cybernetics,* 5 vols. New York: Josiah Macy, Jr. Foundation, 1950–56.

A. N. Whitehead and Bertrand Russell, *Principia Mathematica,* 3 vols., Second Edition. Cambridge: Cambridge University Press, 1910–13.

CH 12 1 Braden, Gregg, *Awakening to Zero Point: the Collective Initiation.* Radio Bookstore Press, Bellevue, Washington, 1997.

2 Blavatsky, H. P., *Collected Writings.* Theosophical Publishing House, 1983, p. 177.

3 Alan, Fred, *Mind into Matter.* Moment Point Press, 2001.

4 Kafatos, Menas and Kafatou, Thalia, *Looking In: Seeing Out: Consciousness and Cosmos.* Quest Books, 1991, p. 163.

5 Amber, Reuben, *Color Therapy.* Aurora Press, 1983, p. 138.

6 Prophet, Elizabeth Clare, *Violet Flame to Heal Body, Mind & Soul,* Summit Lighthouse Press, 1997.

7 Dalai Lama, H. H., "Reality's Emptiness," *Parabola,* Spring 2003, p. 27.

CH 18

1 Yellow Emperor. The Internal Classic of Yellow Emperor. In the *Big Collection of The Classics of Traditional Chinese Medicine*. Shanghai: Hunan Electronic Image Press, 1998.

2 Fu, S. L., et al., Out of Sub-Optimal Health. *The New Perspective of Health in 21th Century*, Shanghai: Shanghai Science and Technology Education Press, 2000.

3 Fu, op. cit.

4 Stenson, J., The Herbal Frontier. *Newsweek*, 2001.

5 McNeill, W., *Plagues and Peoples*. New York: Doubleday, 1976, p. 35-45.

6 McNeill, op. cit.

7 Kiple, K. F., *The History of Disease*. In Porter, R., edit., *Cambridge Illustrated History Medicine*. Cambridge: Cambridge University Press, 1996, p. 17.

8 Porter, R., edit., *Cambridge Illustrated History Medicine*. Cambridge: Cambridge University Press, 1996, p. 378–379.

9 McNeill, op. cit.

10 Kiple, op. cit.

11 Johnson, K. M., Emerging Viruses in Context: An Overview of Viral Hemorrhagic Fevers. In Morse S. S., edit., *Emerging Viruses*. Oxford: Oxford University Press, 1993, p. 46–57.

12 Garrett, L., *The Coming Plague*. New York: Penguin Books, 1994.

13 Kiple, op. cit.

14 Porter, R., *The Greatest Benefit to Mankind: A Medical History of Humanity*. New York: Norton Books, 1999.

15 McNeill, op. cit.

16 McNeill, op. cit.

17 Porter, op. cit.

18 McNeill, op. cit.

19 Speidel, J. J., Population, Consumption, and Human Health. In McCally, M., edit., *Life Support*. Cambridge, MA.: The MIT Press, 2002, p. 83–97.

20 Speidel, op. cit.

21 Garrett, op. cit.

22 Johnson, op. cit.

23 Crawford, D. H., *The Invisible Enemy: A Natural History of Viruses*. Oxford: Oxford University Press, 2000.

24 Clark, W., Managing Planet Earth. *Scientific American*, 1989; 261(3) 45–55.

25 Landrigan, P., et al., Vulnerable Populations. In McCally, M., edit., *Life Support*. Cambridge, MA.: The MIT Press, 2002, p. 258–259.

26 Rom, W. N., *Environmental and Occupational Medicine*, 2nd ed. Boston: Little Brown, 1992.

27 Yang, R., *Toxicology of Chemical Mixture*. New York: Academic Press, 1994.

28 Roe, D., et al., *Toxic Ignorance: The Continuing Absence of Basic Health Testing for Top-selling Chemicals in the United States*. New York: Environmental Defense Fund, 1997.

29 Epstein, P. R., et al., Biological and Physical Signs of Climate Change. *Bulletin of American Meteorology Society*, 1998; 78:410–417.

30 Patz, J. A., et al., Global Climate Change and Emerging Infectious Diseases. *JAMA*, 1996; 275:217–223.

31 Brown, L. R., et al., *Vital Signs 2000*. New York: WW Norton, 2000.

32 Haines, A., et al., Global Climate Change and Health. In McCally, M., edit., *Life Support*. Cambridge, MA: The MIT Press, 2002, p. 98–117.

33 Frank, R., at al., Ozone Depletion and Ultraviolet Radiation. In McCally, M., edit., *Life Support*. Cambridge, MA.: The MIT Press, 2002, p. 135–146.

34 Balbus, J., Water Quality and Water Resources. In McCally, M., edit., *Life Support*. Cambridge, MA.: The MIT Press, 2002, p. 39–63.

35 Thornton, J., et al., Body Burdens of Industrial Chemicals in the General Population. In McCally, M., edit., *Life Support*. Cambridge, MA.: The MIT Press, 2002, p. 163–190.

36 Thornton, J., *Pandora's Poison*. Cambridge, MA: The MIT Press, 2000.

37 Dewailly, E., et al., Innuit Exposure to Organochlorines Through the Food Chain in Arctic Quebec. *Environmental Health Perspective*, 1993; 101:618–620.

38 Thornton, J., et al., op. cit.

39 EPA, Office of Toxic Substances. *Broad Scan Analysis of the FY82 National Human Adipose Tissue Survey Specimens*. EPA-560/5-86-035.

40 Stehr-Green, P. A., Demographic and Seasonal Influences on Human Serum Pesticide Residue Levels. *Journal Toxicol Environ Health*, 1989;27:405–421.

41 Crinnion, W. J., Environmental Medicine, Part One: The Human Burden of Environmental Toxins and Their Common Health Effects. *Alternative Medical Review,* 2000; 5.1:52–63.
42 Landrigan, P., et al., op. cit.
43 WHO. *World Cancer Report.* Lyon: IARC Press, 2003.
44 U.S. Dept. of Health & Human Services, National Toxicology Program. *The Report on Carcinogens,* Tenth Edition.
45 WHO. *World Cancer Report.* Lyon: IARC Press, 2003.
46 U. S. Dept. of Health & Human Services, National Toxicology Program. *The Report on Carcinogens,* Tenth Edition.
47 WHO. *World Cancer Report.* Lyon: IARC Press, 2003.
48 WHO. *World Cancer Report.* Lyon: IARC Press, 2003.
49 WHO. *World Cancer Report.* Lyon: IARC Press, 2003.
50 Carroll, C. R., et al., *Agroecology.* New York: McGraw-Hill Publishing, 1990.
51 Pollan, M., Power Steer. *New York Times,* March 31, 2002
52 Schlosser, E., *Fast Food Nation.* New York, Houghton Mifflin C., 2001.
53 Schlosser, op. cit.
54 The Safefood.org. sponsored by the National Food Processors Association Fact Sheet.
55 Schlosser, op. cit.
56 Pitchford, P., *Healing With Whole Foods: Asian Traditions and Modern Nutrition,* 3rd Edition. Berkeley: North Atlantic Books, 2002.
57 Jones, J. M., *Food Safety.* St. Paul, MN: Eagan Press, 1993.
58 WHO. *World Health Report 2002.* WHO Publication, 2003.
59 WHO. *World Health Report 2002.* WHO Publication, 2003.
60 Sapolsky, R., *Why Zebra Don't Get Ulcers.* New York: W. H. Freeman & Co., 1998.
61 McEwen, B., et al., *The End of Stress As We Know It.* Washington, D.C: Joseph Henry Press, 2002.
62 McEwen, op. cit.
63 U.S. National Center For Disease Control & Prevention. *U. S. Obesity Trend 1985 to 2001.*
64 WHO. *Move for Health Initiative.* 2003.
65 Thompson, T. G., Secretary of Health and Human Services, U.S. Department of Health and Human Services. *The Power of Prevention.* 2003.
66 Antos, J. R., Assistant Director for Health and Human Resources, Congressional Budget Office. Statement of The Magnitude of the Financial Crisis in Medicare. Congressional Hearing, 1997.
67 Antos, J. R., Assistant Director for Health and Human Resources, Congressional Budget Office. Statement of The Magnitude of the Financial Crisis in Medicare. Congressional Hearing, 1997.
68 Thompson, op. cit.
Berry, Thomas, *The Great Work.* New York: Bell Tower, 1999, p. 159.

CH 34 Cousineau, Philip, *The Art of Pilgrimage.* Berkeley: Conari, 2000.
Geertz, Clifford "Person, Place and Conduct," in *The Interpretation of Culture.* NY: Basic Books, 1973 , p. 360–411.
Helmi, Rio and Leonard Lueras, *Offerings: The Ritual Art of Bali.* Singapore: Image Network Indonesia, 1996.
Jensen, Gordon D., and Luh Ketut Suryani, *The Balinese People: A Reinvestigation of Character.* Singapore: Oxford University Press, 1992.
Lansing, Stephen, *Evil in the Morning of the World.* Michigan Papers on South and Southeast Asia, No. 6. Ann Arbor: Center for South and Southeast Asia Studies, 1974.
Eiseman, Fred B., *Bali: Sekala & Niskala, Vol 2.* Singapore: Periplus Editions, 1986.
Suryani, Luh Ketut and Gordon Jensen, *Trance and Possession in Bali: A Window on Western Multiple Personality, Possession Disorder, and Suicide.* Kuala Lumpur: Oxford University Press, 1993.